*Fictional Realism
in Twentieth-Century China
Mao Dun,
Lao She,
Shen Congwen*

Modern Asian Literature Series

Modern Asian Literature Series
Editorial Board

Paul Anderer
Kathleen R. F. Burrill
Pierre Cachia
C. T. Hsia
Donald Keene
Barbara Stoler Miller
Marsha Wagner

*Fictional Realism
in Twentieth-Century China:
Mao Dun,
Lao She,
Shen Congwen*

David Der-wei Wang

Columbia University Press
New York

Columbia University Press
New York   Oxford

Copyright © 1992 Columbia University Press
All rights reserved

Columbia University Press wishes to express its
appreciation of assistance given by the Pacific
Cultural Foundation toward the publication of this
book.

Library of Congress Cataloging-in-Publication Data

Wang, David Der-wei
    Fictional realism in twentieth-century China : Mao Dun, Lao She,
Shen Congwen / David Wang.
       p.   cm.—(Modern Asian literature series)
    Includes bibliographical references and index.
    ISBN 0-231-07656-8 (alk. paper)
    1. Chinese fiction—20th century—History and criticism.
2. Realism in literature.   3. Mao, Tun, 1896–   — Criticism and
interpretation.   4. Lao, She, 1899–1966—Criticism and
interpretation.   5. Shen, Ts'ung-wen, 1902–   —Criticism and
interpretation.   I. Title.   II. Series.
PL2442.W36   1992
895.6'350912—dc20   91 33051
                                                        CIP

Casebound editions of Columbia University Press books
are Smyth-sewn and printed on
permanent and durable acid-free paper.

Printed in the United States of America
Book design by Teresa Bonner
c 10 9 8 7 6 5 4 3 2 1

Contents

	Acknowledgments	vii
1	Introduction: After Lu Xun	1
2	Fictive History: Mao Dun's Historical Fiction	25
	The Historical, the Fictional, and the Real	27
	Emplotting History: *Eclipse* and *Rainbow*	35
	(Re)writing the Past and the Present	44
	"Multifaceted Relations": The Rural, the Urban, and the Metropolitan	49
3	Plotted Revolutions: Mao Dun's Politics of the Novel	67
	Zola or Tolstoy?	69
	The Politics of Gender	77
	The Politics of Betrayal	89
	Collapsing Spheres	101
4	Melancholy Laughter: Farce and Melodrama in Lao She's Fiction	111
	Farce and Melodrama: Transgressions of the Real	113
	Comic Heroes as *Alazons*: *The Two Mas* and *Divorce*	123
	From Mimesis to Mimicry: *The Biography of Niu Tianci* and *The City of Cats*	135
	Camel Xiangzi: A Macabre Farce?	144

Contents

5	"I Love My Country, Does My Country Love Me?": Lao She's Patriotic Fiction	157
	Patriotism as a Problematic	159
	Cremation	168
	Unproblematic Problems: Patriotic Short Stories	174
	Patriotism "Domesticated": *Four Generations Under One Roof*	185
6	Critical Lyricism: The Boundary of the Real in the Fiction of Shen Congwen	201
	Critical Lyricism and Irony	203
	The Uncanny and the Grotesque	210
	Lyricizing Time, War, and History	224
	Eros, Thanatos, and Their Poetic Manifestations	234
7	Imaginary Nostalgia: Shen Congwen and Native Soil Fiction	247
	Toward a Poetics of Imaginary Nostalgia	249
	Random Sketches on A Trip to Hunan and *West Hunan*	253
	The Border Town and *Long River*	265
	The Art of Remembrance of Things Past	281
8	Conclusion	290
	Notes	317
	Glossary	343
	Bibliography	351
	Index	361

Acknowledgments

Portions of the first section of chapter 3 appeared in the article "Mao Dun and Naturalism: A Case of Misreading in Modern Chinese Literary Criticism" in *Monumenta Serica*, 37 (1986–87); an altered version of the second part of chapter 5 appeared as "Lao She's Wartime Fiction" in *Modern Chinese Literature* 5, 2 (1989); and portions of the second section of chapter 8 appeared in "Radical Laughter: Lao She and His Taiwan Successors" in *Worlds Apart: Recent Chinese Writing and Its Implications*, edited by Howard Goldblatt (Armonk: Sharpe, 1990).

I thank the editors and reviewers of Columbia University Press for reading the manuscript and offering valuable suggestions.

*Fictional Realism
in Twentieth-Century China
Mao Dun,
Lao She,
Shen Congwen*

Chapter one

Introduction: After Lu Xun

Lu Xun is *the* inevitable figure in every canon of modern Chinese literature. He is seen as the founder of modern discourse, the engaged intellectual, the conscience of China, the leader of the literary revolution, and the model of revolutionary art. Held in the power of these mythifications, one is almost obliged to suppose that modern Chinese fiction climaxed where it started, that what happens after Lu Xun is at best an echo of the master's voice.[1]

Lu Xun deserves credit for envisioning a Chinese reality in crisis. Given the formal and conceptual range he poses, however, there are writers who are not totally taken in by his power. I am not referring to cases reflecting an anxiety of influence but, rather, to dialogical voices arising within the discursive paradigm set by Lu Xun, voices that valorize Lu Xun's position by questioning and even transgressing its boundaries. To me, Mao Dun, Lao She, and Shen Congwen represent perhaps the three most prominent examples of such voices. Writing after Lu Xun, these writers understand Lu Xun's concept of reality well enough to renew it by revising it. They experiment with narrative modes ranging from the historical/political novel to farce, from melodrama to native-soil fiction. In these experiments, they are extending Lu Xun's initial map of the Chinese landscape and they succeed in pointing out the main directions for the subsequent praxis of modern Chinese realism. The limits reached by Lu Xun's realism are also the limits of realism for some subsequent writers, but are the boundaries where the realisms of Mao Dun, Lao She, and Shen Congwen begin. As the twentieth century nears its end, this wider territory of realism is the one from which the younger Chinese realists take their departure.

Lu Xun wrote his fiction at a historical juncture when the master narratives vindicating China's reality were in a state of disintegration. As intellectuals and literati desperately sought the *Way* to national strength, the question of how to read and write China ranked high on their agendas. The search for a new narrative paradigm was never merely a literary game; it was a crucial part of their cultural-intellectualistic approach to crises: a prevalent conviction that China's problem stemmed solely from the break in cultural/intellectual coherence and could be solved only in immanent, holistic terms.[2] Both rhetorically and conceptually, a renovated narrative paradigm was regarded as the prerequisite for reflecting and rectifying reality. This mode of thinking is evinced by Liang Qichao's propagation of fiction as possessing an incredible power over the Chinese mentality; by Chen Duxiu's hyperbolic manifestos of literary modernization in the magazine *New Youth;* by Hu Shi's proposals to "revolutionize" literature; and by Lu Xun's powerful confession that he wanted to save the minds of the Chinese people before their bodies.[3]

Even at its very beginning, the realist campaign of Lu Xun and his contemporaries entertained a paradox: it called into question the real while at the same time re-essentializing the Real. The movement historicized what had been regarded as sacred, disturbing immanent cultural/political institutions, while it nervously prescribed a replacement, cultivating the old yearnings for an ontology of the Real. Canons such as objectivity and distance were emphasized, if only to serve the purposes of empathy and commitment. As scholars have pointed out, the tragicomic scenario of modern Chinese realism is well summarized as the period of transition from literary revolution to literature in service of the revolution.[4] How this paradox affected modern Chinese realist fiction and how the three authors under discussion came to terms with it will be the main concern of this book.

Lu Xun's and his predecessors' campaign for a new approach to

Introduction

reality can be discussed in terms of formal defamiliarization.[5] Before he could use literature to diagnose the problems of China, Lu Xun was first obliged to constitute a viable narrative means that sustained its own cause; to represent reality, he had to attain the way to represent reality. In this regard, Lu Xun's greatest contribution lies in the fact that he managed to assimilate nineteenth-century European realism to Chinese narrative formats, thereby giving a tentative coda to the late Qing fiction-writers' efforts to represent a recalcitrant reality. Critics Patrick Hanan's and V. I. Semanov's meticulous studies of Lu Xun's reception and revision of nineteenth-century European and Late Qing narrative formats have offered a matrix for further comparative study along these lines.[6]

Any attempt at formal defamiliarization involves the dialogue between the new and old horizons of the real along a time continuum. In the case of modern Chinese realism, this built-in historical motivation is blatantly manifested by calls for reform and revolution that take place outside the text. Even classics well known for their sensitive portrait of reality are denounced by the May Fourth critics as unrealistic, because they fail to meet the need of the time. Setting out to break with the old, unrealistic literary tradition, Lu Xun's fiction reenacts the perennial dialectic between the need to give form to a reality in flux and the commitment to contextualize that form, the desire to transcend time and the impulse to inscribe time, realism for aesthetic catharsis and realism for normative purpose,[7] for mimesis, and for verisimilitude. Let us understand realistic mimesis as a claim to faithful reflection of the world's objective surface, and realistic verisimilitude as the narration of truths deeply ingrained in cultural-historical subjectivity.[8] Neither mimesis nor verisimilitude would be possible without adherence to conventions of intra- and extralinguistic discourse.[9]

Seeing that attempts at representation are conditioned by history and that mimetic practice presupposes verisimilar motivation, the representation of reality is always overdetermined—calling attention to, rather than erasing (as traditionally thought), the terms of its intangibility. This lends light to the antinomies inherent in Lu Xun's moral imperative—"write!"—and in the consequences of writing. He starts out with a declared intention to recapture and reform reality, but he can never provide a coherent meaning for the real without exposing the break between signifier and signified, between form and content.[10] Realism is so practiced as to bring forth its self-contradiction: to name the real is to bring forth either transgression or denial of the Real. The formation of Lu Xun's realist discourse evokes at the same time a counter-discourse, an allegorical subtext that reveals the tension between what the real should be and what the real is. By showing us contemporary society in its immediacy, his stories also tell a story about how Reality has disappeared and reappeared only tentatively, in words.

Lu Xun's first vernacular short story, "Kuangren riji" (Diary of a madman), must be looked at again. Much has been said about the allegorical aspects of the story, but above all its implications, one can argue that "Diary of a Madman" itself stands as an allegory of the way modern Chinese realism came into existence. Spanning intelligible and unintelligible psychological/ideological contexts, readable and unreadable linguistic codes, the story dramatizes Lu Xun's (and contemporary writers') efforts to break with an obsolete representational system and to cry out for a new vision of the real. Significantly this originator of modern Chinese realist discourse amounts to a self-interrogation of its own end. It invites a metafictional reading on the tension between the real as something immanent versus the real as something historically predetermined, on language as a fully functional medium reflecting the real versus language as an arbitrary closure conditioning the real and so on. All these tensions testify to the eternal interplay between reality and vision/illusion, between realism and allegory. Contrary to conventional criticism, the charm of Lu Xun is not that he manages to smooth out these tensions but his tragic awareness of an inability to deal with them.

"Diary of a Madman" is well known for its formal devices of framed narrative and contrasting styles: its short introduction is narrated by an anonymous narrator in classical Chinese, while its central text—the diary of the Madman—is rendered in vernacular Chinese. The framed narrative structure is admittedly an old device, by which a writer claims that he is only a transcriber of the text proper and therefore provides a mimetic illusion by assuming the pose of a transparent intermediary. Besides numerous western examples, Wu Woyao's *Ershinian mudu zhi guaixianzhuang* (Strange things seen in the past twenty years) would be one of the late Qing examples with which Lu Xun must have been familiar. This *framing* narrative contextualizes the central story, providing intelligible referentiality for reading and interpretation and engendering an atmosphere often called realistic. However, the center part of the story also calls for a realistic reading; it is where Lu Xun's motive to narrate originates. Its colloquial language claims itself as more familiar and hence closer to reality. The *framed* narrative then contextualizes the outer narrative, demonstrating that its classical language disqualifies it from direct contact with the real. In a highly graphical manner, Lu Xun doubles the reality in question and draws attention to the paradoxical condition of language and narrative in transmitting the real.

The split in linguistic code leads to the problematic of mediation. Although language reform does not always parallel political revolution, the campaign for vernacular language on the eve of the May Fourth Movement does indicate that the social/political desire to reform reality can be manifested as a matter of speaking and writing about the real. The Madman is confined not only to an "iron house" as carceral space but also to an "iron house" of language. When the Madman expresses himself in vernacular idioms and western sentence patterns, as opposed to the ornate classical Chinese that frames his diary, he articulates problems both of communication and of representation. For him, the signifier and signified, the world he sees and the world he is supposed to see do not coalesce any more, and the diary desperately tries to name the real by means of a discourse which is not (yet) authenticated by his society.

"Diary of a Madman" points to the dialectic of voices as practiced by realist narrative. One of the important traits of nineteenth-century realist fiction is its increasing self-consciousness over its complexity of voice and vision. A writer penetrates the individual psyche, linking it with a mobile social/historical consciousness in the name of objective observation; such observation is nevertheless subject to the implied author's omniscient knowledge. As critics such as Gérard Genette have noticed, *voice* in narrative functions more powerfully than a sheer statement made by the narrator or other character(s). Closely related to viewpoint, voice regulates the relation between narrative and its instance.[11] Whether in the first or third person, limited or all-embracing in knowledge, partially or absolutely trustworthy, the realist voice offers a variety of entry points that link the subjectivity of the author/reader with the objective world under description and demand to be heard.

Lu Xun's obsession with the validity of voice is indicated by the title of his short story collection, *Nahan* (A *call* to arms). "Diary of A Madman" can be read as an exposé of the predicament of speaking out in a society which refuses to listen. As the barrier between the addresser and the addressee becomes too difficult to cross, the Madman's (and Lu Xun's) voice takes an inward turn in the form of a diary. Muted by external reality, the Madman can only address himself. And the question that follows is, why speak? Or more poignantly, why write a story about the gratuitousness of speech? Involved here is not so much a Derridian concern about the mythical precedence of voice over script as a deep moral anxiety about the grounds for any meaningful interlocution. Silence takes over again at the end of the story, voicing the dilemma of the Madman's (and Lu Xun's) commitment to speech. As the Madman's cry falls into ellipsis, the subjective truth represented in him evaporates.

Here we should notice the I-narrator at the edge of the story, a voice usually ignored. The narrator occupies an ambiguous position, being either a complacent spokesman for the sober majority, a passive transcriber of the Madman's mumblings, or an accomplice amplifying the Madman's cries. Whatever role he plays, he calls attention to the Madman's diary by denying it. Especially when the Madman's voice is absorbed by the I-narrator's voice in the frame, there arises a ventriloquist's text, a text that engenders and at the same time suppresses its subtext. We hear the Madman's talk through the I-narrator's voice; we accept the narrator's comments as if this Madman's voice could validate them. The most fascinating aspect of the story lies not in the easy dichotomies we have become used to but in the puzzling dialogical reverberations between the I-narrator's and the Madman's voices.

The major theme of "Diary of Madman," madness, directs us to the psychological/figurative aspect of Lu Xun's approach to reality. Lu Xun is known for his interest in issues related to disease and death, an interest illustrated by such stories and essays as "Yao" (Medicine), "Gudu zhe" (The misanthrope), "Fuqin de bing" (Father's disease), and so on. However, he consistently maintains a greater interest in another kind of sickness—moral illness, disease of consciousness. Lu Xun gave up medicine for literature, as he put it in the preface to *A Call to Arms,* so that he could spend all his time trying to cure the Chinese soul.

Madness, as Lu Xun would have it, does not only refer to a mental/behavioral disorder; it also refers to the idiosyncratic manifestations of a psyche's figuring out of reality and rationality. The primary lesson of "Diary of Madman," we are told, is that the Madman is not mad; it is those persecuting him who exhibit the pathology of reality displacement. In Lacanian terminology, the Madman's babblings bring to the fore the break in the symbolic chain of the normal world and usher us back into the repressed realm of imaginary loss. Madness remains as the other way of seeing and talking about the world, a way which is nevertheless hushed up, excluded, and policed as the chaotic unknown. Seen in this light, "Diary of Madman" can be taken as an allegory of how we narrate in order to define and/or defy the rational and the real.

The symptoms of madness described in "Diary of A Madman" such as paranoia, schizophrenia, claustrophobia, thus call for more than psychiatric interpretation. The story's medical problems demand a metaphorical solution. Insofar as the Madman is comparable to the Mara poet or Nietzschean superman,[12] his symptoms can be regarded as tropological signs, dramatizing a nonconformist writer's insight into the real as well as his desperate attempt to maintain his ability to narrate and rationalize.

Nevertheless, if Lu Xun sees madness metaphorically as the repressed real demanding to be emancipated, he has to deal with a result not unlike an opened Pandora's box. The Madman's radical talk cannot be valorized at the center in its own right: as figured speech, it has to be continuedly subject to an allegorized, socially acceptable reading and re-reading. As the story's frame indicates, the nomination and exclusion of the mad and irrational makes possible a society's differentiation of the object from the subject, the conscious from the unconscious, and the real from the unreal. By contrast, the center of the story triggers a vertiginous interplay between madness and rationality, illusion and reality. To push Lu Xun's narrative strategy to the extreme, one must conclude that any effort to validate meaning in a realist discourse can claim at best a partial and transitory victory. In contrast to the traditional reading of this story, I would argue that Lu Xun's critical position holds only because the Madman is no more or less rational than the cannibalistic society he condemns.

Since "Diary of a Madman" is not really about madness but, rather, about a figurative reading-through of madness, it leads us to the ideological and epistemological conditions of a realist discourse. Indeed, the story provides a locus where claims of different truths compete. Contemporary studies deny the mutual exclusion of madness and civilization: the domain of madness is neither a mysterious realm of darkness nor an island of psychological malaise; it is a space in which different systems of knowledge and rationality are in combat over the power to claim truth and reality.[13] Both the Madman and Lu Xun treat the narrative of the diary as a hermeneutic process, in which the truth will be exhumed and order will be restored from chaos. "Everything has to be studied so as to be made clear,"[14] as the Madman puts it. His diary is directed by an anxious plan that enables him to make sense of what he perceives and receives, to launch a new knowledge system. Thus, the story's introduction serves not only as a realistic context in which the Madman's diary sounds intelligible but also as an epistemological closure that distinguishes the rational from the irrational, the healthy from the diseased, the real from the fantastic.

In Lu Xun's view, this hermeneutic project of defining the real entails political scenes of assimilation and persecution, naturalization and censorship. This is shown not only by the penal and carceral imagery of quarantine, persecution, rehabilitation, stifling ironhouse, and claustrophobia, that permeates the story, but also by the narrative frame itself. Given the abundance of cases of censorship, extrapolation, indictment, imprisonment, and execution in his narrative, the fate of modern Chinese writing is surely predicated in the Madman's condition.

But beyond Lu Xun's premonition of ideological and epistemological exclusion for the unreal and the irrational lurks his most ambivalent desire to embrace what he denounces, to transgress what he confirms. T. A. Hsia has pointed out that, for all Lu Xun's efforts to draw the new boundary of the rational world, he is fascinated with the dark domain he himself rules out, a domain haunted by ghosts, demons, death wishes—the supernatural or unnatural side of the natural.[15] Lu Xun's description of madness, fantasy, nightmare, and macabre custom reveals the haunting existence of the political unconscious where it is most tightly policed. One must especially take note of the carnivalesque treatment of a world turned upside down in "Diary of A Madman." When the Madman ranks human beings with animals and equates cultural rites with a cannibalistic banquet, he not only reveals the barbarous mechanism of any established institutions but also unleashes defiant forces that celebrate this chaos. Instead of submitting to the allegorization of the demonic, Lu Xun's stories return, like the Madman's diaries, to inscribe it again and again.

As an allegory on the conditions of writing about the real, "Diary of A Madman" points to the historical and ontological assumptions that support a discourse of the real. The story proceeds with the Madman's reading of classical texts to the point when he comes to realize that history is nothing but a long record of institutionalized cannibalistic banquets in which family members, teachers, students, and friends all participate. A nonconformist reader, the Madman reveals meanings hidden between the lines of the seemingly unquestionable texts, historicizing the history consolidated by the classics. The ontological basis of history is broken in the sense that the Madman comes to believe that history has to subject itself to continuous rereading and investigation.

The irony is that, after his fall into historical uncertainty, the Madman submits history to a new totalization. This can be seen on two levels. It is customary to deplore the fact that, after his discovery, a realization of temporality in rituals and institutions, the Madman nevertheless rejoins the macabre historical parade when he recovers. While Lu Xun may have expected us to read this way, the more bothersome fact is that, even at his most sensible (or crazy) moment, the Madman thinks in just the way he should have rejected: he bases his condemnation of Chinese history on a piece of totalistic Chinese reasoning. Cannibalism is the new myth he develops to explain four thousand years of Chinese history. Even if the Madman had maintained his irrational conclusions about Chinese history and society, the form of those conclusions would never have broken with traditional Chinese rationality.

Allegory emends the horror of cannibalism, but it does not repair the absurdity of totalism. The Madman's mythology calls forth a counterpart of the cannibal. Modern Chinese history has borne witness to the way the Madman's final outcry, "save the children," can be realized in the most ironic and brutal ways. Despite his suspicion of children's equal complicity in cannibalistic Chinese history, Lu Xun inspires his followers to allegorize the children and the reality promised to the children at the madman's incipient call. Lu Xun's radical hermeneutic courts a radical solution in historical/political praxis. In order to save a generation of Chinese children, millions of

Introduction

Chinese children would have to die for the Revolution; and in order to save China again, millions of Red Guard children would know how to brutalize their parents and themselves.

Lu Xun's "Diary of A Madman" thus introduces a complex of entry points into modern Chinese reality, and reveals a realist writer who is also a Mara poet, an intellectual revolutionary, an allegory writer, an unhappy prophet, a radical historian, an ideologue, and a Madman. Each of these roles points to an aspect of the ever-changing rubric of reality. Lu Xun's success should be found not in his versatility, however, but in his inability to play all these roles; the Madman's story becomes his own story—that of a frustrated realist. The problematic of the real is best posed as he poses it, trying to bridge in vain the breaks between intention and practice, text and context, political consciousness and political unconsciousness. Looking back from the end of century on Lu Xun's pioneering of modern Chinese realism, we should not ask how the master managed to render a new mimetic discourse that influenced writers to come. We should ask how his discourse generated the conditions of writing and reading Chinese reality, and how subsequent writers tried to break away from his conditions. Even as Lu Xun's more pious followers idolized him, they ignored his example. Only a few writers, such as Mao Dun, Lao She, and Shen Congwen, imitated not the works but the man.

Of these three writers, Mao Dun maintains the most apparent kinship with Lu Xun. Mao Dun theorizes the realist discourse initiated by Lu Xun and other early May Fourth writers, while developing a close comradeship with Lu Xun that culminated in the period of the League of Left-Wing Writers.[16] Mao Dun's works persistently explore two of the most challenging aspects of modern Chinese portraiture of the real: the historical and the political. His involvement in ongoing political events and his commitment to Chinese communism have made writing itself susceptible to historical and political investigation.

Insofar as literary form is more than a matter of verbal and structural play, the fact that Mao Dun is one of the earliest practitioners of the modern full-length novel deserves attention. Lu Xun is the pioneer of the modern form of the short story. With a new economy of spatiotemporal structure, emotional input, and linguistic form, his short stories renovated the paradigm of Chinese fiction and demand a different strategy of reading. Lu Xun cannot take credit for his followers' experiments with the mode of the nineteenth-century novel, however. If Lu Xun succeeds in communicating the epiphanic moments of human experience in a tense and immediate form of short story, Mao Dun is good at rendering the prolonged dynamics of time and history, against which an individual's or society's behavioral and psychological patterns are defined. Pursuing the slow flux of time, he develops a panoramic view of a society on the move and of the changing internal and external traits of its inhabitants. He accumulates sensory and cognitive data from his characters as they undergo different stages of life, to the point that the communal scene and the individual landscape are blended into each other.

Compare the opening scene of Mao Dun's *Hong* (Rainbow), in which the heroine stands alone on a boat while it sails through the zigzagging straits of the Yangtze River, with Lu Xun's "Diary of a Madman," in which an intellectual outcast is trapped in a claustrophobic environment. One sees two different visions of reality. Whereas Mao Dun paces his narrative by the passage of the river of time, Lu Xun confines his story to a real or imaginary spatial proximity, and aims at a meaningful figured utterance. Dealing with a woman's political and sexual awareness in the turbulent post–May Fourth days or with the war of stock speculation between Shanghai tycoons, Mao Dun is able to highlight selected characters' conceptual progress from illusion to disillusion/enlightenment, drawing the reader into the situation at the expense of his or her critical position. Featuring the effect of the real in terms of inventoried (social and psychological) fact, local color, and typical figures, Mao Dun banks on our seemingly inexhaustible interest in referentiality and naming. He thus recapitulates the social and psychological intricacy as well as the structural magnanimity of nineteenth-century grand novels by writers such as Balzac, Tolstoy, and Zola.

Mao Dun started to write fiction right after the failure of the first Communist Revolution in 1927, in which he took an active part. To write fiction about the immediate past is not only a way to piece together the crumbled event, endowing it with a coherence of meaning before it fades away into oblivion, but also a counter-move against the distortion of official historiography. At a time when the access to history is controlled by governmental authorities, Mao

Introduction

Dun adopts fiction as a means to probe the real. Mao Dun's fiction enacts the classical confrontation between fiction and history, the discourse of fantasy and fabrication and the discourse of reality. The traditional dualism of fiction versus history has been seriously questioned by scholars in recent years, since both call for a narrative scheme to make sense of the flux of human experiences, past or present, fantastic or evidentially verifiable. A sophisticated adjudication of the problem is beyond the scope of this book; my concern will be with the social/political factors that determined Mao Dun's fictional depictions of history.

Mao Dun emphasizes the importance of the sense of time or the historicity of fiction, by which he means "how people are influenced by their time, and how people's consolidated vitality pushes history into an inevitable new age."[17] Mao Dun's ideological sanction of history and historicism notwithstanding, his works demonstrate at least two approaches to the formation of a historical reality. He inherits the concept of nineteenth-century historical narrative demonstrated by such novelists as Scott, Balzac, Tolstoy, and Zola, a historical narrative that chronicles not only the ironically predictable themes of history, such as wars, political upheavals, man-made or natural disasters, but also the psychological and behavioral changes manifested by people living through a particular era. The reality of history, accordingly, hinges as much on figures and events at a national scale as on non-events and the changing "consciousness" of ordinary people. This conviction of the spontaneous overflow of the sense of time and history culminates in the book *Zhongguo de yiri, yijiu sanliu nian wuyue ershiyi* (One day in China, May 21, 1936), a collection of writings contributed by people all over China on a randomly selected date of which Mao Dun poses merely as editor rather than author.

Mao Dun's historical discourse is also known for its concern with what is happening or what has just now happened. All his major novels, like *Shi* (Eclipse), *Hong* (Rainbow) and *Ziye* (Midnight), share a sense of temporal urgency. With an almost journalistic fervor, Mao Dun puts fresh news and topical events into words for the record, and in so doing creates a sensation that history is something happening around us, furnishing our conception of immediate reality. The way Mao Dun transcribes the ongoing sociopolitical dynamic reflects a volatile time in which events take place at such a speed that they demand quick interpretation before they march on to the next stage. If one takes a closer look at the infinite, linear progression of history reflected by Mao Dun's works, however, one discerns a teleological plan. Besides the objective goal of recording proliferating realities, there is an ideological imperative for Mao Dun to *speed up* his chronicle, in anticipation of the inevitable self-realization of History.

Both approaches to defining historical reality lead us to the political dimension of Mao Dun's fiction, posing such questions as what kind of historical "consciousness" Mao Dun is trying to crystallize, and in what context the immediate reality becomes historically meaningful. The effect of the real does not happen on its own terms. Its intelligibility stems from a design that is prefigured both by ideological and narratorial motivations. Insofar as he writes tendentiously in support of a certain ideology or even party line, Mao Dun can easily be called a political novelist. My interest here is not to what extent he dramatizes his political beliefs in fiction but how realistic fiction serves as a medium to convey his political beliefs, and how the process of fictional mediation engenders a politics of fiction. Mao Dun does not just write about politics; his act of choosing fiction is itself a political statement.

It is also noteworthy that, under the banner of abiding by reality, Mao Dun's works are finished (or aborted) in the midst of problems like censorship, charges of falsification, debates over the correct reflection of the real and, most paradoxically, allegorization. In addition to these extra-textual issues, he has to come to terms with intra-textual problematics. Ideological commitment can be betrayed by its rhetoric, and narratorial closure may have always already presupposed the transgression of the political unconscious. As far as the call for reflecting an arguable reality is concerned, realism is not so much a promise as a pact, pointing to aesthetic, cultural, and ideological terms of writing and reading the real.

Two more aspects of Mao Dun's practice of realist/naturalist fiction deserve attention. First, despite the proletarian theses of his realist/naturalist discourse, Mao Dun is at his best when describing the predicament of bourgeois intellectuals, capitalist businessmen tycoons, and emancipated women. Second, despite his belief in the ideological imperatives of writing, Mao Dun insists on aesthetic craftsmanship as an obligation upon all writers. Good fiction, for him, is worked out by a conscientious writer rather than just written down.[18] Both these aspects, however, are foci of heated debate among his fellow leftist writers, because they contradict the literary theories these writers hold to be true, and therefore threaten to subvert the ideological underpinning of the discourse of the real.

By looking at the decadent, old society objectively and rendering sympathetic portraits of characters whose thoughts and deeds are condemnable, Mao Dun demonstrates that commentator and ideologue are not always identical roles. On the other hand, Mao Dun's emphasis on artistic discipline brings into question the ideas of will and spontaneity celebrated by his radical peers. Structure, plotting, and rhetoric are never merely formal measures, rather they imply a figurative commitment to a certain conception of the real. Both factors, one on the subject matter of the real and the other on the style of the real, proved to be politically threatening in the forties. Mao Dun's personal exploration of ideological and political dynamics eventually gave way to propagandist writing, partly due to the call for "war of resistance" literature (*kangzhan wenxue*) under the united front of rightist and leftist writers, and partly due to the communist literary policy evinced in Mao Zedong's 1942 Yenan lectures. Deprived of both the consciousness in which real history could be enacted and the craft by which consciousness could be made historically manifest, Mao Dun had nothing left to inscribe but the official vacuities of History. But Mao Dun's earlier novels survive, maintaining a polemical space that will be reoccupied by the historically chastened writers of the eighties.

Often lauded as a humanitarian writer, humorist, and master of the Chinese idiom, Lao She appears in sharply different light from Mao Dun. Friends and scholars of Lao She like to describe his benign, straightforward personality, patriotic fervor, witty remarks, and authentic Beijing manner. However, there are aspects of Lao She yet to be acknowledged, especially Lao She the sentimentalist lavishing his romantic or cynic feelings, and Lao She the instigator of farce whose laughter defies all rules and decorum. These aspects form a way out of what Joseph Lau calls a literature of "snivelling and tears,"[19] and represent Lao She's most important contribution to modern Chinese realism.

Viewed in terms of the paradigm set up by Lu Xun, we may say that Lao She's works such as "Yue yaer" (The crescent moon) and *Luotuo Xiangzi* (Camel Xiangzi) continue the hard-core realist style demonstrated by Lu Xun's "Zhufu" (The new-year sacrifice). On the other hand, Lao She's comic and satirical fiction such as *Lao Zhang de zhexue* (The philosophy of Lao Zhang), *Niu Tianci zhuan* (The biography of Niu Tianci), and *Lihun* (Divorce) is reminiscent of Lu Xun's "A Q zhengzhuan" (The true story of Ah Q), "Lihun" (Divorce) and "Feizao" (Soap). Such a comparison tends to make Lao She merely one of the many imitators of Lu Xun when in fact his achievement lies instead in his compulsion to go beyond the verisimilitude sanctioned by Lu Xun's followers. At his best, Lao She either carries out the radicalism inherent in Lu Xun's realist visions or parodies the trickery hidden in Lu Xun's moralist postures.

Both Lu Xun and Lao She make use of realist discourse to explore the realm of the irrational and the unreal. Critics often like to talk about the "dark side" of Lu Xun. There also is a dark side in Lao She's fiction. If Lu Xun's call to arms and wandering comes from his frustrated yearning for a lost rationale of life and from his moral qualms over the conflicting representational systems of the new and old, Lao She's difficulty is that he is incapable of deceiving himself. He is compelled to cast a skeptical look even at those things he thinks he believes in. In contrast to Lu Xun, whose negative critique of society reinforces his desire for the lost plenitude of the Real, Lao She works hard to uphold realist causes, only to find that what he upholds has been hollow from the outset. Given his image as an engaged intellectual and patriot, Lao She's fiction betrays more nihilist elements than Lu Xun's. Life is at best an absurd comedy of mistaken identities and irrational collisions. As he puts it, "things should not have happened like this, but they happened anyway"; the only response left for him is "bitter laughter."[20]

Where Lu Xun opts for emotional restraint, symbolic subtlety, and linguistic economy, Lao She indulges in emotional spectacle, gestural hyperbole, and verbal extravagance. Where Lu Xun aims at bitter caricature and poignant satire, Lao She lavishes wild laughter and tearful excess. In contrast to Lu Xun's toned-down, melancholy love story "Shangshi" (Regret for the past), Lao She's romantic sentiment finds expression in such cases as "Weishen" (Vision), with its windy, pleading tears and sighs, and its dramatic pronouncements on the mechanism of fate. In the face of Lu Xun's comic satires such as "The True Story of Ah Q," Lao She's farcical energy drives him to celebrate the victory of clowns in chaos, as evidenced in *The Philosophy of Lao Zhang* and *The Biography of Niu Tianci*.

Introduction

Even in incipient tearjerkers such as "The Crescent Moon" and *Camel Xiangzi,* Lao She seems to have a dimension of moral extremity that projects an unspoken circus of suffering.

Melodrama and *farce* are the two modes with which Lao She plays in his realism. Both being modes of excess, they illuminate each other in gestural theatricality and in moral and emotional schematization or reversal. The fundamental conflict between farce and melodrama consists in the epistemologies they construct. Melodrama is often bolstered with genuine or self-proclaimed concern about a jeopardized axiological order, while farce defies, transgresses such an order—even if it exists—with demonic laughter and obscene actions. With a strong emotional charge, stereotyped characters, and twisted actions, melodrama enacts the periodic fight between vice and virtue in the arena of the "moral occult."[21] By contrast, farce ushers us into a domain presided over by buffoons and clowns, where rationality is questioned and decorum mocked.

Two questions must be addressed: how Lao She's practice of the farcical and melodramatic can be justified as reflection of the real, and more intriguingly, how modes are mixed in his writing, thus twice complicating the problem of verisimilitude. Compared with his fellow writers who vow to criticize social abuses objectively, Lao She is much less confident in positing a superior position with regard to his subject. In a world where the representational order is already broken, any literary praxis in the name of realism must call attention to its own formal and conceptual insufficiency. This self-consciousness haunts Lao She, leading him to cross the line that differentiates mimesis, the ultimate goal of realism, from mimicry, the phantasmal displacement and degradation of the mimetic effort. For Lao She, melodrama and farce are both the condition which prefigures the outcome of a mimetic endeavor and the means to expose that condition.

Melodrama and farce, accordingly, should be regarded not as the opposites of an authentic realist narrative but, rather, as its ironic approximations. Only through the prism of excessive tears and laughter, can Lao She bring a reflexive dimension to the discourse that salutes objectivity and impartiality. The design of melodrama can be best seen in Lao She's early comic fiction such as *The Philosophy of Lao Zhang* and *Divorce.* Along with structural conventions such as undeserved sufferings, villainous conspiracies, and moral schematizations and suspensions, the reader experiences drastic emotional and intellectual ups and downs, while anticipating a certain order that will counter this chaos. Lao She's stupendous anti-Japanese trilogy *Sishi tongtang* (Four generations under one roof), for all its epic scale, must be appreciated as a domestic melodrama. In the trilogy, the war of resistance is dealt with in family terms, featuring polarities such as national cause versus filial piety, patriotism versus betrayal, moral stoicism versus sensual decadence. Characters, suspiciously good or absurdly bad, talk and act with patent gestures, all designed to throw blame on the ultimate evil—the Japanese.

Even in Lao She's most typical realist or naturalist works such as "The Crescent Moon" and *Camel Xiangzi,* melodramatic registers abound. These works are often approached from a humanitarian viewpoint, as they reflect what would happen in a society devoid of justice and order. Very little attention has been paid to Lao She's desire for a melodramatic presentation of the horror and misery. Lao She not only wants to say something about human suffering, but he also intends to say it *all*. Observing how the mechanism of fate works in *Camel Xiangzi* or how many varieties of suffering Xiangzi undergoes in his rhythmic progress toward final downfall enables one to detect Lao She's penchant for the extreme conditions of the real. His blatant melodramatic touch may contribute to the portrait of a hopeless society, but it points at the same time to the artifices of his realist or naturalist scheme.

The farcical side of Lao She's realism leads him to explore the grotesque and outrageous aspects of the human condition. When tears dry up, it is laughter that conveys an even more sinister comment. Lao She shares Dickens' idea that contemporary society is not only monstrous but also fiendishly funny, and he borrows energy from the late Qing exposé-writers to catalogue social buffoonery in parade format. From his first novel, *The Philosophy of Lao Zhang,* to the last, *Zhenghongqi xia* (Under the red banner), Lao She's impulse to laugh always breaks forth, even at the most miserable moments of his tearjerkers. He creates a long gallery of clowns and grotesques whose slapstick pieces, pratfalls, and obscene postures scare and amuse us at the same time. They add an ironically vivacious dimension to the sullen scene of modern Chinese literature.

Lao She's philosophy of farce goes beyond the stage of social caricature or normative comedy, best illustrated by a writer like Zhang Tianyi. Lao She's laughter often betrays an ontological anx-

Introduction

iety as to the closure of the real. Farce emancipates us from the state of normalcy and celebrates in imagination a world turned upside down; its transgression presupposes a well-defined limit of the real. Under Lao She's treatment, the farcical and the realistic are never clearly defined, to the point that one suspects that his farcical world is the *real* one. This being the case, Lao She's hilarious narrative tends to lure one into a situation of moral ambiguity.

If Lao She's farcical world is built on the basis of a reality just as violent and outrageous as itself, his serious look into reality invites a farcical analogy. In both *The Two Mas* and *Divorce,* Lao She introduces his heroes as victims of their society *because of* their sobriety and self-esteem. The laughter evoked by his works has nothing to do with a villainous power or a corrupt society, any more than with a basic absurd view of human existence.

Lao She's most powerful interpretation of the interplay of farce and melodrama in his realist domain is *Camel Xiangzi.* Depicting a rickshaw driver's sysiphean effort to obtain and keep a rickshaw, Lao She invests the novel with just as much bitter tearfulness as horrendous laughter. Xiangzi's desire and despair can easily be defined by his social environment. But the more Xiangzi shows his obsession with his rickshaw, the more an element of laughter creeps into the supposedly pathetic novel, and the more one suspects the legitimacy of naturalism/realism (a naturalism to which the novel apparently subscribes). Lao She ultimately writes the tragedy of Xiangzi in the same outrageous way that he writes a farce. Hardcore realism cannot be sustained under Lao She's pen without his putting its hardness under the erasure of laughter.

Shen Congwen's fiction sheds light on another facet of Lu Xun's realist legacy. With his subjective configuration of evanescent experiences, refined sentiments, and evocative symbolism, Shen Congwen inherits the *lyrical* side of Lu Xun's discourse. In particular, Shen Congwen's nostalgic descriptions of his hometown, West Hunan, and his ambivalent attitude toward the past remind the reader of some of Lu Xun's finest homecoming stories such as "Guxiang" (My old home), "The New-Year Sacrifice," and "Zai jiuloushang" (In the tavern) as well as Lu Xun's essays about his childhood. Indeed, Lu Xun was among the first group of critics to note the surge of native soil fiction in the post—May Fourth era.[22] Shen Congwen is not unaware of Lu Xun's impact in this regard. As late as the forties, he still gives credit to Lu Xun.[23] Unlike most native-soil writers, however, Shen Congwen notices the intricate relation between plain homesickness and nostalgia, between a hometown on a map and the hometown of the imagination. In a lyrical style, Shen Congwen explores West Hunan both as a geographical territory and as a tropological locus. By all standards, he is the most important creator of the myth of the *homeland* in modern Chinese fiction.

Shen Congwen's conscientious attitude toward prose is a rare thing among his contemporaries. Most of his peers consider the handling of language as secondary to the expression of content. Their obsession with China and their belief in the mimetic power of realist narrative often lead them to downplay the mediating role of language. Shen Congwen takes a different path. Not only does he emphasize the necessity of refining words and rhetoric in a work, he goes so far as to propose an ideal for fiction in the light of poetry—the crystalized form of language. Shen's own works certainly suggest a poetic quality. His *Biancheng* (The border town), for example, has long been hailed as one of the most important examples of lyrical fiction, for its idyllic story, dreamlike imagery, figurative language, and for its highly sensitive treatment of human relationships.

But Shen Congwen's lyricism indicates far more than a benign working of conventional pastoral themes and rhetoric. More often than not, his works deal with subjects which would not ordinarily be classified as lyrical. War, madness, brutal death, political folly, and even unnerving scenes of decapitation are frequently given a lyrical treatment. One of the best examples is *Congwen zizhuan* (Congwen's autobiography), in which ghastly human contingencies and bloody military experiences call forth a young soldier/artist's poetic sensibilities.

Even *The Border Town* is not a naive pastoral romance. Suicide, accidental death, misunderstanding, and inevitable loss compel the novella, making its serenity equivocal. A drastic incompatibility between subject and style drives home the polemic of realist aesthetics: in what way gruesome realities can be treated as poetic subjects, and what the moral/ideological consequences will be.

Shen Congwen's lyricization of an ugly reality may contain a critical intent, indicating in a negative manner what cannot be seen and experienced in the real. This view has been widely adopted by

Introduction

mainland Chinese critics.[24] But I believe his lyrical discourse to be motivated as much by a concern with immediate reality as by a radical rethinking of the generic latitude at which a reality manifests itself. His *critical lyricism* exposes the closure not only of traditional lyrical writing but also of the critical realism still in fashion. The life of the down and out calls for the writer's sympathy and humanitarian treatment, but it does not follow that a powerful work can be written and appreciated only in the bitterness of exposure. Shen Congwen would rather reveal the immensity of perception, letting the darkest realities situate themselves in the music of human memory.

Shen Congwen's advocacy of a poetically magnanimous realist fiction thus posits an alternative to a reality that has been described by Lu Xun's disciples as a dead end, as a treacherous abyss, or as self-indulgent play. Shen Congwen refuses to see language as a set of lifeless signifiers, subject to logical prefiguration or ideological determinism. As he puts it, "writers should reestablish in their works a new principle [of life], and recognize that the perfection of a work creates a kind of order."[25] By calling attention to the "divine" quality (*shenxing*) evoked by poetry and poetic work, he tries to revive the immensely suggestive and figurative power of the word. Shen Congwen's concept of language and poetry never lure him into a Mallarméan predicament, however. The poetic potential of language itself offers as much a textual displacement of Utopia as a verbal confirmation of human choice in the very reality to which one has been conditioned. It is in this sense that Shen Congwen contributes his own extension of the May Fourth humanist and humanitarian ethos.

With such a concept of language in mind, the reader can be more appreciative of the vision of the hometown in Shen Congwen's native soil writings. His hundreds of works, in the form of short stories, novels, sketches, essays, travelogues, and memoirs about his homeland, West Hunan, easily makes Shen Congwen one of the most influential native soil fiction writers in modern Chinese literature. He begins his portrait of West Hunan with an ironic view: that though his homeland has been a marginal area on the Chinese map, an area known for its barbarous ethnic residents, primitive life-style, and superstitious religious customs, it is also the place that allegedly inspired Qu Yuan's *Chuci* (Songs of the south) and Tao Qian's "Taohuayuan ji" (Peach blossom spring).

West Hunan, accordingly, always appears in a double image in Shen Congwen's text, one that embraces such thematic polarities as geographical locus versus textual landscape, reality versus memory, and history versus myth. Shen Congwen plays with these thematic axes, showing how they infiltrate each other's domains and thus implement the affinities beneath the surface oppositions. At a time when most Chinese writers are committed to a monolithic rendering of reality, Shen Congwen's vision of the native soil is much more avant-garde than it first appears to be.

Shen Congwen's writing engenders not only simple nostalgia, a yearning for a lost time, place, or experience, but also *imaginary nostalgia,* a self-reflexive display of nostalgia as a fantastic inscription of textuality and memory in a past which is always already mediated. Shen Congwen does not write *The Border Town* to project a naive utopian dream. The novella indicates as much his own nostalgic longing as his awareness of the artificial quality of that longing in an ongoing historical stream.[26] By contrast, his novel *Changhe* (The long river) is not totally subject to Shen Congwen's wish to bridge the gap between the bucolic past and the realistic present: it contains a mythical incantation against the return of Myth.

More notable in this regard are the two travelogues, *Xiangxing sanji* (Random sketches on a trip to Hunan, hereafter indicated as random sketches) and *Xiangxi* (West Hunan). A recollection of Shen Congwen's homecoming trip in 1934, seventeen years after he left his home region, *Random Sketches* is subtly flavored with references to Tao Qian's "Peach Blossom Spring." Moving between the past and present, between ancient utopian myth and modern harsh reality, Shen Congwen lays bare the historical condition that makes it impossible for Peach Blossom Spring to (re)appear in reality. In so doing, he also advocates the priority of imagination and writing over actual perception and experience, thus tacitly reconfirming Tao Qian's project of writing his utopia. What Shen Congwen does best in *Random Sketches* is the inscription of personal sensibilities and impressions in terms of the fragments of a supposedly lost world, and the fantastic substitution of what should be for what is.

West Hunan, on the other hand, represents Shen Congwen's effort to correct common misconceptions of his home region and to restore the legacy and charm of the decaying Chu culture. But when Shen Congwen maps out obscure towns and rivers and rationalizes bizarre morals and manners, he risks explaining away the mysterious aura that makes the Chu culture what it is. The best part of the travelogue enacts a drama: while redefining West Hunan in a modern light, Shen Congwen himself may want to save a secret place for the supernatural and the uncanny—not in the apparently realist reportage of West Hunan, but in the dark realm of imaginary nostalgia for a home region that subsumes the text.

These considerations direct the reader to rethink the art of remembering and retailing the past in Shen Congwen's native-soil writings. Shen Congwen many times acknowledges the debt his "spontaneous" writing owes to craftsmanship and to Chinese and Western literary tradition. He learned the techniques of understatement from masters like Fei Ming, Zhou Zuoren, Chekhov, Maupassant, and Turgenev. Turgenev, especially, enlightened him on ways of exploring the human landscape. Of the numerous classics he read, Shen Congwen particularly mentions the influences of Sima Qian's *Shiji* (Records of the grand historian) and the early Republican translation of the *Bible,* saying that he learned the "basic knowledge of narration and lyricism from the two works."[27] There is good reason to think that Shen Congwen must have used these texts both to train his historical sense and to heighten the religious/mythical ethos of his prose.

Shen Congwen is one of the most important story tellers in modern Chinese literature. Unlike another fascinating storyteller, Lao She, Shen Congwen attracts his readers neither by melodramatic plotting nor by farcical buffoonery; instead, he covers up the "storiness" of his stories, aiming at an account in which nothing seems to be happening. For him, storytelling encompasses a way of dealing with life. As Shen Congwen puts it in the ending of "Sange nanren he yige nüren" (Three men and one woman): "I feel forever restless because the past returns to haunt me often.... Some things from the past perpetually gnaw at my insides. When I talk about them you would think they were only stories. Nobody could understand how a person feels who lives day after day under the weight of hundreds of stories like this one."[28] To narrate, or, to write, is to translate of memory into art; it is an effort to re-member the pieces of the past in determinate form. Writing (narrating) is not only a ritual of exorcism but also a form of incantation, ushering one again and again into the cavern of memory, throwing different lights on

Introduction

that cavern's dark passages. Whereas the meaning of *homeland* will never lie in the definition but only in the transmission, the future telling of Shen Congwen's autobiographical experience will have to be narrative in nature because there is no way to locate its center directly; it can only be approached through plottings and story tellings.

Shen Congwen's *critical lyricism* and his discourse of *imaginary nostalgia* thus lend a new light to the problematic of reality and its re-presentation. So far as native-soil fiction indulges in the nostalgia to recapitulate the eternally regressive vision of home, past, and origin, it dramatizes the ontological desire for and fear of a realism that proposes an unmediated recapture of the real and the origin. While the homeland in reality never looks as it does in memory, especially as a native soil writer would have it remembered, a realist text always takes the risk of betraying the arguable reality it once set out to recover. What is at stake here is a firm belief in the trans-temporal and trans-spatial power of literary representation. Both literally and symbolically, Shen Congwen makes his quest for a homeland vacillate between reality and Reality, history and originary Being. Through the convention of storytelling, he tells again and again the story of the possibilities and limitations of a realist's task.

Mao Dun, Lao She and Shen Congwen demonstrate three different aspects of modern Chinese realists' definition of realism. Mao Dun shows how realism is conditioned by political and historical factors, and how the claim to reflect always contains the hidden mandate to conceal and exclude, thereby pointing to power struggles in the text as well as in reality. His practice of the historical novel injects a new possibility into this classical genre, redefining the boundary of time. Lao She depicts the real by subverting its closure with melodramatic tears and hysterical laughter. In spite of his public image as a patriotic and humanitarian writer, he flirts with irrationality and chaos and thus casts doubt on the legitimacy of a realism he purportedly defends. Shen Congwen appears with his apparently conservative writings about his homeland, but his lyrical plan proves far more avant-garde than most of his would-be revolutionary peers. His native soil writings rekindle a yearning for a utopia while at the same time repositioning the borders of that utopia within the present.

Introduction

These three writers have opened up a new world of Chinese fiction; their influences are still being worked out, even at the end of the twentieth century, on both sides of China. They prove that with Lu Xun, the Chinese exploration of narrative reality had merely begun. Writing *after Lu Xun,* Mao Dun, Lao She, and Shen Congwen define Chinese realism in the twentieth century.

Chapter two

Fictive History: Mao Dun's Historical Fiction

Mao Dun (the pseudonym of Shen Yanbing, 1896–1981), literary critic, novelist, translator, clique-organizer, editor, playwright, essayist, and advocate of Chinese Communism, is one of the most versatile among the May Fourth generation of Chinese literati. As early as the 1920's, he systematically introduced western literary ideas and masterpieces into China, with the aim of constructing a new paradigm for modern Chinese fiction.[1] His advocacy and practice of nineteenth-century European naturalism even won him fame as the Chinese spokesman for Zola. But just as his pseudonym, Mao Dun (a homonym for *contradiction*), suggests, his critical and creative works contain many layers of contradiction, calling for continual acts of deciphering by his readers.

Mao Dun wrote his first novel, *Shi* (Eclipse) in 1927, while he was seeking seclusion after the fiasco of the First Chinese Communist Revolution, which had taken place earlier that year.[2] Dealing with young urban leftists' illusion and disillusion during the revolution, *Eclipse* won readers' immediate acclaim for its sympathetic treatment of bourgeois revolutionary psychology, its panoramic portraiture of political upheavals in town and country, and its acute presentation of history on the move. Despite this acclaim, the novel also provoked heated debate among critics over such questions as: how can a novelist project reality objectively while adhering to psychological as well as ideological preconceptions? where are the conceptual and perceptual boundaries of the real for the writer in a given intra- and extraliterary context? and, most poignantly, how should history be represented realistically in fiction?[3]

Eclipse represents only the beginning of Mao Dun's fictional approach to the dynamics of modern Chinese politics and history. His works over a period of two decades chronicle such prominent events as the May Fourth Movement (*Hong* [Rainbow], 1930); *Shuangye hongsi eryuehua* [Maple leaves as red as February flowers], 1943); the May Thirtieth Incident (*Rainbow*); the Northern Expedition ("Huanmie" [Disillusion], 1930); and the coalition and eventual split between the Chinese Communist Party (CCP) and the left-wing Nationalist party (KMT) government[4] ("Dongyao" [Vacillation], 1930). Mao Dun also wrote about the Nanchang Uprising ("Guling zhiqiu" [Autumn in Guling], 1933); the rise and fall of the First Chinese Communist Revolution ("Zhuiqiu" [Pursuit], 1930); the stormy Shanghai stock market crash (*Ziye* [Midnight], 1933); the Shanghai Resistance of 1931 ("Chuncan" [Spring silkworms], 1932); the Second Sino-Japanese War (*Fushi* [Putrefaction], 1941; *Duanlian* [Discipline, 1980]); the fall of Hong Kong (*Jiehou shiyi* [Pieces picked up after the calamity], 1942); and the New Fourth Army Incident (*Putrefaction*, 1941).[5] Mao Dun's realist fiction is characterized by an urgency to capture what is still fresh in people's memory before it fades away into the realm of the past, as well as by a tendentious motive to defy what has been sanctioned by official historiographers as the orthodox and legitimate. Moreover, given the fact that his works have always been the target of critical controversy and censorship, Mao Dun's way of writing about history must itself amount to a political event.

There are two challenges at the core of Mao Dun's realistic discourse. First, his claim to transcribe history faithfully contradicts both the truth claims of official historiography on the one hand and, ironically, the inherent illusoriness of fictional writing itself on the other. Second, his effort to imbue his narrative with a political agenda tempts him to walk the thin line between propaganda and art, between a realism of commitment and a realism of impartiality. History and politics are the two hidden motivations that give rise to Mao Dun's realist novel while threatening to undermine the novel every time it seeks to manifest them. How Mao Dun finds his own realist (dis)course between the Scylla and Charybdis of history and politics, and how he redefines the genres of the historical and the political novel in modern Chinese fiction, are the questions explored in this chapter.

The Historical, the Fictional, and the Real

Mao Dun's practice of the historical novel merits attention, not just because the historical novel has enjoyed a long prestige in Chinese fiction, but especially because "History" per se has all along been sanctioned by communist theoreticians as a holy text, one that prefigures China's destiny in the socialist millennium. What makes the case of Mao Dun doubly intriguing is that he came to take up the genre at a time when classical Chinese historical fiction had lost its verisimilar legitimacy, and when the communist plan of historical determinism was under its first severe test, following the failure of the 1927 revolution. As its title indicates, Mao Dun's first novel *Eclipse* bespeaks less the predestined success of Chinese Communism than its uncertain future, less a coherent path of history than its rupture.

In search of a new narrative model with which to "emplot" history, Mao Dun turned to western masters, finding both Zola's and Tolstoy's novels equally appealing, despite the theoretical conflict between Zola's pseudo-scientific naturalism and Tolstoy's apocalyptic vision. One suspects that, even beyond this contradiction, Mao Dun never really broke with the traditional plan of historical discourse underlying classical Chinese fiction, due to his eagerness or even anxiety to ensure the historical meaningfulness of his own fiction. All these preliminary observations must lead one to reconsider the intricate relation between history and the realist fiction in which Mao Dun's works are situated. Before any further inquiry into his individual traits, the context from which Mao Dun's historical discourse is figured must be historicized.

The *historical novel* has been a major genre in both Western and Chinese fiction; its popularity may well be derived from its rather resilient orientation to both fiction and history. The term is generally applied to works that interweave real and/or fictional characters and episodes into a social and causal sequence that calls for the reader's thoughtful attention. Such a novel renders a historical sense not only by offering factual evidence such as the names, dates, and social manners of a given period but also by arousing speculation on the meaning of given events and on the historical dynamics configured by the text.

A definition like this can serve only tentatively and needs to be further qualified. Such problems immediately come to mind as the conditions under which a certain kind of narrative sequence is made into an intelligible account of past events; the endless interaction between language and arguable reality, hence between fiction and history; and the mutual illumination between historiography and historical fiction in the novel's thematics, narrative typology, and ideology.[6] These problems cannot be discussed fully in the limited scope of this chapter, but I will refer my reading of Mao Dun's fiction to them whenever possible.

The traditional approach to the historical novel tends to oppose history to fiction by asserting that the former category deals with verifiable facts and is therefore in alliance with reality or truth, while the latter category stems from imaginary materials or distorted facts, therefore leaning towards fantasy or myth. Such an opposition touches only one level, and a rather superficial one, of the relationships between history and fiction. History, when regarded as a written/oral account or as a type of conception of bygone human activities, must involve a process in which individual events/ thoughts are organized in such a way as to form a narrational sequence.

In other words, history may well be considered a kind of narrative discourse possessing its own brand of discursive norms. As long as language intervenes (as it always does), historical discourse must also be subject to the intertextual qualification of other cultural, ideological, and literary discourses. History and narrative fiction are two particularly related discourses, in that they overlap each other considerably in probing into human experiences which are both imaginative and empirical, fictive and conceptual, to say nothing of the mutual appropriation of narrative strategies. It may well be by straddling these two discourses that the historical novel gains its unique charm and force.

It has been pointed out by many scholars that the central role of historiography must be understood in any study of classical Chinese fiction.[7] One finds in cases as early as the *Shiji* and *Zuozhuan* that the roles of *histor* and *fictor,* if not identifiable, are at least complementary.[8] The greater portion of the corpus of Song and Ming-Qing fiction can be called historical fiction, because it continues to draw on history for its central figures, for its documentary sources, and for its formal and structural devices. Since historiography plays such a pivotal role in validating the meaning of fiction, one can take a step further to describe a historical imperative underlying classical Chinese fiction, an imperative that requires both the author and reader to treat a story, be it realistic or fantastic, as a meaningful account of history. In other words, precisely because history enjoys the prestige of containing *and* prefiguring all Chinese experiences, to relate fiction in terms of a certain historical context seems to help a writer justify his text's reliability and authority—even if the fiction being narrated may be pure fantasy.[9]

Consequently, classical Chinese fiction writers share a historical discourse less for the purpose of achieving a mimetic illusion, as do the nineteenth-century European historical novelists, than for the purpose of attaining the verisimilitude of a *text:* the world implied in the bulk of classical Chinese fiction is one in which everything has meaning as long as it is related in a historical context. In Andrew Plaks' words, "the sense that what is recorded is ultimately true—either true to fact or true to life—remains a fundamental underpinning" in both the historical and fictional branches of the Chinese narrative tradition.[10] It is to fulfill this cognitive imperative that classical Chinese fiction, including the *yanyi* (saga) novels which usually base themselves on historical accounts, constitutes a sequence of events illuminating not so much the changing ethos or consciousness of a specific era but a set of preestablished, atemporal, moral criteria.

Western influences on the Chinese historical novel became discernible in the late Qing period, as evidenced especially by Zeng Pu's efforts to cast the figures and plots of *Niehaihua* (A flower in the sea of sins) in the style of Hugo and Balzac.[11] Deeply influenced by nineteenth century European historiography, Zeng Pu was inclined to see history as a linear, progressive development, full of changes and struggles. Individuals are hurled into the tremendous flux of changing trends; their fates are forged by it. This view must be underlined, however, by Zeng Pu's intention to bracket history within a predetermined moral mechanism. This tendency can be inferred from the novel's title, *A Flower in the Sea of Sins.* In

Fictive History

Chinese, the word "sin" (nie) has a strong Buddhist implication of *samsara,* or spiritual transmigration, pointing not only to the "sin" itself but also to its predetermined cause and inevitable punishment. Zeng Pu's progressive, revolutionary vision is strangely qualified by a nonprogressive, almost cyclical mode of moral retribution. He thus lends to his novel a double historical perspective: his characters are seen both as free spirits drifting along with the torrents of history, in search of their unknown future, and as puppets conditioned by the great Wheel of Fortune that rewards and exacts retribution in terms of their previous lives.[12]

Zeng Pu and his contemporaries' attempt to rewrite history in a different narrative and with a different thematic typology is further developed by the May Fourth generation of writers, among whom Mao Dun is probably the most important. Ideological preoccupations notwithstanding, Mao Dun by and large endorses a mode of writing best demonstrated by such western writers as Scott and Tolstoy; this mode requires its fictional characters to undergo and give expression to the impact which historical events had upon the people who lived through them, with the result that a bygone age is given in personal and immediate terms. As Lukács puts it, the nineteenth-century historical novel aims not at the "retelling of great historical events, but the poetic awakening of the people who figured in those events."[13] While traditional themes such as wars and revolutions, economic and political turmoil still constitute the major indices to Mao Dun's historical discourse, history manifests itself no less palpably in the interplay between environmental mutations and ordinary people's behavioral, cognitive, and psychic responses. At his best, Mao Dun manages to intertwine individual experiences with contemporary sociopolitical turmoil, giving the reader a fascinating sense that history unfolds through people's involuntary, spontaneous reactions to the changes of the external world, while being at the same time manifested in a sequence of important public events.

Mao Dun's contribution to the modern Chinese historical novel can be elaborated further in three of its aspects, each revealing a complex dialogue between the various assumptions of historical writing and novelistic narrative, and between the real and the fictional. First, as mentioned above, Mao Dun began writing novels at a moment of crisis in both his literary and political careers. Before this crisis, he had for years been a well-established literary critic and editor, with close ties with the Chinese Communist Party as one of its most active members from literary circles. The 1927 revolution and its immediate suppression showed Mao Dun the gaps between what should have happened and what really happened, between political belief and political reality, between party mandate and personal conviction. These gaps can even be historically vindicated by his temporary loss of touch with the party, which later resulted in his permanent ejection from the CCP.[14] To write novels at this juncture, therefore, must have represented for Mao Dun not a mere pastime in reclusion but a means to review and rationalize the gaps, to narrate coherently what otherwise might have been seen as broken and illogical.

Personal motives aside, Mao Dun's endeavor to piece the broken past together in fiction subserves an ideological end. Insofar as official history is so inscribed as to justify its power over the past, Mao Dun feels obliged to put down the "facts" he perceives, to tell the other side of the story, as opposed to the authorized version. His historical novel is thus a defiant sign against the truth claims of official historiography, a phantom voice that doubles the monological statement controlled by the government he vows to overthrow. The irony here is of course that, despite their sharp ideological conflict in denying or rewriting each other's interpretation of a given event, both Mao Dun and his censors share the same belief that history provides a neutral ground, one on which truth can be attested and reality sanctioned. Under the banner of the historical novel as the narrative of the Real is a metaphysical absolutism that sees in historical discourse the unfolding of essence in accordance with its own built-in teleological laws.

But, as I will argue later, the phantom voice, or the fictional statement, through which Mao Dun's own historical/political views are articulated may transmit something other than expected. It may turn itself against that which it intends to valorize. This brings to mind the irony that his novel *Eclipse* was most bitterly attacked for failing to tell the prescribed truths of History not by political rightists but by Mao Dun's fellow critics; that his capitalist archvillain in the epic *Midnight* wins the reader's sympathy; and that his *Village* trilogy ("Spring Silkworms," "Qiushou" [Autumn harvest], 1933), "Candong" [Winter ruins], 1933) betrays nostalgia for the ethics of pre-revolutionary days. In these cases, Mao Dun's

Fictive History

discourse presents a truly dialogical scene of history, thereby bringing out more of the full volatility of nineteen-twenties and thirties in China.

The traditional discourse of historical narrative often derives its historical sense from the temporal distance between the narrated subject and narration itself. Be it a war, a revolution, or a famine, the past is recounted in such a way as to be sealed in the closure of pastness. Mao Dun's novels take an opposite direction in envisioning the "historiness" of his material. Faced with increasingly urgent social and political crises, Mao Dun is bent on writing down what has just happened or what is still happening. *Eclipse* was written only half a year after the First Communist Revolution, and novels such as *Midnight*, *Rainbow*, and *Maple Leaves as Red as February Flowers* end in the middle of an action in response to what is going on in actuality; such an action can include Mao Dun's own abortion of the original writing plan. Even decades after their first publication, these works still impress a reader with their compulsion to reflect and make sense of the immediate past in a journalistic manner. History is no longer remote; rather, its presence can be felt as the existential ambiance in which we are living and playing an active role. Suffice it for Jaroslav Průšek to say that Mao Dun's endeavors "to seize and communicate reality is characterized by his preoccupation with topical reality. Few are the number of great writers in the world whose oeuvre is so closely and constantly bound up with the immediate present, with important contemporary political and economic events, as is that of Mao Tun [Dun]."[15]

Průšek is correct in observing Mao Dun's sensitive display of time at work in his fiction, but he may wittingly or unwittingly have overlooked the ideological issue: that such an acute temporal sense presupposes a hidden desire for an atemporal goal. I have pointed out earlier the complex of ideological motives contained in Mao Dun's fictional narrative of history. Here I would address the issue from another perspective. For Mao Dun the ideologue, the historical novel should introduce an agenda that can be appreciated not only in retrospect but also in prospect. His nervous gaze at every fleeting moment of the present may indicate a gesture towards speeding up the procession of history so as to settle it into the mythical frame of History. The ongoing events have to be taken note of, not because they are of any essential significance but because they constitute a transitory stage, an overture, for the final presence of history in the form of revolution. This anticipatory mood is Mao Dun's key for bracketing the present in a past tense. I would argue against Průšek's concept and claim that Mao Dun's endeavor to make history of the present only assures us of what history is not; or, more paradoxically, that his novels justify their own function only before the master narrative—History—comes into existence.

Third, Mao Dun's fictional efforts to fill in the gaps in time brings to the fore the problems of narrativity and imagination in a historical discourse. In order to make sense of what has happened and what is going to happen, a historian needs a narrative structure or a plot that, however well disguised in the name of transcribing the real, integrates scattered phenomena into an intelligible sequence. This is doubly true for a historical novelist such as Mao Dun, simply because against the official historical narrative which is but fiction, he has a different story to tell. The line between historical sequence and fictional narrative is never easy to draw. Especially when the issues of rhetoric and trope are highlighted by the retelling of history as story, one has to take into account the allegorical quality imbued in both the fictional and nonfictional treatment of history. In her study of Mao Dun in terms of the dialectic of allegory and realism, Yu-shih Chen provides valuable insights into the allegorical elements in Mao Dun's fictional version of history vis-à-vis the hard facts of history. But insofar as history exists as a verbal or nonverbal account of the past always already inscribed by narrative typologies, Yu-shih Chen's neat dichotomy between allegory and realism overlooks the allegorical presuppositions of realism and history, and thus appears to stop short in the analysis of the issue.[16]

Mao Dun's way of emplotting China's fate in the nineteen-twenties and thirties is visibly influenced by the nineteenth-century European realists, of whom Zola and Tolstoy are the two major models,[17] but his interest in portraying topical reality reveals his equal indebtedness to late Qing exposé fiction. Novels such as Wu Woyao's *Strange Things Seen in the Past Twenty Years* may not bear direct resemblance to Mao Dun's modernized narrative format, but the way they accumulate contemporary social/political data and feature them panoramically must have offered a viable Chinese example for Mao Dun. At the bottom of Mao Dun's narrative, after all, hides the old precept of classical Chinese fiction, that fiction serves, at its best, as an extension of historical accounts, generalizing the meaningfulness of lived human experience. A narrative makes sense because it deals with an *event* which is remarkable in the light of the archive of historical knowledge. Mao Dun's writing manifests the syndrome of "obsession with China," C. T. Hsia's well-known description of modern Chinese fiction,[18] in terms both of its concern about the current fate of China and of its amplified conviction that fiction's moral bearing helps transmit and explain history as it should be.

Zola and Tolstoy may at first seem an unlikely pair to lend form to Mao Dun's historical vision. Zola's naturalism proposes a scientific survey of human conditions, like an experiment conducted in a laboratory. Although this positivist view theoretically promises humanity's potential for progress, its effect is instead "the solidification of the present in a pre-determined circularity that resembles timelessness."[19] Zola's *Rougon Macquart* series portrays the Second Empire, from the ambuscade of the coup d'état to the betrayal at Sedan, as a slow process of decline in which changes turn out to be repetitions. Trapped in the menacing cycle of heredity and environment, all life seems to exist synchronically, in established boundaries which thwart any individual attempt at breakthrough. The present is consequently conceived of as being at once inevitable and endlessly repeated under the shadow of destiny. This perspective enables Zola to accumulate sensory and cognitive data as if they were always there, evoking a historical aura of atemporality that is close to myth.

Tolstoy visualizes history as a tremendous flux in which everybody's fate is involuntarily involved, yet over which nobody can declare final control. History is no longer perceived only as a sequence of prominent episodes presided over simply by heroes, rulers, and politicians; rather, it is more like an "unconscious, general hive life of mankind" in which "every act of man is in a historical sense involuntary and is related to the whole course of history and predestined from eternity."[20] But in spite of his pose as primitivist and anti-historicist, Tolstoy is strangely affected by his time's belief in progress, by the Hegelian view of the coherence of ages on the one hand, and by the Christian yearning for the sacred experience of apocalyptic transformation on the other. The plotting behind his historical narrative is far more complicated than he claims; it contains both spontaneous and teleological paths, both the seemingly meaningless flow of events or actions and the preordained anagogic leap at certain moments.

Vacillating between Zola's scientific naturalism and Tolstoy's apocalyptical humanitarianism, Mao Dun had a hard time making commitment to either. But as I shall discuss in the next chapter, the dilemma proves to be an advantage to Mao Dun. In his emplotment of modern Chinese history in the 1920's, both Zola's mechanical determinism and Tolstoy's visionary religiosity function as crucial themes. Zola's determinism looms large when Mao Dun writes about the ideological confinement for those who live in a prerevolutionary dungeon, while Tolstoy's religious epiphany surfaces when his Chinese admirer describes a communist apocalypse descending around his characters. Not unlike Zola and Tolstoy, Mao Dun formulates in his novels a historiographical discourse which is rife with allegorical meaning. He endorses the spontaneous awakening of people living in an transitional moment of history, yet at the same time celebrates the *deus ex machina* power of social/political events that dramatically change their fate and bracket their action with a preestablished moral significance.

Emplotting History: *Eclipse* and *Rainbow*

Mao Dun's early novels *Eclipse* and *Rainbow* represent two of his most ambitious attempts at recapturing contemporary reality in historical terms. Encompassing the turbulent period from the May Fourth Movement to the First Chinese Communist Revolution, both novels focus on the ups and downs of young intellectuals' search for personal and political fulfillment in the face of various adversities. They are also pioneering examples of modern Chinese writers' efforts to create full-length works modelled on the European novel. As far as the representation of a historical view is concerned, the two novels contain very different strategies, which consequently form a dialectic, echoing Mao Dun's struggles between realism and historical writing, history and History.

Eclipse is a trilogy composed of three thematically interrelated novelettes, respectively entitled "Disillusionment," "Vacillation," and "Pursuit." Written right after the failure of the First Chinese Communist Revolution, in which Mao Dun was personally involved, the trilogy is Mao Dun's interpretation of urban intellectual

Fictive History

youth's response to the failed revolution. In his own words, the three novelettes describe the three stages of the revolution: "first, young revolutionaries' exuberance on the eve of revolution and the disillusionment when coming face to face with it; second, their vacillation during the intensification of the revolutionary struggle; and third, their unwillingness to accept the desolation and despair after the revolution, and their desire to make a final search for ideal."[21] The novel was vehemently criticized by leftist critics, owing to its depressing portrayal of the failed revolutionary attempt and its distortion of the historical reality they wished to believe in.

To begin with, in spite of the chronological order clearly stated in *Eclipse* and in Mao Dun's self-critique, one wonders if he really endows his novel with a coherent account of the historical progression from one stage to another. There is some overlapping of character and plot among the three novelettes, but the crucial links that relate one story to another, or as Mao Dun has it, one stage of the revolution to another, are missing. Besides the three discrete novelettes, we want to know what happens in between that has brought on the disaster of the revolution. The real forces that propel history forward are strangely left out of his narrative. If one removes the superficial temporal registers in the novelettes, one has a feeling that Mao Dun tells the same story about young revolutionaries' desire and despair three times. As its title, *Eclipse,* suggests, the trilogy deals with the erosion of its characters' love and ideals in both private and public terms. At the core of its narrative, however, is an anxiety about the eclipse of time as progress, the most important factor of history as Mao Dun and his leftist peers understand it. Ironically, this is where the novel's historical vision is most emphatically expressed.

Balzac's and Zola's influence can be easily discerned in Mao Dun's molding of the three novelettes into a static, vertically structured format. Both Balzac's *Human Comedy* and Zola's *Rougon Macquart* series project a vision of society so massive and complicated that any of its slow changes amount to an effect of changelessness. This structure is usefully employed by Mao Dun, as it reflects his perception of Chinese society before and after the revolution. It also enables him to elaborate his sensory and cognitive data in a form of gradual accumulation, to the point where an illusion of continual repetition arises. The opening scene of "Disillusionment," in which the heroine, Jing, sits motionlessly on her balcony and gets lost in daydreaming about her future sets the tone of the whole trilogy. More pertinent to our concern is how Mao Dun inherits Zola's naturalist determinism and transforms it for his own use. Unlike the French master, Mao Dun takes less interest in lower-class people than in urban intellectuals, whose struggles to break away from ethical and social bondage always constitute the most powerful scenario of his fiction. Zola's scientific hypotheses of heredity and environment remain as important themes, but Mao Dun would rather interpret them at an ideological than at a biological level. In a strange logic of replacement, he elevates Zola's naturalist discourse by identifying desires with ideas, instincts with sentiments.

The cyclical movement of time is already well demonstrated by "Disillusionment," the first novelette of *Eclipse*. Through the vain pursuits of love and revolution of two girls, Jing and Hui, Mao Dun depicts how, for those who are eager to find a way out of murky reality, history unfolds itself as a deceptive circle. These two heroines are prototypes for many other Mao Dun female characters. Jing is a sensitive girl from a small-town gentry family. In the name of study, she comes to Shanghai with the hope of experiencing life. In contrast to Jing, her friend Hui has seen the world and now assumes a nonchalant gaiety in order to disguise her basic anxiety and thwarted idealism. The two girls undertake their romantic and political causes alternately throughout the story, yet they find themselves ending up nowhere. Jing falls in love, only to be betrayed by her lover; she participates in the revolutionary government, but soon makes a habit of quitting jobs. She finally marries Qiang Meng, a wounded soldier under her care when she works as a nurse. But before their honeymoon is over, Qiang Meng is recalled to the front lines, leaving Jing again in a state of suspension and disillusionment.[22]

Mao Dun takes pains to suggest the two girls' flaws are hereditary symptoms of the class from which they come. Whereas Jing indulges in a kind of Bovaryism—wishing oneself to be other than what one is—Hui is a cynical hedonist. But what intensifies their case is that, though they become gradually aware of their problems, they are either unwilling or unable to do away with them. History *does* take place around the girls, in terms of political and military events such as the May Thirtieth Incident, the Northern Expedition, the Nanchang Uprising, and so on, but fails to leave any trace on them other than arousing their periodical ecstasy or disillusionment.

Fictive History

The strange gap between what the girls perceive and what they conceive, between the social/political upheavals they are thrown into and the narcissistic closure they dwell on *within* the upheavals, is the locus where Mao Dun's own sense of historicity really takes place. While this gap hints at his sensitive inquiry into the landscape of historical consciousness, hence his indebtedness to nineteenth-century European historical fiction, it also marks where Mao Dun and his fellow leftist critics part.

The second novelette of *Eclipse,* "Vacillation," takes an even more radical look at the paradox of the conceptions of history on the move and history in stagnation. Fang Luolan is a left wing KMT official running an office somewhere in Hubei under the coalition government of the KMT and the CCP. An idealist, Fang Luolan knows too little about local politics to cope with opportunists and conspirators. He is also trapped in a triangular relationship with his worldly colleague, Sun Wuyang, and his meek wife, Meili.

Mao Dun has commented that the story records one of the most critical moments in the First Chinese Communist Revolution: "leftism led to an epidemic of leftist radicalism; when people tried to put down leftist radicalism, they opened the way for the rejuvenation of rightist thoughts, which finally resulted in a tremendous counter-revolutionary riot."[23] But Mao Dun may be simplifying his novelistic presentation of this political scene. The real crisis lies not so much in the power struggle between the leftists and rightists as in the "lack" of any ideological grounding that would have justified a power struggle as such. Fang Luolan vacillates between different categories of values just as much as his wife, his girlfriend, and the reactionary villains around him. He is the leftist in a right-wing party; he is and is not a revolutionary; he loves and does not love his wife and girlfriend. "Vacillation," seen in this light, points to the peculiar moment of history that refuses to make sense to both good and bad characters, both conservative and progressive actions, both rightist and leftist party lines. At the center of his and other characters' vacillation is an anarchist blank that nullifies any logic of action. Suffice it for the reader to see the final outburst of the horrible riots and massacres that turn the Revolution upside down.

The novelette culminates in a surrealistic hallucination, as experienced by Meili. While seeking refuge from the massacre in a decayed nunnery, she seems to see a spider with a human face growing in front of her. "The spider's wrinkled face pants in a mechanical way. Suddenly, this face is turned into a multitude, flying aimlessly in the air. Then from the earth there pop many bloody, naked, headless corpses with huge breasts. The sad faces fly to join the corpses' necks which are still bleeding, all uttering sighs that would horrify any human being to death."[24] Time comes to a sudden halt here; so does the coherent flow of Mao Dun's realistic narrative. The chain that mediates the past to the future can now be described only as a phantasmic hallucination, a nightmare from which one can never wake up. Can this be the other side of the rationale of history? With this scene, Mao Dun brings forth the hidden apprehensiveness of his historical discourse.

Mao Dun's historical drama completes its full cycle in "Pursuit." The young revolutionaries who have survived the revolution are reunited again, fittingly in Shanghai, the place where they first set out for their project. Now at loose ends, these ex-idealists are searching for something meaningful to restart their lives. But whatever they do, they are doomed to fall back into the predestined trap of their environment. History presents itself as a false promise, leading every attempt, selfish or altruistic, cautious or ambitious, to its opposite end. Irony surges up as the dominant mode of Mao Dun's historical perspective. One character gets married and settles for a less ambitious goal of promoting education; both his marriage and career turn out to be disasters. Another tries his hand in journalism yet learns only the lesson of forging sensational news; even his desirable girlfriend is accidentally disfigured by the end of the novelette. More noticeable is the case of Zhang Qiuliu, the female lead of the novelette. A high-spirited, flamboyant woman, Zhang Qiuliu wants to rekindle her own revolutionary passion by rectifying her decadent old classmate who has a suicidal tendency. She never succeeds, and worse, she finds after his suicide that she has contracted syphilis from him.

C. T. Hsia is correct in pointing out that, behind its naturalist façade, "Pursuit" is based on a "melodramatic trick."[25] Indeed, Zola's determinism, from which Mao Dun derives part of his historical imagination, partakes of a clear narrative design as it prefigures the human condition. But what really impresses us is the moral dialectic in Mao Dun's (and Zola's) melodramatic description of reality and history. For Mao Dun the communist, if history means a progression of time through which the revolution is carried out, what happens in *Eclipse* is then a digression of time, and therefore an

Fictive History

unhistorical look at history. For Mao Dun the realist, nevertheless, this unhistorical look precisely brings out the meaningfulness of the revolution, since history registers a too comprehensive sequence of events and non-events.

By sympathetically describing a group of revolutionaries trapped in the cycle of time, unable to move forward, Mao Dun vacillates between two roads: History as a *deus ex machina,* acting out a certain moral plan; and history as a contingency of erratic and intentional human actions. In other words, he mixes History as something in which he believes with history as something he sees and feels. But insofar as history is something always already mediated, transcribed, these two roads may well not be as divergent as they appear. Mao Dun's most vehement critics such as Qian Xingcun might have a point in noticing that the dilemma as shown in *Eclipse* is not unsolvable—you see what you believe and you believe what you see.[26] Still, Qian Xingcun has shown that unconditional commitment to the Communist version of history is never too far from either dogmatism or cynicism. How to find a viable narrative mode for the presentation of history as it is while maintaining a firm ideological ground remains the goal of Mao Dun's next major work, *Rainbow*.

Written in 1929, *Rainbow* is one of the earliest full-length modern Chinese novels, at least as defined in terms of nineteenth-century European fiction. According to Mao Dun, *Rainbow* is only the first volume of a larger project. But judging by its length (over three hundred pages) and plot structure, one may well appreciate it in its own right. The fact that *Rainbow* is long enough to be called a full-fledged novel is important here, not only because it represents a big leap since Lu Xun, who first mastered the skill of western-style short stories, but especially because it posits a different scheme of temporality, one that enables Mao Dun to come to terms with the problematic, surfacing in *Eclipse,* of history/History.

With the novel's built-in sequential flow of time on its narrative level, Mao Dun gains enough latitude to envision a slow but powerful continuum of social and cultural mutations along which the changes of his characters' morals and manners are gradually defined. As time carries on in its irreversible direction, so does history proceed to open up new horizons. In this regard, it is the historical scenario of Tolstoy rather than that of Zola that comes to mind.

Rainbow opens with a highly symbolic scene wherein the heroine, Mei, takes a cruise from Szechuan to Shanghai on the Yangtze River. As the steamship is sailing through the Wu Straits, Mei, amid the other passengers, watches the spectacular scenery and bids farewell to her life in Szechuan. After crossing the Gui Gate, or the gate of the devil (*gui*), she will lead her life on her own.²⁷ By starting his narrative *in medias res,* Mao Dun confers on the novel an epic scope, while at the same time making it clear that Mei is *already* well along into the flux of time. Mei has an unhappy past to forget, just as she has an uncertain future to expect. Mei's voyage down the Yangtze River is a passage from the old land of feudalist oppression to the brave new world of freedom and revolution. It is also a voyage of time from the realm of stagnating myth to the realm of history.

The novel covers a period from the May Fourth Movement (1919) to the May Thirtieth Incident (1925). Just like many other young people at the time, Mei is awakened by May Fourth anti-traditionalism and strives to find her own meaning in life. She stages Ibsen's *A Doll's House* at school, and develops a romance despite a forthcoming arranged marriage. Later on, with great reluctance, she gets married, but leaves her husband after one year's stifling existence. She then supports herself by teaching somewhere else in Szechuan, a job she eventually quits amid rumors of sexual scandal. Mao Dun describes how much the pursuit of independence and freedom might cost a Chinese woman in the 1920s. He is especially good at tracing every turn and twist of Mei's psychological activities in her confrontation with external forces. Given her strong personality, Mei undergoes weak moments as she is lured by self-doubt or the desire for a man's care and bodily proximity. The risk she and other like-minded women struggle against is neatly summarized by one of her friends: "people are being awakened to a new awareness, are being called forward, are moving ahead, but not toward the light, toward darkness instead. The fighters who are shouting war cries to arouse the young have not prepared a bright and happy society into which refugees [from the old one] can be received."²⁸

Mao Dun has laid out for us a winding course of history just as tricky as the Wu Straits Mei crosses through at the beginning of the novel. Mei feels relieved when the steamship leaves the last gate of the straits, but little does she know what is awaiting her. The river mobilizes everything, providing Mao Dun's historical outlook with a factor of change. As has been pointed out, reference to the passage of time on the steamship recurs in many other parts throughout the novel.[29] Instead of the circular pattern of temporality that dominates *Eclipse,* one gets a feeling from *Rainbow* that time propels people forward to meet their unknown destiny. History figures no longer as a trap, as it does in *Eclipse,* but as a series of tests.

Thus, we see Mei dealing with new troubles after arriving in Shanghai and joining underground Communist activities. Enlightened by the revolutionary cause, Mei also finds herself helplessly torn between her secret love for her leader, the firm, mysterious Liang Gangfu, and the party line that calls for a purely fraternal relation between comrades. The irony here for Mei is, of course, that to attain the utopian state wherein free love is asserted, she has first to learn not to love freely. Whether she can relinquish all all personal concerns and dedicate herself to the Revolution is yet to be tested by the end of the novel. Mei is last seen going to a demonstration against foreign imperialism, a demonstration which is later to be called the May Thirtieth Incident.

Insofar as she searches amid the flux of human contingency for a means of self-salvation, Mei's adventure reminds one of those experienced by characters such as Pierre in *War and Peace* and Levin in *Anna Karenina.* The Tolstoyan narrative scheme calls for its heroes and heroines to go through the test of time in pursuit of spiritual metamorphosis; Mao Dun's novel reveals a structural kinship with that narrative scheme by allegorizing the metamorphosis of revolution as a matter of time. Mao Dun does not inherit from his spiritual mentor only the linear temporality that sanctions humanity's pilgrimage toward salvation. While he disbelieves in Tolstoy's religious fanaticism and pacifist posture, the way Mao Dun postpones the moment of reconciliation with history leads one to suspect that the two writers do share the tacit awareness that, no matter how the progression of time contributes to the final salvation, the epiphanic moment comes only as a gift of grace, a mystical encounter that is beyond the human experience of time.

It is this peculiar resemblance that leads one to reexamine the ending of *Rainbow.* In the final scene, Mei joins other demonstrators marching down the crowded avenues of Shanghai on the warm spring afternoon of May 30, 1925, as a street clock marks the time—a couple of minutes past three. This is the moment which will later be commemorated as the beginning of the historical May Thirtieth Incident, and the moment wherein the existential present and history encounter one another. By concluding Mei's six-year-long struggle at this magical moment, Mao Dun provides one way to solve the temporal dilemma revealed by the narrative of *Eclipse*. His compulsion to bracket the meaning of both past and future within the present demonstrates his realist/naturalist fixation on time par excellence. One can never transmit the sense of immediacy in reality better than (re)capturing the fleeting moment of the now. Since this ephemeral segment of time is inscribed by the narrator in such a self-conscious way, it seems frozen into a crystal moment of immanence that ironically transcends its existential bondage. In other words, this present is so framed as to suspend the flow of time and give invocation to eternity.

In contrast to the river image in the book's opening scene that motivates the flow of time and narrative, the huge clock which appears at the end suggests the return of a mythical rhythm that Mei had once been trapped in before she finally left Szechuan. One wants to ask, does the May Thirtieth Incident indicate one of those magic thresholds leading toward the revolution? or is it just a rerun of the May Fourth campaign, awakening Mei only to hurl her into a circle of desire and despair? A more disturbing irony can be sensed if *Rainbow* is put back into the chronology of Mao Dun's writings. His first book *Eclipse,* it will be recalled, opens sometime after the May Thirtieth Incident, when many of its causes are taking roots in reality, in such a way as to result in the failure of the First Communist Revolution. In "Disillusionment," Mao Dun even juxtaposes Jing's first date with the anniversary of the May Thirtieth Incident; she and her nonchalant boyfriend run into its commemorators' parade after they go to the movie suitably entitled *Crime and Punishment*. In an anachronistic way, *Eclipse* takes up where *Rainbow* leaves off, previewing the embarrassing result of what Mao Dun would sanctify as absent cause. The ending of *Rainbow* indicates not so much an epiphanic coda as a human effort at wrestling with time, an effort to call a stop to time before it precipitates once again the incessant variety of history.

Eclipse and *Rainbow*, therefore, teach more about (fictional) writing of history than Mao Dun may have expected. The two novels form a dialectic between history as selective memory and history as hermeneutic inquisition. While the promised sequel to *Rainbow* was

Fictive History

never written by Mao Dun,[30] its predecessor *Eclipse* at least exists as a welcome chronological supplement, revealing efforts to disentangle history from destiny. These novels demonstrate how history is a matter of organizing stories, and how, with the right permutation of narrative order, history can manifest different moods and different implications.

(Re)writing the Past and the Present

In the early thirties, Mao Dun also experimented with other forms of historical narrative such as sketches, reportage, and rewriting of classical texts.[31] Sketches and reportage are often associated with journalistic writing whose generic attributes can refer to anything but fiction.[32] Yet precisely because of their emphasis on reporting topical events, objective accumulation of data, and immediate communication with readers, sketches and reportage may well be considered the kind of transparent writings that best represent reality as it is. By practicing them, Mao Dun also finds a viable form with which to make sense of fleeting impressions and events, thereby reasserting the force of history working beneath evanescent human experience.

For example, "Shanghai danianye" (The new year's eve in Shanghai, 1934) reports the bleak business scene in the spring festival period of 1933; "Guxiang zaji" (Random notes on my hometown, 1933) deals with the increasing shabbiness of life in the countryside after the Shanghai resistance. In both pieces, Mao Dun assumes the role of an unobtrusive spectator, engaged by his subjects but insistent upon distance in writing about them. Under his detached posture and innocent style, one finds just as much narrative design and thematic arrangement as in his fiction; the most straightforward reportage may demand redoubled expertise at cutting and editing to foreground its straightforwardness and to hide its art. Thus, on New Year's Eve, Mao Dun sees not only the empty, dark streets with bankrupt stores, but also the huge crowds in front of the glamorous movie theatres—a contrast that brings out a bizarre eschatological scene of despair and escapade, desolation and decadence. Or, on his homecoming cruise, he quietly observes passengers' self-serving predictions of China's fate in terms of ancient prophesies, their apprehensiveness at seeing soldiers stationed on the banks, and their worries about the sluggish voyage (due to mechanical problems), as their boat slowly sails into the darkness of night—the realm of blindness and inertia.

Mao Dun's most important contribution to the genre of reportage is the stupendous book *One Day in China: May 21, 1936* (1936). Inspired by Maxim Gorky's *One Day in the World* (1934),[33] Mao Dun and his co-editors launched the project by inviting their readers to submit writings about their experience on the randomly chosen date of May 21, 1936, a day otherwise without significance. The result was a huge success. Mao Dun and his colleagues received more than three thousand works by writers from almost every social stratum all over China and from Chinese communities abroad.[34] They ended up selecting four hundred and sixty-nine most representative pieces to compile the book, including subjects ranging as widely as a prostitute's routine business, a house wife's daily chores, a vignette of a theater, a glimpse of a street scene, to an underground agent's new mission in the area occupied by the Japanese. As the advertisement for the project promises, the book encompasses "a cross-section of today's China. In this, we'll see things that make us happy, things that make us sad, things we love, and things we hate . . . things of every shape and color throughout all of China on one day—a big picture."[35]

By recruiting ordinary people to write about their experience on a certain day, Mao Dun pushes to the extreme the naturalist/realist call for a natural writing free of individual authorship and thematic conventions. The published entries, though composed of less than one-sixth of the total number of submissions, demonstrate a panoramic view of Chinese life in the thirties. From family letters to wall posters, from marriage problems to nationalist causes, both the form and the content of the entries could not be more divergent. Yet divergence and variety constitute the core of Mao Dun's historical concept. His version of modern Chinese history is not to be written by one professional historian about predictable subjects such as wars or political upheavals; nor does it involve great figures or celebrities. Rather, it is written by and about the masses, a collective effort that articulates the public's mind and feelings. Absorbing everything in a paradigmatic manner, the book presents an encyclopedic vision of history and it demands a multiple perspective in reading. The domi-

Fictive History

nant image in this historical account is not temporal sequence but the seemingly continued expansion of space, as indicated especially by its classification of entries in terms of geographical areas.

Nevertheless, granting Mao Dun's withdrawal from the scene of authorship, and his concern about the general public's position in historical discourse, one still discerns a tendentious force behind the book. As the book develops, there gradually appears a defiant shadow that belongs to nobody but Mao Dun himself. To begin with, the loose, open form of narrative structure indicates an ironic reversal of the linear sequentiality of traditional historiography. Mao Dun introduces non-events to replace events; he also invokes a polyphonic web of noises with which to disturb the single, pure voice of the authorized historical account. Moreover, in the random impressions, personal correspondences, and other forms of writing in the book, Mao Dun sees a great moral authenticity. The contents of individual entries may be of significance on their own terms, but the book form in which they all appear together exerts a compelling sense about time and national fate hitherto rarely seen in modern Chinese narrative. Mao Dun's rejection of the sequential form of narrative, and his erasure of self-image thus turn out to be only an alibi, one that points to the paradox of both his aesthetic and ideological assumptions, to say nothing of his secret indebtedness to the synchronic structure of ancient chronicles and late Qing exposé fiction. Under his aegis, the day without significance is now loaded with historical significance.

At the other end of Mao Dun's historical narrative is his rewriting of classical tales. Mao Dun's three short stories, "Daze xiang" (The great marsh district, 1930) "Baozitou Lin Chong" (Lin Chong the leopard head, 1930), and "Shijie" (Stone tablet, 1930), though constituting only a small chunk of his oeuvre, deserve special attention; they proffer reinterpretation of ancient material and therefore indicate Mao Dun's attempt to enter into dialogue not just with what is happening but also with what happened a long time ago. "The Great Marsh District," inspired by Sima Qian's account of the uprising of Chen Sheng and Wu Guang in the late days of the Qin dynasty, tells how the masses' rebellious consciousness surges up when the tyrannical pressure finally becomes too heavy to bear any more. "Lin Chong the Leopard Head" and "Stone Tablet," on the other hand, are spin-offs of *The Water Margin;* the first story deals with Lin Chong's first psychological crisis after he is "driven to [the outlaw district] Liangshan" (*bishang Liangshan*), as the proverbial expression has it, and the second with the conspiracy to fake the heavenly mandate by a small group of Water Margin heroes.

Mao Dun is not the first modern Chinese writer to retell the old yarns in a new light; Lu Xun's *Gushi xinbian* (Old stories retold) is the pioneer in this regard. Mao Dun distinguishes himself, however, by calling attention to the intricate concepts of history as implemented in his stories. Yu-shih Chen has pointed out that all three stories share the tendency to substitute class consciousness for individual heroism.[36] Outlaws, runaway prisoners, bandits, or lower-class soldiers are emphasized main characters, replacing traditional history-makers of higher rank; their peasant origins lend the fundamental motivation to their rebellion against the status quo.

Besides these visible signs highlighting collective experience and class struggle, Mao Dun also tries to show how the power of history can be detected in more personal and subjective terms. "Lin Chong the Leopard Head," for example, carries some of the most highly sophisticated passages of interior monologue in modern Chinese fiction, in which Lin Chong's skepticism about the competence of his host, the bandit king Wang Lun, and his anxiety about his future, are touchingly rendered. Taking shelter from the government's search in Wang Lun's territory, Lin Chong feels a restless desire prodding him to do something his near-sighted and arrogant host cannot afford to do. The cause lurks in the back of his mind, yet he is unable to name it concretely. He finally puts away his impulse to kill Wang Lun and waits instead for the predestined moment to mature. Although the story contains no real action at all on its surface, it represents the most crucial moment in Lin Chong's life, a moment in which he realizes his yearning for a utopian community as well as the limitation of his ability to create it singlehandedly.

Mao Dun's rewriting of ancient tales is designed to invoke an allegorical reading; the past, as described in the stories, does not make sense until we read the stories in terms of the present. This tendentious purpose radicalizes one of the most polemical features in the historical narrative. A writer of historical fiction arouses the sense of the past by distancing us from that with which we are familiar; at the same time, he must maintain the intelligibility of his narrative by associating the past with the present. The "historiness" of a text lies neither in the irretrievable past nor in the present reconstruction of it, but rather in the gulf marking the difference between the past and present. For a realist such as Mao Dun, this gulf can be bridged in terms not so much of meticulous mimesis as of a privileged perspective; namely, a Marxist/Communist ideology, one that subsumes both the past and present. In this sense, anachronism is out of the question, since history is identifiable with allegory.

The problem here is that, once the allegorical power of the historical stories is released, it multiplies and even subverts the ideal reading at which Mao Dun originally aims. Both "Great Marsh District" and "Stone Tablet" involve plots that have peasant rebels forging supernatural portents or oracular signs calling for uprisings. In the "Great Marsh District," for example, a piece of silk with the inscription "Chen Sheng shall be the King" is found in the belly of a fish, and a fox crying the same message is said to be heard in the wilderness. By these episodes, Mao Dun seems to be suggesting the innate spontaneousness of revolution shared by the people; as long as the heavenly mandate is but a man-made ploy, an excuse for the old rulers to assert their legitimacy, it can be used just as well by the rebels as a means to justify their end. Given Mao Dun's own ideological vision, however, one may well ask if the immanent quality inherent in revolution is not really rather too close to the old myth of heaven's will. His allegorized history always invites an ironic reading.

This problem is poignantly dramatized in "Stone Tablet," a missing plot right before the epilogue to the seventy chapter version of *The Water Margin*. In the epilogue, the one hundred and eight heroes come together when the ground is opened up by a thunderbolt from the heavens, and a stone tablet is found. On it are inscribed the names of the heroes in hierarchical order; and Song Jiang's name leads the list as a sign of the mandate of heaven. Mao Dun adds his tale to the epilogue by telling us that the stone tablet was actually inscribed by one of the heroes, an ex-stone-cutter, and that the whole episode was set up by Song Jiang's strategist, Wu Yong. Mao Dun's attitude is ambiguous here. While he undermines the old version of the tale by revealing the human reality behind the myth of bandit leadership, he does not disapprove of the necessity for political intrigue as one way to bring the heroes together. The ambiguity extends to the very fact of Mao Dun's choosing to write about the forgery. One may ask, isn't Mao Dun comparable to the stone-cutter of his story, inscribing in his text a modern will of heaven? Hasn't he fabricated this text for an ideological purpose? If so, hasn't he reduced the absolute mandate of Communist revolution, as he and his fellow leftists believe it to be, merely to one of the efficient lies in history? "Stone Tablet" thus becomes a problematic text, threatening to tear apart from inside the total historical discourse on which Mao Dun's works are based.

"Multifaceted Relations": The Rural, the Urban, and the Metropolitan

The early 1930s mark the peak of Mao Dun's career as novelist. Equipped with the two "naturalist treasures" of objective observation and scientific description, as he puts it,[37] Mao Dun conducts his novelistic survey on the changes of China as manifested in both rural and urban areas. For Mao Dun, the early thirties witness the most dramatic moment of China in metamorphosis, a moment whose range of impacts cannot be fully delineated unless one looks at the changes in both town and village, city and country with a simultaneous and organic perspective.[38] Through his surveys and writings, he comes up with a panoramic view of China at the crossroad of contrastive values: agrarian versus industrial models of technology; capitalist versus communist modes of economy; rightist versus leftist leadership; decline versus revolution; past versus future. These axes of value do not have to be paralleled in terms of binary opposition; rather each calls for a more careful definition of its own historical rationale. According to Mao Dun's historiographical discourse, there must be some scheme(s) working behind them, linking them in such a way as to bring about the grand schedule of history's unfolding.

Mao Dun's best works in this period, such as the *Village Trilogy* ("Spring Silkworms," "Autumn Harvest," and "Winter Ruins"), "Linjia puzi" (The Lins' family store, 1932), *Duojiao guanxi* (Multifaceted relations, 1936), and *Midnight,* are products of this keen historical concern. Portraying changes and continuities respectively in country, town, and city, these works deserve critical acclaim in their own right. However, one can hardly capture the magnitude of the social/political/economic interactions contained by them till one

Fictive History

juxtaposes them and reads them intertextually. Modern Chinese history is so complex for Mao Dun that he has to multiply his narrative sequence in order to chronicle its dynamics in full. It is with this intention, both of offering a simultaneous overview of China at every social stratum and of demonstrating a synchronic version of the diachronic process of time, that Mao Dun proves himself to be one of the most ambitious writers in modern Chinese historical fiction.

The move to "spatialize" history is further reinforced by Mao Dun's effort to expand the range of his subjects. History does not find expression only in revolution, as evinced by his previous works like *Eclipse* and *Rainbow;* rather history has to be substantiated by various social and economic activities, whose mutations point more vividly to the winding course of time and to the inevitable rise of revolution. Thus, Mao Dun constructs a picture of China in the early thirties where at least three time/space junctures or *chronotopes*[39]—rural, urban, and metropolitan—coexist. Each is presided over by figures from different classes: producers, traders, or speculators; and each makes agrarian, entrepreneurial, or speculative activities the dominant sign of its economic and technological system.

Mao Dun's purpose is to show that the three most representative social communities are on the verge of breakdown on the eve of a revolution. They threaten each other's existence while they are all well on their own way toward throwing themselves upon the mercy of time. This is the moment when history reaches a finale by gathering all its variegated trajectories onto a single stage. Ideological imperatives notwithstanding, the more interesting issues for the reader are: in what ways Mao Dun conjures up tropes and metaphors to dramatize the coexistence and clash of the three social strata and techno-economical systems; whether he has really carried out his historical vision as he does so, and, even more poignantly, whether his critique of a certain format of historical discourse sometimes betrays a secret endorsement of it.

Mao Dun's *Village Trilogy* is a sensitive portrayal of Chinese peasants experiencing the economic and political storms of the thirties. "Spring Silkworms," the first story in the trilogy, has been especially praised for its compelling exposé of the declining agrarian mode of production in the countryside vis-à-vis the rise of modern technology and speculative investment in the city. Written at the same time as another much bigger project, *Midnight*,[40] the novel of aggressive capitalism set in Shanghai, "Spring Silkworms" represents a part of Mao Dun's historical dialectic that highlights the confrontation of modern machinery with provincial handicraftsmanship; of western know-how with native values; and of a capitalist monopoly with the rural struggle for cultural and socioeconomic autonomy. Mao Dun intends an account that would favor neither side, since to him real history manifests its meaning only amid a pre-revolutionary setting. Contradictions and conflicts are what he aims to describe; there are moments, however, when fewer contradictions surge up than expected, and when conflicts take place out of their set context. This exposes the gaps in his historical discourse and its privileging of an external position.

The question at the center of "Spring Silkworms" is the future of Chinese textile technology; the story raises the issue of a changing work ethic, a concept of management, a marketing strategy, and even a locale for those who are involved in this technology's various stages of practice. In "Spring Silkworms," through the tale of the old farmer, Lao Tongbao, and his family's bitter experience with raising silkworms, Mao Dun brings to light not just the procedures of the traditional form of sericulture but also its sociopsychological impact. The peasants take care of the silkworms with a religious fervor otherwise reserved for ritual. From speaking to eating, every facet of life must be devoted to the nurture of silkworms; every sericultural taboo must be cautiously avoided. During the incubation period, husbands are even forbidden to sleep with their wives, who hatch the eggs of the silkworms in their bosoms. The critic C. T. Hsia points out the humanitarian ethos underlying the story: "Although it is [Mao Dun's] articulate intention to discredit this kind of feudal mentality, his loving portrayal of good peasants at their customary tasks transforms the supposed Communist tract into a testament of humanity."[41]

As a result of their hard labor, the peasants reap an abundant crop of cocoons. But the harvest soon turns out to be a disaster; most silk factories have shut down as a consequence of the armed conflict between the Chinese and Japanese in the Shanghai area, and there is no demand for cocoons. Lao Tongbao's family is forced to sell their crop at a great loss and falls deeper in debt than ever for all their season's hard work and worries. The same ironic disaster of over-

Fictive History

production happens in "Autumn Harvest," part two of Mao Dun's trilogy. Lao Tongbao and his family try their luck in growing rice but, once again, the more they harvest, the more they lose. By the end of the story, Lao Tongbao, dying in bed, finally concedes to his rebellious son, A Duo, that there is something else working upon man's fate: "How come you should prove to be the right one? How strange it is!"[42]

Notice how the naturalist treasures of scientific observation and objective description work here to transmit an unprecedentedly close look at the process of sericulture. Mao Dun may not necessarily be an expert on the silkworm raising industry, but by detailing a farm family's hardships in the new naturalist-scientific way, he manages to usher his readers into a world where the diseased mode of production is still under way, even though history has evolved to the next stage of its set course. Without the practice of a new narrative discourse, the old silkworm raising business would not have been so conspicuously scrutinized by writers who behave like scientists, nor would it have set itself off so poignantly as something disappearingly quaint for the delectation of enlightened readers. Mao Dun thus makes himself at least sound more persuasive than traditional storytellers when he describes the recession of the old technology as a stage of Chinese history, generating a new rhetorical power in his seemingly neutral discourse.

Nevertheless, Mao Dun's scientific accounts carry gaps and inconsistencies, pointing to a deep-lying dispute within both his narrative and his ideological discourses. In order to accentuate the vulnerability of the traditional silk industry in a time of rapid political and economic changes, Mao Dun is committed to adding more and more blows to the family of Lao Tongbao. In so doing, he reveals his predilection for melodramatic arrangement in the name of naturalist experimentalism, with the visible difference that a Chinese version of communism has been brought in to substitute for the old Darwinian positivist hypotheses. Before things get better as a result of revolution, they will first have to get worse in every perceivable way. The deterministic elements of Zolaesque theory are again neatly reinterpreted by Mao Dun as a heritage of feudalistic consciousness and an environment of precapitalist society, which predetermine the Chinese peasantry's fate; the old concept of the Wheel of Fortune cycles through another turn.

Fictive History

The problem goes deeper. A well-known leftist writer, Mao Dun is theoretically writing to document the downfall of traditional rural technology on the eve of the impending capitalist monopoly of China's economy and industry. But, as has been pointed out by critics, he describes the peasants' hard work and unfaltering trust in the Deity with such an understanding tone that the story comes out more as a celebration of their endurance and patience than as a critique of their superstition and conservatism.[43] Even the title of the story, "Spring Silkworms," suggests an overtone of romantic melancholy, with its allusion to the famous lines from the Tang poet Li Shangyin's poem, "Untitled":

> And the silkworms of spring will weave until they die
> And every night the candles will weep their wicks away.[44]

Lao Tongbao serves as the spokesman for values which are admittedly out of date, but judged by his family's current predicament, one wonders if the superstitions of the past may not have been better comfort than the promises of the present. Has Mao Dun unintentionally revealed a reactionary consciousness? Or, more equivocally, has he suspended ideological and moral judgment, and made his text a space of uncertainties?

It is due to this ironic narrative potential that the story enhances rather than settles the tension that arises between old and new concepts of technology at a historical juncture. Mao Dun's political point of view leads him to see history as a progressive evolution toward a communist millennium—thus the stage of rural manual labor has to yield to that of capitalist investment and mass production, as reflected exactly by *Midnight*. Yet one discerns from this formula the bothersome paradox that, before the final revolution comes, history manifests a regressive development, with each new stage of social structure (and mode of production) being one degree inferior to the previous one. If, as critics have pointed out, the Marxist scheme reenacts the plot of the fortunate fall of Christianity, in which paradise is lost in order to be regained, and in which each age is more sinful and miserable than the last, in preparation for the Millennium,[45] then Mao Dun's interpretation of Marxism is further bolstered by a Chinese concept of the cyclical mechanism of history. Revolutionary anticipation and reactionary nostalgia thus coalesce, reflecting a simultaneous affirmation of inevitable progress and increasing alienation; one in which progress is only apparent because of one's awareness of ultimate salvation, not from any contemporary evidence.

The two parts of the trilogy, "Autumn Harvest" and "Winter Ruins," present farmers simply trapped deeper by the gratuitousness of their labor. Before his younger son, A Duo's, revolutionary consciousness is acted upon, Lao Tongbao and his family are living in an increasingly worsening condition; for this reason, Lao Tongbao's nostalgia for the arguable "good old days" is not absolutely blameworthy. Situated in such a self-contradictory vision of historical movement, Mao Dun's nostalgic record of the old customs of silkworm raising is not necessarily a sign of his latent reactionary consciousness; rather, it could serve as an indicator, hinting at his foreknowledge of how the forthcoming capitalist age would be even less rational and human in both economic and moral terms. In a way unexpected by Mao Dun and orthodox leftist critics,[46] this inconsistency in reasoning reinforces the drama of the trilogy while posing a more serious question: has Mao Dun's wholesale introduction of new narrative and economic/historical models also paved the way for a new mythology?

The peasants' burgeoning desire for revolt and revolution provides the major motivation of the trilogy. Contrasted with it, nevertheless, is a less noticeable (but just as powerful) yearning for the return of the mythic Order of Heaven. Mao Dun makes it clear that the former is based on human will and volition while the latter derives its power from nothing but passive superstitions about heavenly grace. Ideally, we are supposed to witness the two contrasting forces crossing each other somewhere in the trilogy—the death of Lao Tongbao, for instance, or the peasants' robbery of local rich men's barns—with one incident losing its mysterious spell and the other winning more and more recognition. But the way Mao Dun writes about these forces solicits a different reading. Throughout the trilogy, the two forces never really exchange positions but, rather, parallel each other, gaining more strength. One still remembers how the prophetlike Taoist monk, Huang, spreads rumors about oracular signs and omens and gathers more and more followers, as A Duo and other young farmers organize themselves to stir up troubles against the rich and powerful. By the end of "Winter Ruins," A Duo and his fellow rebels finally rise against the local authorities, amid rumors of the descent of the new Heavenly Prince.

Fictive History

In this sense, the ending of the trilogy is highly ambiguous. The allegedly descended Heavenly Prince, a poor, naive kid, is arrested by nervous, local armed forces. It is A Duo who unexpectedly comes to his rescue while attacking the prison. Laughing at his discovery of the identity of the "Heavenly Prince," A Duo sends him away and thus reaffirms his own cause. This rescue emblemizes less a cancellation than a replacement of the mythical heavenly mandate. The confrontation between the leader of farm insurgents and the chosen candidate for heaven's will leads the reader to wonder if they share any common ground in reflecting the utopian wish of the Chinese peasantry. According to Mao Dun's plan, the climax of his *Village Trilogy* portrays a progression of history towards the goal of Revolution. Given the novel's hidden yearning for a regressive mode of rescue from time, however, one may take one step further and say the linear development in either progressive or regressive form is only part of a cycle, an alternation of chaos and order underlined by the periodic return of revolution. Last but not least, Mao Dun intends to write an initiation story about Chinese peasants' voluntary fight against the powers of Nature and Heaven, but just as the titles of his three stories indicate, the mythical rhythm formed by the cycle of seasons is only too well reestablished at the level of discourse.

After *Village Trilogy,* Mao Dun's geohistorical itinerary leads next to the towns and small cities, intermediary areas linking the countryside, where Lao Tongbao and his family take up residence, and to metropolitan Shanghai, where capitalist tycoons and investors thrive. These towns form a second chronotope, a temporal/spatial context that regulates human relations less in terms of labor than in terms of commercial transaction. The change of the chronotopic mode must affect the representational system that makes reality what it is. Instead of farmers, small shop proprietors and provincial enterprise owners constitute the prominent class of this society.[47] Money, rather than commodity, is the new metaphor that gives meaning to the society under discussion.

One can hardly forget the long list of Tang Zijia's bank accounts, loans, mortgages, rent incomes, pawnshop earnings, uncashed checks, houses, realty investments, land, and other valuables that appears at the very beginning of the novel, *Multifaceted Relations;* or the meticulous reports of the financial fluctuations of Mr. Lin's grocery store throughout the story, "The Lins' Family Store." Indeed, Tang Zijia and Mr. Lin represent two stereotypes in Mao Dun's gallery of smalltown figures. Tang Zijia is a landlord now turned into a modern entrepreneur. He lives by collecting rent from his tenants, and running a pawn shop and a silk factory. Mr. Lin, on the other hand, manages a grocery store which is also a private credit union for lower-class people. In a strictly Balzac-like manner, Mao Dun depicts these two characters' business activities as if they were indices to a monstrous mechanism from which nobody can escape. *Midnight,* as we shall see soon, also deals with the power of money. Whereas to characters in "The Lins' Family Store" and *Multifaceted Relations* money means more or less a contractual emblem for goods, thereby taking on a certain material value, money exposes its abstract nature in the hands of the tycoons, stock brokers, and speculators in *Midnight,* proliferating or diminishing in such a relentless fashion as to threaten the whole sign system of commerce. The conception of money, therefore, is endowed with a new moral exchange-value at each stage of economic/historical development.

The three enterprises run by Tang Zijia in *Multifaceted Relations,* land, pawnshop, and factory, neatly form a web that capture most farmers like Lao Tongbao and his family. Tang Zijia rents his land and structures on the ground to tenants, reinvesting his rent income in factories that make products far beyond the farmers' ability to acquire. To ease the financial stringency of the poor, his pawnshop is always ready to buy things for a price much lower than their true value. Linked together, the three enterprises supplement each other's needs, thus enabling Tang Zijia to accumulate fortunes indefinitely, as time surges forward in its linear fashion.

But the novel is not about how well things are going for the landlord entrepreneur. Instead, it tells a story of the way the machine of fortune runs out of gear at a time full of unpredictable economic and political upheavals. As early as chapter three, we are informed that Tang's pawnshop has gone bankrupt, followed by the news that his clerks are having trouble collecting rents in the countryside. Worse, the workers of his silk factory are about to launch a strike in protest against unpaid work. Throughout the novel, Tang Zijia runs around to find support to fill in his financial holes, but his banker friends all turn him down simply through fear of high risk. The problem involved here, nevertheless, is that Tang Zijia is as much a loser as his financier friends. If Tang suffers from an overstock of goods in his factory, his friends suffer from an overstock of money in their safes. Just as he sighs at the end of the novel, "This is really a bizarre year! So many stores and factories are paralyzed because of running out of reserves; but the financial business is paralyzed, too, only because of keeping too much money out of circulation—it is going to be stifled to death."[48]

A similar problem happens to Mr. Lin in "The Lins' Family Store," though both his fortune and business are much smaller in scale than Tang Zijia's. A tailor-made character representing the petit bourgeois class in China, Mr. Lin runs his grocery store in an old fashioned way.[49] He buys things cheap in large quantity and sells them at a higher price to his customers, while at the same time he absorbs their extra money and runs it like a private credit union. According to Mao Dun's moral standard, Mr. Lin may not always be an honest merchant, since he makes money by taking advantage of buyers and creditors, but he is otherwise a good person among family members and friends. This makes him a much more complicated character than Tang Zijia, especially when he is faced with the fate of impending bankruptcy. Mr. Lin has no intention of failing the clients of his small credit union, but, when customers cannot afford to buy his goods and business runs more and more slowly, he finds himself unable to live up to his reputation as a trustworthy man.

From the viewpoint of vulgar communism, one may easily conclude that neither Tang Zijia nor Mr. Lin deserves sympathy, because they are exploiters of the majority, as in the case of the family of Lao Tongbao. But Mao Dun has something else to say about their downfall. He sees in it a signal through which the forces of time and history are made themselves intelligible to people living amid them. In the *Village Trilogy,* as we remember, not until the final moment of the farmers' insurgence is time passively felt by them in terms of the cycle of nature and of the Wheel of Fortune. In the cases of both Tang Zijia and Mr. Lin, however, time is a much more active element. Timing, on top of time, is the key factor determining their gains or loses. They see the right moment to buy and sell commodities, and they reinvest their earnings at a time most favorable to their interest. News and rumors about political or economic jolts happening far away in Shanghai have a significant effect on their businesses. Time and timing correspond to each other but do not necessarily form a causal relation. Bad times such as war, famine, or flood may actually provide a good chance for a Mr. Lin or Tang Zijia to make money—particularly if they time every move shrewdly.

Insofar as Tang Zijia and Mr. Lin recognize the irreversible passage of time and consciously make the best use of every fleeting moment, history demonstrates itself in "The Lins' Family Store" and *Multifaceted Relations* more as a linear flux of forces involving visible signs of human awareness and effort than in *Village Trilogy*. The question posited by Mao Dun, nevertheless, is why, given all their perception of time and timing, both Tang Zijia and Mr. Lin fail so disastrously. History seems to contain a sly power that outwits even those who are on full alert. One can certainly find easy explanations on the surface of Mao Dun's narrative account. Cheap foreign goods, especially things made in Japan, are said to be the major evil cause of disturbance in the otherwise stable Chinese market. But just as the center part of "The Lins' Family Store" demonstrates, even if Mr. Lin and his competitors sell Japanese products, despite the students' nationalist campaign against them, they find themselves still losing money. There must be some element yet unperceivable to Mao Dun's businessman characters, turning them from victimizers into the victims of their time.

Besides money, a correlated emblem of the ongoing commercial activities is the credit contract. Contracts are regulative mechanisms designed to guarantee the terms of an exchange between individuals in a set temporal context. For investors, credit contracts promise a return of their capital plus interest by the end of the stated amount of time. In "The Lins' Family Store" and *Multifaceted Relations,* when money is running short, credit contracts are in immediate jeopardy, too. Since Mr. Lin's personal credit union is nurtured especially on the savings of low-income people, the bankruptcy of his store brings about pathetic family tragedies. The story ends with a widow going insane after she loses all her life savings. Whereas man's contract with Heaven is already broken, as shown by works such as *Village Trilogy,* men's contracts among themselves are still doomed to fail. It is here that Mao Dun reasserts the ironic moral conclusion he has reached in *Village Trilogy:* time betrays, both in the sense that it fails people's trust in their fate or future, and in the sense that it reveals the falsity of such a trust. But the story is not over yet. *Midnight* represents the climax of Mao Dun's grand scenario of time and history.

Published in 1933, *Midnight* is a novel of five hundred and seventy pages (in one Chinese edition), encompassing as many as seventy characters from capitalist businessmen to communist activists, from intellectuals to socialites. In his autobiography, Mao Dun relates that he originally intended to write a macroscopic portrait of modern Chinese commerce based in Shanghai, of which the current version of *Midnight* is only the first part. Like Mao Dun's many other aborted plans for grand novels, the project was never carried out.[50] Still, given the size of its plot structure and gallery of characters, *Midnight* is the closest to the ideal epic novel as conceived by Mao Dun.[51]

The novel's central theme is the futile struggle of a group of Chinese capitalists to establish viable industries in competition with foreign economic aggression, and their involvement in a ferocious native game of stock speculation. Beneath this major plot, there are at least half a dozen subplots, including the capitalists' conspiracy to annex small domestic industries, their confrontation with the workers they exploit in the name of nationalism, romantic liaisons run by rich women and girls, sexual and commercial intrigues between socialites and their millionaire customers, and the ups and downs of underground communist activities amid the proletariat. Critics have long noticed the resemblance between *Midnight* and Zola's *L'Argent* in terms of plotting and characterization, but Mao Dun denied the French novel's influence on him.[52]

Mao Dun selects Shanghai as the setting of his drama. Not too far away from the village in his *Village Trilogy* or the town in "The Lins' Family Store" and *Multifaceted Relations,* Shanghai is the center of China's techno-economic activities and the paradise of international capitalists' financial games. Of course, it is also the place where the fates of farmers like Lao Tongbao and small businessmen and entrepreneurs like Mr. Lin and Tang Zijia are thrown in for the final trial. Shanghai represents the stage where reactionary and revolutionary forces are engaged in the starkest conflict.

The novel opens with an arresting depiction of the Shanghai landscape on a late spring evening in 1930:

> The sun had just sunk below the horizon and a gentle breeze caressed one's face. The muddy water of the Soochow Creek, transformed to a golden green, flowed quietly westward. The evening tide from the Whangpoo had turned imperceptibly, and now the assortment of boats along both sides of the creek were riding high, their

decks some six inches above the landing-stages. Faint strains of music were borne on the wind from the park across the river, punctuated by the sharp, cheerful patter of kettledrums. Under a sunset-mottled sky, the towering framework of Garden Bridge was mantled in a gathering mist. Whenever a tram passed over the bridge, the overhead cable suspended below the top of the steel frame threw off bright, greenish sparks. Looking east, one could see the warehouse on the waterfront of Poodong like huge monsters crouching in the gloom, their lights twinkling like countless tiny eyes. To the west, one saw with a shock of wonder on the roof of a building a gigantic neon sign in flaming red and phosphorescent green: LIGHT, HEAT, POWER!⁵³

Mao Dun carefully sets up two groups of imagery in this narrative. Whereas the ancient Suzhou (Soochow) River quietly flows westward at dusk, with some soft music from the Riverside Park, Shanghai is now enlivened by the noises of trams and steamboats, and lit up by the lights of foreign firms' warehouses as well as by the neon sign in English atop the international settlement. Investing naturalist details with an impressionist atmosphere, the scene is immediately reminiscent of Zola's famous description of the mine in *Germinal*. Shanghai, as Mao Dun would have it, is the major character in his saga of the capitalist wars in China, a chameleon-like monster which plays with the ambitions and defeats, gains and losses of investors, opportunists, merchants, and politicians.

Particularly pertinent to our concern is the neon sign carrying the words (in English), *Light, Heat, Power*—linguistic registers of a new mode of knowing, desiring, and possessing. Shining in "flaming red and phosphorescent green" atop the foreign settlement, the sign addresses in the most blatant way both the ends and the means of China's way to modernization. Light, heat, power are the basic forces making modern technology and production possible. But the neon sign is not just a reminder that equates basic social/political dynamics with techno-economic power and achievement. It is also a material emblem suggesting the aura of the future, a symbolic text that gives form to people's yearning for what is promised for the future.[54] The problem is that, given China's position in the 1930's, light, heat, and power exist at the price of the open door policy in politics and economics, and at the cost of the welfare of tens and thousands of Chinese farmers like Lao Tongbao. As Marián Gálik puts it, the "new mythical beasts" of capitalism and international imperialism "[embody] 'light, heat, and power' in all possible manifestations."⁵⁵ Especially by putting light, heat, and power in English, Mao Dun calls attention twice over to the foreignness of the promised utopia, as opposed to the familiar signs of China. The split in modern Chinese history is indicated not only by the description of economic and political systems but also by the symbols of these systems.

The most important human character in *Midnight* is Wu Sunfu, owner of a large silk factory and by all standards a competent and resourceful industrialist.⁵⁶ As the story opens, Wu has succeeded in taking advantage of declining traditional manually-oriented industry by means of advanced foreign technology and large capital investment. Far from being discouraged by the worsening economic and political situation, Wu considers the crisis an excellent opportunity: he can capitalize on the insolvency of the smaller companies by absorbing them. Wu is ambitious to establish his own empire without the intervention of foreign capital and management. He had even once planned to make his hometown a model of rural industry, before it was destroyed in the battles of a civil war.

The complicated ideological motivations of Wu Sunfu's business adventure will be discussed in the next chapter. At issue here is how, as a capitalist tycoon, Wu Sunfu is different from a provincial entrepreneur like Tang Zijia of *Multifaceted Relations*. As far as his ambition of establishing an empire of industries is concerned, Wu appears to be only a richer and more worldly version of Tang Zijia. The way he accumulates his fortune is based on buying and selling commodities shrewdly along the linear development of time, though the commodities here are not just grain and silk but whole factories. Tang Zijia could be one of the small factory owners in *Midnight*, hopelessly losing their enterprises to Wu's cunning manoeuvres. But as the story continues, one finds that a new economic mode has surfaced, one that projects a new vision of time that is crucial to an understanding of Mao Dun's historical discourse. To carry out his plan of establishing his own industrial empire, Wu Sunfu enlists the help of his brother-in-law, a wealthy banker, in setting up a trust company, which besides giving loans to the entrenched national capitalists, also engages in speculation. In doing this, Wu is unaware that Zhao Botao, a "compradore financier" who has the backing of foreign capitalists, is just as ambitious as he is to swallow up others' declining businesses with the money he makes from stock manipulation. Stock exchanges become the arena where the two capitalist villains wage their war of life and death.

Stock investment and speculation furnish Mao Dun's *Midnight* with a kind of reality hitherto unseen in modern Chinese fiction, a reality that is ironically based on the most fictitious of dealings in money and commodities. The mechanism of the stock exchange allows its buyers and sellers to conduct dealings *as if* they meant an actual transaction between money and commodities, while in fact they profit mainly from speculating on the fluctuations in the price of things in which they are purportedly interested. Speculation produces a source of profit for a new class of investors who neither produce nor consume commodities but play with their abstract values. These speculators recognize in money a quirk of identity that makes it possible to transcend the limitations of any actual fact. For a farmer like Lao Tongbao who lives in the world of an agrarian economy, the idea of value is sanctioned by the tangible existence of products; for master speculators like Wu Sunfu and Zhao Botao, silk or rice seem to take on a life of their own, proliferating or diminishing moment by moment, as their value proliferates or diminishes.

Not unlike Tang Zijia and Mr. Lin, Wu Sunfu and Zhao Botao's primary concern is the continued accumulation of money as time goes by. But if Tang Zijia and Mr. Lin are still conditioned by the material side of money, as indicated by their manipulating the price of goods, the two Shanghai tycoons celebrate the abstract nature of money by creating false demand and selling short, thus bypassing the physical stage of transactions. Moreover, they do not just sit, closely watching the fluctuations of money as affected by economic and non-economic factors in a given historical context; they produce fluctuations through their connections so as to create the best possible chance for profit. In terms of their creativity in conjuring up various prospects of money, and their total embrace of the symbolic system of a monetary economy, Wu Sunfu and Zhao Botao demonstrate their desire and ability to remake reality according to their own vision. They are artists of finance.

The question is, given Wu Sunfu's and Zhao Botao's speculative adventures, how they present a different look at time and history. As suggested above, in order to profit from highly volatile stock exchange activities, these speculators do not just watch and seize the right time when it comes up; they race against and even ahead of time. On each of their competitions, the two tycoons play bull or bear alternately, depending on tips they have received about tendencies in the economic/political dynamic. A scheduled military move, a possible political power struggle, or a secret business takeover may instantly change their decision to bet on the rise or fall of stock prices. At the core of their game is neither the past nor the present but, rather, the uncertainties of the future. Their maneuvering speeds up the process of transaction and make time itself the final stake in their speculations. Losing any set scale of movement, time presents a different format: it can mean the cyclical run of the Wheel of Fortune just as much as the linear progression or regression toward a certain destination, or the whirling around at top speed toward final disintegration. The sense of time is disoriented, not because it is short of meaning, but because it is overloaded with meanings. Mao Dun thus envisions the crisis in the capitalist stage of history in an entropic form.

The disorientation of time affects not only the way history is represented, but also the way one represents history. Fictitious dealings and speculation bring to light the self-subversive potential of the sign system hidden in our perception of reality. When money is no longer a stable sign for the value of commodities, when stock prices rise and fall precariously from one moment to the next, the fundamental laws of identity between value and goods, the signifier and signified, threaten to collapse. All unities fall into pluralities, just as the neon sign, "Light, Heat, Power," in the novel's beginning illuminates the inconsistency between what it is and what it symbolizes in the given historical context. But the most outrageous result of the breakdown of the system of value and reality, one may argue, is not that it ruins the cohesive relations underlying social verisimilitude so much as it triggers a representational link among things we would otherwise have considered divergent or even contradictory. Things exist in the paradoxical state of a "disintegrating ensemble."[57] Disintegrating, because they do not contain an authentic raison d'être that they allegedly have had; ensemble, because they hang together in terms of a phantom analogy.

Wu Sunfu starts out as a patriotic business mogul with an ambition to revitalize domestic industry against foreign economic invasion. But the way he exploits his workers also makes him the archetype of a capitalist villain. As the novel develops, the cause of nationalism and the cause of Mammon coalesce and strangely become two sides of one coin. Moreover, to the extent that Wu Sunfu and Zhao Botao work hard to create values out of their fictitious dealings, their speculation produces its own kind of harvest; while even a stubborn practitioner of agrarian economy such as Lao Tongbao is not totally free from speculation while raising silkworms or growing rice. If the speculator, by generating money, is a kind of producer, isn't the producer a kind of speculator by modulating his production against the fluctuation of market? There exists, of course, a moral hierarchy behind the different degrees of speculation. But the point for Mao Dun is that, when the representational system is out of control in the given historical context, nobody can be shielded from the disorder of identity and nothing can be dealt with authentically in realist terms any more.

If Mao Dun intends to make the world of *Midnight* the dark period before *Power, Heat,* and *Light* come, or to figure reality on the eve of revolution, he invests the novel with a mythical economic capital which is a most unexpected dividend of the entropic world of speculation and fictitious dealings. The capitalist world of Shanghai will fall, only to beget the new paradise. Therefore, speculation, in its extensive sense, is not formidable force, precipitating the total destruction of the world; rather, it is part of the grand dialectic of History, giving rise to the return of order. Time has never lost its meaning. The periodical rhythm of rise and fall inherent in the stock market echoes to the rhythms of mythological time. And critics have noticed how the capitalist villains in *Midnight* are modeled after the battling gods of Scandinavian myth,[58] taking on larger-than-life proportions. The novel never shows the total breakdown of the Chinese capitalist world; it ends with Wu Sunfu's temporary downfall in his latest combat with Zhao Botao. Chances are high that, after taking a vacation in Guling with his wife, Wu Sunfu will stage a comeback. All of which reminds the reader that Mao Dun's historical plan encompasses a full circle, returning to the stage illustrated by *Village Trilogy*, in which myth is the dominant mode of time and reality.

Speculation, accordingly, can be regarded as a theme that defines not only economic but other aspects of human activities in *Midnight*. Take the romantic affairs in the novel as examples. One finds that even an emotional capacity such as love or hate can be codified as a kind of currency, fluctuating along with other objects in the market. Wu Sunfu's wife, for example, carries on a platonic affair with her old sweetheart, the military liaison officer Captain Lei, while she has no intention of giving up what she already owns with her rich husband. Captain Lei, on the other hand, is one of Wu Sunfu's most important sources for information concerning military activities at the front. As their secret liaison goes on and off, one can never be sure if Mrs. Wu is playing with fire or just acting out the drama of unrequited love so as to add more flavor to her emotional life. We are reminded repeatedly that *The Sorrows of Young Werther* is Mrs. Wu's favorite reading; wherever she goes, however, she tends to leave the novel behind.

Other men and women in the novel fall in or out of love as if they, too, were betting on the value of each romance. Of these, the most blatant examples are Xu Manli and Feng Meiqing. A popular socialite in Shanghai, Xu Manli deals with love in just the same way as her tycoon friends speculate on stocks. By putting herself on the market of lust, she always goes along with the winner of each turn of the stock exchange. In contrast to her is Feng Meiqing, daughter of the provincial landlord Feng Yunqing who has squandered most of his fortune in speculation. In his desperate attempt to gain back what he has lost, Feng Yunqing manages to persuade his daughter to make love to the fiendish Zhao Botao, hoping she will bring her father back some profitable tips for his speculations. The result is disastrous. Not only does Feng Meiqing lose her body to Zhao Botao, she also obtains false stock information, which hastens her father's fall into the abyss of bankruptcy.

Even military and political activities in the novel are tainted with speculative color. The troops in the north move forward or retreat often, not purely for military purposes, but in coordination with the rise and fall of the stock market. In order to carry out their projections, the bulls and bears conduct secret deals with generals of the troops to stage victories or defeats, thus mixing military tactics with monetary manoeuvres. Mao Dun also spares no efforts to caricature urban bourgeois youth's changeable attitude regarding political causes. In the middle of the novel, Wu Sunfu's cousin Zhang Susu and her boyfriend carry out their romantic whims by attending the May Thirtieth anniversary demonstration. They thus turn the historical date into their own date. Driven away by fire hoses, the excited young couple take shelter in a restaurant, where they run into other like-minded friends, and engage in exchanges of stock information and flirtatious chatter.

Most noticeably, young men and women communists appear in *Midnight* as speculators. Under the so-called Li Lisan line, a party line that calls for urban proletariat organization and violent action, the revolutionaries launch strikes and demonstrations at a time least favorable to their scheduled uprising. For Mao Dun, the revolutionaries' unconditional dedication to the party line is nevertheless overshadowed by a strange individual desire to risk themselves, at the price of the cause if necessary. More poignantly, the party leadership gambles on the future of the revolution by putting its members' faith and competence at stake. Both the party and its members bet on the ideal of revolution in the way speculators bet on their stocks: with endless motion, with inexhaustible but misdirected energy, all share in a high-strung, manic-depressive syndrome, which Mao Dun must have thought characterized the ethos of the time.

A tentative conclusion can be drawn with regard to Mao Dun's description of the entropic tendency of history in *Midnight*. If history at the capitalist stage is permeated with an evil force that corrupts every facet of reality, on what ground does Mao Dun reserve for himself a transhistorical position? Writing at a time when all forms of reality, ranging from politics, to commerce, to revolution, are seen as floating values subject to speculation, doesn't Mao Dun propagate his ideal in no less speculative a fashion? For all its ideological assumptions, *Midnight* contains a capacity to resist the limits of Marxist-Christian ideology, and to refuse its own claims of transcending time. It solicits a paradoxical reading. Describing the capitalist world as one rapidly becoming estranged from itself, Mao Dun offers a rare chance to look into the dazzling interplay between values and objects, words and world; especially so, when his skepticism reflects an estrangement of its other: ideology. *Midnight* is thus a major achievement of modern Chinese realist fiction, not because it presents Mao Dun's social critique in a communist vein, but because it threatens to demythologize, however tentatively, the values inherent in various forms of history, including Mao Dun's own, and thereby drives home a polemic on the illusions of reality and realism.

Chapter three

Plotted Revolutions: Mao Dun's Politics of the Novel

Mao Dun joined the Chinese Communist Party as early as 1921,[1] and afterward served as one of the most persuasive interpreters of Communist causes by means of his literary criticism and fiction. Before he became a member of the literati, he was first a party member and an ideologue. Given his firm commitment to ideology and literature, to the provocative treatment of social/political issues, and to an involvement in the power struggles within and without the party, Mao Dun deserves to be considered one of the most prominent political novelists of the thirties. But if Mao Dun is still interesting to us today, it is not so much because his realist/naturalist fiction lends light to any political fact or ideological truism, as because he engenders in his discourse some different voices which, however unwelcome, clamor for our attention just as much as the monologic ideology Mao Dun intends to articulate.

Mao Dun creates in his fiction a locus where his juggling of realist aesthetics and Communist politics, truth-claims and party lines, themes of betrayal and themes of conversion, can be so dazzling as to confuse the very issues he means to clarify.

For example, Mao Dun's theory and practice of the naturalist novel led to one of the most heated debates among leftist critics on the verisimilitude of realism, thereby ironically revealing the existence of surveillance and self-censorship in a discourse dedicated to telling the truth in toto. His self-proclaimed vacillation between Zola and Tolstoy, or between the causes of "art for life's sake" and "art for revolution's sake," indicates one of the most classical cases of the May Fourth writer's dilemma—except that the vacillation at issue may prove to be only a posture, backed by an inherent ideological fixation. That Mao Dun maintained a dubious tie with the CCP after his mysterious loss of membership in the late twenties highlights all the more the intricate mechanism of politics working behind his social profile as a writer and behind his writings. As his pseudonym suggests, *contradiction* (maodun) is at the center of Mao Dun's writing, giving rise to a configuration of meaning(s) while at the same continuously threatening to deny itself.

By political novel, therefore, I mean not only a novel in which political ideas and milieux are taken as dominant indices to the intelligibility of the narrative, but also the inter- and intra-textual dynamic which gives rise to the writing and reading of a novel. In other words, I am dealing not merely with novels about politics but also with the politics of the novel.[2]

In finding novelistic expression of a political subject matter, the writer is obliged to acknowledge that the textual combat he or she is always engaged in can be just as treacherous as the political one it is designed to portray.[3] From a contemporary view, literary form can be the locus engaged by the endless struggle between ideologies; text and language betray as much as they confirm. The dichotomy between politics and aesthetics, if it exists at all, is thus much less clear-cut than critics such as Irving Howe used to claim.[4] In the limited space of this chapter, I will approach only four aspects of Mao Dun's political discourse. The first part will deal with how Mao Dun came up with his own theory of the naturalist novel by misreading his foreign predecessors; the second part will delineate the politics of gender and desire as shown by Mao Dun's feminine/feminist themes and characters; the third part will define the dialectics of betrayal and self-denial in two of Mao Dun's most blatantly party oriented novels; and the last part will reassess Mao Dun's political discourse from the ironic viewpoint of collapsing spheres.

Zola or Tolstoy?

Although literary reformation does not necessarily parallel political mutation, May Fourth fiction was politically motivated and thus calls for a reading in terms of ideological dialectics. The term political novel was first borrowed by Liang Qichao from the West via Japanese translations. In the famous essay entitled "Lun xiaoshuo yu qunzhi zhi guanxi" (On the relations between fiction and ruling the people), Liang Qichao sanctions fiction as the most powerful cultural medium that can transform the mentality of Chinese readers and thereby strengthen the country.[5] Both C. T. Hsia and Doleželová-Velingerová have pointed out that the two merits of the political novel celebrated by the late Qing literati—psychological impact and didactic function—are not derived from Western fictional tradition so much as from classical Buddhist/Confucian teachings on the effects which literature should entail.[6] The concept that fiction can serve a political purpose is further substantiated by May Fourth intellectual writers such as Lu Xun, as evidenced by his idealistic description of the Mara poet,[7] and by his autobiographical account of relinquishing his medical studies in favor of literature in 1906.[8]

Mao Dun and most of his fellow writers believe that modern Chinese literature should serve a serious cause and that intellectuals are obliged to enlighten the common people, helping them to recognize their socio-historical status. In an essay written in 1923, Mao Dun declares, "Literature is capable not only of driving away melancholy and of elating people who keep aloof from reality, but it can also stimulate them to activity. Especially in our age we hope that literature may take upon itself a great and important task: to awaken the masses of the nation and give them strength."[9]

Mao Dun merits attention in this context for two reasons: he directs the then general call for fiction with a political function onto a specific ideological track—Chinese Communism, thus injecting a formal rigor into an otherwise vague discursive flux; and he tries to work out a viable framework that would support both his Western literary knowledge and his political commitment, both his aesthetic belief and his fictional praxis. The result is his own brand of naturalism. Critics have sometimes argued that Mao Dun's naturalism is but a different term for trendy realism in that he does not fully indicate the naturalist treatise of Western masters such as Zola and

Hauptmann. This is, nevertheless, precisely where I would start my inquiry. Even if propagating naturalism only for the sake of a name different from realism, Mao Dun already expresses a polemical point of view. Mao Dun's misreading of Western naturalism may of course be due to insufficient references and other contingent reasons, but at stake here is the possibility that, even if he had a full knowledge of naturalism, he might have chosen to misread it in order to accommodate to new social/historical environments.

To put it in the crudest way, one may say that Mao Dun's naturalism represents a strange amalgam of at least four sources: Zola's deterministic view of the human condition, Tolstoy's yearning for religious epiphany and metamorphosis, the Chinese Communist ideal of volitionism, and elite Confucian didacticism in the radical guise of a political novel. Each of the four notions has its own special historical and ideological orientations and appears understandably in conflict with the others. By laying them on top of one another for his own purposes, Mao Dun indicates how his naturalism is unnaturally constructed, pointing to the hidden strains and cracks of his seemingly autonomous discourse. But his misreading also sheds light on the common grounds shared by those sources. In the process of unraveling the theoretical fabric of Mao Dun's naturalism, therefore, one can pause and wonder if Tolstoy and Zola are really as far apart as they appear; or if Chinese Communist interpretation of art is any more radical and progressive than the Confucian teaching that literature should promulgate the Way.

In response to his fellow leftist critics' vehement attack on his novel *Eclipse* for its depressing reflection of the first Chinese Communist revolution, Mao Dun wrote in "From Guling to Tokyo" that

> Zola explored human conditions because he wanted to be a novelist, while Tolstoy started to write novels only after he experienced the vicissitudes of life. Despite the two masters' different starting points, their works shocked the world equally. Zola's attitude towards life can be summarized as cool detachment, which is in sharp contrast to Tolstoy's warm embrace of it; but the works of both are criticisms of and reflections of reality. I like Zola, but I am also fond of Tolstoy. At one time I enthusiastically propagandized for naturalism. Yet when I tried to write novels, it was Tolstoy I came closer to.[10]

Plotted Revolutions

This self-critique indeed gives a neat description of Mao Dun's indebtedness to both Tolstoy and Zola. But a closer reading of his critical and fictional works will show that the story of influence and reception is more twisted than he admits. Both Zola and Tolstoy, for one thing, suffer from an identity problem in Mao Dun's critical treatise. By labeling Zola "cool and detached," Mao Dun may have captured only the posture of Zola as a scientific literary experimentalist, ignoring his warm side indicated by his championing of the Dreyfus case and by his 1898 essay "J'accuse." In novels such as *Germinal,* Mao Dun also bypasses Zola's strong humanitarian concerns and his fascination with mythical topoi. On the other hand, Tolstoy impresses Mao Dun and other contemporary Chinese intelligentsia more as a larger-than-life moral paradigm than as a novelist; he is seen as "the source of progressive thought in this century and the major ideological impetus of the modern world."[11] Ironically, these conceptions provide us a chance not only to see Mao Dun's own ideological standpoints but also to reapproximate the affinity between Zola's and Tolstoy's realist/naturalist notions. As a matter of fact, Mao Dun advocates Zola's scientific methods because of a Tolstoyan concern with his own society's moral degeneration.

Mao Dun's concept of literary history provides the general context in which the juxtaposition of Zola and Tolstoy becomes possible. Mao Dun derives the basic tenets of naturalism and literary evolution from such foreign books as William Lyon Phelps' *Essays on Modern Novelists* (1910), Frank Wadleigh Chandler's *Aspects of Modern Drama* (1918), and Shimamura Hōgetsu's *Naturalism in Literature* (1921).[12] For Mao Dun, "Western fiction has already passed from romanticism to realism, symbolism, and neoromanticism," whereas Chinese literature "has stopped before coming close to realism."[13] Though he personally favors symbolism and neoromanticism, Mao Dun declares that he is obliged to promote a realist/naturalist movement since it best meets China's current needs. One notices here a strong moral imperative in Mao Dun's literary evolutionism. This imperative does not stem from those foreign references he consults, but echoes the Chinese version of Darwinism which Mao Dun shares with other May Fourth intellectuals. As Benjamin Schwartz observes, the Chinese intelligentsia at the turn of the century and afterward have tended to see Darwinism not only as a hypothesis concerning the nature of biological evolution but also as a "singularly appropriate cosmic myth epitomizing and supporting all the values of Western civilization."[14] Thus, when Mao Dun and other contemporary critics apply such an understanding of Darwinian evolution to the interpretation of literary history, they find that realism and naturalism represent a watershed distinguishing "human" literature from the "inhuman" literature that is the sum total of classical Chinese literature.[15] Traditional Chinese fiction is barbarian, vulgar, and insincere (hence inhuman); by contrast the nineteenth-century European realist/naturalist novel shows a "human(e)" characteristic by stressing individual dignity and social justice.

To drag Tolstoy into the trend of literary and social evolutionism may first sound a little odd. Yet just as René Wellek points out, in spite of his primitivism and strong anti-historicism, Tolstoy "is strangely affected by the belief of his time in progress and by the basic Hegelian view of the coherence of ages: the view of art as a collective expression of its society."[16] He regards art, like speech, as a means of communication and progress. The evolution of knowledge takes place by new and better knowledge replacing the old; the evolution of feelings proceeds by means of art. Good art, according to Tolstoy, is infectious because it "destroys in the consciousness of the recipient the separation between himself and the artist, and not that alone, but also between himself and all those that receive this work of art."[17] Tolstoy's Chinese admirers are obviously not interested in the Russian master's belief that art at its best serves Christian brotherhood. What most impresses them is his humanitarian concerns and the promises in his works of evolution and change. Hence in "Tolstoy and Contemporary Russia," Mao Dun writes, "when Tolstoy speaks about art, he admits that popular art is his main concern. . . . Tolstoy believes that if art becomes alienated from most people in human society, it is of no use and has no creative power. The strength of Tolstoy's popular works enabled him to penetrate the whole world of Russia. Hence, the world acknowledges his view on art and there is no doubt that it shows the way to future development."[18]

Mao Dun understands that Zola's naturalism indicates a codified version of the literary practice and the scattered ideological theses of his nineteenth century predecessors. He considers Flaubert to be, if not the father, at least "the predecessor of naturalism in terms of his impassibilité."[19] He also notices the influences of Darwin, Taine, the Goncourts, and even Balzac on Zola.[20] In his reading of Zola and his naturalist assumption, Mao Dun particularly emphasizes three aspects: the attitudes of scientific observation and objective description, the demand of impersonality, and the concept of determinism.[21] While treating the first two aspects of naturalism as skills enabling a writer to represent life as it is, Mao Dun is ambivalent in his attitude towards the Zolaesque concept of determinism.[22]

In "Naturalism and Contemporary Chinese Fiction," which is probably the first serious Chinese document on naturalism, Mao Dun maintains that "weak human beings under the pressure of environment and determinism" are facts of life rather than fabrications of the naturalists.[23] On the other hand, he notes that the naturalist deterministic vision of the world is confined by a subjective bias that presupposes the depravity of life.[24] In an effort to find a middle ground for these two contradictory observations, Mao Dun argues that, insofar as Chinese writers adopt only the naturalist methods of accurate description and scientific observation, their novels do not necessarily render the same gloomy vision as those of their European predecessors did. "Western naturalist novels expose only the animal side of humanity in terms of determinism and are full of despair and pathos. But this is due to the fact that life in nineteenth-century Europe is ugly, subordinated to the fate of mechanical materialism."[25] But, Mao Dun asks, if the social condition of contemporary China is as ugly as that of nineteenth century Europe, "should we pretend ignorance and refuse to describe all the problems of our society?"[26]

Zola's determinism is important in the sense that it draws one's attention to the drama of the conflict between individuals and a society controlled by a monstrous, obsolete, cultural/ideological mechanism. What bothers Mao Dun, however, is its pessimistic implication that humanity's sad fate is everlasting and unchangeable. Although in Zola's positive/naturalist schema there is a temporal level assuring man's potential for progress, his novels show instead the solidification of the present in a predetermined circularity which resembles timelessness.[27] All life is seen to exist within the established synchronic boundaries that are also the basis of his biological and pathological "experiments." For Mao Dun, this biological/pathological vision of the human condition means an unthinkable perversion.[28] First, his Tolstoyan concern with humanity leads him to respect man's consciousness and his ability to perceive and improve his condition; secondly and more importantly, Mao Dun's Communist notion of historical revolution forbids him from accepting the Zolaesque static historical discourse. As argued in the previous chapter, Mao Dun is obliged to "emplot" history as a dynamically changing process in terms of revolution and class struggle. To honor Zola's deterministic social outlook would be opposed to both the Tolstoyan vision and the Chinese Communist project of revolution.

Paradoxically enough, this theoretical predicament eventually proves to be the turning point of Mao Dun's revolutionary naturalism. Contrary to Mao Dun's open declaration, Zola's deterministic view is never given up; rather, via a Tolstoyan twist, it is transformed into the most convenient stepping stone on the pathway to his Communist agenda. From a comparative angle, one finds that neither Zola nor Tolstoy is a strange figure to contemporary European leftist critics from Lenin to Lukács. Zola has long been noticed for his powerful dissection of society under the regime of the second Empire, but he has been blamed for sticking to an undialectic conception of the organic unity of nature and society.[29] "Thus Zola's subjectively most sincere and courageous criticism of society is locked into the magic circle of progressive bourgeois narrow-mindedness."[30] By contrast, Tolstoy has won much praise thanks to his epic presentation of the totality of life at a historical juncture between feudal and capitalist modes of production.[31] The irksome elements of Tolstoy's vision are, of course, his religious fanaticism and his philosophy of nonviolence in the presence of evil. As Lenin said of Tolstoy, "On the one hand we have the most sober realism, the tearing down of all and sundry masks; on the other hand we have the preaching of one of the most odious things on earth, namely, religion."[32]

Mao Dun adds an even richer Chinese dimension to the spectrum of the love-hate relations Western leftist critics have maintained with both Zola and Tolstoy. Although Mao Dun is a well-known interpreter of Chinese Communist literary theory, he derives his Marxist/Communist concepts less from orthodox readings than from secondary foreign references and other contemporary Chinese leftist critics, even including Lu Xun.[33] Together with fellow comrades, he upholds a revolutionary thesis that combines both determinist and activist elements, with a special emphasis on the consciousness which calls for a voluntary reaction to the alienation entailed by a capitalist mode of social production.[34] Since China in the 1920s lacked the material conditions for the realization of a Marxist/Socialist revolution, its Chinese advocates did not always read *Capital* as a scientific exposition of the laws of capitalist production; sometimes the book was read as a moral indictment of the injustices and dehumanizing influence of capitalist industrialization. Moreover, in response to the pervasive claim of nationalism in the May Fourth era, Chinese Communists maintained that, since China lacked a developed urban proletariat to carry on the class struggle, the whole nation must be looked on as part of the worldwide forces of the proletarian revolution. If the economic preconditions for the realization of socialism were absent in China, then the socialist reorganization of Chinese society was all the more necessary in order to achieve these very preconditions.[35]

In Mao Dun's theoretical discourse of "naturalism," both Zola's mechanical determinism and Tolstoy's humanitarianism function as crucial factors, demonstrating the two sides of his understanding of Marxist/Communist dialectics. By linking the two masters' literary theses together in the light of Marxism/Communism, he unwittingly shows us that they are, after all, products of the same age: they are bound to a total vision of reality, and prefigure a holistic discourse of determinism (be it labelled as genetic, religious, or economic) in approach to that reality. As mentioned earlier, Mao Dun criticizes Zola's deterministic assumptions of heredity and environment but never really rejects them. He subordinates them instead to the determinism defined not by Zola but by Marx. Accordingly, unlike Zola, whose novelistic practice foregrounds the miserable and vulgar condition of the lower classes driven by their instincts, Mao Dun is able to envision a bourgeois society doomed to disintegrate under the forthcoming proletarian revolution, and to contend that a naturalist writer's duty is to expose the corrupt bourgeois scene as accurately as possible.

But Mao Dun's Marxist conviction will not allow him to stop at merely attacking the steadily decaying capitalist society; rather it obliges him to proceed with predicting a transformation that will take place soon. He expects bourgeois intellectuals like himself to fight their way to an ideological conversion and to become activists leading the revolution of the masses thereafter.[36] At this point, his criticism is charged with the Tolstoyan theme of spiritual metamorphosis, which, nevertheless, is originally directed to Christian belief. Where Tolstoy showed his religious yearning for the apocalypse, Mao Dun now sets up a moral imperative in the name of the Communist revolution.

For all his iconoclastic posture in favor of the Communist thesis of literature and revolution, one question remains. Why does Mao Dun show far more concern with urban intellectuals than with the proletariat he is commissioned to rescue? Judging by his political essays and fiction, Mao Dun—at least in this period—was neither familiar with, nor interested in, proletarian activities, beyond paying them lip service. Numerous examples indicate that he is more at ease in dealing with the painful ideological transformation of young urban intellectuals from a bourgeois to a Marxist mentality.[37] For him, these young people's awakening to their historical role and their subsequent struggle to liberate themselves from the decadent status quo represent one of the most touching aspects of modern Chinese history up to 1927. In spite of their frustrations as they fumble for a new ideology, there is an implicit promise in Mao Dun's criticism and fiction that the educated youth will become the key figures in arousing a proletarian revolution.[38]

Lurking behind Mao Dun's argument may very well be the traditional mode of thinking that stresses the priority of cultural/intellectual change over social/political/economic transformation,[39] as well as the superiority of intellectuals over the less educated common people in directing a historical transition in its proper course. Described by Yü-sheng Lin as the cultural/intellectualistic approach, which can be traced back to the early stage of the development of Confucianism in Chinese history, such a mode of thinking confirms the crucial position of intellectuals in reforming the common people's mentality; this is the first step toward solving the nation's other problems.[40] We may say that Mao Dun—as a typical member of the May Fourth literati—is very conscious of his elite position and eager to contribute his efforts to accelerate a social/political reformation. It is with such a Confucian scholar's devotion to society that he, like most of his fellow leftist writers, receives Marxism as an ideal plan for reconstructing China and embraces its predetermined schedule concerning historical revolution. This gives an ironical explanation to the question of why both the Marxist notion of voluntaristic consciousness and the Leninist canon of elite leadership were readily accepted by Chinese leftist intellectuals. Furthermore, Mao Dun leads us to wonder whether he is, in fact, a Confucian-minded scholar taking on a radical Marxist mask. In this sense, he is still writing in the vein of late Qing scholars such as Yan Fu and Liang Qichao.

The preceding discussion has demonstrated how Mao Dun borrows the novelistic premises of Tolstoy and Zola for the formation of his political novel. This novel is ideologically motivated by his commitment both to the vision of Communist revolution and to Chinese traditional elite didacticism, a motivation not immediately visible on its surface. His argument clearly indicates that the environment of contemporary Chinese society is morally so degraded that no one born into it can be immune from depravity. Hence a critic/writer's duty is to expose with scientific accuracy the stagnating, decaying status quo. On the other hand, Mao Dun's elite concept and the voluntaristic part of Marxist-Leninist ideology lead him to expect some selected young urban intellectuals, like himself, to fight to achieve an ideological conversion and become activists leading mass revolution. At this point, both the themes and the characterization of Tolstoy's novels such as *War and Peace, Anna Karenina,* and especially *Resurrection,* are borrowed by Mao Dun to recount the long struggle of a young intellectual in search of "reality" or the "meaning of life"; the difference being that, whereas Tolstoy's heroes like Pierre, Levin, and Nekhlyudov are undergoing spiritual trials to attain Christian humility, Mao Dun's promising critic/writer/revolutionary has to pass all sorts of tests in quest of the apocalypse of Marxism. In short, Mao Dun's critic/writer (presumably coming from a bourgeois educational background) is required not only to depict the ugly features of his own heredity and environment but also to undergo a Tolstoyan ideological metamorphosis, in order to complete the drama of the birth of a modern Marxist critic/writer.

The Politics of Gender

One of the most remarkable traits in Mao Dun's novelistic project of politicizing contemporary Chinese reality is his predilection for feminine discourse. Not only does he feature in his works a long gallery of female characters, he is also at his best in dealing with social/political issues from a female viewpoint. His earliest work,

Eclipse, for example, introduces almost a dozen female characters, through whose ups and downs the meaning of the first Chinese Communist revolution finds a dramatic definition. In his second novel, *Rainbow,* Mao Dun depicts modern Chinese history from the May Fourth to the May Thirtieth period in parallel to a woman's psychological and ideological growth. Moreover, the five stories in his first short story collection, *Ye Qiangwei* (Wild roses, 1929), are five accounts of modern Chinese women's triumphs and failures, desires and fears, in confrontation with drastically changing social/political values. Mao Dun's "feminine" quality is best described by C. T. Hsia, who contrasts Mao Dun and Lao She by saying that "Lao She represents the North, individualist, forthright, humorous, and Mao Dun, the more feminine South, romantic, sensuous, melancholic. Mao Dun is distinguished for his gallery of heroines . . . record[ing] the passive feminine response to the chaotic events of contemporary Chinese history."⁴¹

Hsia's comment calls attention to the fact that, more than writing about women, Mao Dun writes like a woman. Hsia sees in Mao Dun's writings a discourse whose stylistic register, perceptive capacity, and general system of symbolism call for a "feminine" reading. By making such an observation, Hsia has already revealed his endorsement of the traditional binary oppositions based on gender difference, such as masculinity/activeness/straightfowardness versus femininity/passiveness/introvertedness. His conclusion that Mao Dun is at his best in depicting women's "passive" responses to national upheavals further indicates that he willingly subscribes to a male-centered view whenever issues such as politics or revolution are at stake. The fact is that Mao Dun's female characters are far more active than their male counterparts; their "passiveness" is more imposed on them by external forces than inherent in their characters. But, ironically, this does not necessarily mean that Mao Dun is more in alliance with women than is a commentator like C. T. Hsia. There is something more than a man/woman dichotomy to discuss in Mao Dun's writing. As I will argue later, his feminine discourse, while celebrating the political and sexual awakening of modern Chinese women, enacts a drama of conceptual transvestism, one which has nothing so much to do with his gender preference as with his gender-oriented ideological posture.⁴²

Critics have repeatedly pointed out that, by writing extensively about women, Mao Dun renders a vivid picture of the burgeoning feminist movement in China.⁴³ At a time when all traditional values were threatening to collapse, women were left in a condition twice as vulnerable as men; their struggle to redefine their identities on both domestic and social levels naturally begets moving scenarios, pointing to a country's painful process of recasting every aspect of her image.

Nevertheless, beneath its apparent concern with the fate of women, Mao Dun's writing from a feminine view may well suggest a tactical move, one that allows him to assert his marginal (and therefore feminine) position on a political ground occupied by the patriarchal power of the Nationalist Party. In other words, he is acting out a "martyrology" of gender in the fight against his political victimizers.⁴⁴ Mao Dun lends his voice to the traditionally oppressed sex, exposing the injustices that have been done to them and the desperate need of changing the status quo under the current regime; in so doing he gains a mobile, nonconformist power, which enables him to disturb from the outside the normative closures built by male-centered authorities.

Chinese literary history is full of examples in which male writers assume a female voice in articulating a certain political point; Qu Yuan's *Songs of the south* is but one of the most prominent cases. What distinguishes Mao Dun from his classical predecessors is that, beyond playing the game of sex change in literary imagination, he does have a historical case of a feminist movement in sight and he is ready to offer a political scheme to deal with it. Women's cries for rights of education, free marriage, economic independence, etc., are louder and more urgent than ever, forcing (male) writers like Mao Dun to declare their own grounds in both fiction and reality. Mao Dun's feminine discursive posture, as it were, (en)genders politics, making gender consciousness part of the agenda of the revolution.

But by calling attention to a politics of gender, Mao Dun at the same time subjects himself to the vertiginous interplay between the values of the two sexes. Reading his fiction, one may at least raise two questions. First, one may ask whether Mao Dun, as a male writer writing like a woman, throws himself into the limbo of linguistic transvestism, thus revealing the existence of sexual surveillance in the text; in other words, whether he really accommodates this ambiguous sexual/textual position to his political convictions. Second, given Mao Dun's attempt to propagate women's sexual liberation through political revolution, one also has to ask whether he has resituated man's position in response to woman's changing role. Both questions, I would argue, shed light on the deep-seated ambivalence in Mao Dun's discourse of male feminism. For all his feminine linguistic façade and profeminist statements, his sympathy sometimes spells anxiety, and his campaign for women's liberation leads to new constraints.

Take Mao Dun's first short story collection *Wild Roses* as an example. All of the five stories deal with women's tragicomical encounters with a new, liberated environment. The heroines of the stories are enlightened in one way or another by May Fourth thought, but in an effort to further their pursuit of self-identity, they are thwarted either by their (male) partners who had once encouraged them, or by their own weakening will to withstand forthcoming hardships. The women's longing for love and adventure constitutes the major motivation of their stories, but this romantic yearning must mean a personalized projection of a desire yet too remote and too radical to be speakable.[45] Before the revolution comes, these heroines' happy or unhappy affairs with men work only to intensify rather than resolve this insatiable desire. Ideally, these women will do away with the temptations of sex and passion, and march toward a true liberation. Xianxian in "Chuangzao" (Creation), for example, walks out on her husband like a Chinese Nora, while Gui in "Shi yu sanwen" (Poetry and prose) asserts her dignity by sneering at her double-minded suitor.

Nevertheless, those who are weak are often trapped in a state of *ressentiment*—they turn their discontent with their objective surroundings inward as self-depreciation and self-deception, each of which alternately gives them both pain and pleasure.[46] Thus, in "Tan" (Haze) Miss Zhang expresses periods of happiness and dejection in her adventures of falling in love and being deceived by it; while Qionghua in "Yige nüxing" (A woman) is deeply hurt by the game of love, only to choose to keep playing the game at the risk of her life. Miss Zhang tries to solve her problem by running away from it; in Qionghua's case, death is her only way out. "Zisha" (Suicide) has a similar story, in which Miss Huan stages a mock-martyrdom by hanging herself, after she finds herself no longer able to cope with external pressures.

In these stories, one can already discern a tautology in Mao Dun's feminist scheme. Liberation of body and thought is what Mao Dun's heroines are supposedly chasing after. But when they try out their luck in reality, the first moral lesson they learn is that, before their desire is fully realized in the future realm of freedom, no form of existential experience such as love, family, or even life itself can be trusted or appreciated as a projection of that state of plenitude. For all Mao Dun's feminist talk, there lurks in his discourse a highly evasive *and* austere demand. Evasive, because his heroines are promised a complete womanhood only in a continued regressive fashion; austere, because women's liberation presupposes an ideological commitment whose harsh terms are exempt from any foretaste. For the present, accordingly, Mao Dun's realist brush can only draw either women's painful disillusionment with regard to love or life, or their courageous breakaway from the status quo with a vague hope of revolution in mind. This leads one to wonder if Mao Dun is too harsh to his female characters by putting so much burden on them and, more arguably, if he is in fact writing about women from an ideological viewpoint no less patriarchal than the one he aims to attack, however feminine he might sound.

Of particular significance is "Creation," a story of the way in which a woman is ushered by her husband into the modern world, only to find him the biggest barrier to her continued pursuit of the total self. Xianxian is enlivened and enlightened by her husband Junshi after their marriage, but as time passes by, the more progressive knowledge she acquires, the more foibles she finds in her husband. When she cannot stand his petty hobbies and reactionary political positions any more, she leaves him. "Creation" is often read as an initiation story in praise of women's awakening to a new revolutionary call. But at the center of the story is Mao Dun's remake of the Pygmalion myth, a myth that is solidly based on man's fantasy of creating an ideal woman.[47] Although Mao Dun mockingly lets the ideal woman Xianxian fly away from her husband/creator at the end of the story, thereby asserting his feminist attitude, one senses a condescending overtone, with even a touch of anxiety, throughout his account. Though refusing to be the object of desire of her own husband, Xianxian, as Mao Dun's creation, is nevertheless the (male) passive ideal to be imitated by his implied women readers.

Mao Dun, after all, cannot afford to go all the way toward rewriting the Pygmalion myth. Deep in his mind, he understands that a true reversal of the process of creation in favor of women may bring a disastrous outcome for the patriarchal society. The story of

Zhang Qiuliu, the flamboyant lady in "Pursuit," part three of Mao Dun's trilogy *Eclipse,* comes to mind. Most of the female characters in the novel suffer either from melancholy sentimentalism or from self-indulgent hedonism, both symptomatic disguises of their chronic resentment during the eventful period of the first Chinese Communist revolution. Zhang Qiuliu may not be free of these syndromes, but she is probably the only female who believes in the power of her liberated femininity vis-à-vis the oppressive post-revolutionary environment. In the midst of her ex-comrades, who have become pessimistic and cautious after the failure of the first Communist revolution, only she stands out and vows to continue her fight with no compromise, however hyperbolic she might sound. Her immediate project is to recreate the image of her old classmate, Shi Xun, who has been leading a dissolute life haunted by suicidal wishes.

Mao Dun certainly cherishes an emotional attachment to the complicated personality of Zhang Qiuliu, a character who is both decadent and lively, high-spirited and frivolous. But the way he describes her rescue task betrays his ambivalent attitude toward woman. In the name of guiding Shi Xun back on to the normal track of life, Zhang Qiuliu actually helps accelerate the tempo of his self-destruction by going along with his dissipated lifestyle. With other friends who are suffering from post-revolutionary nihilism, they drink, fool around, and make love without restraint. In Zhang's daring, splashy personality, there gradually emerges an almost vampirish menace, one that threatens to devour Shi Xun's manhood. Shi Xun finally does commit suicide, while Zhang Qiuliu finds that she contracted syphilis from him before his death. Implicit in Zhang Qiuliu and Shi Xun's disastrous affair is Mao Dun's submerged acknowledgment and fear of the sexually independent woman, whose erotic empowerment refuses the conventional assumption of feminine passivity. In contrast to the ironic comedy of the creation of Xianxian by her husband, a woman like Zhang Qiuliu cannot turn the tables and set out to (re)create her man. If she insists on doing so, she invites the destruction of both of them. Setting Xianxian and Zhang Qiuliu side by side, one thus sees both Mao Dun's fantasy about and fear of women's desire for liberation and transgression in a masculine world.

Mao Dun's dialectic of sex and politics finds a more systematic expression in *Rainbow,* one of the pioneering novels about Chinese women's pursuit of self. As mentioned in the last chapter, *Rainbow* delineates modern Chinese history from the May Fourth Movement to the May Thirtieth Incident by focusing on its heroine Mei's pilgrimage toward sexual and ideological enlightenment. The novel has a mythological structure: in a letter to Zheng Zhenduo, Mao Dun writes, "Rainbow is a bridge, by which the Goddess of Spring leaves the Kingdom of Death and comes to the world again."[48] In each of the three parts of the novel, Mei undergoes an ideological crisis which is paralleled to her changing relations with men. In part one, we see a Mei first enlightened by the May Fourth Movement and the campaign for free love and marriage. She participates in the performance of Ibsen's *A Doll's House,* propagating women's rights, while carrying on a love affair with Wei Yu, an effeminate young man, and defying her father's wish to marry her to the businessman Liu Yuchun. She eventually loses her battle and marries the man chosen by her father. The case is complicated by the fact that, Mei's married life is not all miserable. She does not love her husband, whose awkward efforts to please her and accommodate her new thoughts only repulse her more, but to her secret embarrassment, she knows she is attracted to the part of their marriage involving physical touch and sex. There is a split between Mei's desire for bodily pleasure and her yearning for spiritual transcendence; this split thrills and exasperates her at the same time.

In dealing with a life gap like this, Mao Dun drives home the realist/naturalist endeavor to expose the inconsistency in the human condition between the arguable body and spirit; between the object of desire and desire; between reality and dream. As C. T. Hsia points out, Liu Yuchun's confession to his high-minded wife of his pathetic early experience and his intellectual inferiority is one of the most touching parts of the novel.[49] Mei feels sympathy for her husband, but she has to leave him for a higher goal. She divorces him and leaves her hometown to teach somewhere else. While Mei's decision is necessitated by the hidden ideological plan of the novel, one can already see a self-contradictory force at work. Along with Mei's gradual initiation into seeing her sexual and social role in a new political light, she also wrestles with repugnance against the sensation she feels in her mature female body, that very body that should be serving as the basis for all her feminist awareness. This ambivalence constitutes the second part of the novel, in which Mei teaches at a small school and becomes involved in the game of love and lust with her colleagues and a local warlord. Mei is both amazed and scared by her female sexuality. She rejects men's advances just as much as she is tantalized by the desire to be chased by them. As far as her sexuality is concerned, it is no longer easy to distinguish whether she is a seductress empowering men or an erstwhile victim being empowered by men. This confusion is only highlighted by the ambiguous role she plays in the faculty's moon-watching party, which turns out to be an orgiastic chaos.

The third stage of Mei's metamorphosis takes place in Shanghai. Mei now tries hard to probe for a new rationale to sustain the feminist cause which has been so thwarted by her teaching experience. Looking back at her previous adventures, Mei finds herself bothered by a question: "In the past, I struggled against reactionary forces. I have run away from home and led an independent life. Later on, I got divorced. After all, I did not fail [as a liberated woman]. But what good has my struggle done for the country?"[50] In dejection, she "randomly picked up a book, *Marxism and Darwinism*. The two 'isms' sounded so familiar yet so strange to Mei,"[51] and she simply cannot resist the temptation of reading them. Her eyes "shine greedily" as she reads on, to the point where she is overwhelmed by the thrill the book produced. Instead of individualistic Ibsenism, Mei sees the final step toward the completeness of her womanhood in the communal campaign for revolution.

Notice how Mao Dun lavishes sexual imagery on Mei's first contact with Marxism, and how he ends up substituting a causal relation between sexual and political revolution for the paradigmatic one which underlines the first two parts of the novel. Communist revolution is now revealed as the prerequisite of any meaningful sexual emancipation, though in fact the two causes may only be commensurable rather than inextricable. The problem is further intensified by Mei's secret love for Liang Gangfu, the leader of the underground organization she joins. Cold, determined, and inscrutable, Liang Gangfu acts out the ideal features of Communist heroism; these features are ironically reminiscent of the chivalric virtues of classical Chinese vernacular fiction. In front of Liang Gangfu, whose name, after all, means "stern man," Mei "becomes so weak, losing all control over the unnameable restlessness in her mind . . . she is helplessly obsessed with his image."[52] Liang Gangfu is not only the ideological mentor but also the emotional idol of Mei's new life. Mei's body and character may indeed be feminine, but the signification they bear is written and interpreted solely by males.

Nevertheless, if Liang Gangfu embodies the virile, rational quality of the Communist revolutionary movement, one must rethink the blatant feminine style Mao Dun has applied to his fictional discourse all along; the question must be asked whether Mao Dun's discourse betrays a phallocentric fantasy by consistently submitting only his heroine to such harsh tests. Assuming the mobile, subversive voice of the "other" sex in challenge against the authorities, he plays with the female gender merely as a mediator, aiming at foregrounding the new genre of Communist fiction which is as male-centered as the old, reactionary one he sets out to overthrow.

Unsurprisingly, in order to carry out her historical mission as revolutionary, Mei gives up her emotional attachment to Liang Gangfu. To love a man and to love a party line become exchangeable; sexuality is subordinated to seemingly neutral politics, and woman is again made submissive to man. The strange circular logic embedded here is that, in anticipation of the future where all desires will be fulfilled, one's private wishes have to be checked for the present; or, even more ironically, desire had better remain unfulfilled in both passive and active terms as long as it is the major impetus for the revolution that satisfies all desires. In order to be a woman liberator, Mei has to cease (at least for the present) from becoming a liberated woman.

The trickiest part of Mao Dun's feminine/feminist discourse, therefore, is its hidden tendency to desexualize Mei's newly found gender awareness. The underground Communist organization demands a discipline of fraternity that means women and men comrades work and live together like brothers and brothers. This wish to degenderize sexual difference throws into question not only Mao Dun's apparent concerns with women but also an unspeakable homosocial desire/anxiety.[53] Chivalric, heroic brotherhood lies at the bottom of Mao Dun's ideal revolutionary activity; on the other hand, inhibited by the homoerotic threat it hides, this brotherhood cannot be fully articulated except in heterosexual terms. One may say that there coexist in Mao Dun's characterizations of women contrary impulses to establish and subvert the fundamental difference between hetero-eroticism and male affections, desire and its sublimations.

Mei's love for Liang Gangfu is consummated in the May Thirtieth demonstration. She shouts amid crowds and is driven this way and that by policemen. Her thin blouse totally drenched by fire hoses, she last appears almost half-naked, standing next to her beloved Liang Gangfu and readying herself for the next move. But this highly erotic scene only suggests sexual anxiety. For Liang Gangfu, Mei's feminine sexuality is transparent, in the sense that she is but a "brother." The libidinal Communist fraternity can be fulfilled only through a mediating female, the other sex. This insistent ideology of heterosexual mediation, and its corollary anxiety about independent feminine sexuality, parade Mao Dun's stylistic and symbolic transvestism throughout his text, laying bare his impotence to differentiate in sexual terms his leftist political convictions from the rightist mores he writes against.

In *Midnight,* Mao Dun's feminine/feminist theme is evinced not only by the complicated relationships among characters but also by the temporal/spatial images of the novel. Shanghai, for instance, appears under his pen like a woman. The feminine quality of Shanghai is first transmitted in the opening chapter through the eyes of Wu Sunfu's father. After he arrives in Shanghai, he is escorted home by his daughters in a fashionable Citroën. As the car penetrates the streets of Shanghai, Mr. Wu gets more and more uncomfortable. The towering skyscrapers, the kaleidoscopic colors of neon signs, and the endless stream of monster-like cars drive him over the edge of nervous breakdown. Even more horrible are the images of women sitting next him and walking on the streets: "Old Mr. Wu felt his heart contracting with disgust and quickly averted his eyes, which, however, fell straight away upon a half-naked young woman sitting in a rickshaw, fashionably dressed in a transparent, sleeveless voile blouse, displaying her bare legs and thighs. The old man thought for one moment that she had nothing else on. The text 'of all the vices sexual indulgence is the cardinal sin' drummed on his mind, and he shuddered."[54]

Through the window of the Citroën, Old Mr. Wu sees a montage composed of parts of female bodies. Quivering breasts, naked legs, red lips, come together in his first impression of Shanghai. But there is a blatant sense of voyeurism implied in his indignant, helpless "gaze" at the world outside his car window, making us wonder whether Old Mr. Wu's excessive fear bespeaks the excess of his repressed desire. This rhetorical montage is even more exuberantly delineated as Old Mr. Wu enters the luxurious mansion of his son, in which he is surrounded by women with heavy perfume, sensual smiles, and "startling red lips." "Their light silk dresses barely concealed their curves, their full, pink-tipped breasts, and the shadow under their arms. The room was filled with countless swelling bosoms, bosoms that bobbed and quivered and danced around him,"[55] so much so that he finally collapses, and soon dies from shock.

Starting his novel with the burlesque overture of the death of Mr. Wu from seeing too many naked women, Mao Dun, of course, intends to caricature the old man and the moral values for which he stands. But in the light of the novel's overall vision of Shanghai, one cannot but suspect that Mao Dun's caricature points no less to his own narrative standpoint. His social critique on Shanghai seems to begin where old Mr. Wu's repugnance leaves off. Whereas, to old Mr. Wu, the last vanguard of Confucian feudalism, Shanghai means a "devilish cave,"[56] to Mao Dun the Communist ideologue, it means equally a city of capitalist evil. In a most paradoxical way, Mao Dun sees the city through the eyes of the old gentleman he laughs at. For all their ideological difference, both project a sordid, voluptuous, female image on the city. Shanghai is like a vamp, mysterious, seductive, and dangerous. Woman's body is again used as a mediating place for the conflicts of ideology.

As *Midnight* develops, it becomes clearer that Shanghai is the place where one can buy and sell everything; "the place to which virtually everybody comes," in a "promiscuous mingling" of groups, factions, trades, professions, classes.[57] Promiscuity indeed provides the thematic matrix in *Midnight* for the interlinking of the different worlds of commerce, politics, warfare, literature, and romance: it spreads metaphorically across the text in the way in which it spreads out over society. The stock market, as a corollary, is the center where this promiscuous social activity is foregrounded. The stock market brings together what should be kept hierarchically apart, and thus blurs the contours of the social map. It is at once a "meeting-place" and a "melting pot." Bankers, merchants, politicians, landlords, opportunists, revolutionaries, intellectuals, poets, socialites, and callgirls, find themselves mixed with each other, all engaged in the fast circulation of money, financial tips, political intrigue, news, gossip, sex, and power.[58]

The vamp image of Shanghai is best represented in personal terms by the socialite Xu Manli. With her mercurial adaptability and inexhaustible energy, Xu Manli is one of the most active characters in the novel. She has the instinct that enables her to keep away from danger and to gain access to where money is. Xu Manli is a decadent woman. But who else is better qualified for ushering us into a world in which corruption and decadence prevail as the normal? Thus, in the third chapter of *Midnight,* she performs a striptease on a billiard table to four selected "pillars of society" in the billiard room of the Wu mansion, while outside the room, the funeral in memory of old Mr. Wu is proceeding.[59] She is the priestess presiding over a danse macabre. Later in the novel, we see her again with Wu Sunfu and the other three businessmen on a late night cruise on the Huangpu River. Fed up with the bad news about the civil war that is ruining their business, the men try to relax themselves by playing an erotic parody of Russian roulette with Xu Manli. Asked to stand on one leg atop a table, Xu Manli is supposed to bring luck to the one who catches her in his arms as she loses her balance in the wind. Meanwhile, the steamboat, now renamed Manli, runs at full speed on the river, sinking a sampan that stands in its way.[60]

As if directly borrowed from the gallery of Zola's sensuous women like Nana,[61] Xu Manli uses her body in exchange for the good life and for money. Put in the context of Chinese fiction, however, she reminds one more of the famous *femme fatale* Sai Jinhua in the late Qing exposé novel, *A Flower in the Sea of Sins,* by Zeng Pu.[62] One can see her through a double perspective. Like Sai Jinhua, Xu Manli is an unscrupulous opportunist, but given her carefree behavior and her sexual power over men, she appears ironically the most liberated of the more than dozen female characters in *Midnight* who are searching for freedom via either romance or revolution. On the other hand, the characterization of Xu Manli takes on a strong sense of moral retribution; modeled after other *femmes fatales* in history, her badness finally embodies a moral agency, whose mission is to corrupt the devilish capitalists, exposing their licence and self-destructive impulses.

The double reading brings one to the basic indecisive attitude Mao Dun has held all along in his treatment of women and politics. Xu Manli flirts her way through the moral, political, and economic downfall of the Nationalist regime, therefore representing "a" force of liberation, but the power of her sexuality, once unleashed, posits a new challenge to the stoic discipline of the male Communist revolution. Xu Manli could appear to be a formidable character, threatening to laugh away not only the old moral/political canons but also the new, revolutionary ones yet to be established. She releases forces which may run beyond the author's presumably omnipotent control. In conclusion, from a model woman like Mei in *Rainbow* to a bad woman like Xu Manli in *Midnight,* one witnesses Mao Dun's ambivalent definition of woman's roles in the revolutionary years. His feminine style, at its best, is but a costume drama. Take away his profeminist mask, and he shows a misogynist face.

The Politics of Betrayal

After Mao Dun published his first novel, *Eclipse,* he was vehemently attacked by his fellow leftist writers and critics. The crux of the charges against Mao Dun was that he had betrayed his ideological convictions by exposing the negative side of the First Chinese Communist Revolution. Dealing with the easy disillusionment of the young urban intellectuals' pursuit of love and revolution, their vacillation in the midst of divergent political causes, and their desperate, nihilist struggle to survive the pain of the lost revolution, *Eclipse* is a novel full of skeptical overtones, in sharp contrast to the hyperbolic, affirmative statements Mao Dun makes in his critical essays on the function of literature.[63] Moreover, as an ideologue, Mao Dun betrays his political conviction by writing about young Chinese revolutionaries who feel betrayed by what happened in the revolution.

The issue of *betrayal* is important here, not only because it is one of the themes of the novel but also because it involves the political consequences of writing any novel. Before being a writer, Mao Dun is first a party member; any writing deliberately against the interest of the party should naturally be subject to censorship. But on the other hand, the realist/naturalist aesthetics Mao Dun has propagated calls for an exposure of what has been unspeakable and unperceivable; a conscientious writer's work naturally "betrays" things happening in reality, good or bad, happy or dejected. By regarding betrayal (and self-betrayal) as the center of both the theory and praxis of Mao Dun's early realist/naturalist fiction, I am thus referring to the double meaning of the word: to betray means both to turn back on a cause (country, ideology, contract, and so forth) or a person and to reveal unknowingly what would otherwise be concealed. The politics of betrayal is the last taboo of Mao Dun's ideology; it serves also as an aesthetic guideline in his realist/naturalist treatise. The two definitions of betrayal are not always well separated. In the case of *Eclipse,* one sees the two sides of betrayal interfere with each other, turning an apparently aesthetic issue into a provocative political debate. What compounds the issue is the problem of self-betrayal, which sees a seemingly well-defined writing, theory, position, or belief turning against itself, thus revealing the innermost threat hidden in any self-sufficient claim.

In response to his critics, Mao Dun wrote a long article, "From Guling to Tokyo," in which he details his motive and overall process of writing *Eclipse* in the wake of the failure of the revolution. In this article, he reasserts that modern literature cannot ignore bourgeois readership, though its goal is to enlighten the proletariat on the revolution.[64] Mao Dun is certainly discontented with the writing of propagandist literature in the name of serving lower-class readers. He questions how many farmers and workers would be interested in new literature in exchange for the traditional forms of literature and theater. "You want to awaken the proletariat by means of literature, but the kind of literature you produce cannot bring about any impact on them in reality. Isn't this a waste of energy?"[65] His cynicism is emphatically expressed in the following statement: "If you write fiction about the sufferings of the proletariat, you obtain praise from everybody as revolutionary writer; but if you write about the pain of the bourgeoisie, you are guilty of anti-revolutionary activity."[66]

Together with its rejoinders, "From Guling to Tokyo" serves as firsthand material about the debate among leftist critics/writers over the purpose of literature; it also sheds light on the inherent paradox Mao Dun would play with for the next two decades. We can approach the paradox from at least two angles. First, both Mao Dun and his critics betray an elite perspective by declaring that literature represents the interests only of a special group of readers, labelled either as bourgeois or proletariat. The debate as to whom literature should serve leads us to the fact that, while condemning elitism, distinction, discrimination, and so forth, Communist literary ideology itself establishes a hierarchy of taste, a priority list. In the name of representing life to the fullest, Mao Dun and his critics argue about how exclusive a realist literature can be rather than how it can contain as many facets of life as possible.

Second, one has to examine the wild paradox in Mao Dun's

argument that the Communist revolution should not rule out support from the middle classes, that a writer is entitled to write for and about them in order to win them over. Ideally, a Communist work is not something that rules out that which finds hideous because they constitute part of the real; a conscientious leftist writer should not reject the inscription of the useless and wasteful elements of society. Here Mao Dun espouses a strong humanist tenet that highlights, in effect, the utopian vision of Communism. But the danger implied in such an argument is that, when he pushes the humanist side of Communism to its logical end, Mao Dun seems to propagate a literature that betrays itself and embraces what is radically different and unassimilable. In other words, the human must contain rather than ignore the inhuman; the authentic, leftist, realist writer can be so only by setting out to embrace what he aims at eliminating in the long run. The ultimate goal of mimesis is to represent even what is not (or should not be) representable. But in so doing, the seeds of betrayal and self-betrayal have been already planted. This is what Mao Dun's critics are most afraid of.

The doubling of betrayal sheds light on a self-deconstructive inclination in Mao Dun's early works, while at the same time it bespeaks most emphatically his utopian desire to include everything. Take *Eclipse* as an example. The intellectual youth in the three novelettes suffer in one way or another from a guilty conscience. They are lured to take part in the revolution that projects a moral and rational sphere free of the threats of chaos and irrationality, but in reality they find that such a revolutionary aim has to be subsumed in a contrary sphere, one of revolt that is constituted by aimless whims, violence, useless love affairs, wasted lives, and other contingencies.[67] How the young people reconcile their impulse to revolt with their yearning for revolution has often been seen as the main theme of the novel. But only by looking from the perspective of Mao Dun's discourse of betrayal can we understand that the thematic conflict may amount to a duplicity. All the oppositions are already removed from a simple origin and implicated in doublings and repetitions. Hence Mao Dun's sympathy with his characters and his complicity with what he appears to be against.

In "Disillusionment," the theme of betrayal is first dramatized by Jing's love affair with Baosu. Jing has come from the countryside to pursue a new life, but she is soon disappointed with the boredom of life even in the Chinese metropolis. The appearance of Baosu brings the romance she has been yearning for all along. Openly called the "dandy" by his classmates, Baosu has had a long history of romantic conquests, and Jing is but his latest prey. In contrast to Baosu, Li Ke, nicknamed on campus as "the rationalist," often sneers at Baosu's boasting of his romances with the statement, "here goes yet another recital of his romantic fiction."[68] Li Ke's repeated reference to the word fiction is a key image here, because it later becomes apparent that Baosu is indeed a person with a fictitious façade. He catches Jing's heart, sleeps with her, and then deserts her. Worse, he is a spy working for the warlord government. With neither scruples nor substantial beliefs, Baosu betrays because he has nothing to lose from the outset. His whole personality is a dangerous void. Jing's being betrayed by him is an inevitable fact. The irony, nevertheless, is that Jing's violation initiates her into the fictional, rootless side of the pursuit of the real.

This chain of delusion and (self)betrayal sets the tone of the trilogy; by describing how the chain works, Mao Dun dramatizes his concept of reality, which hinges exactly on its self-denial as illusion. In this regard, Baosu's dandyism deserves special attention. As a fashionable young-man-about-town, Baosu moves smoothly within and without campus, blurring the focus of social recognition. His identities and origins cannot be established, and his appearance is a defiance of the fixed structure of differentiation. Dandyism is an art of betrayal and self-betrayal. Like a disease eventually prevailing over the whole trilogy, it confuses characters' ideological and psychological orientations, obscuring the line between flirtation with a cause and commitment to it, between fashion and obligation. In short, the love affair between Jing and Baosu brings together a politics and an aesthetics, calling attention to Mao Dun's worried awareness of the crisis brought about by a degenerate illusion of mimesis.[69]

Accordingly, after Jing recovers from her sorrows and sicknesses, she goes out to find a new rationale for her life, this time in the campaign of the Northern Expedition. Mao Dun acutely spots that Jing is not free of the dandyism Baosu once embodied. She switches from one job to another, caught in the circular track of illusion and disillusionment, till her beloved, Qiang Meng, appears in time to save her. But as the ending of the story makes clear, even her happy marriage with Qiang Meng turns out to be a bad joke, as duty calls him to the front before their honeymoon is over. The lesson for Jing

Plotted Revolutions

is that the supposedly concentric spheres of order, love, and revolution cannot be grasped as One: each unfolds into its Other, chaos, desertion, and dissatisfaction. For Mao Dun, description of the "irrational" side of the real is where the art of realism/naturalism begins.

The dialectic of delusion and betrayal in both the political and romantic realm is even more graphically depicted in "Vacillation." The menace of self-contradiction and expenditure is reflected by the setting, the collaboration government of the Nationalists and Communists in the Wuhan area; by the mixed ideological identity of Fang Luolan, the hero of the novelette, as a liberal Nationalist, or a leftist in a right-wing party; and by his simultaneous love for his conservative wife and his liberated colleague. An idealist, Fang Luolan is nevertheless thrown into a condition where his reform projects, together with his love affairs, are all turned upside down. By the end of the novel, he brings only pains and confusion to himself and to the people he vowed to serve.

As Mao Dun puts it, "The period in which 'Vacillation' takes place represents the most serious stage in the history of the Chinese Communist revolution. The novelette deals with the vacillation between revolutionary concepts and policies—leftism leads to an epidemic of leftist radicalism; when the people try to put down leftist radicalism, they open the way for the rejuvenation of rightist thoughts, which finally results in a tremendous counter-revolutionary riot."[70] Fang Luolan ends up making himself just the opposite of the revolutionary he wants to be. What goes wrong with his character? Even more poignantly, if a Communist Party or political platform is supposed to foresee a future rationalized society, how can it let a collaboration government incur the disaster shown at the end of the novelette? Or, was the collaboration itself a waste "by design," aiming at the success of the future revolution at the cost of current chaos?

The novelette is neatly placed in a temporal context starting with an ideal of revolution and ending with the fact of revolt. Though involving both radical moves and violence, "revolution" and "revolt" mean two distinct categories of human action to Mao Dun; the former points to a rationalized goal, while the latter points to a sheer release of destructive power. "Vacillation" deals only with the blurring of the distinctions between the two categories; it therefore smuggles into its discourse an element of seedy defiance. On the superficial level, Mao Dun attributes the collapse of the revolutionary ideal to the archvillain Hu Guoguang, a slimy opportunist who manipulates the weak-willed Fang Luolan for his own political and commercial ends. Hu Guoguang thrives at a time when anarchism rules. In C. T. Hsia's words, he is a "power-driven man bent on self-aggrandizement, a frequent protagonist in naturalist fiction."[71] Nevertheless, if one takes a closer look at Hu Guoguang, one finds that he is as much a parody as he is the opponent of Fang Luolan. Not unlike Fang, Hu Guoguang also vacillates in his own way, between the leftist and rightist causes and between wife and mistresses. Hu Guoguang is the most unwelcome participant in Fang Luolan's mission, yet he exists to testify to the gratuitous part of Fang Luolan's seemingly neat scheme of revolution. As if in complicity, he cooperates with Fang Luolan, carrying out Fang Luolan's plan in the worst possible way. Insofar as they are doubles, Fang Luolan is not betrayed by Hu Guoguang so much as by himself. His revolution contains its own seeds of riotous revolt.

Betrayal spreads and saturates everything in the third part of *Eclipse*, "Pursuit." The revolution has failed, and those who have taken part in it are now left to face up to the bitter question why an action devoted to Justice and Reason should result in cruelty and waste. As the novelette's beginning indicates, these young ex-revolutionaries meet where they had parted to pursue their individual goals just a couple of years previously. Ironically, it is in this moment of disillusionment, in the retrospective yearning for a lost reality, that reality makes itself most poignantly felt. As the grand plan turns out to be but a dream, trivialities—things which would have been considered redundant or useless in the heyday of revolution—are brought in to fill up the now unbearable void. Goals such as a convenient marriage, self-serving commitment to primary education, a job in journalism, or the pursuit of carnal pleasure constitute the major part of "Pursuit." But even these humble goals cannot survive the trials of reality. The most dissipated character in the novelette, the suicidal Shi Xun, fails to commit suicide, but dies from tuberculosis at the moment he least wishes to.

Zhang Qiuliu stands out among the ex-revolutionaries mainly because she approaches the condition of betrayal and self-betrayal by means of a different strategy. As she declares, "it is more significant to lead a short but passionate life than a long, dull one. I have a strong belief in mind: no matter what I am going to do, I want my life to leave an unforgettable mark on this gray world. My motto is: Don't be an ordinary person!"[72] She injects radical negativity into the placid reality which threatens to devour all the differences between things, turning them into an indistinguishable muddle. Another extreme case is Zhao Chizhu, who works as a prostitute to support herself and her husband, while anticipating the next revolution.

For the critics of "Eclipse," these characters are held responsible for the failure of the revolution, in that they are longing for a doctrine of discipline and rationality while at the same time embracing a life of decadence. Their alliance with Communism is a sham, unrealistic in essence. But Mao Dun's point is that, even if this were the case, these bourgeois intellectuals' exaltation and abjection underscore the complicated facts of the revolution as it was. They affirm the cause of revolution by acting out the excess of the rational cause, or by betraying it. Mao Dun the leftist writer's predilection for the intellectual's rise and fall becomes itself a betrayal of the literary policy of the party. It nevertheless indicates a utopian denial of the status quo based on ideological and literary dualism. In it is staged the excited interplay of writing and politics.

In 1941, Mao Dun published a novel entitled *Putrefaction*. Compared with *Eclipse,* the novel appears strangely familiar, in terms of Mao Dun's sympathy with women's fate and his intricate descriptions of their ideological and psychological agitation in a time of political turmoil. There is also an overlap in the two novels' Chinese titles. But there is a clear shift in Mao Dun's political concerns. Whereas *Eclipse* deals with the disillusionment and fruitless pursuits of Chinese Communist revolutionaries in the late twenties, *Putrefaction* reveals the moral degeneration of those youths when they ally with the Nationalist Party in the late thirties. Mao Dun's shift of angle makes good sense at first glance, because ever since the early thirties, his commitment to the Communist Party line has become more and more clear, and a novel like *Putrefaction* may represent one of his increasingly tendentious critiques of life under the KMT regime. But the phantoms of *Eclipse* haunt this novel, forming a dialogical subtext which challenges its apparent anti-Nationalist theme. Moreover, *Putrefaction* has a peculiar discursive format—a secret confession of a KMT spy in the form of diary, which is purportedly copied and publicized by Mao Dun in his persona of leftist intellectual. It is this framed diary narrative that provides a textual arena showing how conflict in writing and conflict in politics are as tangled as ever in Mao Dun's fiction.

In the preface, or the frame, of the narrative, Mao Dun the writer claims that he once found a small package containing two pictures and a diary at a bomb shelter in Chongqing. Unable to identify the writer of the diary, Mao Dun transcribes it and makes it available to the public. The reason for doing so is that the diary contains a woman's painful confession about her degradation in the KMT regime, and it therefore articulates the mind of many other young people who have shared the same fate. In the center part of the novel, the reader learns that the background of the diary is the mid-period of the second Sino-Japanese war, and that its writer's name is Zhao Huiming. Beautiful and intelligent, Zhao Huiming appears to be an intellectual lady involved in patriotic activities. Yet she is also a KMT spy engaged in checking up on Communist suspects. The diary, now left in fragmentary form, tells of her mission and her increasing disgust with her job. At its center is Zhao Huiming's love for a man named Xiaozhao, who happens to be a Communist activist. Their love affair ends tragically with Xiaozhao's arrest and execution; meanwhile, Zhao Huiming has gradually been awakened to the cause he represents. The abrupt cessation of the diary indicates either that she has given up her job or, more possibly, that she has been arrested by her fellow spies.

Written in the form of a fiction within a fiction, the novel situates itself in a realistic context which calls for a different ideological verisimilitude from that which the center of the text offers. This device reminds one of Lu Xun's "Diary of A Madman," in which the narrator also plays the role of innocent transcriber, copying and therefore framing with a safe, rational closure a diary that spreads radical, crazy thoughts. The device can also be traced back to late Qing exposé novels such as Wu Woyao's *Strange Things Seen in the Past Twenty Years*, in which the journal of a person, whose pseudonym is "Jiusi yisheng" (survivor of disasters), is discovered and published by the narrator. The introduction of Wu Woyao's novel, it will be remembered, describes China at the turn of the century as a dungeon full of "ghosts, demons, and spirits,"[73] which sounds just like Mao Dun's description of China in the anti-Japanese war period: full of "foxes and demons."[74] The framed story presumably cultivates a distance from the sensitive subject for the narrator and implied reader. But just like Lu Xun's and Wu Woyao's works, *Putrefaction* is so burdened with the paradoxical desire to conceal and reveal an ideological purpose that a rhetorical modulation such as a framed narrative only duplicates what Mao Dun originally intends to denounce in a negative way.

With the treacherous theme of betrayal in mind, one can develop at least three readings of *Putrefaction*. To begin with, *Putrefaction* is a confessional novel about a woman spy's regrets for what she has done. Piecing together Zhao Huiming's random references to her past, one realizes that her participation in the KMT spy network is due not to her political commitment but to her desire to revenge her unhappy family life and her being impregnated and deserted by an irresponsible man. This motivation sounds familiar, as many female characters in Mao Dun's early works, like Jing in "Disillusionment," choose politics as a escape from, or compensation for, their domestic failures. What makes Zhao Huiming's political move more dangerous is that, having been betrayed by her boyfriend, she has then taken up a profession whose highest achievement is nothing but expertise in betrayal and complicity. The image of mutual deception and betrayal expands as the novel develops, to the point where the whole Chongqing government is seen as a huge network specializing in lying and fraud. Not only do bureaucrats cheat on each other for political and commercial advantage, but the government itself is said to maintain a secret tie with the puppet regime supported by the Japanese in Nanjing, thus undermining its own political legitimacy.

Zhao Huiming's hardest job comes when she learns that her first love Xiaozhao, now a leader of underground Communist activity, is under arrest and that she has been assigned to pursue him to reveal the names of his other comrades. Vacillating in the classical dilemma between love and duty, Zhao Huiming fails both. Always watched from behind, she never succeeds in saving Xiaozhao (who suspects her motives anyway) while in the meantime she has exposed her emotional weakness, which will only cause her more trouble. In her desperate action to rescue Xiaozhao on account of love, Zhao Huiming betrays not only her party but also Xiaozhao's will to die for his own cause. After the death of Xiaozhao, Zhao Huiming is reassigned a job on a university campus where she gets involved in a new love triangle, only to be sold out while she is again about to betray her own mission for the sake of love.

By placing Zhao Huiming in an endless chain of deception, betrayal, and complicity, Mao Dun must have meant that this is what reality in the Nationalist regime is all about. But he cannot reach such a conclusion without taking as truth Zhao Huiming's confession, which is a defiance of her profession to begin with. Zhao Huiming's diary betrays, in a double sense, in that it reveals what should have been hidden and turns back on what should have been held as undeniable. This double image of betrayal involves again the phenomenon of language and writing, thereby bringing us to the second reading of the novel.

The diary begins: "the greatest pain I have felt recently is that I cannot find a person to speak to. My mind is full of things to be let out, but I cannot find the right person so that I can pour out what I have in mind."[75] What increases her desire to speak is that she has "memories" which make her "unable to forget my past. These memories suck my blood like poisonous snakes, driving me to the verge of a nervous breakdown."[76] As a result, she can only talk to herself in the form of diary. She becomes her own confidante.

But there is a basic contradiction in Zhao Huiming's action of writing a diary. In the diary, she creates a written self to whom she expresses the full spectrum of her own feelings and thoughts, good or bad, happy or unhappy. She denies what she does in reality, utters what she cannot speak to other people, and confirms what she lies about. She shares a secret world with this written self, which may well be called an alter ego, a conscience, or an unhappy consciousness. But Zhao's self-inscription leads to a treacherous twist she would have least expected. Zhao Huiming writes to evoke the true self, with whom she wishes to identify, but that self, once posited in text, seems to take on its own life and eventually rises against Zhao Huiming by means of nothing but mimicry. It proliferates to accommodate the different images Zhao projects of herself at different times. The self (in the diary) is an innocent girl, a sexy woman, a cunning spy, an unmarried mother, a romantic lover, a professional student, a compassionate humanist, and a reluctant traitor, all turning each other in for the sake of what Zhao calls her "real" self.

Therefore, in her diary where the last true self will be preserved, Zhao Huiming actually duplicates what she is and wants to be in reality. She is no more or less than what she writes about herself. Her revelation is actually a masquerade, engendering rather than terminating the gallery of roles she plays as a spy. In other words, the confession of the diary turns out to be both an alibi and a verdict, depending on Zhao Huiming's shifting consciousness. A crisis of self-contradiction or self-betrayal looms large in Zhao Huiming' intent of confession as the diary continues, not because it tells the truth and endangers her safety but because it threatens to reveal her for what she is, denying what she believes to be true. This finally makes the diary the reflection of the treacherous political wars from which she has tried to take refuge in her writing.

Putrefaction invites a third kind of reading, if Mao Dun the author is brought back onto the scene. According to the preface of the novel, Mao Dun is only a transcriber of the diary, copying or rewriting what is already there. This is, of course, an old trick. As far as authorship is concerned, Mao Dun is, after all, the writer of the original diary which he now denies to be his own work. Mao Dun's "rewriting" is never a transparent project; it always involves a theatrical process of simultaneous self-erasure and self-exposure. In this sense, he is not unlike Zhao Huiming in the diary, who also continuously shuffles back and forth between her various identities. Yet the frame of the diary is more than just a rhetorical ploy. As previously mentioned, the frame serves as an ideological closure, capturing what is in the flux of Mao Dun's will to truth. In the name of (re)presenting what it is, Mao Dun's (re)writing has secretly doubled the original and inscribed in it a Communist guideline of (re)reading.

This ideological motivation, nevertheless, evokes more complicated problems in regard to writing in the given political context. Mao Dun lost contact with the Communist Party after the failure of its first revolution. As the PRC prime minister Hu Yaobang revealed at Mao Dun's memorial service in 1981, by the end of the forties, Mao Dun had tried twice in vain to renew his party membership. He first submitted an application in 1931, but was simply ignored by the extreme leftist leaders in power. He tried again in 1940 and was denied for a more subtle reason: that "he will contribute more to the 'people' if he maintains the status as a nonpartisan."[77] Mao Dun was ordered to play a double role, promoting the Communist party line on the one hand while keeping a neutral position as a progressive on the other. However thinly disguised, this double role gives Mao Dun something in common with the fictional Zhao Huiming. Both assume different identities to carry out a certain political end. Mao Dun's denial of what is really his own authorship, besides creating an ironic reading, also plays with the codes of hiding and betraying that constitute his new vocation.

There is a more important historical factor looming behind *Putrefaction*. The novel was written in the summer of 1941, just a couple of months after the New Fourth Army Incident, in which Chiang Kai-shek launched an surprise attack on the New Fourth Army—the major Communist force in the united front against the Japanese—and almost wiped out the Communist Party's military involvement in the War of Resistance. Since this incident is traditionally considered to be the KMT's second anti-Communist campaign in the history of the Chinese Communist revolution, the timing of Mao Dun's writing of *Putrefaction* is suggestive.[78] It reminds one that his *Eclipse* was written right after the KMT's first anti-Communist campaign in 1927. Both novels are motivated to explore the sociopolitical ambiances that threaten the revolution, but there is a remarkable shift of angle. Where *Eclipse* exposes the disillusionment of young Communist revolutionaries, *Putrefaction* describes the dissipation of young KMT followers. *Eclipse,* as it will be recalled, has been harshly criticized because it touches on the unspeakable scenes behind the failed First Communist Revolution. In *Putrefaction,* instead of talking about the problems that might have taken place within the CCP, Mao Dun emphasizes the disintegration tion and corruption of the KMT. Mao Dun thus posits a new formula for his (re)writing about Communist revolution. The new formula may reflect Mao Dun's changing conception of the objective environment; it also serves just as well as a belated reply to his alleged betrayal of the cause of revolutionary literature thirteen years before.

But Mao Dun's rewriting evokes the ghostly return of the controversial discourse of *Eclipse*. The political confrontation in *Putrefaction* may appear only as a front. At the core of Zhao Huiming's diary, one finds problems similar to those once besetting Jing, Fang Luolan, or Zhang Qiuliu in *Eclipse:* private and public causes infiltrate each other's spheres in such a way as to problematize the rationale of revolution. They all portray Mao Dun's inquiry into the other side of politics as motivated by narrow self-interest and murky ideological dialectics. In the diary form, Mao Dun pushes to the extreme Zhao Huiming's disgust with the political reality and her yearning for an authentic existence under the purest of ideologies. These are feelings the young Communist revolutionaries in *Eclipse* once entertained. As the party's name changes, what was considered as unrealistic and unquestionable in *Eclipse* is now ironically liberated and legitimated in *Putrefaction*. If Zhao Huiming wins wins more of our sympathy than our condemnation, it is because she, not her Communist boyfriend Xiaozhao, has acted out the treacherous rules of revolution. In a manner of isomorphic displacement, Mao Dun brings to light in *Putrefaction* what has been repressed since *Eclipse*. A novel about dissimulation, *Putrefaction* allows the face of an ideologically troubled age to hide itself, disguised as the enemy, and so momentarily eluding recognition; but *Putrefaction* also discloses its own betrayals, leaving only a few more layers between the reader and a final unwrapping of corruption.

Collapsing Spheres

For Mao Dun and most writers of his time, writing at a time of social/political rampage means finding a tenable form not only to contain the volatility of politics but also to make it intelligible to the reading public. Writing, in its ideal state, provides an ideal realm in which social problems are reflected and ideological complexities are articulated. Whatever its subjects are, writing in itself projects a utopian wish, mediating human conflicts at different levels and letting truth speak on its own terms. By introducing naturalism and realism to Chinese literature, Mao Dun means to incorporate into existing literary discourse a new mode of writing which is capable of exposing the chaotic status quo in such a way as to arouse his readers' desire for a brave new world. Mao Dun intends to *emplot revolution*.

But when we come to Mao Dun's actual works, we find that this utopian wish can best be named only in a negative way. Mao Dun's writings are at their best when dealing with collapsing spheres during a period in which nothing can sustain its own meaning but hinges on the displacement of something else. As previously discussed, the private and the public, the sentimental and political infiltrate as well as clash, creating a blur of surfaces, in which partisan vocation and romantic longing, discipline and transgression, the expected and the aleatory tend to become indistinguishable. By dealing with these confusions in the form of naturalist/realist writing, Mao Dun aims at sorting them out and putting them in an order anticipated by the doctrine of revolutionary literature. But this project is thwarted, both by the party line which plays with, rather than makes distinction between, the fusion and confusion of spheres, and by the action of writing per se. He sets out to write about reality critically, but both the aesthetic assumption and the ideology he resorts to prove insufficient to serve as a solution to the crisis disclosed, or to stand up to the ironic and parodic forces unleashed. As a result, his own writing becomes one of the collapsing spheres to which it gives witness. The *revolution* appears only to have been a *plot*.

One of the most prominent examples is the story "The Autumn of Guling." The story appears in an incomplete form, dealing with a mysterious Master Yun's trip to Jiujiang and Guling with his friends. It details their boat trip and their difficulty finding their hotel, and the ending offers no answer to the riddles contained in the action. The story is so diffuse that it has tantalized many critics. In her research, Yu-shih Chen concludes that the novella refers to the failed Nanchang Uprising in 1928, and that the characters are mostly based on figures from real life.[79] Young Master Yun, for example, could be a projection of Mao Dun himself. That Mao Dun wrote the story in such a crude and obscure way may be due to the tremendous pressure of censorship and to his unstable life while seeking a hiding place. Mao Dun later added an afterword to the story, indicating that there are four chapters missing from the current text; for various reasons, he decided to leave the incomplete version the way it was.[80]

The story evokes an allegorical reading, as Yu-shih Chen suggests in her study. It illustrates what realist writing can and cannot do in a political context such as China in the late twenties. The story is full of detail: a crowded boat, nervous but aimless chitchat among characters, a mysterious fog in Jiujiang, the big detour Young Master Yun takes before he reaches the hotel, the sudden decision to visit Guling, etc., all written in such a meticulous way as to produce a lifelike atmosphere. But, not unlike the fog in Jiujiang that confuses Young Master Yun, these realistic references may well constitute a verbal fog which leads the reader astray. The missing four chapters are supposed to fill in the gaps. Yet given the current content of the story and the general political environment in which Mao Dun wrote, one wonders if they could really provide anything substantial.

This erasure on the part of the author poses a serious question for the paradigm of naturalist/realist narrative to which Mao Dun adheres. On the one hand, the excessive reference to details provides no transparent look into reality but rather gets a noisy but empty text which demands a studious reading yet offers no resolution. On the other hand, the visibly missing parts of the story lure one into the censored realm of real politics. The unspoken and the unspeakable seem identified with each other; both point to the arguable "real" meaning of the story. The sphere of writing (or inscription and voice) is subject to the challenge of the sphere of silence. Writing turns out to be a camouflage which covers up rather than reveals the truth, or even more radically, an excuse for the nonexistence of that truth.

The question of an incomplete text redirects us to the missing chapter of Mao Dun's autobiography. For literary historians and scholars of Mao Dun, one of the most puzzling questions about his life is why and how he lost his membership in the Chinese Communist Party in the late twenties and became an independent writer—almost at the same time "Autumn in Guling" was written. One of the earliest members of the CCP, Mao Dun lost contact with the party after the failure of the First Chinese Communist Revolution. Although his tie with the Communist Party became only closer in the thirties, and though he expressed strong wishes to rejoin the party, he remained a fellow traveller in support of the Communist cause for the rest of his life. Mao Dun's autobiography sounds extremely evasive about what happened between him and the party, and scholars were unable to reach any conclusion till Hu Yaobang gave an account on behalf of the party in 1981: Mao Dun remained outside the party as a result of a political scheme, because his identity as an independent writer helped to propagate revolution.[81]

By calling attention to the missing part in both Mao Dun's autobiography and "Autumn in Guling," I am not suggesting that there may be any causal connection between the two. What interests me here is not the "real" story behind the scenes but how both cases shed light on the intricate relations between writer and party, between writing and politics, that entangle Mao Dun (and contemporary critics). Politics and writing are discussed by Mao Dun as two distinct spheres, brought together only to reinforce each other's strengths in carrying out the utopian goal of revolution. Both Mao Dun's personal experience and his works provide an opposite view, however: that any writing about politics inevitably calls attention to the politics of writing. Mao Dun's reluctance to write about his relation with the party provides all too dramatic an example, showing to what extent his transparent writing presupposes political motivations. The missing chapter of the autobiography leads one to wonder if the existing parts are also motivated by a politically allegorical framework. Also, Mao Dun's posthumous readmission to the party makes one wonder if Hu Yaobang's account is not itself an emplotment of the past, for revolutionary purposes, an enrollment of Mao Dun's text into party service, a writerly filling-in of the novelistic gap in the biography. The realms of life, fiction, autobiography, and party line collapse into one another and give rise to an infinite interplay of meanings. Behind its pure, utopian façade, writing is not a value-free activity: nor is submission to the party.

The second example I would like to deal with concerns the much-discussed problem of the mutual interference of the sentimental and political spheres in Mao Dun's fiction. Whereas in novels like *Eclipse, Rainbow* and *Putrefaction,* characters are thrown into the conflict between desire for love and desire for politics, through which the meaning of revolution is crystallized, in "Shuizaoxing" (The story of marsh hay, 1936), Mao Dun offers at least one counterargument that, if not resolving it, complicates the thematic tension he sees in the process of revolution.

The story takes place in a small southern village. The villagers are so poor that they collect marsh hay in winter and make it into a substitute fertilizer. At the center of the story are Caixi, a sturdy middle-aged farmer, Caixi's nephew Xiusheng, and Xiusheng's wife. The three live together, and, because of Xiusheng's poor health, Caixi is actually the main support of the family. Life in the village is getting worse, as government taxes and other commissions take more and more of their meager income. But what really leads the family to crisis is that Xiusheng's wife finds herself pregnant and that the father of her baby may not be Xiusheng but Caixi.

Caixi and Xiusheng's wife commit the sin not only of adultery but also of incest. Xiusheng is not totally free of blame in this family scandal; though his poor health has long disabled him from making love with his wife, he keeps the virile, strong Caixi at home to help him run the farm. The irony is that, apart from beating his wife and making insinuating remarks, Xiusheng is either unwilling or unable to find any way to punish his uncle. In fact, when winter comes, they team up as usual to collect marsh hay in competition with other villagers.

Mao Dun takes a sympathetic attitude toward his three characters. Instead of describing the adultery between the uncle and his nephew's woman à la Zola, he injects into the story a strong compulsion to transgression and revolt that goes so far beyond the instinctive level as to amount to a total denial of all existing human institutions. The desire that drives Caixi and Xiusheng's wife to violate sexual taboos also prompts them to rebel against other aspects of life. Mao Dun invests the character of Caixi with a particularly tough robustness. Caixi never feels truly guilty for what he has done with his nephew's woman. In his view, "that a woman commits adultery because her husband is sick and useless has nothing to do with whether she has a conscience or not. Besides sleeping with another man, she has not changed a bit, she is still Xiusheng's wife. She has done her best to do everything a wife should do."[82] Later on, Caixi becomes a heroic leader in organizing the villagers to stand together against the coercion of the government. In particular, he saves the diseased Xiusheng from being drafted to serve as a coolie for the local office and thus plants the seed of future trouble. But the story has a "happy" ending; farmers sing songs as they collect marsh hay: "They laughed, they yelled, they sang songs conjured up at will. Amid all these voices, Caixi's long scream pierced the sky, sad but strong, like a protest, and like a battle cry."[83]

In this story, Mao Dun produces a radical nonconformist tone rarely seen in his other stories. Gone is the old tension of desire versus ideology that paralyzes his bourgeois characters. Caixi and Xiusheng's wife's passion for each other is actually the first sign of the defiant spirit which will make revolution possible. Desire is so expressed as to betray its roots in the political unconscious. Mao Dun thus combines a story about instinct and desire with a story about ideology and will, a tragic plot of domestic scandal with a comic plot of political awakening.

The story creates more questions than it solves, however. Mao Dun has a hard time conveying to his readers whether the peasants are the privileged social class for starting a revolution or but walking emblems inscribed by an elite writer to probe the limits of established social morality. One wonders, moreover, what will happen to Xiusheng's ménage à trois. Will Xiusheng die a convenient death and solve the problem of incest, or will Caixi restrain his personal desire in pursuit of the apocalypse, like most idealized heroes? More poignantly, if the adultery of Caixi and Xiusheng's wife is derived from an unleashed libidinous force that knows no decorum, won't it implant a seed of chaos in the forthcoming revolution?

The causes and effects of the family scandal are never satisfactorily delineated. As a matter of fact, in his attempt to demolish feudal taboos, Mao Dun has tacitly established a new moral mythology of the sublation of desire. For Caixi, the sin of incestuous passion can be atoned for by the deed of revolution; for Xiusheng, the shame of impotence and cuckoldry can be expunged by joining the collective uprising. Judged by the ending, where the peasants march together toward their predestined fate, under Caixi's leadership, the story stages a most peculiar kind of morality play.

The role of Xiusheng's wife is more bothersome. A silent but vivacious woman, she first appears as the center of the domestic tragedy. Trapped in a Zolaesque situation, she gives in to instinct and triggers the family crisis. But as the story continues, Mao Dun's sympathy for her gives way to an increasing concern for Caixi. She becomes less and less important, ending up a marginal character who echoes Caixi and Xiusheng's rebellious calls. Given Mao Dun's dubious feminist stand (discussed in the second section of this chapter), the story of Xiusheng's wife provides just one more example that woman is given no priority on his agenda of revolution. Not even given a name, "the woman" humbly assimilates herself to the body of men, now called "the people," at the end of the story.

The last problem I would like to deal with is the dilemma of technology versus ideology in *Midnight,* as manifested especially in the character of Wu Sunfu. A pivot of all the problems and contradictions in the novel, Wu Sunfu demonstrates in his actions the conflicting resources pertaining to the implementation of national industry. He is a capitalist heavily dependent on foreign technology and finance, but at the same time he is a strong advocate of domestic enterprise; an exploiter of his factory workers, but a conscientious planner of the rural economy; an unscrupulous villain in absorbing smaller factories, but a tragic hero in fighting against foreign powers.

While describing the Shanghai tycoons' fierce competition among themselves, Mao Dun spares no efforts to depict workers' actions vis-à-vis their bosses' oppressive manoeuvres. For the first time in modern Chinese fiction, workers, their own brand of problems, and the space where these problems take place, i. e., factories, are introduced, forming a new stratum of Chinese "reality." Along with the subject of the advances of foreign technology and industry, there arises in Chinese fiction a new chronotope, one which is in sharp contrast to the scenes of domestic handicraft in "Spring Silkworms." Workers are hired to work in different timeslots; they are also assigned to specific positions on the production line. Whenever workers feel maltreated, they get together to adopt a new kind of action to express their frustration and anger; in the case of *Midnight*—demonstrations and strikes.

But demonstrations and strikes are not enough to define the tensions between Shanghai workers and their managers and bosses. Mao Dun goes further, revealing that behind picket lines and bargaining, there exists another struggle among progressive workers—this time over leadership and interpretations of the party line. Under the direct guidance of Li Lisan, then the leader of the Chinese Communist Party chosen by the Soviet Comintern, union organizers seek to paralyze factories by armed violence and large scale strikes, only to meet failure when most workers readily accept their bosses' small concessions on wages and other benefits. In view of the shaky solidarity among workers and their unions, Mao Dun criticizes the immature strike plans, as well as the leftover bourgeois/romantic revolutionism that deludes followers of the so-called "Li Lisan line." For him, the historically appointed time for technological *and* political revolution is not yet at hand. What one can do is to bear witness to the fatal struggle of national capitalists like Wu Sunfu and their eventual downfall at the hands of foreign powers.

By smashing the workers' strikes, Wu Sunfu serves ironically as an agent legitimizing Mao Dun's historical determinism in two ways: Wu Sunfu's blind investment speeds up his own downfall, and his cruel control over his workers bespeaks the eternal antagonism between the capitalist and the "people," however nationalist his goal may be. As it seems impossible to win over his rival Zhao Botao either financially or politically, Wu Sunfu puts his last hope in a wild stock speculation with Zhao Botao; he loses even this final bet. By the end of the novel, threatened with new strikes and impending bankruptcy, Wu Sunfu leaves Shanghai to take a vacation in a summer resort. The novel winds down in suspense.

As far as the subject of Chinese industrialization is concerned, traditional criticisms of *Midnight* tend to fall into simplified accounts, either of Mao Dun's leftist bias against Nationalist economic and technological policy, or of his insights into the diseases of the Chinese socioeconomic system. According to Marián Gálik, Mao Dun succeeds in producing a Chinese version of Zola's *L'argent* by exposing the sordid deals and desperate competitions among Chinese entrepreneurs.[84] But the most intriguing aspect of the novel, I would argue, is Mao Dun's attempt to politicize the issue of technology and industry, and the fact that he becomes caught in the very conditions he evokes and purports to solve.

Beneath Mao Dun's naturalist treatment of the predicaments of Chinese industry, one finds an intricate texture of presuppositions which derive from the writer's own ideological convictions. In Mao Dun's view, China can be strengthened only when she is fully fitted out with modern technology, i.e., Light, Heat, and Power. This proposition, simple as it is, must be qualified by a historically necessary sequence of contradictions and sublations. China's technological and industrial future hinges on the victory of modern equipment and knowledge over traditional craftsmanship; the victory of nationalist capitalists over international imperialist investors; the victory of an enlightened urban proletariat over their bourgeois capitalist bosses and managers; the victory of the project of rural industrialization over urban commercialization; the victory of the Chinese Communist Party over the Chinese Nationalist Party; and the victory of the Maoist leadership over the anti-Mao "Li Lisan line." The novel sets out to deal with the conditions that would benefit Chinese technology and industry, only to entangle itself in the ideological and historical conflicts it raises, thereby leaving very small leeway for "technology."

Mao Dun's dilemma derives not so much from the way he exposes the conflicts and contradictions that underlie China's economy and industry, as from the way he explains them in the light of Communist historicism. Under the influence of the nineteenth-century Western ideology he has imported to diagnose modern Chinese industry's diseases, he is lured into seeing all contradictions and conflicts as integral parts of a grand historical plan. While Mao Dun may be entitled to approach China's problems from a foreign vantage point such as Marxism, it does not follow that he or anyone can implement its totalizing visions. If *Midnight* provides a testimonial to China's experience with modernization, it is due not only to Mao Dun's revelation of the social/economic forces as mentioned above, but also to the cracks left in his (unsuccessful) effort to inject these forces into a single, intelligible mechanism.

Two particular terms compete with each other in Mao Dun's discourse on the rise of technology in China. In the wake of so-called critical realism, Mao Dun is laying out in a negative way the thesis that China's industry cannot be built up until a strong, healthy political entity, namely, a consciously Marxist government, is founded. On the other hand, he indicates just as cogently that no political power, leftist or rightist, can be fully instated, unless China is first transformed by modern technology and industry. This explains why the character Wu Sunfu is especially interesting in the novel. In a sense, Wu Sunfu is set on a mission with a self-contradictory goal. He deserves credit because he is a patriotic businessman working toward the ideal of a politically and economically autonomous China, but he must be condemned for attempting to take a capitalist route to reach his goal.

The imagery of the neon sign, *Light, Heat and Power,* that Mao Dun creates in the novel's beginning, comes to mind again. For those who are dazzled and fascinated by the neon sign in its English letters, isn't Marxist theory yet another foreign commodity imported by cultural compradores like Mao Dun? There is a good reason for Mao Dun to sympathize with Wu Sunfu, since they *are* in the same historical marketplace, striving for a purchase on Western technology and modern ideology. Mao Dun's theoretical position collapses into the practical position of Wu Sunfu; and the position of both of them collapses into that of old Mr. Wu, once their gaze has been caught by that lurid, enticing, imported historical promise, of *Light, Heat,* and *Power.*

Mao Dun's fiction presents a mapping of conceptual and perceptual spheres, spheres whose radii trace out the traffic of theory and practice, science and prophecy. These spheres were understood as substantiating a project of realism/naturalism, an enterprise of modern humanity. And Mao Dun indeed builds in his works a realistic edifice rarely achieved by his peers.[85] But the spheres of this cognitive map cannot be hinged upon any one narrative scheme, at least not one expected to fulfill the desire for the single, final mimetic closure. The spheres of realism overlap, reciprocate, infiltrate, or

Plotted Revolutions

contradict each other, bespeaking at best the impossibility of mimesis—a transparent representation of the real. Nor do the spheres finally appear as one, as the Same: incommensurability remains. As his pen name suggests, Mao Dun's fiction brings about a continuous sense of conflicting and collapsing spheres, which ironically and dramatically manifest the politics of the real.

Chapter four

Melancholy Laughter: Farce and Melodrama in Lao She's Fiction

One of the most important novelists of the 1930's, Lao She (pseudonym of Shu Qingchun, 1899–1966) presents us with a double image. Few readers will be left unstirred by the hilarious plots, dangling narratorial postures, and paraded clowns that enliven his early works. But when engaged in a critical survey of his merits, readers have been more apt to praise his vivid portrayal of ordinary life, his compassion for the underdog, or the warmth of his humor. While his *Luotuo Xiangzi* (Camel Xiangzi, 1938) has been acclaimed as one of the best works of modern Chinese fiction written before the eve of the second Sino-Japanese war,[1] novels such as *Lao Zhang de zhexue* (The philosophy of Lao Zhang, 1928) and *Lihun* (Divorce, 1933) have received much less attention. To regard Lao She as a humanitarian realist or good-hearted humorist is certainly justified, but in so doing one overlooks his comic talents and makes him merely a good practitioner of the kind of orthodox realism initiated by writers such as Lu Xun. In fact, what truly distinguishes Lao She from other May Fourth writers is not so much his mimetic exposure of social abuses as his exaggeration of them in terms of both farcical and melodramatic discourses. These discourses derive their powers from excessive displays of laughter or tears, the dramatic reversal or parade of moral/intellectual values, and, most important, the compulsion to defy the sanctioned mode of representation.

Lao She was born to a Manchu family of limited means in 1899, a time when the Manchu name ensured neither social privilege nor a secure future. His father, a guard of the Imperial Palace, died protecting the forbidden city in the Boxer Rebellion, while the Emperor and the Imperial Dowager had fled to the west. Lao She and his mother survived the bayonets of looting soldiers only by miraculous luck. But these infantile traumas bring not so much sadness as muffled laughter to Lao She's recollections. One discerns a sense of absurdity when he relates his father's sacrifice for an empty cause, or his own survival under most unlikely conditions.[2] He "remembers" how, as a baby, he survived the "foreign devils": "I was sleeping soundly when they entered our house. If I had awakened, they would have sliced me up with their swords, since they were angry not to find anything valuable in our home."[3]

This sense of absurdity provides the basic tone of Lao She's laughter, laughter directed not only at a world full of irrationalities but also at Lao She himself trapped in such a world; not only at amusing subjects but also at subjects which could elicit indignation or tears. This ambiguous laughter can be heard when Lao She describes, in a self-mocking tone, his marginal identity as a Manchu growing up in the Republican period,[4] his poor family situation,[5] his lonely overseas experiences as a language teacher,[6] and his untimely absence from two of the most important scenes in modern Chinese history—the post–May Fourth days and the Chinese Communist takeover of the mainland—due respectively to his teaching commission in England and to his tour in the United States.[7]

But Lao She might have burst out with his most outrageous laughter in the Great Cultural Revolution, a historical event he would have hoped to miss. Years after being designated as a "People's Artist" by the government,[8] Lao She found himself the "enemy of the people" in the heyday of the revolution. When things are suddenly deprived of the meanings they should have, nothing is left but infinite chaos punctuated by a peal of demonic laughter. It should be no surprise that Lao She chose to end his own life by drowning himself.[9] For a king of laughter, suicide may well painfully recapitulate the ironic telos of his philosophy of laughter, in that it carries out to the extreme the auto-destructive tendency always embedded in his mockery and self-mockery, while indicating a final scorn at the absurdities he had been through all his life.

Laughter is the means by which Lao She questions the cultural/moral codes that sanction the concept of the real in his society. This profane laughter cannot be fully appreciated till we pay equal attention to Lao She's pursuit of melodramatic tears: "Although I am not opposed to tearjerkers, I wish I could write something that will bring down the house, and make people really feel exhilarated. To tell the truth, laughter and tears are actually two sides of one coin."[10] In this chapter, I will attempt to analyze the laughter in Lao She's fiction in two ways. First, I will reassess Lao She's comical/satirical fiction in terms of the modes of farce and melodrama, drawing out the carnivalesque impulse in his discourse of laughter and tears, and describing its nihilist undercurrent. Second, I will point out the link between the two seemingly contradictory images (or styles) of Lao She, the compassionate humanist and the cynical joker, by showing how his most flamboyant and hilarious narratives contain a poignant inquiry into the absurdities of life in modern China, while his "hard-core" revelations of human suffering can evoke a dubious mood of festivity.

Farce and Melodrama: Transgressions of the Real

Lao She's comic/farcical discourse is drawn from two major sources: the kind of grotesque realism perfected by Dickens and the rhetoric of buffoonery of Late Qing exposé fiction. Lao She taught Chinese at the University of London School of Oriental Studies from 1924 to 1929, and finished his first three novels in London. As his critical essays indicate, he is quite familiar with eighteenth and nineteenth-century English writers ranging from Fielding to James and Conrad; among these writers, Charles Dickens stands as his major model.[11] Lao She admits that his first novel, *The Philosophy of Lao Zhang*, is an imitation of Dickens' *Nicholas Nickleby*.[12] Lao She's indebtedness to Dickens' novels is best manifested in his exuberant language, melodramatic plotting, and huge gallery of grotesques. Both writers tend to consider social evils and irrational institutions not only monstrous but absurd as well. Yet this parallel should not keep one from noticing that Lao She was a diligent student of classical Chinese fiction and folk performing arts such as story telling and *xiangsheng* (a Chinese form of comic talk show).[13] As Jaroslav Průšek observed a long time ago, to give his comic fiction a special ironic effect, Lao She revived the story telling technique of classical

Chinese vernacular fiction.[14] It is equally clear that he drew upon late Qing exposé fiction as a source for the modes of buffoonery and burlesque.[15]

Lao She's first novel, *The Philosophy of Lao Zhang,* can be read as a good example of the author's farcical/melodramatic discourse. In the novel, Lao She ridicules the chaotic situation of modern Chinese society, caught in a drastic transformation from the old to the new. The novel's dominant character is Lao Zhang, a villainous rural schoolmaster and a cunning moneylender. The "philosophy of Lao Zhang" is to grab money by whatever means possible—a "threefold way of pilgrimage for cash."[16] Lao Zhang's businesses include a tiny school with only one class, a grocery store selling things "ranging from green onions to opium," geomancy, and a position in local government. Lao Zhang converts from one religion to another freely, depending on the fluctuations of the meat market. With Volpone-like energy and ingenuity, Lao Zhang's desire for money is amplified to lust for power and women; the novel is a record of the way in which he fulfills all his goals. The novel also has several subplots, including the account of a squire's attempt to marry an educated concubine, a Chinese Salvation Army officer's thriving career as a preacher, and two idealistic students' aborted love affairs. All related to Lao Zhang's businesses of money lending and teaching.

In characterizing Lao Zhang as a moneylender and a vicious school master, Lao She may have in mind the images of both Ralph Nickleby and Mr. Squeers of Dickens' *Nicholas Nickleby*.[17] Lao Zhang also reminds the reader of Quilp of *The Old Curiosity Shop* (which was translated into Chinese as early as in the late Qing period), in that both enjoy harrassing youngsters and enslaving their own wives. Whereas Dickensian grotesques are portrayed as egoists who fabricate a self-centered world in the form of ostentatious routine, or practice strange mannerisms as an (unconscious) defence mechanism,[18] Lao She's clownish characters like Lao Zhang act with an aggressive force that knows no restraints. Unlike Dickens, who tends to reveal the psychological motivations of his characters' grotesque behavior, Lao She creates Lao Zhang as an invulnerable robot. Neither social norms nor moral criteria are barriers to Lao Zhang's lust and ambition; instead, he makes use of those norms to develop his own system of values. Thus we have the doubtfully pleasurable expectation of seeing Lao Zhang continuously step beyond the limits he sets for himself to work out something more outrageous. In fact, the novel is organized like a series of spectacles presided over by Lao Zhang, with each one more hilarious (abusive) than the last.

Satirical comedy is too general and benign a term to describe Lao She's vision of the real as conceived in *The Philosophy of Lao Zhang*. With all the gratuitous violence and ambivalent laughter, what he really tries to create is something like a farce. Celebrating in an ironic manner a world turned upside down, *The Philosophy of Lao Zhang* may well be the first modern Chinese novel written deliberately in the farcical mode; Lao Zhang is the lord of misrule and his "philosophy" is the norm of chaos.

When treated as a narrative mode, *farce* refers to a type of writing that uses outrageous comedy to defy formalistic and thematic conventions, attack preestablished values, and test audience sensibilities. It often highlights a series of carnivallike episodes in which physical actions (collision, abuse, mockery, disfigurement, and so on) temporarily overpower intellectual and emotional control.[19] The agents of farcical action are clowns who present themselves either as laughable victims or comic assailants, or as a combination of the two. Through the clowns' radical behavior, farce also implies a mentality or even an ideology which, in Bakhtinian terms, "disintegrates" the existing order in terms of imaginative "degradation."[20] But at the core of farce is its ambiguous view of chaos: its characters' irreverent, comically violent attacks on each other and the surrounding society generate a certain new order; the audience's pleasure derives both from distancing the embarrassing or uncomfortable circumstances and from imaginative involvement in them.[21]

A definition of farce such as this does not, of course, apply to all of Lao She's comic fiction. In the case of *The Philosophy of Lao Zhang,* I shall argue that Lao She tends to add a dimension of sentimental melodrama to his farcical discourse, so as to salvage his fiction from the total denial of meaning. In some of Lao She's short stories, nevertheless, one finds a full-fledged expression of the farcical mode. "Kaishi daji" (The grand opening, 1933), for example, deals with four quacks running an expensive charity hospital like a three-ring circus. Almost without any medical knowledge and facilities, they nevertheless manage to attract many dupes looking for magical cures. They encourage an old lady with ulcers to eat as much Beijing duck as she wants, and prescribe a shot of jasmine tea as a new medicine for an officer with venereal disease. At one time, they almost mistake a fat man for a pregnant woman; at another, they bully a patient with hemorrhoids to pay more for anaesthetic treatment—right in the middle of his surgery. The story contains a relentlessly festive atmosphere hitherto unseen in modern Chinese fiction, celebrating the quacks' undeserved prosperity and laughing at their patients' pain. Similar examples can be found in other short stories: "Baosun" (Grandson, 1933) in which a grandmother feeds her pregnant daughter-in-law so well that she is the focus of a hilarious horror when she delivers a thirteen pound baby; or "Liucun de" (A woman from the Liu village, 1934) in which a monstrous shrew persecutes her husband, family, and even the whole village, in the name of God, since she is a converted Christian.

On the other hand, Lao She's concept of farcical norms may well be traced back to late Qing exposé fiction such as, say, Wu Woyao's *Strange Things Seen in the Past Twenty Years,* a novel deriving its vitality from the absurd events and characters it openly denounces. Just like Wu Woyao, Lao She feels indignation over the stories he himself is recounting, but he assumes a so called extroverted attitude, collecting, studying, and classifying the stories as if he were enjoying the lavish display of his own social knowledge. Even more noticeable is the fact that Lao She projects in his novel an order highly reminiscent of that conceived by the late Qing exposé fiction, one where, as Doležélová-Velingerová has described it, "evil always defeats good," and "the great evil defeats the minor one."[22]

In *The Philosophy of Lao Zhang,* we find that, with stylized gestures reminiscent of the clowns in traditional Chinese theater, Lao Zhang appears to the reader as dangerous *but* funny. Though he personifies an emancipated energy that transgresses all social and moral norms, we are so attracted by his seemingly inexhaustible imagination and protean mannerisms that we tend to neglect the offensiveness and radicalism embedded in his absurd actions. The new values forged by Lao Zhang and other minor villains in the novel are the opposite of those endorsed by a sober society. The label, "modern education," ensures nothing but higher enrollments and richer administrators; a "democratic election" is a new euphemism for winning a governmental job by bribery; "freedom of the press" allows journalists to slander and blackmail at will; "liberalism" inspires rich men to marry as many women as they want—

girls with a modern education being especially welcome. Thus, Lao Zhang "is indeed an important figure in the town of Erlang! If Lao Zhang were unfortunately to die, it would be a disaster even bigger than losing a saint, because, after all, what saint could be like him, mastering both the pen and the sword, and communicating with both the living and the dead."[23] The plot develops through a procession of slapstick interludes all starred in by Lao Zhang. He and his friends thrive in the novel all the way to the end. It is the good or sensible characters who are expelled from the scene.

Though the laughter Lao She aims to arouse remains as ambivalent in essence as ever, his comic/farcical scheme is more elaborate in terms of caricature and mockery than his late Qing predecessors. In *The Philosophy of Lao Zhang,* he creates a plural narrator "we," referring to a group of spectators who observe the ongoing chaos from a safe position. In no danger of finding themselves persecuted, they can make condescending jokes at the expense of those who are suffering. This plural narrator sounds most like the classical storyteller when he adopts colloquialisms and clichés to establish the linguistic illusion of intimate, direct communication with readers, and when he takes a detached middle distance to judge the story narrated. Lao She also adds to his voice a pompous style by practicing Dickensian formality of syntax and figures of speech.[24] The oily, ostentatious rhetoric runs in such a way as to blur social values, dissolve the pain the characters should feel into a miming of it, and turn an otherwise sad story into a hilarious extravaganza. As if speaking for the public, the "we"-narrators invite readers to join "them" and relish the comic villains' performances. And as readers, the most embarrassing moment is when we find ourselves not only laughing *at* Lao Zhang and his friends but *with* them.

Lao She is clearly uneasy about the subversive undertone suggested by this kind of laughter. He continuously interjects into the second part of the novel voices of sober-minded characters or his own as implied author. With the remarkable increase of narrated monologues, authorial interruptions, and sententious descriptions, all punctuated by heavy sighs and/or tearful gestures, one cannot help noticing that the young and innocent characters are fighting a losing battle against Lao Zhang and his cohorts. Amid the outrageous laughter, there arise cries, however muffled by the comic villains, which attempt to spell the name of the evil, to articulate the pain and sadness the good has undergone, and to solicit the full range of emotional responses from the reader. These interpolations deflate the coherence of the novel's farcical effect, and point to the narrative mode of melodrama, the mode highlighting excessive expression and moral hyperbole.

This melodramatic tendency can especially be seen on the level of plot. As the novel progresses, Lao Zhang falls in love with his student's beloved and wants to take her as his concubine. He plans to have a magnificent wedding in Western style, and will invite only those friends who have concubines as his guests. Lao Zhang's dark force is now looming ever larger, threatening to break the ethical relation between teacher and student, to violate the virginity of the heroine, and to disintegrate social order completely.

By *melodrama,* I refer to a narrative mode that espouses an exaggerated presentation of moral and emotional conflicts, in such a way as to intensify the values of life in a theatrical form. Aiming at inflated and extravagant expression, a melodrama features extreme situations or states of action.[25] Among its major characteristics are the indulgence of strong emotionalism, moral polarization, and artificial plotting. It often begins with the persecution of the good and ends with the reward of virtue, via such actions as dark conspiracy, suspense, and breathtaking adventure. However frivolous it may appear, at the core of melodramatic writing lies a deep concern with the moral consequences behind our everyday life and actions; its aim is to restore the lost social order and ethical imperatives. This pursuit of what Peter Brooks calls the "moral occult,"[26] the quintessential meaning of life, foregrounds conflicting values otherwise relativized or even naturalized in the continuum of our daily existence. Seen in this light, an effective melodrama acts out both our anxiety in the search for the hidden moral configuration of lived experiences, and our fantasy of carrying out such a configuration in a moment of wish fulfillment.

Because of its polarization of good and evil, indulgence in hyperbolic rhetoric, and refusal to cast characters and their actions in the ordinary way, melodrama has always been considered as the opposite of realist/naturalist writing. But insofar as any representation of the real needs a narratorial pattern or dramatic arrangement, the difference between realist and melodramatic writings, as some critics have pointed out, is a matter of degree rather than of kind. Nineteenth-century European fiction by Balzac, Dickens, and even Flaubert and Zola has provided numerous examples along this continuum. In the case of Lao She, therefore, the question I would like to raise is not whether his melodramatic imagination has transgressed the boundary of the authentic discourse of realism, but whether this transgression has brought any new perspective on the Chinese reality under discussion.

The question becomes even more intriguing, when one places melodrama next to farce, and asks how Lao She mixes the two modes in telling his realist stories, and what moral and psychic results he brings forth. Both farce and melodrama are used by Lao She as a heightened literary response to a reality immersed in contingency and chaos. In a world where values have been thrown into question, one can rely only on extreme rhetorical measures to define the blurred image of the real. By means either of radical laughter or of polarized sentiments and overt moral schematization, Lao She tries to bring to the fore facts that can no longer be mediated in ordinary language. He thus sees the meaning of the real not in the reflection but the refraction of the objects he encounters. Compared with his peers, Lao She's realist strategy partakes of a strong skepticism concerning its own function, while his pessimism about the possibility of representing the real as it is, and his play with rhetoric forms give his writings a modernist touch.

Beneath the two modes' formal recourse to the rule of excess and theatricality, however, there is a fundamental difference between their epistemological assumptions. Whereas melodrama aims at the nomination of the manichaean struggle of good and evil behind chaotic reality, thereby projecting a longing for the return of a certain order, farce ventures to laugh away any such efforts. If melodrama celebrates the search for the moral occult, farce defies that search as one of the world's dirty jokes. Throughout Lao She's career, the effect of farce may seem less and less visible, as melodrama remains the persistent force of his narrative. But a sophisticated reader will find that Lao She's melodrama is made possible only because it is subsumed by a farcical impulse. Even his sad works contain a titillating element, ready to turn sentimental expressions into hysterical giggling. Beyond the level of plot, therefore, one must notice a battle between the two forms which is just as melodramatic.

This tension can be seen in the ending of *The Philosophy of Lao Zhang*. Whenever Lao She tries to speak in clear language about the menace of evil and the eventual triumph of morality, he ends up doing so amid chuckles.²⁷ Lao Zhang's wedding does take place as promised, and to nobody's surprise, it turns out to be a circus of follies. But the wedding is never completed, because of the last minute intervention of a member of the local gentry, Regional Commander Sun, and a rickshaw puller with a chivalric spirit, Zhao Si. The two rescuing figures appear to be stereotypes from classical Chinese vernacular fiction: Regional Commander Sun enacts the traditional role of the impartial judge, while Zhao Si revives the chivalric spirit of a knight-errant. Both, however, undergo a certain degradation in Lao She's world. Sun must buy Lao Zhang off in order to stop the wedding, and Zhao Si is simply ignored by everyone. The lofty ideals of justice and chivalry are jokes in Lao She's world. His moral scheme is articulated only at the expense of immediate laughter.

In the epilogue, we are told that Lao Zhang was never thwarted by the aborted marriage. He eventually fulfills his ambition of not only becoming a provincial commissioner of education but also buying two concubines at the price of one, "and the bargain has become one of the memorable achievements of his life."²⁸ The young lovers, however, are never reunited. Lao Zhang's student is forced by his parents to marry a country girl, and his girl friend wastes away and dies.

Lao She thus mixes two possible endings together, a farcical one that acknowledges a society turned upside down by the prosperity of villainous clowns and buffoons, and a melodramatic one that asserts the horror and pain that results from the persecution of the good by the wicked. At issue here is not which ending leans more closely toward reality, since both farce and melodrama are derived from a systematic distortion or exaggeration of the real. What is noteworthy is that the two modes undercut each other's aesthetic and moral premises, thereby forming a phantasmal vision which indicates a critical mockery, rather than a mimesis, of the real. Whereas Lao She's melodramatic wish brackets the chaotic world with a plenitude of meaning, his farcical impulse reinscribes such a wish in terms of parody, portraying not an order restored but an ordered chaos.

The dialectic of melodrama and farce is even more forcefully expressed is Lao She's second novel *Zhao Ziyue* (Zhao Ziyue, 1928), which deals with post–May Fourth student activities in Beijing. The novel mocks those students who, in the name of revolution and patriotism, are in practice undermining social and cultural order. While Lao She never gives up his predilection for physical collisions and slapstick gestures, the laughter evoked thereby conveys a pensive undertone. Compared with *The Philosophy of Lao Zhang, Zhao Ziyue* has a clearer theme—the conditions of patriotism—to deal with; it is possible that Lao She might be imposing some didactic meaning on his burlesque narrative in response to critics' attacks on the frivolity of his first novel. But beyond these possible motivations of social/political critique, I suggest that the comical discourse of *Zhao Ziyue* brings to light what has already germinated in *The Philosophy of Lao Zhang*, namely, Lao She's preoccupation with the irrational side of life as a force forever menacing with violent conflict and laughter, and his compulsion to play with this dark force at the cost of losing his own moral ground.

Through its ambiguous mirth, the novel also throws into question the model of representation as seen in conventional fiction. No longer do Lao She's villains possess recognizable traits like Lao Zhang's; rather they are hypocrites and impeders who conceal their malice behind the mask of friendliness or naiveté. Life now takes on the symbolism of theater in which everybody plays and exchanges roles. The demarcation line between vice and virtue, imposture and sincerity, is often emphatically presented, only to turn out to be a misjudged line, a fake boundary. How to define the real, and how to turn down the temptation of the irrational forces of life, become the two complementary goals of Lao She's inquiry into the malaise of his society.

The novel's leading character is Zhao Ziyue, a "student" who spends most of his time gambling, drinking, chasing after women, and daydreaming. Modeled after Mr. Pickwick of Dickens' *Pickwick Papers,* Zhao Ziyue undergoes a series of adventures in Beijing. His naïveté, gullibility, and basic good-heartedness always bring him into unexpected troubles, but thanks to his good luck, he survives one disaster after another. Throughout the first two-thirds of the novel, one laughs at Zhao's wanton adventures which range from taking part in antigovernment rallies to staging amateur Beijing operas, from campaigning for women's rights to fooling around with professional ladies, and from getting in and out of colleges to tutoring the stupid son of a local politician. Two of Zhao's friends are particularly important: Ouyang Tianfeng, a handsome playboy who always seduces Zhao into debauchery, and Li Jingchun, a student dedicated to patriotic activities. Swinging between the two friends, Zhao Ziyue happily carries on with his flamboyant life in Beijing; what concerns him most is how to get rid of his wife in the countryside and how to win the heart of a pretty Miss Wang.

But the novel takes a drastic turn when Ouyang Tianfeng is exposed as a villain who has squandered Zhao's money, raped and bullied Miss Wang, and been working as an undercover agent for the warlord government. In the meantime, Li Jingchun turns out to be a patriotic terrorist who, after a failed assassination attempt, has been arrested and will be put to death. While the novel best demonstrates Dickensian melodramatic mechanisms in terms of its twisty plotting, exposure of hidden villainy, and blatant indulgence in sentimentalism, one should also note how Lao She's laughter is nurtured on, and easily overrun by, violence and irrationality. When slapstick causes real pain, and when clowns attack and kill, melodrama intrudes on the aesthetic confines of farce.

The moment of revelation brings a crisis to the novel's system of representation. *The Philosophy of Lao Zhang* has already indicated Lao She's skepticism concerning the compatibility between what the world appears to be and what it is; Lao Zhang is dangerous not only because he bullies good people and damages the social order but because he threatens moral and ethical norms *in their own name*. In *Zhao Ziyue,* the crack between appearance and reality deepens: characters are in one way or another engaged in a show and one can no longer identify the origin of fraud and villainy merely by appearance. Most of the major characters lead a double life, and the motif of theatricality permeates the whole novel. Zhao Ziyue comes to Beijing as a college student, yet what he really learns is the complicated codes of imposture and forgery. Ouyang Tianfeng undoubtedly dramatizes villainous imposture of the most dangerous kind, but even Miss Wang, the symbol of purity in the novel, conceives a secret in her mind concerning Ouyang Tianfeng.

At the end of the novel, Li Jingchun is executed; moved by his martyrdom, Zhao Ziyue decides to do something by joining a new assassination plot. By highlighting the tearful scene of Zhao Ziyue's last visit to Li Jingchun before the execution, and by concluding the novel with Zhao Ziyue's dramatic change into a patriotic activist, Lao She obviously demands not logic but empathy from a reader who, not long before, was still laughing at these students' wanton adventures. Li Jingchun's death, though described as a martyrdom, does not produce the kind of tragic moment at which Lao She seems to be aiming. At best, Li serves as a scapegoat, redeeming the violence and outrage seen throughout the novel, while anticipating the return of a kind of social order. More ironically, given its demand for excessive tears and its spurious claims upon the tragic, the farewell scene renders a sense of artificiality that is not inconsistent with the frivolous part of the novel. In light of Zhao Ziyue's and his friends' eagerness to do something to commemorate Li's death (one becomes a really "good" student; one tries to stop the government from selling foreigners the Temple of Heaven; and Zhao himself wants to becomes an anti-warlord terrorist), one may even talk about a mood of secret festivity that lingers at the end of the novel.

Despite the ending, which superficially promises a change, one can detect Lao She's feeling of uncertainty. The melodramatic sentiments he invests do not bring about catharsis; nor do they reveal themselves as plastic entities subject to theatrical rules. After all, the villain Ouyang Tianfeng is at large, and the corrupt official whom Li Jingchun attempted to kill survives the assassination attempt. As C. T. Hsia observes, "In his want of solid learning and constructive usefulness, the reawakened Chao [Zhao Ziyue] can only abide by terrorism, a caricature of the ideal *hsia* [knight-errant], celebrated in popular Chinese fiction."[29] I would go one step further and argue that, by making his protagonist an assassin, Lao She never intends a plausible ending (as Hsia supposes), but instead drives home the outrageous essence of farce in realist terms. When the terrorism anticipated by Zhao Ziyue is legitimized in the name of patriotism or knight-errantry, a clear line can no longer be drawn between law and its transgression, between order and chaos. Transgression is prized by both revolutionary and cynical clowns. From the narrator's acquiescence to violence and the prosperity of villains, we find in the novel's ending the equivocal mentality that has already marked the conclusion of *The Philosophy of Lao Zhang*.

Comic Heroes as *Alazons: The Two Mas* and *Divorce*

Lao She's *Erma* (The two Mas) and *Divorce* were published respectively in 1931 and 1933. The two books may at first look very different in terms of setting and of characterization. The last work

Lao She wrote in England, *The Two Mas* summarizes his overseas experience in a mildly melancholy tone, while *Divorce* represents his attempt at return—return not only to his favorite locale in both life and fiction, Beijing, but also to his early farcical style—after experimenting with other modes such as children's stories (*Xiao Po de shengri* [Xiao Po's birthday], 1934) and Swiftian fantasy (*Maocheng ji* [The city of cats], 1933).[30] When one takes a closer look at the characters and actions of the two novels, a dialectical relation can be discerned beneath them. They represent an effort to explore the psychological depth of the modes of melodrama and farce, and to explore the possibility of combining the superficial and the serious, the extroverted and the introverted. But most importantly, both novels introduce a new type of clown—the *alazon* or comic intruder—as opposed to the comic assaulters presented in *The Philosophy of Lao Zhang* and *Zhao Ziyue*.

In each of the two novels, Lao She introduces a romantic and sensitive young man who feels trapped by the pull of contradictory forces in an unfamiliar environment. He is seen and felt as an outsider, physically and psychologically colliding with those inside the community. Consequently, the self-conscious hero, precisely because he sees himself as a sensitive person, realizes that he is an intruder in the society with which he has refused to identify and that he must run away in order to preserve his sanity. In both cases, though we find ourselves agreeing with the hero's judgment, siding with him against his adversaries and preferring him over his peers, we are never allowed to forget his comic potential or to lose our perspective. The narrator invites us to laugh at the hero's self-pity and priggish attitudes towards social norms, yet this laughter always contains a melancholy flavor.

Set against the exotic background of London, *The Two Mas* deals with the painful experiences of Chinese who lived overseas earlier in the century. Its story focuses on the generation gap between Mr. Ma, an old-fashioned Chinese gentleman who comes to England to take over his late brother's curio shop, and his son, Ma Wei, a young romantic patriot who reluctantly moves with his father to the country he considers most directly responsible for the fate of China in the past half-century.[31] The conflict between father and son is dramatized by their different attitudes toward their current situation. Indulging in romantic fantasy and rootless patriotism, Ma Wei can not (or will not) see that all his ideals become petty whims in an indifferent foreign country. In contrast to his son, Mr. Ma is determined to maintain his old ways as a gentleman scholar, only to find that his outdated mannerisms amuse the British and feed into their fixed ideas about the Chinese and their life-style. The conflict is further strengthened by the father's and son's romances with English women. Mr. Ma, a widower, falls in love with Mrs. Winter, his widowed landlady, but the romance is soon broken up by social prejudices against Mr. Ma. Ma Wei, on the other hand, is tantalized by Mrs. Winter's coquettish daughter, Mary, who reacts to Ma Wei's infatuation only with amusement.

To intensify the clash between the father and son, Lao She foregrounds the foreign setting of London as well as his English characters' mannerisms; the city and its citizens each constitute a major source of his comedy. Before meeting Mr. Ma and his son, Mrs. Winter thinks that all Chinese eat mice and smoke opium, not to mention engaging in other vices such as robbery and rape. Another character, Father Evanston, who has spent years preaching in China, is a self-proclaimed expert on Chinese affairs, and never misses a chance to show his "kindness" to Mr. Ma and his son. One of his favors is to invite them to a family dinner of fat roast beef and rice pudding—because he and his wife think the Chinese "must" love fat meat and rice. Mrs. Evanston never allows her children, who were born in China, to study Chinese for the simple reason: "there will be no future for an English baby starting his language lesson with Chinese—If you water an English eggplant with Chinese water, how can it grow up to be big, juicy, and thin-skinned?"[32]

C. T. Hsia contends that *The Two Mas* "treats the patriotic message in more or less tragic terms."[33] But a reading in the light of Lao She's farcical/melodramatic scheme leads one to conclude that the novel is really about a supposedly tragic hero, Ma Wei, who is trapped in a genuinely comic situation. He becomes an *alazon*-like character in a world where absurdity is normal. As Northrop Frye points out, "an *alazon* is some one who pretends or tries to be something more than he is."[34] There is always an ambiguity in the characterization of the *alazon*: whether his action is tragic or comic hinges on the reader's interpretation of it as either obsession or imposture. In the realm of comedy, the so-called *blocking characters* often assume the traits of an *alazon,* though it is more frequently "a lack of self-knowledge than simple hypocrisy" that characterizes them.³⁵ The tragic presentation of the *alazon,* on the other hand, can been seen in a figure who is "made dizzy" by his fixations on a certain idea or by his hubris. Shakespeare's Hamlet is such a case, in that he is so preoccupied with a philosophical posture vis à vis the immediate call for action that he is paralyzed by the posture.

My reference to Hamlet is by no means a coincidence, because his figure has deeply affected Lao She's literary imagination. Though Lao She's interpretation of the Hamlet syndrome remains mostly comical, he recapitulates the Danish prince's problems: procrastination, prolonged anguish, and self-torturing philosophical poses. Lao She has used the name of Hamlet in the titles of his works. "Xin hanmuliede" (New Hamlet, 1936) is a short story which deals with a weak-willed college student's failure either to carry out his revolutionary ideals or to help his businessman father withstand local turmoils in the name of revolution. Named Tian Liede, the hero declares, "I am Shakespeare's Hamlet; we share the same first name [*liede*/Ham *let*]."³⁶ He "always looks at himself in the mirror, a long, thin face, with a wide and pale forehead. His eyes look languid; he has big mouth and thin lips, which often form a long line in between." And "he is very proud, very serious. He plans everything thoroughly, and he ponders all the time."³⁷ On the other hand, Lao She's anti-Japanese patriotic drama, *Guiqulaixi* (Homecoming, 1942), was originally called *Hamlet;* its central character is clearly based on Shakespeare's creation.³⁸

Ma Wei in *The Two Mas* may well be one of Lao She's earliest parodies of the image of Hamlet. He is the first clown in modern Chinese fiction with a sullen face and melancholy posture, a clown who is as vulnerable as he is laughable. Ma Wei has a clear cause to fight for—patriotism. He despises his father's deeds, but he cannot find any way to justify his own indignation. Nor does patriotism keep him from chasing after Mary. Throughout the novel, he undergoes one humiliation after another, yet his sighs and grumblings, tears and screams develop only into familiar stage gestures. The father and son have, of course, very different characters. But trapped in the hostile environment of London, old Ma's mannerisms, those of an old-fashioned Chinese gentleman, are no more hollow than his son's petulant patriotic outcries. "Ma Wei is aware of his predicament; his heart is filled up with [indecisiveness and melancholy]. Not only does his heart leave no crack to let other things come in, his whole body has refused to be directed by it . . .

He has forgotten the whole world. He wishes the world and himself would be destroyed at the same time."[39]

The above quotation indicates the state of Ma Wei's mind after he has been through all his bitter London experiences and is thinking what he should do next. But because the novel is narrated in a flashback form, it appears on the first page. Thanks to its flashback form that tells of what has happened in the frame of what will happen, the novel creates a cyclical effect that makes the ending the beginning.[40] In view of Ma Wei's Hamlet-like idiosyncrasy to pose and think, this narrative format neatly reflects his psychological habit of looking back and thinking rather than acting. Technically speaking, the major part of the novel, Ma Wei's London experience, appears only in a retrospective mood, devoid of a substantial link with the present and future. By the end (or at the beginning) of the novel, Ma Wei seems to reach some decision. He will break away with his father and flee England—but to France, not back to China. Ma Wei's decision or nondecision anticipates the ending of "New Hamlet": "run away, run away, run away!"[41]

Lao She writes *Divorce* as if he wanted to answer the question, what would happen if an intellectual like Ma Wei had, after all, gone back to stay in China? The protagonist of *Divorce,* Lao Li, a married man with two children, is literally an older and more subdued Ma Wei; the novel's setting is switched from London to Beijing. Lao Li takes a job in Beijing. He brings his family with him, hoping to make a modern woman of his country bumpkin wife and obviate the possibility of the fashionable divorce he has already considered. Like Ma Wei, Lao Li is a romantic dreaming about an existence in which happiness and beauty would be living experiences rather than abstractions, but he is thrown into a situation in which ideals are jokes and norms are distortions of norms.

As the only sober-minded person in a novel crowded with grotesques and clowns, Lao Li nevertheless becomes the most laughable figure, not because he has a hidden funny character, but ironically because he refuses to laugh with the buffoons and clowns around him. In this sense, Lao Li shares similar comic traits with Ma Wei. Both are blocking characters in a carnivalesque situation, and their defeats usually mark not so much their moral superiority as their ignorance and incompetence in coping with a perverse society. The novel ends with Lao Li retreating to the countryside in order to curb the extravagances of a wife now emancipated beyond all restraint.

Divorce contains several subplots, including Lao Li's wistful yearnings for his neighbor's wife, and his Chaplinesque efforts to solve a friend's problems. What links the plot and subplots is the modern idea of divorce that both scares and tantalizes every married man and woman in the novel. In many ways, the novel can be regarded as the best illustration of Lao She's fusion of farce and melodrama. Cyril Birch even considers it "Lao She's first and last comedy."[42] By putting Lao Li in a small governmental office in Beijing, Lao She furnishes us with a gallery of petty bureaucrats, each of whom is grotesque in his unique way. They are descendents of clowns from late Qing fiction such as *Guanchang xianxingji* (Exposé of the officialdom) by Li Baojia, while their psychological fixations and behavioral gestures reveal a secret kinship with Dickensian grotesques. Here is only a glimpse of some of them: "What is the chief of the office? A bureaucrat and part-time bandit. Little Zhao? A fraud and part-time clerk. Big Brother Zhang? A male matchmaker. Wu Taikai? A small potato and part-time acrobat. Mr. Sun? A scoundrel and part-time connoisseur of Beijing accents. Mr. Qiu? An 'emblem of melancholy' and part-time clerk."[43]

These bureaucrats and their wives constitute a miniature Beijing society that is shallow and snobbish, self-aggrandizing and sadistic. They give the Li family a welcome dinner at a Western restaurant, knowing that Mrs. Li is totally ignorant of Western table manners. Thus, allied with the tricky hosts, steak and brandy seem to become animate enemies bent on revealing Mrs. Li's provincial origins. While Lao Li is terribly embarrassed by his wife, she really enjoys brandishing her knives and forks. Approached by a waiter bearing a huge tray of hors d'oeuvres, she clears her place, saying, "put them all down here."[44]

Two of Lao Li's "friends" are closely involved in the main action: Old Brother Zhang, a self-satisfied man enjoying matchmaking more than his own job, so much so that "even his character has been feminized,"[45] and Little Zhao, the typical archvillain of Lao She's comic world, whose unscrupulous hypocrisy assures his success in corrupt Beijing bureaucratic circles. The novel's crisis arises when Old Brother Zhang's only son is arrested as a Communist and nobody but Little Zhao, who has a certain mysterious relation with the police bureau, can save the young man. While all of Old Brother Zhang's friends turn their backs on him, it is Lao Li who volunteers to bargain with Little Zhao. However, his efforts (including selling his own house to pay off Little Zhao) prove fruitless, because Little Zhao insists on having Old Brother Zhang's daughter as a reward. When nothing can be done to change the situation, Little Zhao is mysteriously murdered; his death is followed by the release of Old Brother Zhang's son. Lao Li is the only person who knows the killer: he is the parasitic relative of the Zhang family, Second Master Ding, a drunkard despised by almost everyone in the novel.

With the rollercoasting of plot, permeation of villains and grotesques, mysterious murder and revenge, as well as blatant sentimentalism, *Divorce* stands out as a highly entertaining melodrama. But Lao She shows considerable reservation in laying out the scheme of the moral occult in the conventional way. Undiscriminatingly putting together themes ranging from classical chivalry to underground Communist activity, from marital tragedy to bureaucratic exposé, he is willing to entertain the total absurdity of every action involved in his world. By using Second Master Ding as *deus ex machina*, Lao She obviously intends to caricature not only the archetype of knight-errantry but also the easy poetic justice in a middlebrow popular novel. Precisely because Second Master Ding's heroic act is brought in too abruptly to be convincing even on a melodramatic plane, one is led to notice the increasingly radical tendency in Lao She's fiction. Second Master Ding simply acts out what Zhao Ziyue would have done had he been given a chance. Lao She seems to indicate that one can rely neither on government forces nor on public justice to counter social irrationalities and abuses, but rather on one's own action—action that may be just as violent and desperate as the villains'.

In the wake of the tentative endings of his previous novels, *Divorce* does not end with the murder of Little Zhao. Instead, it ends with Lao Li's escape from Beijing, a move recapitulating Ma Wei's self-exile at the end of *The Two Mas*. But now Lao Li is wandering in his own homeland and there is really no way out. Nor does he leave Beijing by himself; he takes his two children, his wife—who has become an unbearable shrew—and, most surprisingly, Second Master Ding. The two men are now paired up like a bizarre Chinese version of Don Quixote and Sancho Panza. The sense of incongruity surrounding this odd couple proves once again that, in Lao She's comical/farcical world no one is privileged to carry out a heroism that exists only in fiction. The real winners are the buffoons in Lao Li's office who dominate the city of Beijing. The novel closes with Big Brother Zhang sneering: "You just wait and see, Lao Li will have to come back sooner or later! How can he really forget Beijing?"[46]

In the melodramatic world of both *The Two Mas* and *Divorce,* love, and its related themes, sex and marriage, occupy the center position. Given Ma Wei's and Lao Li's romantic temperaments, it is no surprise that their search for love constitutes the most crucial part of their emotional journey. One English translation of *Divorce* is even entitled *The Quest for Love of Lao Lee*.[47] Precisely because love is so emphatically thought of, talked about, and gestured at by the characters, it becomes the most prominent target of Lao She's farcical laughter.

Lao She has always felt uncomfortable about the concept of love as conceived by Chinese society and its literature. As his English article, entitled "The Romantic Fiction of the Tang Dynasty," points out, it is to be deplored that "people think of marriage whenever love is mentioned; and the family comes to mind next whenever marriage is mentioned . . . [the Chinese feudal system] allows no freedom of marriage. In other words, love and marriage are totally irrelevant to each other."[48] Lao She's adoption of Freud's theories of sexuality in the early thirties further reinforced his discontent with the Chinese institutions of love and marriage. In a blatantly Freudian tone, he once postulated that "the repression of sexual desire can be considered almost as the origin of human suffering. The wounds hidden in men's unconscious are exactly what drives them to behave abnormally."[49] He goes so far as to announce elsewhere that the romantic theme he explores in fiction "has nothing to do with the so-called love triangle, etc. Put in a more frank way, it is mainly about the problem of sexual desire."[50]

The key issue in Lao She's criticism of the Chinese concept of romance is its split between love and sexual desire.[51] Whereas love means the unique spiritual communication between two individuals, sexual desire refers to a blind mechanical repetition of a bodily instinct. Lao She recognizes the outrageous comedy in the biological mechanism of sexual desire, and in the perverse ways Chinese people invent to cover that desire. It will be remembered that one of Lao Zhang's biggest ambitions is to carry out the idea of free love; he achieves this ambition by buying two concubines at a bargain price. Ouyang Tianfeng in *Zhao Ziyue* and Little Zhao in *Divorce* consummate their villainous desires by deflowering virgins. What makes Lao She's laughter even more bitter is the institution of (arranged) marriage, which arbitrarily binds two people together and legalizes their physical relations. Instead of individuated love, Lao She sees in traditional marriage only a systemized repetition of sex, which is also a most hilarious way of controlling otherwise free libidinal energy. Besides *Divorce,* Lao She's laughter at the Chinese version of love, sex, and marriage is best illustrated by the short story "Yeshi sanjiao" (A different kind of triangle, 1934) in which two bumpkin runaway soldiers are eager to start a family life; since they have no money to run two families, they end up buying only one woman and take turns at enjoying their marriage!

It is with Lao She's radical critique of the Chinese way of love and marriage in mind that we find the two love affairs in *The Two Mas* both funny and sad. The two Mas' romance with the English women is their first "love" experience in life, and both cases are doomed from the beginning. I am not talking merely about such superficial reasons as racial discrimination and class consciousness, both of which bother the characters in their love affairs. I am also talking about the cynical narrator's tongue-in-cheek tone in regarding love as something so rare and fragile that it will inevitably evaporate like a bubble when the bodily factor of sex intervenes. The two Mas' foreign affairs intensify rather than mitigate the barriers of their search for love. The model character of the novel, Li Zirong, is described as an honest and hardworking student, whose goal is to finish his studies, go back to do something for his country, and marry a simple and strong woman. Lao She highlights Li Zirong's realistic plan in order to satirize the two Mas' rootless romantic fancies. Judged by Lao She's assumptions about Chinese marriage, Li Zirong is in fact even more a dupe than the two Mas.

Ma Wei's romance must also be read in juxtaposition with his patriotic sentimentalism. We laugh at Ma Wei because his pompous nationalist pose is continually undercut by his nervous, adolescent approach to the coy British girl. Especially so, as he is denied love by Mary and consequently escapes from all other obligations. Ma Wei reminds us of Yu Dafu's nameless overseas Chinese student in "Chenlun" (Sinking) who, after a cluster of romantic failures, drowns himself, while faulting his country for all his sexual frustrations. Yu Dafu's story is already underscored by a touch of self-irony, while Lao She pushes that irony one step further by depriving Ma Wei of the chance to carry out not only the sexual fantasy but also a dramatic action like the suicide in "Sinking." What has been left instead is but echoes of lovesick whines and grouchy posturing, signifying nothing.

The tension between romantic idealism and biologistic cynicism becomes even clearer in *Divorce*. The male matchmaker Big Brother Zhang is just as vicious as Little Zhao, so far as his contribution to the Chinese marriage system is concerned. In the novel, almost all the characters, male and female, have good reasons to get divorced. Divorce indicates a release from the ceaselessly repetitive, tediously predictable routine of married life, and a second chance to look for a dreamed-of unique romantic experience. All the characters use the word "divorce" either to intimidate their spouses or to conceal their own anxieties. By the end of the novel, however, no one has been divorced. What might be thought to be the most deviant, stimulating, shocking concept turns out to be carnivalesque mockery, verbal self-abuse. As a result, every couple remains the same, living "happily" in a world in which the matchmaker Big Brother Zhang thrives. At this point, the novel reveals a metafictional overtone, in that it proposes to deal with a serious subject matter only by laughing away its seriousness, and that it depicts the supposed singularity of love and emancipated marriage in a mirrored parade of repetitions where each individual unwittingly mocks the next.

The theme of divorce even partakes of a historical reference. In 1930, the KMT government passed a kinship law, which spelled out items such as the equal position of men and women, monogamy, and freedom of divorce. But the law had a strange loophole in defining the status of monogamy: "marrying a concubine is not a legal marriage, and therefore it does not involve the problem of double marriage."[52] The novel, in this light, serves as a farcical interpretation of the self-contradictory law and as a fictional mockery of the hypocrisy of the society that endorses the law.

Like those of most of his colleagues, Lao Li's marriage is arranged by his parents. After he moves his wife and children to Beijing on the advice of Big Brother Zhang, he finds that the emotional and intellectual gap between him and his wife grows so rapidly that neither can cross it any more even if he or she wanted to. While the wish for divorce tantalizes him, Lao Li cultivates a secret love for the discarded wife of Ma Ketong,[53] a beautiful and lonely woman living in another part of the same residential compound. In his wildest fantasy, he even dreams of running away with her to some tropical island. This self-delusion is soon tested by the news that Ma Ketong is coming home. Lao Li is anxious to see what will transpire between the couple. He hopes that they will break up. But when Ma returns from Shanghai as a Marxist and brings with him a comrade-mistress (whom he later dismisses), it does not take long for Mrs. Ma to forgive his brazen neglect and impudence. By nightfall when the estranged couple stay together in their room, Lao Li's dream is crushed.

> When night came, his heart went completely numb. Comrade Ma had gone to sleep in the eastern room, Mrs. Ma's bedroom! The world of Lao Li was shattered like a piece of old pottery crashing down from the air. "Poetic sense"? There was no such thing in this world. Beauty and grace and independence: all these terms were now void of meaning. Life was only a compromise, slipping by and dragging along without ideals. Other people might do it, but she, she was also like that! Perhaps in her eyes Comrade Ma was attractive. But why?[54]

Lao Li feels heartbroken because he finally has come to realize that even the most sacred love has to be subjected to infamous wedlock and bodily instinct. The woman Lao Li enshrines turns out to be a priestess not of love but of folly. More laughable is Lao Li's realization of what kind of fool he has made of himself. When everything means something else, when heart is exchangeable for body, love for sex, romantic melodrama must give way to farce.

The problem of love and marriage is but the tip of the iceberg of the Chinese reality which Lao She condemns. The next question is what, after all, is the source of the irrationalities? This leads to the second theme most frequently dealt with by Lao She's melodramatic discourse, the definition of evil. In Lao She's first two novels, *The Philosophy of Lao Zhang* and *Zhao Ziyue*, evil is basically interpreted in terms of vice and villainy, as personified by wicked clowns like Lao Zhang, Ouyang Tianfeng, and their followers. By contrast, in *The Two Mas*, one no longer encounters this kind of character with such easy labels as fraud and hypocrisy. This novel is indeed one which does not have bad characters. Even Ma Wei's father and those snobbish lower-middle-class Londoners are merely grotesque rather than wicked. But given Ma Wei's increasing moral anxiety throughout the novel, some insidious power must be sensed at work behind the scenes. Frustrated patriotism and unrequited love are the superficial symptoms Ma Wei suffers from in combat with a dark force. What Lao She really wants to depict is a kind of force which, unlike simple immorality, is not hostile or indifferent to particular values but, rather, to the whole idea of value as such. It evokes incredulous mocking laughter by letting us witness the sheer self-delusion of an idealist's pathetic belief that there is ever anything more than facts or floating "reality." In other words, Lao She's most threatening laughter stems from his and his heroes' realization of a human condition that is based an ontological void, of which the visible villainy is only a part.

The same observation applies to the case of Lao Li in *Divorce*. Despite the return of an obvious villain to the book, embodied by Little Zhao, Lao Li has a far more mysterious demon to fight against, an invisible force harvesting malicious delight from destroying value wherever it finds it. Beijing and London project a strikingly similar environment in which Lao She's Hamlet-like heroes carry on their vain struggle. Both cities are known for their cultural/historical heritage on the one hand and their codified systems of social manners and morals, which confuse and intimidate any outsiders, on the other. Tear down their genteel façades, and one finds a kafkaesque atmosphere of malice and treachery. Whereas Ma Wei may justify his loneliness on account of living in a foreign city, Lao Li finds the city of Chinese culture just a capricious and tricky an environment. We should, therefore, pay more attention to the absurdist tendency in Lao She's fiction, a tendency that flirts with realistic attempts to name personal and social evils and finally points to something beyond representation. What Lao Li and Ma Wei have been resisting turn out to be a vision of . . . *nothing* at all. For them, no action seems efficacious; every escape comes to naught. In this sense, Lao She demonstrates modernist sensibilities best reminiscent of his favorite writer—Joseph Conrad.[55]

To sum up, what makes *Divorce* and *The Two Mas* so grippingly funny (in spite of their basic pessimistic undertones) is that they dramatize the pomposity and vulnerability of intellectuals' search for meaning in a world already suffering either from too much or too little meaning. It is hard for Lao She to restrain a burst of hysterical laughter at the sight of Ma Wei's and Lao Li's self-important endeavor to think and do things in their own way, only to find that they are caught in the incompatibility between what they think and what they do. "What I seek are some poetic ideas. Family, society, nation, world, are all so prosaic and lacking in poetic meaning. . . . I am probably a little insane, and this insanity, if I can understand myself, is that I dare not become a romantic but have only daydreams. I see society filled with the forces of darkness and evil, yet hope for immediate peace and tranquility; I know the fate of man, yet conjure up visions of eternal paradise."[56] When love and lust, humor and hopelessness, are made indistinguishable, laughter sounds like crying.

From Mimesis to Mimicry: *The Biography of Niu Tianci* and *The City of Cats*

Lao She's farcical/melodramatic world takes on another dimension in the novels *The City of Cats* and *Niu Tianci zhuan* (The biography of Niu Tianci, 1936). Written to seem like an animal allegory, *The City of Cats* depicts contemporary society in its totally deformed state, while *The Biography of Niu Tianci* reveals the phantasmal essence of reality by telling of a boy's initiation into a society that is an endless masquerade. Both novels shed important lights on Lao She's changing strategy for dealing with Chinese reality.

Given its narrative framework of fantasy, *The City of Cats* may not be strictly discussed in terms of realistic fiction. But behind its thin disguise, one finds Lao She's most cynical dialogue with reality and the mode of realism. By reducing Chinese people to animals, transforming their country into an outlandish dystopia, and previewing their extinction by other animals, Lao She's farcical scheme presents the meanest configuration of the "real" world we have yet seen. In sharp contrast to the heavy satire of *The City of Cats, The Biography of Niu Tianci* impresses with its seemingly weightless flamboyance. Through a foundling's unbelievable fortune, it introduces a society in which everybody, good or bad, young or old, is an imposter, involved in a massive game of fraud. Values form and evaporate like bubbles, and morals *are* but a matter of manners. The state of unbearable lightness in *The Biography of Niu Tianci* makes the reader no less uneasy than the deadly gravity of the *The City of Cats*. The two novels are related like the print of a film and its negative, furnishing the contradictory and complementary sides of a Lao She snapshot of reality.

The City of Cats tells of a pilot's visit to the Cat Country after his plane crashes on Mars. Lao She once mentioned that the novel was inspired by H. G. Wells' *The First Man in the Moon*,[57] but with its reversal of the positions of animal and human being, its fake erudition in enumerating the absurdities in the Cat Country, it reminds us more of *Gulliver's Travels,* especially Gulliver's visit to the country of Yahoos.[58] Lao She's choice to allegorize his subject represents a way to detach himself from reality so as to see it from a refreshed perspective. Acknowledging this attempt at defamiliarization, one is in a position to notice Lao She's constant farcical implications. Farce, again, is a comic mode relying heavily on grotesque gesture and burlesque mimicry; mimicry of animals can be regarded as one of the highlights of the farcical expression of bodily movement.[59] In view of the fact that Lao She's clowns like Lao Zhang, Zhao Ziyue, or Big Brother Zhang have demonstrated a considerable number of nonhuman qualities, it requires only one more step to let them "become" animals. Mimicry involves an intentional exaggeration, distortion, and most importantly, simplification, of things conceived and perceived. When the Chinese representational order has broken down, mimicry is the inevitable result for Lao She of any desire for mimesis.

After the plane crash, the narrator tries to take shelter in a nearby village where he makes his first encounters with residents of Cat Country. It does not take long for the reader to realize that the cats are identifiable with the Chinese, especially those who would be described by a writer like Lu Xun, in terms of cowardice, greediness, ignorance, spinelessness, cynicism, and the self-deluding rationalization which turns physical defeat into "spiritual victory." The cats are a collection of Ah Q's in animal disguise.[60] The first-person narrator is then involved in the cats' fight for *miye* or fantasy leaves, a kind of narcotic plant that makes one forget all worries and cares. How to grab fantasy leaves is the only goal of life in Cat Country, where almost every citizen is an addict. The narrator is later commissioned as a guard, by one group of cats, taking newly harvested fantasy leaves to the capital, the City of Cats. The Chinese Gulliver thus gets a chance to visit the city and give the reader a first-hand report. Amazed by the size of the city and its population, he cannot but feel it is well on its way to decline. Possibly modeled after Lao

She's hometown, Beijing, the City of Cats has a glorious past; now dirty, shabby, and chaotic, it just hangs on, in anticipation of inevitable downfall.

What concerns the narrator (and us) most here is the macabre festive atmosphere permeating the City of Cats. Just as the narrator observes, "like a dying person who often shows a sudden burst of energy right before death, a dying civilization doesn't have to carry on to its end without hustle and bustle."[61] The City of Cats is a noisy and crowded city, shrouded by a most strange mood of happiness. Its streets are always full of cat residents, aimlessly rushing from one end of the city to the other "like waves." "No one walks straight forward along the streets; no one proceeds without getting in the way of the others."[62] The cats are cruel and bloodthirsty. When they do not fight with each other, they entertain themselves by watching scenes of others' bloodshed. Totally weakened by fantasy leaves, the City of Cats has no power whatsoever to defend itself against foreign invasion. Nobody seems really worried about it, though they enjoy "talking" about it. "The Cat Country is full of excitements and noises. But in the midst of the hustling I see the fingers of destruction, which move as if to peel off people's skin and flesh, turning the City of Cats into a dumping ground for bones."[63]

For all his sharp criticism on the culture of the City of Cats, the narrator finds it hard to resist the temptation of being part of it. "As you try to get close to it, you find yourself already glued to it."[64] Shortly after he arrives in the City of Cats, he is talked into enjoying the fantasy leaves. Since the narrator represents the perspective we must rely on, his ambivalent attitude toward the country he openly attacks leads us to wonder where our standpoint should be. "The Cat Country is like a vortex in the sea, sucking in whoever comes near. If you enter Cat Country, you had better follow its ways."[65] The narrator's friend, a cat named Xiaoxie (literally Little Scorpio), is such a case. Coming from a rich and powerful family, Xiaoxie is a conscientious young cat who had once been eager to do something, but his patriotic sentiment has died down after several aborted attempts, and he has since become a cynical hedonist. It is here we find Lao She's pessimistic view about any reform or revolution that might happen to China. The old country, like the Cat Country, has a magical power to soften even the most hard-hearted reformer.

One of the most unnerving facts Lao She's narrator finds in the civilization of Cats is its language system. The Cat language is one of the simplest in the world. Its vocabulary contains no more than five hundred words, and the trick of expressing yourself is to arrange the words at will. If you come cross things and ideas you can hardly articulate, you stop talking about them. Besides a limited amount of nouns, the Cats have few adverbs and adjectives. "They rarely use pronouns and they practically have no relative pronouns. It is a childlike language. You can speak as long as you remember a couple of nouns, and verbs can mostly be conveyed in hand gestures."[66] As a result, the Cats either talk about totally different things as if they were identical, or eliminate from their knowledge system once and for all things they cannot clarify.

The phenomenon of linguistic carnival in the Cat Country drives home Lao She's farcical view, which highlights the triumph of bodily action over verbal expression, aberration over sensibility, chaos over decorum. When "freedom" means a license to bully and oppress others, and "national soul" refers to money; when "party" is substituted by the word *hong* (or fighting together), and the Russian-sound "vsky" is added to any word in order to make it sound modern, one finds an outrageous chasm between objects and language, deeds and words. But two ironies arise at this juncture. Precisely because their language is lacking in grammatical and semantic nuances, the Cat people make it the most useful medium to "communicate" so as to confuse one another. For Lao She, the misused vocabulary, randomly coined words, and redefined terms render more vividly the reality he takes pains to denounce.

This linguistic skepticism also throws into question Xiaoxie's and the narrator's lengthy critiques. As one of the few sensible cats the narrator has ever met, Xiaoxie calls attention to the irrational phenomena of his country and sadly predicts its impending destruction. There is admittedly a strong indignation and pathos in his comments on the educational and political status quo of the City of Cats, but as he continues talking, one gets a feeling that his indignation verges on becoming empty posture, that his pathos may turn into no more than bathos. Moreover, if the Cat Country is comparable to China and the Cat language is a reflection of Chinese, the question that follows is how much one can take the narrator's or Lao She's words as "real." Isn't the narrator like Xiaoxie, who speaks only to deny the authenticity of what he says?

By the end of the novel, the foreigners do invade the City of Cats. The Cat soldiers, instead of fighting back, flee from the front lines and loot their own people, while politicians and scholars run around arguing about the best possible "ism" or regime they should now endorse. The revolutionary students who have been busy overthrowing teachers and principals now worship a huge rock as the icon of their latest ideological/religious enlightenment. Thus Xiaoxie sighs, "[The Cat people] mimic each other to show off their worldliness and intelligence. . . . When disaster comes, they throw away all the new terms and hark back to the most laughable and stupid thing—the rock at the bottom of their mind. This is because they are hollow to begin with, and they reveal this original emptiness whenever they are in perplexity."[67] Xiaoxie finally commits suicide. In response to "the most laughable hollowness" of his and his country's existence, the only way out is self-annihilation. In view what happens to Lao She and China in the next several decades, *The City of Cats* is a novel of striking prophetic perception; at a moment of farcical allegorization, one sees Lao She's most horrible revelation of Chinese reality.

With its continuous proliferation of caricatures and burlesque actions, *The Biography of Niu Tianci* may first impress one as a new version of *The Philosophy of Lao Zhang* or *Zhao Ziyue*. The novel traces the first twenty years of Niu Tianci (literally, "given by Heaven"), a foundling raised by his foster parents (described as stereotypical Chinese petty bourgeois), and shows how his environment can mould the young, innocent hero into a successful middle-class intellectual. As the narrator declares, he wants to describe "the education of a little hero of petty bourgeois class."[68] It is only when one finishes reading the "happy ending" that one realizes that Lao She's pessimistic view of reality has led him to employ a more systematized means than before to "catalogue" absurdities and draw the genealogy of an imposter. Beneath Lao She's flamboyant narrative, one finds a radicalism surpassing his preceding works, to the extent of celebrating chaos. The novel also indicates Lao She's most cynical attempt yet in exhibiting the disparity of social mimetic networks as well as the bankruptcy of the system of signs.

C. T. Hsia notices the novel's striking parallel to Fielding's *Tom Jones:* "The hero is a foundling; his foster parents, his nurse, his amah, his boyhood friend Si Huzi, and his tutors all have their comic counterparts in Fielding's novel."[69] But this novel is in effect less an imitation than an outrageous parody of Fielding's novel.

Consciously identifying himself with the virtues of the gentry, Fielding allows in his novel the triumphant vindication of a good and generous heart. By way of contrast, Lao She tries to prove that, in the given Chinese society, his hero's generous impulses can only be gradually deadened by his home, school, and small town environment, until what remains is channeled into greed and a desire for social conformity. Insofar as it traces the boyhood and adolescent years of a young man's growing encounters with society, the novel serves also as a mock *Bildungsroman,* indicating the process of the hero's dehumanization as he prepares himself to enter society.

On the other hand, as early as the thirties, critics were pointing out the remote resemblance between Niu Tianci and Lu Xun's Ah Q.[70] One can certainly compare the two characters, in terms of their infamous background, the volatile circumstances that predestine their degradation, and the hybridized narrative style used to describe their adventures. However, there is a basic difference between Lu Xun's and Lao She's thematic premises. Lu Xun uses Ah Q to explore and expose the cannibalistic side of the Chinese moral/cultural system, in which Ah Q is both victim and victimizer. Whether we like it or not, we are haunted by a moral anxiety and despair in watching Ah Q's degradation. Lao She refuses to locate such a moral imperative at the center of his discourse. Contrasted to Ah Q, who is burdened with idées fixes and moral biases, Niu Tianci seems as innocent as a piece of blank paper. The moral anxiety Niu Tianci's action should have evoked is so deliberately trivialized that it might as well not have been mentioned at all. Whereas Ah Q is made a scapegoat by his callous society, Niu Tianci is turned into a hero-to-be by the end of his adventure. Such a frivolous posture, as I have argued above, can be more bothersome to the reader, because it marks a paradigmatic change in the discourse of the real.

Lao She lavishes his comic talent mocking Niu Tianci's various learning experiences. Niu Tianci's discipline actually begins in his cradle. One month after being adopted, his arms and legs are bound together all the time by Mrs. Niu, "lest they be deformed someday."[71] Whenever he shows a sign of crying, his mouth is fed with all sorts of medicine. Niu Tianci's body appears as if made from plastic, helplessly subjected to the care (or abuse) of his foster parents, wet nursing, maid, male servant, doctors, and dozens of family friends in turn. Never has Lao She been so skillful in poking fun at the body reduced to a living "thing," an animated toy for capricious adults; and never has he been so observant in satirizing the social rules, superstitions, and disciplines imposed on a body as young as one-month-old baby, who nevertheless responds with adult feelings. "Raising babies is fun, because it lets adults show off their talents. Babies should put up with [these talents], or they cause themselves big troubles."[72] Niu Tianci acquires both traditional tutoring and modern education, both family training invented by his foster mother and experimental lessons conducted by his reformist teachers. As a result of these contradictory policies, Niu Tianci becomes more confused than ever.

The characterization of Niu Tianci represents yet another type in Lao She's gallery of clowns. With a big head whose back is as flat as a board, a pair of small eyes, and skinny arms and legs, Niu Tianci is born to be a comic victim, a perpetual loser, who makes one laugh ironically when he suffers. It is outrageous that Niu Tianci undergoes so many troubles at home and school. But one feels caught between a vulnerable boy silently enduring torture at the hands of family, school and society, and a mature narrator who, as perpetrator of the account, administers with impunity the most ridiculous scenes in a lighthearted style. We feel sorry for a character like Niu Tianci, but we also want to see how awful his fate could become. The problem with Niu Tianci's meek, pitiable look is that, we often tend to ignore the threat he may bring to us. Whereas a comic villain like Lao Zhang offends us by exhibiting obscene gestures and farcical assaults, a comic victim like Niu Tianci mocks us equally by allowing his body to be abused and deformed. His suffering becomes an insidious means with which confuse our sensibilities and dissipate any standards of decorum.

While Niu Tianci's foster mother manipulates his life at home, his teachers use him as a weapon for reviling each other at school. Eventually, Niu Tianci is the victim chosen to be expelled from the school. His expulsion is the beginning rather than end of his education. Following fashionable trends in town, he participates in the post–May Fourth student movements, advocating the revolution of society, and joins a "Cloud Society" organized by the imperialist gentry. At one time, he appears as a modern symbolist poet, troubled by the feeling of ennui; at another, he is dressed in an old-fashioned long gown, reciting ornate classical Chinese couplets. Niu Tianci completes his apprenticeship only after he loses his parents and fortune and, therefore, his popularity among friends. The final blow comes as his identity is questioned by relatives of the Niu family over the issue of inheritance. It is then that Niu Tianci thinks that he has learned his most important lesson: "Money is everything. All of society is built with the foundation of money. . . . We are all salesmen, faking, defrauding, and cheating."[73]

The themes of imposture and charlatanism are clearly indicated throughout the novel. Almost all the characters play roles in a society that is a masquerade. Insofar as Niu Tianci is a foundling, his origin is opaque and his identity nothing but a cipher, a zero. "Like clouds, our hero has no roots."[74] He is adopted by luck and brought up *like* a middle-class child by the Nius. Despite their infertility, Mr. and Mrs. Niu assume the roles of parents, taking care of their foster son by following cheap clichés about raising children. The art of mimicry is so practiced as to produce a confusion and a travesty throughout the whole of society. Switching from one role to another, Niu Tianci's education testifies to the social fact of total epistemological anarchy. Niu Tianci's first mentor, Mr. Wang, is originally an accounting clerk who is less interested in teaching than in running a pawn shop with Niu Tianci's father. Even the elegant poets of the Cloud Society are a group of imposters. "They had picked him up because he was amusing and they knew that he had money . . . They never mentioned the word money but news about money reached them quicker than anyone else."[75]

On top of the theme of imposture and masquerade is the issue of legitimacy of the representational system as conceived and put into practice by the characters of the novel. One of the hidden threats throughout the novel is Niu Tianci's mysterious identity. Where he comes from and how he becomes the adopted son of the Nius is always the hot topic among his schoolmates, friends, and "relatives." He is a son without real parents, a sign without grounding signifieds. "Illegitimate kid" is the nickname often used behind his back. Mr. and Mrs. Niu worry not only about whether Tianci looks like either of them but also about how he can be legitimatized as the only heir to the family fortune. Greedy relatives from both sides of the Nius have always been ready to give away their own children as heirs to the old couple; the appearance of Niu Tianci simply shatters their dream. While Niu Tianci is himself the focus of an uncertainty concerning societal recognition and classification, the problem of legitimacy of representation develops to become a leitmotif underlining almost all social/political activities. Teachers and principal fight at school over the real modern pedagogical method, warlords' troops attack each other to authenticate their political power, and even the Nius' maids watch each other for the right of the kitchen. Reality is seen as a strange amalgam of all kinds of claims for public recognition.

What tentatively links the themes of imposture and illegitimate representation and gives stability to a society such as that in *The Biography of Niu Tianci* is money. Behind the procession of superficially irrelevant episodes, we find a unified motivation that drives all characters to the worship of money. This concern about the social value of money also marks the fundamental difference between Niu Tianci's and Ah Q's worldview. Whereas Ah Q lives and dies in an old world where cannibalistic morality still rules, Niu Tianci grows up to imagine that he is nothing but a product of the system of money and exchange. He is first found by a peanut vendor and given to the Nius in exchange for twenty dollars. He himself is fetishized as an assessment for both his parents and his friends. His face value, nevertheless, fluctuates along with the ups and downs of his financial position, teaching him in return a knowledge endlessly diversified and relativized—signs, identities, beliefs, currencies. To survive the murky social transactions and convertible moral values, one has to master the art of appearing to be what one is not, to give out the sign of value which is in fact false. It is in this examination of the symbolic function of money that Lao She echoes Mao Dun's position in the novel *Midnight*.

According to Lao She's melodramatic scheme, Niu Tianci's predicament should not last long. To rescue the young man from his crisis, the humorist sends a *deus ex machina* in the form of Tianci's first tutor, Mr. Wang, now a successful businessman getting rich by smuggling opium and Japanese goods. Wang owes the Niu family an amount of money he borrowed years ago to start his "business." To express his gratitude, Wang arranges to send Niu Tianci to study in Beijing, since a college education will be a shortcut to making money. Niu Tianci has his worry: he has never received a high school degree. But his mentor easily solves the problem by offering to buy a diploma for him.

Compared with Lao She's previous novels, *The Biography of Niu Tianci* contains a smooth, lighthearted narrative that seems rarely interrupted by his immediate concern with reality. For this reason, Lao She's narrator sounds doubly tongue-in-cheek while recounting

Niu Tianci's various endeavors. By the end of the novel, his tone has become so ambiguous that one finds it hard to decide whether to sigh over Niu Tianci's degradation or to welcome his initiation. The novel's biggest irony is that, though he sees through the unscrupulous nature of his society, Niu Tianci chooses nevertheless to join it and, as the narrator promises, will become a successful man in the future. Mocking and deriding, asserting and denying, Lao She's sense of farcical ambivalence has never been so jubilantly expressed as in this novel. In this jubilant ambivalence one can detect Lao She's cynicism, a cynicism was never so acutely discernible in the novels discussed previously. When Lao She decided to drop this farcical strategy, he wrote *Camel Xiangzi*.

Camel Xiangzi: A Macabre Farce?

Once lauded as "the finest modern Chinese novel before the second Sino-Japanese War,"[76] *Camel Xiangzi* marks not only the climax of Lao She's career but also a milestone of hard-core realism in modern Chinese fiction. Chronicling the process whereby an honest young rickshaw boy in Beijing is degraded to the level of a social misfit, the novel is not only a powerful indictment of social injustice but also a sympathetic portrait of the desire and despair of lower-class people in quest of a fortune. Rich in passages about the manners and customs of Beijing, the novel is yet another of Lao She's accounts of his hometown. Compared with other full-length fictions we have so far discussed, *Camel Xiangzi* constitutes a drastic turn in Lao She's stylistic strategies. One finds in it neither a hilarious parade of characters nor slapstick action but, rather, a display of the overwhelming environments against which men fight their ever-losing war. Indeed, both Lao She's pessimistic representation of reality and his deterministic mechanism are so emphatically pronounced in the novel that most readers have agreed with scholars like Joseph Lau who read it in terms of the tenets of the naturalist novel.[77]

Lau contends, "In [Xiangzi's] character, there is nothing to suggest that his downfall is his individual responsibility. . . . His defeat can only be explained in terms of the society in which he moves, which nullifies all his efforts towards independent and honest living."[78] Stressing the environment as the factor that destroys Xiangzi, Lau calls our attention to the naturalist dimension of the novel. But given the strong theatrical elements of the novel's plot and action, and remembering Lao She's philosophy of laughter and tears, one feels that the novel contains something more than just a cruelly objective slice of life.

I would suggest a different reading of *Camel Xiangzi,* one that listens to its melodramatic and farcical overtones. Much has been said about the novel's humanitarian concern for social underdogs and its naturalist depiction of the oppressed and the insulted, but very little attention has been paid to its formal structure, and next to nothing has been said of its genealogical link with Lao She's comic works. Lao She's funniest writings had in fact always implied the grimmest of visions of the human condition; can *Camel Xiangzi* be governed by the converse of this strategy? does a force intervene in this naturalist presentation of life as it is—a force that can express itself only in suppressed laughter? By calling attention to the melodramatic/farcical subtext contained in *Camel Xiangzi,* I do not mean to override the traditional course of interpretation; rather I want to add a new dimension to an understanding of the novel and to recognize the dialectical relation between the pathetic and the farcical sides of Lao She.

Lao She writes about Xiangzi's degradation in terms of a classical comic convention: the incrustation of something living with something mechanical.[79] The novel, to begin with, is about the love affair between a rickshaw puller and his rickshaw. An orphan growing up in the slums of Beijing, Xiangzi is an honest young man with a very limited ambition—to own a rickshaw—and he does have the ability to achieve his goal. Xiangzi works hard toward this dream and, unlike his peers, his self-esteem keeps him from indulging in various forms of self-debasement such as opium smoking and whoring around. While there is nothing wrong with Xiangzi's humble wish, the way he expresses it is definitely to be understood in romantic terms. After Xiangzi gets his first rickshaw, he pulls it in a manner as if he were making love with a woman:

> After six months this lovable rickshaw of his seemed alive to what he was doing: every time he swerved, bent a leg or straightened his back, its response was immediate and most satisfactory. They were never at cross-purposes in the least. Whenever they came to a flat open stretch, Xiangzi would run with only one hand steadying the shaft, the soft swish of rubber tires behind spurring him on to run swiftly and steadily. On reaching their destination, his clothes would

be wringing wet, as if just fished out of water, and he would feel tired but happy and proud.[80]

Xiangzi is fully justified in loving his rickshaw like a woman, but there is something amusing about the relation. One can even discuss the comic routine of mistaken identity in Xiangzi's romantic gesture. The rickshaw is his first love. No woman, not even his confidante in the second half of the novel, Fortune (Xiao fuzi), can take its place in Xiangzi's affections. Xiangzi buys a second-hand rickshaw later in the novel, which is nicknamed "little widow" by his malicious peers, partially because it is decorated in funereal colors—black and white—and partially because it is being "remarried" to Xiangzi.

Xiangzi's love for rickshaws has nothing to do with fetishism in a semicapitalist society, as some socialist critics claim,[81] or not more than it has to do with the absurd fixations of universal human behavior. In Lao She's comic fiction, one comes across a long list of good or bad characters obsessed with things or ideas ranging from money, matchmaking, and patriotism to modern wives. Xiangzi is but one more entry on the list, though his is a long, sad entry. "If you are crazy about something, you will end up paying your life for it," so declares Lao She's sarcastic narrator in "Lian" (Predilection, 1943), another short story about man's excessive love for things.[82]

But no sooner has Xiangzi fulfilled his dream than he is inadvertently drafted into the army as a coolie and his rickshaw is taken away from him. Although he later manages to escape from the barracks, taking along with him three army camels, which he sells for a cheap price and thereby gets his nickname, "Camel," the theft "nevertheless represents the first step in his downfall, because his integrity has suffered."[83] Xiangzi's first downfall is of course full of melodramatic power. As he vacillates between the tests of virtue and vice, so his readers are torn between sympathy and disappointment. Though we do not agree with Xiangzi's theft, we are somehow willing to forgive his misdeed because of his lovable personality and the external environment in which he is placed. We share a complicity with Xiangzi as we watch him sell the camels and start to save money for the next rickshaw.

Nevertheless, as the novel goes on, we come to realize that Xiangzi's loss of his rickshaw and theft of camels are only the overture to more bad luck, which proliferates at an amazing speed in the rest of the book, to the point that there arises a rhythm of mechanical repetition of misfortune. Three times chance seems to favor his hope of owning his rickshaw, money, and a beloved woman; three times he ends up losing everything. In the course of the novel, Xiangzi is robbed by the army, harassed by secret police, maltreated by his clients, seduced and fooled by Tigress (Huniu) and another woman, cheated by his boss, addicted to gambling, afflicted with venereal disease, and finally rejected by the occupation he once loved. Not only does he lose his rickshaw twice, he also loses his wife, his son, his benefactor (Professor Cao), his confidante, his fortune, and, finally, his self-pride. Right along with his unbelievably bad luck, a new image of Xiangzi surfaces—Xiangzi the unlikely loser, whose touch on any thing or anybody causes immediate disaster. While the parade of disasters highlights the melodramatic essence of the novel, indicting a society devoid of justice and sympathy, it also evokes, perhaps unexpectedly, a tacit humor: like the predictable Chaplinesque victim, Camel Xiangzi finally enacts farce. So much misfortune calls attention to itself: Camel Xiangzi the loser joins Candide and Schlemihl in the march of ridiculously unrelenting persecutions.

Besides investing his story with a mechanical rhythm, Lao She shows a strong tendency to express to the extreme the adversities Xiangzi is thrown into, so much so as to pile on his pains and suffering in a spectacular form. Critics have often noticed that the bad time in which Xiangzi grows up and struggles can be no worse, but they tend to ignore how neatly the timing for the bad luck which falls on him is arranged. Right after Xiangzi owns his first rickshaw, it is stolen away by warlord troops; once he saves enough money for another rickshaw, he runs into the secret police who takes everything from him; once he gets his second rickshaw, he has to sell it to pay for his wife's and son's funeral; and the moment he pieces together his last remaining self-confidence to start a new life, he finds that his confidante Fortune has committed suicide. Each seemingly better situation later proves to be a step taken closer to catastrophe. One can thus discuss the formal design of the ups and downs of Xiangzi's life. Originally, one keeps one's fingers crossed, hoping that something good will turn up to drive away Xiangzi's bad luck. But when suspense turns out to be a routine, anticipating only a worsening situation, and a *deus ex machina* is but a familiar device precipitating a downfall, the magic of melodrama wears off.

One is left with a growing ironic curiosity that leads one to wait and see just how bad things can become.

Our changing attitude toward the spectacle of Xiangzi's misfortune not only reveals our psychological self-defense mechanism in operation but also points to Lao She's own ambiguous outlook on the irrationalities of the human condition as well as on any realist/naturalist attempt at describing them. If Lao She's comic/farcical vision involves subsuming objects to inappropriate concepts or turning social norms and ethics upside down, it is equally true of his most pathetic look at life. The novel's obsessive exhibition of human suffering and its indiscriminate conversion of the lively to the living-dead, of differences to identities, are bound to be amusing, however tragic the actual outlook.

As mentioned at the beginning of this chapter, Lao She considers contemporary reality not just monstrous but absurd. Xiangzi's sysiphean effort to fight back against an absurd world turns him into an ironic embodiment of that world's absurdity. Whereas Lao She's early novels exaggerate social abuses by means of a Dickensian parade of grotesques and buffoonery inherent in late Qing exposé fiction, *Camel Xiangzi* reverses the comic/farcical discourse and substitutes surface tears for surface laughter. Beneath both laughter and tears, however, lurks the same kind of outrageous impulse, amounting to a flirtation with chaos and self-negation. Melodrama lavishes emotion in the name of probing the lost moral occult in the world, while farce celebrates the excess of emotions on account of the loss of moral and behavioral norms. Right at the juncture of the modes of melodrama and farce, *Camel Xiangzi* is as excessively pathetic as *The Philosophy of Lao Zhang* is radically hilarious. Both kinds of novels derive their theatrical absurdity (and horror) from Lao She's skepticism about the boundary of the real and his cynical response to any effort to better the status quo.

Lao She's predilection for explicit bodily gestures shows another sign of his indebtedness to the melodramatic/farcical imagination. Since Xiangzi is an inarticulate person, one of the ways to gain access to his world is to decipher the mute gestures he acts out. When language falls short in uttering the extremes of emotional landscape, nonverbal signs and bodily gestures take over in "posturing" Xiangzi's pains and happiness. But body language intensifies meaning at the risk of simplification; it may well be suggesting a deficient sign system. The language used by the cats in *The City of*

Cats, it will be remembered, highlights bodily gestures. Indeed, there are moments in *Camel Xiangzi* when characters' physical gestures are comparable to miming, one of the most direct sources of clowning. Miming turns ideas and emotions into a sculptural sign, stylizing and distancing any emotional authenticity entailed thereby. Miming stuns and amuses us at the same time as it calls attention to the exaggerated movement of the body itself, foregrounding the non-human quality in an otherwise sensible human movement. Both the seduction and the wedding scene of Tigress and Xiangzi, for example, proceeds like a mime, so theatrical yet so gruesomely real.

The high points of the mute dramaturgy of bodily gestures are, of course, the scenes of Xiangzi pulling his rickshaw. Time and again in the novel are we brought to "see" Xiangzi pulling his rickshaw: the clumsy first experience which brings him sores and pain; his happiness in pulling his own rickshaw as if entangled with a woman; the fatigue that results in an accident at night; and his despair as he limps along with his shabby rickshaw at the end of the novel. On the melodramatic level, we are invited to see how pulling a rickshaw, being a physical labor in itself, serves also as plastic representation, an animated trope, of the moral and psychic state of Xiangzi vis à vis the outside world. On the farcical level, nevertheless, we see how Lao She's naturalist style verbally exploits the bodily gesture, laying layers of meanings on it, to such an unbearable extent as to confuse the reader: we are no longer sure if we are watching a pathetic display of gratuitous human labor or a verbal celebration of the body's malleable performance.

One of the best examples demonstrating Lao She's employment of bodily gestures for the melodramatic presentation of a moral meaning is the summer storm scene in chapter eighteen. The scene opens with descriptions of Beijing in a sultry summer that is like a burning inferno, scorching and grilling those who have to make a living on the streets. "The street was bone dry and glaring white. Dust rose from the footpaths to meet the gray miasma, forming a vicious veil of sand that scorched the faces of the passersby. Every place was parched and stifling as if the whole ancient city were one lighted brick kiln."[84] Then comes lightning and thunder, and in a minute the hot and dusty city of Beijing is turned into an island in a deluge. "Wind, dust, rain, all mingled in one raging cold, murky vortex so that neither trees, earth nor clouds were distinguishable. . . . the downpour continued, pelting vertically down in a solid mass. Countless arrows shot up from the earth, thousands of waterfalls cascaded down from the roofs."[85]

Yet Lao She's lengthy, elaborate passages indicate an attraction to the disaster. With the most decorative diction and ornate imagery, Lao She presents Beijing as a bizarre expressionist theater, staging the primordial war between man and nature. He aims at a pathetic revelation of Xiangzi's suffering, while carrying on with a secret carnival of symbolism on his own terms. In the midst of the revelry of thunderstorm, Xiangzi helplessly runs with his rickshaw. He wants to find a shelter, but his customer orders him to go on. We can barely see his figure trying hard to march on, a figure drenched in the rain as if it would soon be washed off from our sight by water. The chapter cannot be any more melodramatic in transmitting the message that the good are abused and the virtuous, tortured. But given its verbal extravaganza, its almost sadomasochistic exhibition of Xiangzi's suffering body, and its relentless indulgence in moral schematization, one senses—beneath his luxurious presentation of pathos—the ambivalence of Lao She's desire.

The end of the novel, accordingly, is not about Xiangzi's passing knowledge of self-delusion, so much as about his degradation to an inanimate living-dead, a thing. The blows of life deprive him of his rickshaw, making him part of the majority he used to look down upon, practically converting him to a machine. In other words, the comic machinery has run full circle in the novel, turning its human agent into an automaton. All along Xiangzi has sensed this change, over which he has no control. On his wedding night with Tigress, for instance, he feels that, "manipulated in everything, he himself resembled an old yet new ornament, a strange, unrecognizable object."[86]

This fact leads one to think twice about the first chapter in which Lao She generalizes the life of Beijing rickshaw pullers as one dominated by the mechanical run of fate. It is within this narratorial frame that Xiangzi's story is singled out as representative, since his ups and downs are just like a "specific screw in the machine."[87] Be it called a cannibalistic society, a naturalist machine without a god or a big wheel of fortune, the machine runs in its monotonous, unchangeable way, threatening to devour anyone's effort or desire to run away from it, and moulding all different lives into one identical type. Xiangzi's ghastly comedy lies exactly in that he feels this, but never completely understands that he is dealing with such an infamous machine till it is too late.

Insofar as he is a romantic trapped in an insensible environment, Xiangzi is a more humble and wretched version of Ma Wei of *The Two Mas* and Lao Li of *Divorce*. Like his counterparts, Xiangzi fails to understand that, in a society full of injustice and unexpected exploitations, any effort to accomplish an idealistic goal will become a meaningless joke; he is the victim of his own great expectations which are laughable from a cynical point of view. Driven on by a desire to idealize, Xiangzi's character is less tragic than obtuse. By the end of the novel, nothing could be more obvious to the reader than the fact that the world is an unfathomable black hole and any project to make sense out of it is always a ghastly mistake. Only romantic self-delusion could keep one from that laughably self-evident truth. "Life is nothing but a prank . . . I used to think of this, but now I understand it," says Lao She in the epigraph to his short story, "Duanhun qiang" (Soul-shattering spear, 1935).[88]

Xiangzi's marriage with Tigress and his close relation with Fortune may remind us of the triangle between Lao Li, his wife, and Mrs. Ma in *Divorce*. But as suggested above, the rickshaw remains always the hidden fourth element in Xiangzi's romantic dream, competing with the two women for Xiangzi's attention. In the beginning of the novel, Xiangzi dreams of marrying a robust and honest country girl someday after he makes enough money. This dream is demolished when he submits himself to the seduction of Tigress the night he leaves his new long-term client, the Yang family. Critics usually call attention only to Xiangzi's exchange of lofty self-esteem for bodily instinct in this episode. But one should notice that Xiangzi falls prey to Tigress only after he has lost his first rickshaw, quit his job at the Yangs, and seen little hope of earning his second rickshaw. Again, Xiangzi's affair with her can be read in a comic light, in the sense that Tigress serves as an unlikely replacement for the lost rickshaw, a double mistaken identity that mocks Xiangzi's sense of judgment.

Tigress is one of the most unforgettable characters in Lao She's fiction. An extra-large-size "princess" of the slums, Tigress' very existence already implies farcical potential, to say nothing of her looks and temperament. Lao She seems to despise this character so much as to develop a fascination with her. Kept as an old maid by her selfish father so that she can run the rickshaw rental, Tigress finally revolts by seducing Xiangzi and marrying him. Life has made her "another strange object, old yet new, girl yet woman, female yet male, human yet beast-like."[89] One remembers most vividly her facial complexion, which changes from grayish green to reddish black, hinging on her cosmetic skill, and her insatiable appetite and sexual desire. A shrew, Tigress' immediate predecessor is the female trickster in "A Woman from the Liu Village" who beats her husband and father-in-law, maltreats the women of the family, and rules the village in the name of Christianity. In both cases, the shrews are grotesques who intimidate and amuse one at the same time. Given all her foibles, Tigress is not a villainous woman; she is at most a self-complacent, aggressive clown, who thrives on bullying the meek.

Tigress's comic dimension cannot be fully appreciated until she is compared to the weak and pale Fortune. From the point of view of both physique and personality, the two are already in sharp contrast. Placed side by side, they act out not only a naturalist interlude about the persecution of the good by the bad but also a black comedy of the triumph of the victimizer over the victim. Tigress gets her fun either by charging the innocent Fortune with seducing her husband, or by lending the poor girl a room so that Tigress can peep at Fortune while she entertains her customers, after the two are reconciled; the reader is also embarrassingly amused by the two women's dramatic styles of self-aggrandizement or self-depreciation.

The overtone of black farce can be detected even in Lao She's treatment of the two women's deaths. Neither Tigress' death in childbirth nor Fortune's suicide after she has been sold to a whorehouse of the lowest kind is amusing in itself. Xiangzi discovers Fortune's suicide, as we remember, from an old whore who is nicknamed "Bleached Flourbags," for her two huge, pendulous breasts. With five ex-husbands who all died "like empty lice" shortly after marriage, the woman now enjoys her profession and entertains visitors by "flipping her huge breasts over her shoulders."[90] The scene where this gifted whore assesses Fortune's performance and relishes her suicide conveys an emotional effect which is anything but sad in a melodramatic sense. In Lao She's absurd world, nobody, not even meek, pitiable Fortune, is spared cynical laughter.

Death is a beginning rather than an ending, a beginning of obscene mirth.

The same farcical laughter is heard at the deathbed of Tigress. Due to her age and to overeating during her pregnancy, Tigress has a hard time delivering the huge baby. Lao She wryly observes that other pregnant women in the neighborhood have to work hard right up till the time of delivery. Because they had little to eat, their babies are never too large, which, ironically, makes for easy births. While problems for the poor women come only after their delivery, Tigress's are just the opposite. "Her privileged position now proved her undoing."[91]

In the short story "Grandson," Lao She had described the outrageous consequences for a pregnant woman overfed with goodies by her mother-in-law; here, with just as much comic malice, he narrates how much Tigress eats and how little she exercises, actions and inactions that promise the same disastrous result. Yet the pain Tigress suffers becomes all too real. As if reflecting her personality, Tigress dies one of the most noisy deaths in Lao She's fiction. For two weeks, she rolls in bed, her groans and cries horrifying all the neighbors. Even so, Tigress has time to order everybody around. When her personal deities have failed to come to the rescue, Tigress sends for the "Toad Spirit," a woman medium, and her acolyte—a middle-aged ponce with a yellow face.

The two frauds fake trances, forge and burn an oracle, and direct Tigress to swallow its ashes, while themselves enjoying hot sesame-paste biscuits and braised pigfoot, bought by Fortune. When they find Tigress is dying, they run away. The two imposters make the death scene even busier and noisier, yet paradoxically, they best demonstrate what human suffering and death are all about in Lao She's mind: "Folly and cruelty are part of the natural order of this world, for reasons beyond our understanding."[92] No emotional expression of Lao She's world can be rendered in its pure form; melodrama has to subject itself to the defiance of farce. Besides tears and sighs, he aims at arousing laughter, laughter that reveals both despair and mockery of that despair.

Tigress' and Fortune's deaths serve only as preludes to Lao She's climactic celebration of death and decay at the end of *Camel Xiangzi*. The last chapter of the novel, which was suppressed by Lao She for the 1955 edition,[93] presents a macabre carnival in the most grandiose *and* grotesque style seen in Chinese fiction since the execution scene of Lu Xun's "True Story of Ah Q." It also provides an extremely important sign of Lao She's adherence to the discourse of farce and melodrama; this discourse enters even into the most hopeless moment of his story.

The chapter does not add anything to the sum of miseries already in the plot, offering only a general look at life in Beijing when spring comes again. But exactly because it seems to be telling of nothing, it becomes an empty coda, questioning the formal and thematic sufficiencies of a novel overloaded with miseries, deaths, and misfortunes. Vivacious and prosperous, Beijing is seen as a city full of activity and fun in the spring. Lao She's style is so light-hearted and mesmerizing that it sounds as if it were borrowed from a totally different text.

> Fun was everywhere. Bustle was everywhere. Noise and color were everywhere. The early summer heat was like a magic charm which brought glamour to every corner of the old city. Ignoring death, ignoring disaster, ignoring hardship, when the time came she had shown her strength. She had captivated the hearts of a million people who, as if in a dream, were singing her praises. She was grimy, she was beautiful, she was run-down, she was lively, she was motley, she was relaxed, she was lovable.[94]

But it does not take long for the reader to realize that, for all its lively appearance, Beijing is shrouded with a ghostly veil of nostalgia. Just as its euphemism "Gudu" (old capital)—homonym of "Gu" du ("dead" capital)—suggests, Beijing is a phantom city thriving only in and for the past. No longer at the political center, the people of Beijing hang on to the past by observing obsolete customs, recalling old glories, and cultivating wistful airs. But no matter how hard they try, there is an artificial quality infiltrating their lives, making everything only "look" real. In exposing both the real and unreal Beijing, Lao She exposes his ambivalent love for his hometown.

Beijing is also the "City of Cats," peopled by heartless residents who, in the name of courtesy and decorum, practice cannibalistic rituals as routine entertainments. Lao She writes, "there was no good or evil in the hearts of these people living in Beijing. They didn't understand virtues or vice, nor could they distinguish right from wrong. They could cling to a few moral rules handed down to them and were willing to be called civilized people, yet they loved to watch the slicing and carving of their own kind—just as cruelly and enthusiastically as a little boy might chop up a puppy."⁹⁵ In fact, this final chapter culminates in the execution of Ruan Ming, a professional student who had once betrayed Xiangzi's benefactor Professor Cao and now is in turn betrayed by Xiangzi. With the callous and curious Beijing people watching this scene of bloodshed, Lao She plainly reinvokes Lu Xun's indignation over the Chinese crowd syndrome. But even as he is criticizing the bloody carnival scene, Lao She seems carried away by his own exuberant language, to the point that the now-familiar critique sounds just as empty as the Beijing manners and morals it criticizes.

Far away from these crowds we find Xiangzi. Totally despairing (emptied) of any meaning in life, Xiangzi is now a walking deadman, a mean-spirited loafer parading for small pittances in Beijing's endless wedding and funeral processions. Life in these processions strikes Xiangzi as no less logical than life anywhere else. He has become a living prop, furnishing the last spectacle the rich and elegant can still afford. "When somebody got married, he'd parade the banners; when somebody had a funeral, he'd hold up the wreaths and mourning scrolls. He didn't rejoice, nor did he weep. He just went along with somebody's parade for the sake of a dozen or so pennies."⁹⁶

We last see Xiangzi amid a funeral parade. To yield to parading in homage to the dead has become an irresistible temptation to Xiangzi, not only because it assumes a spurious grandeur but also because everything outside it has begun to look lifeless, meaningless, and unreal. Both Xiangzi's gruesome gestures and the pomp of the processions give one a strong sense of decadent theatricality, a deadly sensation. Nowhere else can one find a more emphatic example to show how Lao She's farcical strategy works than watching Xiangzi turned into a human robot, mechanically throwing out funeral money in a funeral parade.

It is noteworthy that, by the end of the novel, even the narrator, who has been sympathetic with Xiangzi, turns his back on his hero. Throughout the last chapter, the narrator's rhetoric becomes noticeably more and more ostentatious and formal. The novel's last paragraph reads as follows:

> The honorable, ambitious, dream-filled, enterprising, robust, magnificent Xiangzi walked with other people on any number of funeral

marches; who knows when and how he will eventually bury himself—this degenerate, selfish, unfortunate offspring of an ailing society, this hopeless wreck of an individualist!⁹⁷

C. T. Hsia comments that "in the account of [Xiangzi's] final degradation, one feels the intrusive presence of satire, which is incongruent with the sympathetic texture of the main body of the novel."⁹⁸ In fact, it is only now apparent that the main body of the text has become congruent with this empty and mechanical "manprop" and with the empty and mechanical "cityprop" around him, due to the cumulative and insidious rewriting of naturalistic formulae into their own deconstructions. It is only now that one senses acutely the carnivalesque impulse that has always existed in Lao She's novels. Through most of the novel the narrator backs his hero up against the invisible destructive forces of his environment, yet when the fight turns out to be a hopeless one, he seems to give up and let deterministic forces take over not only his hero's fate but also his own ground. The sudden shift in the narrator's attitude from tender sympathy to bitter sarcasm suggests to the reader a self-mocking narratorial position which reflects the fickle mentality of Beijing citizens, Xiangzi among them. It also marks Lao She's last joke, a joke on his own self-destruction/creation.

Lao She might have had a good reason to delete the last chapter from the novel's new edition under the Communist regime, not because the chapter is too inconsistent in tone or too irrelevant in structure with regard to the rest of the novel (as he himself and some critics claimed), but because its "happy" ending proves disturbingly appropriate to a tearjerker, and its farcical panoramic view of reality threatens to summarize Lao She's philosophy of life only too well. By removing the last chapter, Lao She and his critics and censors might contend that they are offering a more realistic presentation of life in the thirties; it is in fact the missing chapter, with its repressed laughter, that speaks to that reality, both in the old world of thirties and in the new world of the fifties.

Chapter five

"I Love My Country, Does My Country Love Me?":[1] Lao She's Patriotic Fiction

On the evening of November 15, 1937, Lao She left his home in Jinan for Wuhan. Jinan had fallen to the Japanese army earlier that month, and for a well known writer like Lao She, self-exile seemed to be the only way to maintain dignity and safety. In the midst of bombs and explosions, he was escorted by a friend to the railway station, which, surprisingly, was still doing business. He barely bought himself space on a train already overloaded with refugees, soldiers, and ammunition, and he waited half sitting and half squatting in crowds for another five hours before the train moved. Lao She went without eating all the way to Zhengzhou, where he finally was able to buy some buns when transferring from one train to another, but he almost choked to death at his first greedy bite into the buns.[2]

Even years later, Lao She felt deep sorrow at recalling the scenes of his departure from home and his subsequent journey to the south. He left behind his pregnant wife and two little children, with whom he was not reunited till the fall of 1942. As he puts it, there were moments when he wished either that the train had not gone after all (so that he could have gone back home with a solid excuse) or that the train had been bombed on its way to Wuhan (so that he would have been killed and freed from all national and domestic concerns). "The two different wishes conflicted in my mind and ironically made me numb. I could not make any decision on my own but entrusted my fate to whether the train would go or not."³ Lao She arrived in Wuhan on November 18, 1937, and moved to Chongqing eight months later, when Wuhan was under threat of capture by the Japanese.⁴

Compared with his days in Beijing and Jinan, Lao She led an extremely active life during the wartime period. As if determined not to be bothered by personal worries, he plunged himself into various anti-Japanese campaigns, running magazines, experimenting with new literary forms, organizing writers into a united camp, and visiting the front. In particular, he cofounded the Chinese Writers' National Anti-Aggression Association and was appointed its secretary general. He was also editor in chief of the association's magazine, *Kangzhan wenyi* (National resistance war literature), one of the most important wartime magazines in China.⁵

As secretary general of the Chinese Writers' National Anti-Aggression Association, Lao She of course felt more obliged than anybody else to demonstrate how the war was directing his literary concerns onto new paths. For him and his fellow writers, the performing arts were to be a more intimate and immediate medium for transmitting patriotic messages to the general public. Thus he learned to write drum song lyrics and other popular forms of northern Chinese folk art like *zhuizi*. He also tried his hand at both Chinese opera and Western theater. In spite of their immense popularity, Lao She was never satisfied with the results of these new efforts of his. He felt especially inept at creating Western-style drama, because he tended to write his scripts in the style of narrative fiction.⁶ Even so, in his better plays such as *Mianzi wenti* (The problem of face), he managed to transplant to the stage certain trademarks of his comic fiction such as melodramatic plotting, Dickensian characters, and witty sarcasm, thereby earning due applause from his audiences. Little did he know that, with all this wartime training, he was going to become a major playwright of the first decade of the People's Republic of China (PRC) regime.

Lao She felt most at home writing fiction. But because of his poor health, his commitment to folk arts and drama, and his editorial and administrative burdens, he produced only a handful of works during the wartime period. They include a dozen or so short stories, and two novellas, collected in two volumes respectively titled *Huocheji* (Train, 1939) and *Pinxueji* (Anemia, 1944), and four novels, *Tui* (Metamorphosis, 1938), *Huozang* (Cremation, 1944), *Minzhu shijie* (Democratic world, 1945), and *Sishi tongtang* (Four Generations under one roof, 1946–1950, hereafter abbreviated as *Four Generations*). *Metamorphosis* and *Democratic World* were never finished, while *Four Generations,* invested with epic scope, is composed of three separate parts, titled *Huanghuo* (Bewilderment, 1946), *Tousheng* (Ignoble Life, 1946), and *Jihuang* (Famine, 1950). As its publication date indicates, *Famine* was written after the war—actually during Lao She's visit to the States from 1946 to 1949—and was published even later. In terms of its thematic framework, however, it should be regarded as a continuation of Lao She's wartime fiction.[7]

Critical reaction to Lao She's wartime fiction has been less enthusiastic than to his pre-1937 works.[8] The reason is not difficult to guess. More often than not, Lao She was writing with an overt patriotic purpose which could easily turn a work into simpleminded propaganda. Even the trilogy *Four Generations,* acclaimed for its lyrical yearning for a traditional life-style and its deep pathos over China's fate, can hardly avoid didactic passages and sentimental interpolations. This fact, however, should not keep one from noticing the variations Lao She tries to work out on the given formula; nor should it let one ignore the frequent tensions between what he intended and what his works led to. As I will discuss in detail later, it is precisely because Lao She labored hard, probably too hard, to put into practice the ill-defined concept of "national resistance literature" that he ended up turning his fiction into a drama of polemics. Private desires and fears, public concerns and ideological commitments meld in such a way as to manifest, not so much his original patriotism, as his anxiety and skepticism towards all causes.

Patriotism as a Problematic

Aiguo (love of one's country, patriotism) has been one of the most important causes of modern Chinese fiction, and Lao She well deserves to be claimed as one of the most exuberant voices in support of the cause. Lao She was once an important advocate of the idea of "art for life's sake," the major canon of post—May Fourth realist fiction. When the war broke out, it was only natural for him and his fellow writers to see such a slogan in a new light and to campaign for the idea of "art for *battle's* sake." While the concept of "national resistance literature" arose in a definite historical context, imposing ideological *and* moral imperatives twice as strongly as had prewar literature, it nevertheless provided very weak generic guidelines. As critics have pointed out, in contrast to dynastic powers that take loyalism for granted as natural and inherited, "nationalism asks about 'rights' and thereby opens up the problem of *representation:* who has the right to speak for whom and under what circumstances?" (italics mine).[9] In other words, nationalism (and nationalist literature) derives its power less from an essentialism based on a divine order than from a more egalitarian comradeship. At the center of the feeling of nationhood, patriotism can be regarded as a "cultural artifact";[10] it is overdetermined, reducible neither to an ideological effect nor to an ethical/religious institution. It involves a process of mediation by a complex system of symbols, narrative, and narrated events. The concept of nation and nationalism propagated by Lao She thus invites a careful reading. As we will see, China as an independent nation in a modern sense is intertwined with China as a cultural/historical entity. Patriotism is seen both as a political mandate backed up by a nationalist call, and as a moral imperative reminiscent of the traditional concept of loyalty (*zhong*); both as an innate capacity shared by the Chinese people and as a modern obligation that is made known through pedagogic means.

Questions as to patriotic literature's formal boundaries and thematic adequacies were raised even at the beginning of the war, as reflected by the 1938 debate on what subject was most relevant to war literature. In a feature essay of the literary supplement of the *Zhongyang ribao* (Central daily news), December 1, 1938, Liang Shiqiu, then its editor in chief, complained that writers had been so preoccupied by the theme of anti-Japanese invasion that they were producing more and more propagandist clichés. He called for a literature including, but not limited to, the subject of the war. As he wrote, "We most welcome materials concerning the war, but it is just as well to have things which are not related to the war, as long as they are realistic and fluent. It is not necessary for writers to force the war theme on everything they produce. As for 'eight-legged' anti-Japanese clichés, they are of no significance to anybody."[11]

Liang Shiqiu's essay immediately caused a battle over whether wartime literature should not necessarily be war literature. Partly due to the commanding tone assumed by the essay, and partly due to Liang Shiqiu's being on unfriendly terms with leftist cliques before the war, the debate on the aesthetic premises of war literature soon turned into a fight over ideological legitimacy.[12] Lao She had rarely been involved in politically oriented disputes before the war. But since he was now in charge of the Chinese Writers' National Anti-Aggression Association, he was commissioned to draft an open letter in protest against Liang Shiqiu's frivolous attitude. Therein he retorted that everything undertaken by a writer during the wartime must be relevant to the war, and that only after a writer recognizes such an obligation can he start to write powerful works.[13]

Liang Shiqiu's essay never did manage to switch the ongoing trend of Chinese literature. Paradoxically enough, it best served as a starting point for a highly strident discourse called "national resistance literature." Under its banner, writers were told that their only mission was to boost readers' morale against the Japanese: "Writers should, like the troops with their guns at the front, use their pens to stir up the people, protect the fatherland, pulverize the invaders and win victory."[14] Such a hyperbolic demand did not sound strange. It echoed the militant rhetoric of the literati in their endless debates during the May Fourth period and thereafter, such as the dispute on "revolutionary literature" between the Creation Society and the Society of Literary Studies in the twenties, and the League of Leftist Writers' internecine fights over slogans concerning national defense literature in the thirties.[15] Most of these arguments circled around the formal or thematic legitimacy of a certain kind of writing, such as critical realism versus socialist realism, while the innate value of *Writing* as a magic medium, capable of revealing the meaning of any subject and of triggering any desired socio-political reform, remained completely unexamined.

The confrontation between Liang Shiqiu and Lao She dramatizes once again the arguments about the function of literature. A student of Irving Babbitt's neohumanism, Liang Shiqiu is arguing for retaining the autonomy and decorum of literature in a classical sense.[16] Lao She is emphasizing a didactic, utilitarian course for literature, one that is never too far away from the aims endorsed by the May Fourth literati. Granting the superficial divergence of their theoretical propositions, they actually share (with each other, and with their predecessors), the same mimetic assumption, expecting to gauge literature by what it apparently reflects. They also endorse the same kind of humanist concern, with the difference that Liang Shiqiu encourages writers to depict an amplified human condition, of which the war is a part, whereas Lao She aims to highlight the immediate subject of the war, of which the human condition is a part. Were it not for irrelevant political reasons, the debate could have been resolved with ease. It simply recapitulates the tautological theses underlying modern Chinese realism after the May Fourth generation of writers.

Fifty years after the controversy, one can discern from the bulk of anti-Japanese literature that Liang Shiqiu did have grounds for his warning. He might have had a better chance of convincing contemporary writers, had he argued that what most writers were practicing was only a very narrow type of war literature, and that, given its wartime context, a powerful work does not necessarily have to make any obtrusive reference to the war to ensure its relevance to the war. As for Lao She, the eventual inconsistency between the theme and practice of his own war fiction will serve as the critique of his theory: his most blatantly patriotic rhetoric often shakes the foundations of rhetorical patriotism.

Looking at Lao She's wartime fiction in more personal terms, one finds that, patriotic rhetoric notwithstanding, it registers Lao She's changing sentiments over a turbulent decade. Compared with the jerky, high-strung style of the late thirties fiction, his mid-forties novels, such as *Four Generations,* impress one with their meditative or even cynical undertone. But if the war spurred Lao She on to chronicle new experiences such as exile, starvation, massacre, and the constant fear of sudden annihilation, he in turn invests these experiences with the themes that had previously concerned him. His ambivalent attitude toward chaos and absurdity, his indignation at social injustice, and his chivalric fantasy are never dropped; they appear instead in a manner more poignant than ever, thanks to the compelling historical conditions in which they are now situated. Moreover, Lao She's Manchu background must add a dimension of self-irony to his patriotism, an irony that mocks his fervent nationalist gesture in the most subtle way. It would be only too naive, therefore, to describe how the war suppressed or solved any social or private conflict formerly posed by Lao She, as has been done by one critic.¹⁷ The fact is that the stark light of war brought some painful clarity into Lao She's once barely discernible obsessions.

Lao She dealt with the theme of patriotism as early as his second novel, *Zhao Ziyue*. Through the adventures of naive, good hearted Zhao Ziyue, Lao She speculates on the role of students in the post— May Fourth social/political turmoils and on their responsibility for the national fate. Students played an important part in the May Fourth Movement and in patriotic campaigns thereafter, such as the May Thirtieth Incident. At a time when students were honored as the vanguard of political reform and the voice of social conscience, Lao She questions the limits of their patriotism. He sees in student movements a pure, energetic force that propels social/political reforms otherwise unlikely to have taken place; at the same time he senses the thin line between patriotic fervor and fanatic aggression, between the call for self-sacrifice and the opportunity for self-aggrandizement. One of the best examples in *Zhao Ziyue* is, of course, the student riot on campus. Dissatisfied with their president and teachers, students launch a "revolution" that essentially turns the campus into a slaughterhouse: "Outside the President's office lay a broken strand of rope: the President had been tied up and beaten. In the hallway were five or six satin slippers: the teachers had escaped barefoot. Pinned against the door-frame of an office by a three-inch-long nail was an ear with its blood already congealed: it had been lopped off the head of a faithful, prudent (his crime!) supply clerk of twenty year's standing. On the green near the hothouse was a patch of blood that had turned purplish-black: it had poured forth from the nostrils of a gardener whose income was ten dollars per month."¹⁸

C. T. Hsia notices how such a scene sheds light on Lao She's indignation over a social misconduct in the name of a noble cause. I suspect that Lao She's apprehension goes deeper than this. His graphic accounts of violence and irrationality lead one to notice the skepticism deeply hidden in his mind, a skepticism that throws doubts not only on surface social absurdities, such as students rioting in the name of moral order, but also on hitherto unquestionable deep assumptions, such as the mandate of patriotism itself. Lao She must have been bothered by this dangerous doubt looming on the horizon of his text. He once apologized that *Zhao Ziyue* failed to depict reality in more positive terms because he had never taken part in student patriotic activities and was ill-informed about what "really" happened.[19] The irony is, that while the novel may not report the May Fourth Movement firsthand, it does raise questions that even writers who were present were not willing or able to consider. It documents the dark side of a noble campaign and reveals the self-complacent logic of patriotic imperatives. Compared with the student demonstration scene depicted by a writer such as Mao Dun, Lao She's differently focused attention bespeaks a very different reality.

As mentioned in the last chapter, *Zhao Ziyue* has a hard time rationalizing the means and the ends of patriotism. In quest of his own way of serving his society and country, Zhao Ziyue vacillates between the villain Ouyang Tianfeng and the patriot Li Jingchun. By the middle of the novel, Lao She has made it clear that China is so corrupt that any reform attempt will itself be absorbed into the larger mechanism of self-corruption. To save the country, extreme measures must be taken; Li Jingchun's assassination project represents one of such measures. After Li Jingchun is executed, Zhao Ziyue takes up Li Jingchun's unfulfilled wish and dedicates himself to terrorism. An old hand at melodrama, Lao She thus produces a spectacular moral finale by exaggerating Zhao Ziyue's self-sacrifice for the good of his country. This desperate ending produces more questions than it can answer, however. One wonders if Zhao Ziyue will carry out his patriotic goal without falling prey to individual heroism and if terrorism will not bring back the horror and chaos seen earlier in the campus riot scene. Beyond the level of moral considerations, one also notices that Lao She's definition of patriotism as terrorism betrays his secret flirtation with violence and self-destruction—an irrational embrace of a rational cause. These questions will recur in Lao She's fiction written during the War of Resistance.

Lao She's other two novels, *The Two Mas* and *The City of Cats*, present an odd pair of moves within Lao She's strategy of patriotic verisimilitude. In both cases, China is not depicted in such immediate terms as to arouse direct feelings for her; rather China is distanced or defamiliarized, in such as way as to appear as the "other" country with which ambivalent relations are maintained. Whereas *The Two Mas* deals with the paradox of overseas patriotism, *The City of Cats* highlights the blindspots of a total patriotism. Both, of course, serve as reverse testimonies to Lao She's obsession with China.

One of the earliest modern Chinese works of fiction dealing with life and thoughts of expatriate Chinese, *The Two Mas* anticipates the fiction about the "expatriate Chinese syndrome" that prospered four decades later. It also prefigures the pitfalls of the patriotism many expatriate Chinese step into. The novel provides a model plot and setting for the problematic of overseas patriotism: exiles trapped in a hostile foreign environment, conflicts between those who are concerned about the homeland and those who have resigned themselves to the brave new world, a mixture of unquenchable desire for the homeland and severe criticism of the homeland, frustrated romantic adventures with foreigners, etc., all emphatically addressed through Ma Wei and his father's quests for new identities overseas. Thanks to his own expatriate experience, Lao She believes that patriotism does not wane after one leaves one's country; rather it becomes all the more poignant, testifying to one's cultural and emotional ties with the homeland.[20] But Lao She also knows that there are moments when such a disoriented patriotism may engender a strange sentiment, a sentiment composed of nostalgia and xenophobia, of guilty conscience and self-importance.

By all means, Ma Wei can be seen as a good example of Lao She's condescending yet sympathetic portrait of the patriot as a young man. Cut off from his motherland, Ma Wei struggles to maintain his patriotic tie with that motherland on his own. While geographical distance may hinder him from responding to the immediate needs of his country, it nevertheless strengthens his imaginative bond with it. As the real China fades bit by bit into to the back of his memory, Ma Wei's patriotism grows stronger and stronger. There is a decisively inward turn in the patriotic discourse of *The Two Mas*. In view of Ma Wei's psychological changes, the China he loves may well be an extension of his own image, and his patriotism only the other side of his narcissism. This partially explains why, by the end of the novel, Ma Wei runs away from the foreign Britain, only to exile himself in France. He loves China, but only from afar. His failure to go back to China has become an original sin that preconditions his patriotism.

By this, I do not mean that Ma Wei is a hypocrite. I have previously discussed Ma Wei's "procrastinated" love for China in the light of his Hamletian complex. On the other hand, Ma Wei's problem may also serve as a sign of Lao She's own speculations on the terms of patriotism. Lao She himself left London for China after he finished *The Two Mas*. In reality, he carried out what his hero fails to do. But Ma Wei's self-exile may well have remained as an alternative to Lao She's own patriotic decision. Self-exile may be a cowardly behavior, but it does at least help to sustain one's romantic yearning for the lost motherland. Especially so, if the country one is obligated to return to is as hopeless as that of the City of Cats.

In *The City of Cats,* Lao She changes perspective again, dealing with patriotism in negative terms. In spite of its long civilization and moral heritage, Cat Country knows little about patriotism. The Cat people love themselves just as much as they ignore the fate of their nation. When invaders enter the City of Cats, its residents either run away or surrender immediately. Neither action saves their lives. Lao She's question is simple: if China is comparable to the Cat Country, is she still worthy of our love and sacrifice? By raising such a question, Lao She has put himself in a double bind. Patriotism may as well not exist if it presupposes one's country as lovable; patriotism is best tested precisely when one's country is in crisis. But if one commits oneself to a country which is indifferent to its people's dedication and hostile to any change toward better conditions, one's love tends to become gratuitous.

Although Lao She understands that patriotism can never be rationalized on an abacus of give and take, he keeps a nervous eye on the absurdities in its rational structure. Thus in the case of the Cat spokesman Xiaoxie, we see a strange combination of perseverance and self-abandon, of tragic elitism and cynicism. Xiaoxie represents the intellectual class of the Cat people who foresee the fate of their country yet choose to struggle to the end. Through his scathing remarks about his country, one learns that the Cat Country has lost all its powers to survive the modern world:

> The real reason for the fall of the Cat Country is that smart people think only of leading the revolution, but they are short of any knowledge necessary for reconstructing their country. They set out to solve political/economic problems, but end up getting themselves caught in those problems. As for the general public, they have gained 'class consciousness' but remain ignorant of everything else; they know they have been fooled but can find no way out. . . . With this fatal wound, the Cat People will not resist invasion even when the fall of their country is in sight.[21]

By the end of the novel, Xiaoxie commits suicide, thereby fulfilling his bittersweet ideal of self-immolation. But I would ask, does he die for his country, justifying all the moral values he used to sneer at? or does he die for himself, asserting personal choice in a chaotic world? Xiaoxie's suicide can thus be seen either as reluctant martyrdom or as existentialist rejection.

All these problems are temporarily suspended at the beginning of the war. But as I will discuss in the next pages, Lao She cannot do away with his uncertainties, a fact that makes a model work of patriotism like *Four Generations* a somewhat dubious affirmation. His lack of confidence—in his own country as well as in himself—makes even his most vehement patriotic propaganda sound hollow. Lao She's passion for China is rekindled after the success of Communist liberation, but it takes less than a decade for him to find himself again troubled by the rationale of the ultimate national cause. He articulates his doubts most emphatically in the drama, *Chaguan* (Tea house, 1957). In this play, the hardworking Beijing teahouse proprietor, Wang Lifa, lives through three political regimes in modern Chinese history: the Republican era at the turn of the century, the Warlord government in the twenties, and the KMT regime in the forties. He tries to accommodate to each regime by putting up with all sorts of taxes, troubles, and unjust rules. But on the eve of the Communist revolution, even a tough, resilient person such as Wang Lifa comes to realize the hopelessness of his teahouse. In despair, he performs with two old friends a funeral ceremony in memory of their deaths to come, and then hangs himself. Wang Lifa is not an articulate patriot; his life experience has taught him that his fate hinges only on the regime in power. But deep in his mind, he knows he loves China. His puzzlement about the capricious terms of patriotism later amounts to an absurdist torture, one that is best expressed by his friend Fourth Master Chang: "I love my country, but does my country love me?"[22]

This question underscores the existential anxiety that has always haunted Lao She's patriotic discourse. *Teahouse* was banned, along with Lao She's other works, as counterrevolutionary, in the heyday of the Cultural Revolution. When Lao She stepped into Taiping Lake on the night of August 24, 1966, he acted out the gesture of his character. One wonders if he thought of Fourth Master Chang's desperate line as he drowned himself. "I love my country, but does my country love me?" Fourth Master Chang's cry referred to the dark periods before Communism, but it unhappily fits the Socialist new era. One also wonders if Lao She thought of Ma Wei, whose patriotism survived because he had the wisdom never to return to

China, and more intriguingly, if he felt an ironic relief at the end of his lifelong quest for the right cause for self-sacrifice.

Lao She pondered the social and political conditions of suicide throughout his whole career. The poor prostitutes in "The Crescent Moon" and *Camel Xiangzi* commit suicide because life has proven to be unworthy of their struggles, while the soldiers and civilians in wartime fiction such as *Cremation* and *Four Generations under One Roof* die to maintain their dignity and patriotism. Yet the motive of Lao She's own suicide must have been more complicated, involving an altruistic determination amounting to self-sacrifice as well as a desire for self-destruction; a despair about the status quo as well as a flirtation with the deadly unknown. It reminds one of the peculiar deaths in his early stories. In "Dabeisi wai" (Outside the Dabei temple, 1933), a teacher willingly dies in a student riot, with an almost masochistic posture. His self-sacrifice later produces a life-long obsession in the leader of the rioting students, ruining his life in every way—a most menacing revenge. In "Heibai Li" (The black and white Li, 1934), a man nicknamed Black Li is determined to sacrifice his own welfare—including love, fortune, family, and even life—for his flamboyant brother who is a revolutionary. He finally achieves idea of total brotherhood by being mistakenly arrested and executed in the place of his brother. He dies for the revolutionary cause, but only by a trick of mistaken identity.

Lao She's other names contain the final irony of his patriotism. His literary name *She Yu* derives from the two separate parts of his family name, *Shu,* and literally means "self-sacrifice." Several times in his life Lao She asserted his wish to sacrifice his own life for the national cause.[23] But as Lao She's son Shu Yi notes:

> The real moment of self-sacrifice finally came, but at a time it should least have happened, in a place it should least have taken place, to a person who should have least deserved it, and in a plot which should least have been possible.[24]

Shu Yi's comment summarizes most succinctly the ambiguous aspect of Lao She's patriotic discourse.

Cremation

Cremation is the only full-length novel Lao She completed in the wartime period, and it remains the only attempt Lao She ever made to deal with the war directly. In many ways, the novel best indicates the problematic of the patriotic novel with which Lao She struggled to come to terms. Both the critics and Lao She himself regarded it as a big failure.[25] The novel, in Lao She's own words, "sets out to describe the war, telling people how cowardice and malingering during war will result in nothing but self-destruction. This premise, nevertheless, cannot compensate for its failure, a failure due not to that it deals with the war . . . but to that I knew too little about the war."[26] Moreover, Lao She was working on the novel under extremely unfavorable conditions. His physical weakness and administrative distractions simply would not allow him any chance to concentrate on writing this novel, or to revise it after he finished it. Lao She once thought of destroying the manuscript, but his financial straits kept him from doing so.

Knowing Lao She always discusses his own works in an excessively apologetic manner, one has to learn not to take what he says at face value. Indeed, for all the obvious reasons he gave to account for the failure of *Cremation,* his self-critique comes to an ironic conclusion. He implies that even such a failure as this can be relished, since *Cremation* is a *war* novel. "What can be more formidable than war? It transforms rich farms into wasteland, changes the course of the Yellow River, and turns cities into ruins, weak women into strong men, scholars into warriors, and a body of flesh and blood into a weapon against steel arms. But most of all, it has exposed the deadly antagonism between ideal and delusion."[27] What will a writer be, Lao She queries, if he avoids writing about war with the excuse of his unfamiliarity with the front and life in the occupied areas?[28] Failing to write a war novel is insignificant, but failing to write about the war *is* significant.

In the light of Lao She's self criticism/defense, *Cremation* becomes interesting demonstration of the mutation of literature into politics. It shows how a novelist's concept of writing can be redefined in a special historical context, and how, under such a condition, his act of writing and the work he produces constitute a new intertextual dialectic. As mentioned above, Lao She understands well that he is not good at writing war novels, but in the case of *Cremation,* he feels obliged to make an attempt even if failure is foreseeable. Since the war has become the *raison d'être* for writing, there is simply no way for him to carry on if he does not confront this ultimate theme, however incompetent he may be. This move gives rise to a paradoxical logic: Lao She writes headlong toward failure, as if only through the failure could he convince both himself and readers of his unconditional patriotic heroism. Outside the novel, Lao She is the tragic hero on the scene of writing. He is acting what he is not, thereby following in the steps of those intellectual figures he criticizes in so many of his novels and short stories.

Set in a fictitious town in Hebei, the novel deals with the way in which the townspeople's cowardice and indifference toward the war cause their own disasters, and how they are finally awakened by a local guerrilla's suicidal act of sabotage in the town. The novel culminates with a big fire that claims many lives of the townspeople, the enemy, and the guerrillas. A scenario like this is certainly not too original, but it invites a metaphorical reading, in the sense that it dramatizes the moral Lao She would have drawn from the problematic of national resistance literature. Just like the guerrilla heroes who were left in the town to fight a hopeless but psychologically rewarding fight, Lao She acts out his share in a suicidal attempt by writing something worthy of a fiasco. Lao She the writer becomes an imitation of the heroes in his novel. What happens *in* the novel and what happens *to* a Lao She writing the novel form a queer parallel.

Ironically enough, an impulse of self-abandonment follows in the wake of Lao She's self-martyrdom in his writing. Whereas he is treating a theme he would not have taken up had he been put in a different historical context, he makes stylistic misjudgments he could have avoided had he been writing more conscientiously. As a whole, the novel shows a Lao She who is tempted to try out many new possibilities he cannot handle, at the expense of the conventions which will at least make his a mediocre novel. Thus when it fails, the novel fails in a spectacular way.

The novel has a promising beginning, describing the group of guerrillas anxiously waiting for a chance to sneak into the besieged city, Wencheng, to prepare to sabotage it. Two characters are immediately contrasted: the leader Shi Lei, a stout, clever peasant hero versus the deputy leader Ding Yishan, a young urban intellectual now committed to a new military role. Unsurprisingly, there is a certain incongruity in temperament and class consciousness between the otherwise brotherlike heroes. To add more flavor to this contrast, Ding Yishan happens to be the prospective son-in-law of a traitor who is a member of the town's gentry, while Shi Lei has given up his family for his country for almost ten years.

Given such a beginning, one would have expected something melodramatic to happen, a plot more in the vein of contemporary Russian war novels. Such novels had exerted visible influence on such popular prewar guerrilla novels as *Bayue de xiangcun* (Village in August) by Xiao Jun. For example, Fadeyev's *The Rout* has won a great popularity among Chinese readers, owing to Lu Xun's translation and promotion. Depicting the exploits of a roving band of Red guerrillas in far eastern Russia during the Russian Revolution, it is a story of heroic defeat, not victory. Besieged by White armies and Japanese troops alike, a group of about one hundred and fifty guerrilla fighters is eventually routed; only nineteen members survive. Lu Xun particularly stresses the confrontation between two members of the guerrillas: Metchik, the oversensitive "superfluous man," and Levinson, the guerrilla leader, a gnomelike Jewish Communist.[29]

If a novel such as *The Rout* sheds some light on the kind of war novel Lao She might have had in mind, we may well suppose that, at the very least, the two characters in *Cremation,* Shi Lei and Ding Yishan, would have had more conflicts between their ideological origins and life-styles; that Ding Yishan would have had a hard time solving his dilemma between romantic love and patriotic dedication; and that the thirty-two guerrillas would have established a miniature society during war, showing the variegation of human nature under testing. But all these possibilities are already stunted by the end of chapter one, where Ding Yishan is mysteriously shot to death on a mission to the town. Shi Lei is now left to star in a one-man show, with the part-time job of finding out who killed Ding Yishan.

To make up for the sudden death of one potentially interesting character in the novel, Lao She then allows his heroine, Ding Yishan's fiancée, Menglian, to take up the job left by her beloved. She is going to help the guerrilla leader Shi Lei carry out his mission. A crucial figure in the novel, Menglian appears to be presented in such a way as to testify to Lao She's well-known incompetence at creating romantic heroines.[30] Not only do her postures, ranging from pouting to grieving, indicate a lack of depth, her transformation from a frivolous rich girl to a slogan ridden patriot also presents too easy a fantasy. Throughout the novel, she has new experiences: her fiancé's death, her father's defection, a local traitor's proposal, a desire to help the guerrillas; but she responds and acts so rigidly that she simply illustrates how a character will be if she is drawn purely according to a formula.

Lao She seems also to have lost his confidence in caricaturing villains, one thing he enjoyed and was good at in his early fiction. Liu Ergou, the biggest traitor of the novel and instigator of Ding Yishan's murder, is described as a nerd. Despite his alleged cruelty and unscrupulousness, he is excused from doing anything as ingeniously wicked as Lao She's other villains. Just like Menglian, he is entrusted with a big role yet fails to come up to it. As one critic complains, the novel severely attenuates the tension of the war because it lacks any substantial portrait of the Japanese, and, worse, it lets a petty clown like Liu Ergou run all evil doings on their behalf.[31] Menglian and Liu Ergou are at their best only when they are seen in moments of hide-and-seek between a clownish suitor and a reluctant beauty, moments modeled on a classic comical routine in Chinese theater.

The long-awaited war scene comes at the end of the novel. As all the preparations for a big act of sabotage are under way, the guerrillas are suddenly notified to retreat because the major troops they have been assigned to cover have completed a mission outside town and will soon leave. Reluctantly, the guerrillas take the order, only to find that they have already been spotted by the Japanese army. A fatal combat thus starts, though not without a touch of anticlimax. With his thirty-one guerrillas fighting hundreds and thousands of Japanese soldiers, Lao She must have set out to conjure up a tragic scene like the final debacle in *The Rout*. But what we see instead are groups of people—enemies, awakened civilians, and guerrillas—busily stumbling over each other and running about chaotically. Lao She's lack of expertise in dealing with combat scenes can even be detected by the sudden shift of viewpoint and style here. Instead of the objective, sarcastic tone of a third person narrator, he uses a plural "we" to evoke a mood of communion shared by the narrator and his characters.[32] As well-intended as the device sounds, the narrative is however modeled on an ostentatious journalistic style and results in the opposite effect: by referring to "we," "our men," and "our people," it never brings forth any sense of immediacy but suggests a nervous self-serving rhetoric, one that exposes rather than covers up the writer's absence from the scene.

In the midst of gunshots, bombs, and smoke, the only visible character is the guerrilla leader Shi Lei. Lao She retains an unusual respect for this character, who personifies everything Lao She and his intellectual characters are not. In the middle of the novel, he behaves like a classical chivalric knight, running around on his own to investigate Ding Yishan's murder. But his heroic quality is not fully displayed till the combat scene. In chaos, "Leader Shi Lei knows clearly where his people are and what they are doing. He is very busy, but very calm, like a powerful whip, tied to the top of a combat. . . . He runs, he jumps, just like a panther ready to fight. He has forgotten that he is a creature of flesh and blood . . . He feels as long as he is marching forward, nothing can withstand him. He is a flying, whistling bomb which will penetrate a mountain."[33] Indeed, Shi Lei is not a creature made of flesh and blood. He fights with such Boy Scout courage and earnestness that he becomes a grown-up version of the Little Wooden Puppet (*Xiao mutou ren*)—the character in Lao She's patriotic children's story. The combat ends up with a grand explosion of the Japanese ammunition dump.

Lao She seems to have become obsessed with the destructive power of the explosions and the fires they cause. This scene happens twice at the end of the novel. His hero Shi Lei survives the first explosion, runs out of town, and takes shelter in a country house. When he realizes that Japanese soldiers are approaching his hideout, he throws his last grenade at them, and starts a fire to burn himself to death. Both explosions and fires remind one of the scene of burning hell in "Train," which will be discussed in the next section. Although violence and death are now described as necessary evils in war, Lao She has not quite ended his meditation on the irrational forces they bring forward, forces that plunge every value and every individual into the same vortex of annihilation. When the combat reaches its most vehement moment, guerrillas, Japanese soldiers, and civilians clash, and all die together. Lying on the ground, "head to head, hand to hand," one can "no longer tell winners from losers; invaders' ambition and avengers' aspiration drive everybody to shed each other's blood."[34]

For the Lao She who has a long record of ambivalently tempting the threats of death and chaos, there is probably no better way to end his novel than have Shi Lei commit suicide. It may well be argued that Lao She not only reiterates the significance of a death for the war through his martyrdom, but also secretly rationalizes the tantalizing power of self-destruction. To recapture the metaphorical reading, one could say that Lao She must feel relieved when his book comes to its own end, with the suicide of Shi Lei. Thus Shi Lei is "waiting to be burned into ashes. He is completely free of worries, only feeling his life gushing out of his body like his blood. Slowly, the smoke permeates the thatch house, blinding his eyes. He feels suffocated but peaceful, because he has accomplished his duty as a soldier."[35] Only in the last chapter does Lao She's narrative regain a poetic composure he has not hitherto been able to attain. Like Shi Lei, Lao She has also completed his obligation to the war. For good or bad, it is what he has done, not what he has achieved, that counts.

Unproblematic Problems: Patriotic Short Stories

Lao She published only two collections of short stories and novellas during the wartime. Though written under the same banner of patriotism, the two collections project drastically different images of the war and thus dramatize Lao She's changing attitude toward the cause of national resistance literature. As we have seen, Lao She began as one of the veteran writers dedicated to carrying out the concept of war literature, at whatever cost. But as the war went on, his own writing not only exposed holes in that theoretical fabric but sometimes struck devastatingly (if unwittingly) at the forces it purported to serve.

The 1939 collection, *Train,* contains works Lao She wrote either on the eve of or at the beginning of the war. Only three out of the total of nine stories bear no obvious connection with the war, and a comparative reading of the two groups of stories will show how the concept of national resistance literature gradually had effect on Lao She. The novella "Wo Zeyibeizi" (This is my life) extends his humanist concern with social underdogs evinced in the novel, *Camel Xiangzi*. "Big cities often prepare two tracks [of life] for poor people: being a rickshaw puller or a policeman."[36] The novella is an old policeman's recollection of his past, detailing how fate has tricked him once and again, finally driving him over the edge of despair. In the manner of a dramatic monologue, the old man tells us stories about his adolescent apprenticeship as a funeral decorator; about his happy days as a smart, popular young man among relatives; of his "perfect" marriage, which ended up with his wife's running away with his best friend, leaving him two children; about the hardships a policeman goes through; about political upheavals in Beijing; of the sudden death of his son, also a policeman; and about his most recent burden, the raising of his grandchildren.

Just like *Camel Xiangzi,* the novella triumphs in providing a vivid, sympathetic picture of lower-class life in Beijing. The story may be pathetic, but Lao She's fascination with Beijing life, good or bad, is unmistakable, and carries a tension that will surface much more clearly later, in *Four Generations.* Judged by Lao She's autobiographical novel, *Under the Red Banner,* one finds in the novella clues that indicate that he had especially poor Manchu communities in mind. The old policeman, for instance, may well be based upon memories of Lao She's father and one of his cousins, [37] while the descriptions of family circles and their manners also suggest that social stratum.

What strikes one most is Lao She's handling of the novella's narratorial voice. In a weary, bittersweet tone, the first person narrator imbues his reminiscences with such an introspective sensibility as to salvage them from becoming either a sheer social indictment or a hard-core naturalist story. The old policeman's is not a simple character. Though looking back from a miserable position, he never loses ability to modulate what he was and what he is. He does relish old expectations and small successes, however deceitful his eventual life proves them to have been. He also observes the political stage of Beijing with an earthy wisdom acquired from his work experiences. Throughout the novella, nostalgia and cynicism, memorable hopes and inescapable despair are made to interpret each other, leading one to think again the transpersonal implication of the novella's title—this is "my" life.

Another story which shows no discernible influence of the war is "Tu" (Rabbit). A chilling exposé story, it deals with the sudden rise and downfall of a female impersonator of the Beijing opera, who leaves his fate completely in the hands of underworld patrons. At the center of the story are the homosexual deals between the young impersonator and his sponsors, in which Lao She sees a decadent and irrational temptation, dooming the young man's fate. But if the story deserves more attention, it is because in it Lao She tries out a different approach to the problem of evil.

Lao She had been good at ridiculing social evils in a Dickensian mode. Under such a treatment, villains are often not just hateful but also laughable. "Rabbit," however, casts a much more sullen and sensual image on the villains and their undertakings. Describing how the ambitious young man is lured step by step to his fall, Lao She evokes a world vision reminiscent of Balzac's Paris stories, in which power, money, sex, and evil weave themselves into a magic network, arousing every social climber's desire and then ruining him or her in every way possible. As narrator, Lao She seems helplessly to witness a wicked power whirl away the young man's fame, fortune, and, finally, his life. Only his ability to face up to the last-minute victory of chaos and death remains. The story ends with the narrator's report of the young man's futile struggle to survive the theater, and of his death shrouded in mixed horror and cathartic relief.

By all standards, "Train" must be regarded as a masterpiece among Lao She's short stories. Written before Lao She escaped from Jinan by train, the story nevertheless appears to be a fictional rehearsal of his life experience, because what happens in the story seems to anticipate Lao She's despair and irrational fantasies on the train leaving Jinan.[38] The story takes place sometime before the war. Instead of taking refugees away from home, a train is taking passengers home for family reunions on the eve of the Chinese New Year. In no danger of being bombed by Japanese airplanes, the train is, however, threatened by a big quantity of firecrackers carried by a group of soldiers for their general's birthday party. More, all the passengers on the second-class car hold free passes which actually do not belong to them. These people obtained the passes via the backdoors of their more powerful friends, who nevertheless did not give the favor away till the last moment. As for the soldiers, they do not bother to travel with any kind of pass.

This second-class car neatly symbolizes a small society of petty bureaucrats, opportunists, middle-rank officers, and soldiers. A snobbish society, too, in which the rule of hypocrisy and imposture is enforced in its strictest way. But deep inside everybody's mind is an anxious yearning for home and family reunion. Had they been more "resourceful" on their jobs, they would not have had to wait to go home free on New Year's eve. While sparing no mercy in caricaturing these people's manners and morals from the outset, Lao She does show understanding for their pettiness and small-scale greed. There are points where he even comes to identify with them. After all, as Lao She sees it, nobody in the car is a real winner in life. When the line of sympathy and cynicism gradually blurs, the image of a more mature and meditative Lao She takes shape.

The story's style is terse and crisp. Lao She is clearly striving to produce a rhythm suggestive of the train's movement as well as of its passengers's impatient and excited mood. He gives quick sketches of characters' gestures, nervously switches his camera eye from one scene to the next, and piles up clusters of short sentences and clauses in a breathtaking tempo. The whole narrative is rendered as if in a highly unstable situation, about to blow up into fragments at any moment. Lao She thus turns his realist passages into a patchwork of impressionist pictures:

> New Year, go home! New Year, go home! Thus the train wheels hurried on. But the train moved very slowly. Under the starry sky, trees, tombs rushed backward. The train pierced through one darkness, and ran into another. Sparks and smoke spurted above, moving toward the back. Steam leaked from the bottom of the train and was left behind. Run, run, don't pant, gallop. A lump of darkness, complexly dark, gone. A load of darkness, emptily dark, gone. A puddle of snow, a procession of hills, bright at one moment, dark at another, all gone. But, too slow, too slow, New Year, go home! On the car, bright light, warm air, restless mind. Can't sleep. New Year, go home![39]

The story then takes a drastic turn. Two passengers have made friends and gotten deadly drunk together. One of them lights a cigarette and throws the match aside, which immediately kindles the alcohol fumes pervading the air. What follows is one of the most unforgettable scenes in modern Chinese fiction. The two passengers are set aflame on their faces, bodies, and luggage. In extreme pain, they rush at sleeping passengers and set everybody on fire. Meanwhile, all the firecrackers start to blow up. One waiter (and part-time opium smuggler), already stoned by drugs, "suddenly sits up in the midst of smoke and firecrackers. He sees nothing. The opium he carries is giving forth an extremely fragrant smell. Hot. His legs cannot move; the opium smoke rises upward enclosing him within a big globe, just like a cocoon."[40] Sensations and illusions merge at the climax of the fire:

"I Love My Country"

> As if in ecstasy, the tongues [of the fire] lick out, one protruding, one reaching far, one half hidden in the smoke, one suddenly skirting outside the window, one wandering around, one flickering left and right. Hundreds of tongues [of the fire] dance together, forming thousands of charming shapes. They gradually merge into a big lump, like a fireball, a comet, rolling or shooting around; now they spread out, in red or green, once bright and once dark. Suddenly from the clouds arise new flames, flowing as fast as surf; they squeak, burn flesh, parch hairs; noises become more and more mixed; things fall down; men scream, forming a fire parade; the whole car is burning, thick in smoke and violent blaze, a most horrible cremation![41]

While the disaster takes place, the train is running through one station after another without any stop. People at the stations seem to see one car caught in fire but choose to ignore it. Moreover, the fire finally spreads to a third-class car, causing more deaths.

Most readers will be stunned by the amount of violence and cruelty the story is charged with. Realism and fantasy meet exactly when Lao She envisions his train galloping on a snowy winter night, over the plains of northern China, with one full car of clownlike people screaming fire and jumping out of the windows to their deaths. Yet even in its most horrible passages, one can hardly ignore those images full of theatrical power, like the dancing parade of fire tongues quoted above. Lao She is always bent on decorating his pathetic subjects with black humor and scenes of a *danse macabre;* even the dejected funeral scene at the end of *Camel Xiangzi* conveys a sense of mute festivity. But none of his previous works has shown such a desperate wish for a total destruction, to say nothing of a destruction in a truly spectacular way. In this sense, the fire does shed a most equivocal light on the patriotic novel *Cremation,* where fire is also a central event.

One may well surmise that "Train" is symptomatic of Lao She's tense feelings toward his and his country's fate on the eve of the war. Yet beyond its autobiographical references, the story illuminates Lao She's speculations on the hopelessness of (any kind of) effort in an irrational world, with or without war. The birthday firecrackers, free passes, opium, and homecoming wishes might all be taken as feasible signs, mocking people's frail vanities or illusions. Although the story's raw material seems to have nothing to do with the impending war, the story actually proves to be a more complicated work that captures the edgy, volatile mood of a society waiting for something disastrous to happen.

"I Love My Country"

The other six stories in *Train* are dominated by an anti-Japanese theme. To say these stories are all crudely written is unfair, but they do manifest an urgent sentiment that either commits Lao She to the most sensational plotting or keeps him from digging into things in the way he used to. In these stories, Lao She mainly wants to sample how the war has changed people's ways of living and their prospects, for good or bad, and to point out the "correct" way for his readers to follow. There is no denying that the war tremendously affected one generation's behavior and thoughts, yet at stake here is how Lao She is accounting for these changes in his various narrative modes. By watching the formation of a new verisimilar typology, one can gain access to Lao She's own changing ideological assumptions.

From the outset, the war is seen by Lao She as awakening China to a new consciousness of its moral and ethical existence. As the title of the unfinished 1938 novel, *Metamorphosis,* suggests, the war forces the Chinese people to undergo a painful but necessary metamorphosis, mortifying and preparing them in every aspect for a new life. Therefore students now come to realize their duty outside the classroom, governmental employees work harder at their jobs, and even older people are willingly covering young guerrilla activities ("Rentong cixin" [We are on the same boat]). Such a wish for a magic transformation pervades Lao She's patriotic stories, to the point where generation gaps are filled in ("Shagou," [Killing dogs]); true love is defined ("Yikuai zhugan" [A piece of pig liver]); fraternal friendship is strengthened ("We are on the Same Boat"); marital relations are tested ("Yifeng jiaxin" [A letter from home]); and the bad elements of a society are sorted out for public ridicule ("Dongxi" [East meets West] and "Yunu" [Bath slaves]). One almost feels that, for all the brutal arrests, humiliations, and killings under the Japanese occupation, the wartime society promises a better chance for social reform than the prewar days.

Nevertheless, despite the patriotic rhetoric on the stories' surface, Lao She betrays an uncertainty whenever this wishful thinking needs to be presented in more substantial terms. This can be seen clearly in Lao She's dealings with his major characters, who are mostly students and young urban intellectuals. He tries to inject positive elements into them, yet he often ends up describing them as people playing roles larger than themselves. They easily stumble or get frustrated by the war, not because they are lacking in the will to act but because they assign themselves to do something they are not competent to do. Consequently, quite against Lao She's intention, what is meant to be a patriotic drama of metamorphosis often risks becoming a tragicomedy of mistaken identity. The student assassins in "We are on the Same Boat," for example, are closest to Lao She's ideal heroes. But even their assassination attempts do not exhilarate the reader so much as make him or her worried about their competence. Other characters like Du Yifu in "Killing Dogs," Lin Lei in "A Piece of Pig Liver," and Lao Fan in "A Letter from Home," are twice as vulnerable. They are ready to dedicate themselves to the war, but their deliberation over what action to take is strenuous, and their action, if taken after all, is sloppy. Torn by wasted anxiety and guilty conscience, these characters remind us once again of Lao She's Hamlet-like characters such as Ma Wei in *The Two Mas* or Lao Li in *Divorce*.

Lao She must have sensed this unintended weakness of his characters and tried to do something about it. The heroes from his two prewar novels could find their way out by self-exile, but nobody in wartime is allowed to excuse himself from his duty. Thus Du Yifu's father, an illiterate boxer, teaches his educated son the true spirit of perseverance by withstanding Japanese soldiers' persecution, and Lin Lei is humiliated and deserted by his girl friend for philosophizing on the war. But for Lao Fan in "A Letter from Home," an action like leaving wife and family in Beijing and working alone for the wartime government in Wuhan is still not enough. A patriotic, hardworking person, Lao Fan unfortunately has too much love for a wife who is unworthy of him. After Beijing falls to the Japanese, she chooses to stay for the easier life. Lao Fan works twice as hard to satisfy her needs, only to be bombed to death one day just as he receives mail from home demanding more money and care—a cruel lesson for anyone (including Lao She himself?) who might let homesickness distract his mind from his country's crisis.

If Lao She could be so harsh to his intellectual heroes, one wonders why, at least in his early war stories, traitors and opportunists often survive his machine of retribution only to thrive. In a way, they are put in a different category, one reminiscent of the gallery of grotesques in Lao She's prewar fiction. We do not just look down upon them; we laugh at them. Accordingly, in "East Meets West," two former overseas students, one coming back from Japan and the other from England, are reunited after the Japanese have occupied Beijing. They are studying how to make best use of their foreign experiences in the new puppet government. Their ingenious calculation leads them to seek positions at the bureau of social welfare, so that they might be granted the right to excavate tombs (for treasure). They are given a strange license to follow the steps of their predecessors in producing hilarious chaos and unexpected fun for the reader.

A more interesting case is "Bath Slaves," in which two Beijing bath-house attendants see a source of profit in their new Japanese customers. In the name of catering to the Japanese custom of bathing, they are planning to start a private business of "bathing companions," which will essentially turn the bathhouse into a brothel. They are doing so without their boss's permission, counting on his being intimidated in silence by anything related to the Japanese.

So far the story sounds just like a sarcastic portrait of two petty wartime opportunists. What confounds one is the result of their new enterprise. Following their understanding of Japanese taste for women, the two "bath slaves" bring in a plump, white-skinned woman, "typical of Chinese beauty,"[42] as their first bait. She, however, turns out to be a chaste widow seeking a chance to avenge her husband's death on the battlefield, and in the next scene, she strangles her customer to death and then runs away! The two bath attendants are never punished; it is the boss who is executed without ever straightening out the matter.

Again, Lao She's poetic justice works in a tongue-in-cheek way. His fat heroine bounces about like a parody of those pretty, chaste ladies of Chinese opera. Yet she twists one's low expectations of her by accomplishing her mission only too beautifully. If the woman acts out an unlikely heroic deed, the boss of the bathhouse simply dies a gratuitous death. We could say he is guilty of keeping his bathhouse open after the Japanese arrive in Beijing, but what about the two "bath slaves"? and other, bigger traitors? Beyond dramatizing the idea that everybody is in danger under the capricious Japanese rule, Lao She demonstrates in this story the sense of insecurity and cynicism already characteristic of his prewar fiction. The irony of life works in such a way that, when an unearned disaster befalls, one can only laugh helplessly and yield to it. The story says more about the irrational undercurrent of Lao She's comic vision than either Japanese cruelty or the necessity of patriotism.

Lao She's second collection of wartime stories, *Anemia*, came out as late as 1944. Compared with *Train,* it shows distinct signs of a transition in both subject and style. The sluggishness of the war has worn away Lao She's former fantasy of an overnight win at the front, and hard life, ongoing corruption, and governmental bureaucracy in unoccupied areas have also drained off his hope of a total social rejuvenation. The hyperbolic slogans and romantic adventures that prevail in *Train* have been dropped. There arises instead, in his new works, an increasing awareness of the clash between what should be happening and what is happening. This ambivalent posture can be no better stated than by the title and content of the story, *Bucheng wenti de wenti* (Unproblematic problem).

Presented in a form of allegory, *Unproblematic Problem* is in effect a poorly disguised satire on the social problems of the wartime capital, Chongqing. The story happens on a beautiful farm far away from the front. Everybody on the farm seems amiable and hardworking, but something is going wrong: the farm grows quality, profitable food, but its accounts never break even. To save the farm, a new director is brought in to solve problems. To his amazement, behind its prosperous, harmonious façade, the farm is being undermined bit by bit by bureaucratic inefficiency, incompetent labor, embezzlement, and theft. The source of all the problems lies nowhere else but in the former director, Ding Wuyuan.

The sociopolitical allegory implied here is only too easy to decipher. More interesting is the characterization of this former director Ding Wuyuan, who, because of all his evil deeds, represents the latest champion in Lao She's parade of comic villains. Unlike Lao She's previous creations, Ding Wuyuan appears without any tags of buffoonery or grotesqueness. Cordial, humorous, and worldly, he is a "nice guy" of the best kind, and a perfect master of ceremonies for all fun and games. He is so "nice," however, as to allow bribery and theft, so "popular" as to organize the workers against the new director, and so "friendly" as even to bribe the director's wife to spy on her husband. Under the enchanting spell of this Chinese Tartuffe, the farm runs in a state of happy hypnosis. It is the new director who has become the public enemy; his final days are doomed in advance. The story has its root in a prewar short story, "Tieniu yu bingya" (Iron bull and sick duck), which also deals with the confrontation of two farm administrators, with victory going to the wicked one. But in rendering a pessimistic picture of a society completely deprived of its ability to spot evil, it reminds one more of *The City of Cats*.

Lao She not only lashes out at the social majority, who willingly let themselves be deceived and used by hypocrites, thus sharing the sin of complicity. He also condemns a person like the new director, who is deficient in any skill to fight against bad guys other than a self-proclaimed integrity. Still, Lao She's deepest indignation is reserved for his archvillain. Ding Wuyuan behaves in an insidious way unknown in Lao She's former repositories of evil doings. Whereas his former comic villains gain the reader's attention by means of obscene postures and offensive laughter, the villain in *Unproblematic Problem* is so naturalized that he has become one of us. Siding with his hero, Lao She's narrator of course recognizes the hypocrisy in Ding Wuyuan's obtrusive benignity. But by the end of the story, both the narrator and the old director must withdraw from the scene.

"Unproblematic Problem" does refer to the ongoing war from time to time, only to make the story sound even more bitter. Hundreds of miles away from the front, the crisis on the farm can not be attributed to the enemy. Lao She poses a serious question here: at a time when everybody is supposed to work honestly and diligently for a national cause, what has gone wrong *within* us? Problems happen where they should have had the least chance to happen. A sense of absurdity dominates the story, driving home Lao She's cynicism.

The short stories in *Anemia* also contain elements revealing Lao She's equivocal motives. "Predilection" (Lian), for example, impresses one with its sympathetic depiction of a traitor's mentality on the eve of his defection. The story describes how an intellectual is forced to accept a Japanese job offer in order to keep his beloved collection of classical Chinese paintings. Probing the complex psychology of a reluctant traitor, Lao She deplores the fact that people's reactions to the war may vary; he understands, however, that, right or wrong, weak or strong, these reactions are all only too human. It is notable that the style of contemptuous flamboyance seen in his previous tales about traitors, such as "East Meets West" for example, is replaced by a more meditative one, which has hitherto been saved for his positive characters. Although this should not be taken as a move of concession in regard to Lao She's persistent attack on traitors, it does show that he is ready to deal with the story of the war, especially the other side of it, at a more realistic level.

"Xiao mutouren" (Little wooden puppet) is meant to be a children's tale. A bad remake of the adventure of Pinocchio, it features a little puppet seeking revenge for his uncle, Mr. "Mud," who was smashed by Japanese bombs. With the extreme frailty of the young hero and the great mission he sets himself to fulfill, "Little Wooden Puppet" serves less as a patriotic story in it own right than as an allegory of Lao She's war heroes in general, one that now addresses their "wooden" quality on the fantasy level. Everything the puppet does must have something to do with the patriotic goal. Realist concerns intervene wherever fantasy is about to take off. When Lao She tells us that Little Puppet could use a Boy Scout's string to hang himself onto a flying Japanese bomber, or that he can destroy a Japanese air base with a single grenade, he only convince one of the impossibility of the mission, and thereby unintentionally insinuates his cynicism toward the adults' war.

"Bataiye" (Grand master eight), portrays a country ne'er-do-well, Wang Ertie, who wants to become a modern Robin Hood in Beijing. It is a comedy of anachronism, since the days for chivalry have long passed and, worse, Beijing is now occupied by the Japanese. Wang Ertie is inspired to kill the Japanese, and, after a successful one-man ambush, he is caught and executed. Both the story's plotting and characterization suggest that Lao She is writing a story of a rehabilitated wartime Ah Q, but while so doing, he gives it a very dubious ending. Unlike the old Ah Q, the ne'er-do-well finally does something worth his death; yet this martyrdom wins him neither public applause nor his dreamed-of decapitation, both of which, according to the narrator, are to be taken as silly anyway.

There is a confusion of values at this point. Insofar as Wang Ertie does undertake an action and is capable of seeing the meaning of his action, be it a patriotic sacrifice or a search for personal glory, he is better than Ah Q. It is Lao She's narrator, ironically, who assumes the posture of Ah Q and insists, under the original Ah Q logic, on commenting on any of Wang Ertie's changes. In a condescending tone, the narrator praises Wang's heroism, only to confirm his own belief that Wang Ertie *is* a country bumpkin and that his deed never meets a "worldly" standard. One is thus left to wonder whether one should laugh at Wang Ertie's untimely concept of heroism or admire his courage at ambushing the Japanese. The noble theme of the story—that everybody should be committed to fighting the Japanese—is unduly weakened. Instead of reconciling the patriotic formula and the cynical thesis of Lu Xun's "A True Story of Ah Q," as he thought he had, Lao She is simply juxtaposing them, in such a way as to make his story even more devastating a satire than Lu Xun's original attempt.

Patriotism "Domesticated": *Four Generations under One Roof*

After the heroic disaster of *Cremation,* Lao She decided that he should never confront the war directly again but turn back to familiar things. The result is *Four Generations under One Roof,* a wartime family saga in the form of a trilogy. In every way, the novel represents the biggest undertaking of Lao She's career to date, not just because it is long (in fact, the longest of Lao She's oeuvre) but because it introduces a grand cast of characters and recapitulates almost all the major themes and motifs of his earlier works. Particularly in terms of the national resistance literature Lao She has continuously worked to define, the novel marks a climax of his efforts. In the novel, individual sensibility and propagandist demand, realist account and melodramatic plotting are brought to clash and coalesce with each other, so much so as to form a new model of literary discourse, one that has since prevailed in modern Chinese fiction, on both sides of the Taiwan straits.

Judged by the magnitude of its theme and structure, Lao She must have intended his novel to be an epic in the manner of a Western nineteenth century historical novel like *War and Peace.*[43] By 1944, the war had dragged to its seventh year, causing many painful transformations of the Chinese way of living and thinking. Understandably, ambitious writers all entertained a desire that some narrative accounts should be undertaken to chronicle what had happened to China over the past couple of decades. *Four Generations* is Lao She's answer to such a desire. Describing the vicissitudes of a big family and their neighbors during the war—their mistaken judgment and suffering, their cowardice and betrayal, their humiliation and perseverance, and their heroic deeds and sacrifice—*Four Generations* is rife with the typical plots and characters of the standard historical novel. But instead of working from a Tolstoyan paradigm which highlights in both perceptual and conceptual terms an inevitable historical force on the move, Lao She is more bent on dealing with the perennial dynamic of good versus evil, and with a promised return of poetic justice after evil's periodic rampage. Moreover, lavishing on the novel either tear-jerking scenes or grotesque interludes, Lao She writes to solicit immediate emotional responses from his readers. If the novel does not qualify as an epic, it is certainly a successful historical melodrama.

One finds at least three major modes of the real interwoven underneath the novel's narrative structure. From the outset, Lao She is working on a patriotic story, aiming to name the evil—Japan—and to define individual responsibility in a national crisis. The novel is also a semiautobiographical work, revealing both the writer's own conflict-ridden conscience as an urban intellectual who did not go to the front and his nostalgia for his hometown, Beijing. He is nostalgic for acquaintances from different social strata, for local customs and street scenes, and even for his old residence.[44] Moreover, *Four Generations* is an exposé novel in the tradition of the late Qing fiction of exposure, and provides a grotesque panorama of a society turned upside down.

Each of the three narrative modes demands a unique form of discourse to articulate its realist thrust. Accordingly, there is a melodramatic discourse for Lao She's patriotic story; a lyrical discourse for his inquiry into his past and the turbulence of his psyche; and a farcical discourse for his caricature of social evils. Lao She has been well trained in all three types of discourse, as his prewar works demonstrate, but at issue here is not so much how he recapitulates familiar narrative typologies as how the three discourses are blended into a new historical context, thereby underlining *and* contradicting each other's aesthetic and ideological premises about the real.

The novel takes place in Xiaoyangjuan, an old fashioned Beijing residential compound with an open courtyard, which accommodates a dozen families or so. Its main plot develops around three families. The Qi family is the central one. With four generations living under one roof, this family also lends the novel its title. For Lao She, the Qis symbolize a typical middle-class Chinese family, hardworking, courteous, and self-sufficient. When the war happens, each member of the family makes his or her judgment and decision; the different consequences arising therefrom, and their mutual impact constitute the novel's main action.

The second family is the Qians, an intellectual family which suffers the most during the period of Japanese occupation. The head of the family, Qian Moyin, was a secluded, unworldly scholar-poet before the war. After one of his two sons was killed during an act of anti-Japanese sabotage, Mr. Qian is arrested as a conspirator. Having survived all kinds of torture in jail, he is released a half-dead man, only to find that his wife and his other son are already dead. He eventually joins the anti-Japanese underground.

The third family is the Guans, the most affluent and unscrupulous family in the compound. Mr. Guan and his wife, nicknamed Big Red Melon for her fondness for red dresses and her fatness, are shrewd opportunists. They first win the favor of the Japanese by selling out the Qian family. There is also everlasting war going on within the family, between Mr. Guan's wife, his concubine, and his two daughters.

As if extending the thematic patterns of the three families, the three grandsons of the Qis further demonstrate "emblematic" temperaments: the eldest one, Ruixuan, is a sensitive, conscientious family man torn between filial and patriotic obligations; the second, Ruifeng, is a not very smart opportunist; the third, Ruiquan, is an impetuous student who finally leaves home to join guerrilla troops. Each brother's action serves as a point of reference, leading us to view a different side of Beijing life during wartime. As the story continues, the three discursive modes listed above are by and large prescribed for the three types of people foregrounded by Lao She.

A structural similarity between *Four Generations* and Ba Jin's *Jia* (Family) has been noticed by scholars.[45] Both novels derive their social and political criticism from probing the traditional family system. But it is the basic difference between the two families under discussion, The Qis in *Four Generations* and the Gaos in *Family*, rather than their remote resemblance, that sheds light on Lao She's intention. In a way, Lao She *is* writing a 1940's version of *Family*, but with an aim to confirm, not condemn, the value of the traditional family system. Whereas the young men in *Family* choose to leave the family because it is the root of a chain of social corruptions, the heroes in *Four Generations* are obliged to do so only because their love for their family presupposes their dedication to their country.

Putting words into the mouth of a British character, Mr. Forsham (*Fushan*), Lao She lays bare his views on the Chinese family:

> [Mr. Forsham] considers the Qis a really strange family. They are Chinese, but they are so complicated and changeable. The most amazing thing is that these people should live in one courtyard, and

get along well, as if everybody were ready to change, yet still held together by some force in the process of their change. In this strange family, each member is loyal to his own time, but does not vehemently reject others' times . . . they are following history, yet at the same time fighting against history. Each of them has his own cultural orientation, yet they tolerate and forgive each other. They are marching forward while at the same time seeming to step backward.[46]

Indeed, it is the family that provides the ultimate shelter for everybody in hard times, including even a bad son like Qi Ruifeng, and sustains his or her hope of living on. Lao She's vision of a Chinese family may well show his conservative inclination, but, writing at a time when thousands of families were shattered or separated, the idea that four generations live under one roof simply recapitulates the soothing dream everyone most cherishes.

Besides celebrating the stabilizing power of the Chinese family in a turbulent time, Lao She takes a step further, interpreting the war and its correlated political turmoil in terms of domestic dynamics. The three families quite clearly represent three political as well as three moral postures. While it is a deplorable exception that a decent family like the Qis should have a black sheep, Ruifeng, a traitor's household like the Guans is degraded in every way. Lao She may have a good point when he bases his moral/political accounts on individual family cases, but when he stretches the metaphor of family on every level of his novel, he risks "domesticating" the war in particular and politics in general, assessing otherwise highly complicated matters on a scale of family feuds and squabbles.

As a matter of fact, Lao She could have written something more complicated than the domestic triad in *Four Generations*. For one thing, he is not unaware of the problems a traditional family might have. A good example of his awareness can be found in such a novella as "Xinshidai de jiubeiju" (An old tragedy in a new time), where he exposes the struggles between brothers and in-laws, the greed and stubbornness of the old patriarch, and the eventual breakdown of the total hierarchy. The most striking thing about the novella is Lao She's ambiguous view of domestic and societal values: that a cunning hypocrite *can be* a filial son, and that a man dedicated to family honor *can be* an unscrupulous conspirator. The traditional Confucian doctrine that individual cultivation paves the way for a harmonious family and society is a benign rule for moral progress, but in a real world, values are more likely to clash than to harmonize, and the road to progress is never easy to discern.

In *Four Generations,* however, everything tends to be reduced to a black-and-white conflict. Lao She tries hard to even out any potential contradictions between domestic and public causes. He repeatedly invokes the maxims that the interest of the country precedes that of the family, and that in wartime one should give up his family concerns for the welfare of his country. But there are moments indicating that Lao She does not always feel at ease with such a neat and simple logic. The didactic statements of *Four Generations* are frequently undercut by an implied debate over whether a "sensible" person should desert his family for his country, a question whose answer should have been settled before the novel starts. Paradoxically, it is this painful deliberation, instead of action, that assures the novel's major appeal.

At the center of the drama of deliberation and procrastination is Qi Ruixuan, the eldest grandson of the Qis. A high school English teacher, Ruixuan is an intellectual endowed with an artist's temperament. Lao She obviously has the strongest sympathy for him, frequently using his viewpoint to see the changing social manners and sentiments in wartime Beijing. But Ruixuan has been living with a guilty conscience. As the eldest of the third generation of the Qis, he has been so caught in family obligations that he has given up the wish to leave Beijing for a higher cause. His problems sound familiar, nevertheless, if we recall the tragedy of Gao Juixin, the eldest grandson in *Family*. It is as though Lao She takes up an angle Ba Jin created yet never developed, and works out an apologia for those who do not or cannot achieve anything heroic in a period of revolutions or wars that calls for breaking family ties.

Ruixuan can also be regarded as the summation of a series of characters Lao She has been describing over a span of more than ten years. Since Ma Wei in *The Two Mas,* Lao She has been fascinated by intellectuals who do not fit well into their social surroundings. They are born romantics, full of ideals which can hardly flourish in a soil full of sprouting mediocrity, injustice, and chaos. They share a melancholy, indecisive, and slightly self-pitying mood, one which demands an understanding and care they cannot find among their friends and family members. Stretched between reality and self-proclaimed ideals, they become their own torturers. They are all Hamlets in modern China.

This "Hamlet syndrome" continues into Lao She's early wartime stories, as previously discussed in the cases of "Killing Dogs" and "A Letter from Home." As pointed out in the last chapter, Lao She even planned to name a patriotic drama *Hamlet,* for which he substituted a new title, *Homecoming,* at the last minute, merely for fear of confusion.[47] To recapitulate, the young hero of the play, Qiao Renshan, is having a hard time deciding what he should do in the war, given his immediate duty to fight for his country. Although Lao She's wartime Hamlets uniformly take action after a long delay, he does have reservations with regard to their physical and psychological competence. It will be remembered that, at his most extreme, he allows Lao Fan in "A Letter from Home" be bombed to death in order to redeem his sentimental, hesitant personality, even though the poor man has left his family behind in order to do his work in the midst of the country's impending crisis.

Qi Ruixuan is spared the trouble of going anywhere, and stays in Beijing. Thanks to Lao She's increasingly complex attitude toward the war, he is not punished by any *deus ex machina* as is Lao Fan. One sees him helping his youngest brother run away, consoling the unfortunate Qian family, sighing, shedding indignant tears, taking over one funeral after another (including his father's), self-condemning, and agonizing, yet he has every reason for *not* confronting the final decision; in the main, he is the only person left to take care of his grandpa, his mother, and the children. He is suffering, or seems to enjoy suffering, from a guilty conscience. On hearing that the powerful politician Wang Jingwei, known as a patriotic revolutionary in his younger days, betrayed China in order to establish a puppet regime in Shanghai, he feels that, he, too, should be held responsible for Wang Jingwei's defection. He even compares himself with the traitor:

> What Wang did in old days now looked like a fake. How about himself? He knew all too well that he should leave home for the national crisis, but instead he was staying peacefully at home; he knew all too well that he should show more love for his country, yet he ended up loving his family more; wasn't all this a fake? If revolution and patriotism always turned into a fake in the hands of Chinese, could there be any hope left for China? . . . He felt himself no longer a man; he was only sitting here playing his petty magic. . . . All this was fake, there was no real difference between himself and Wang Jingwei.[48]

Thoughts like this continue for page after page. Had his youngest brother not come back, almost at the end of the novel, to teach him a lesson and send him to join the underground work organized by Mr. Qian, Ruixuan could have lived through the whole war without doing anything "positive," thereby making himself an excellent example of the "superfluous man" of wartime.

The novel's comic side is presided over by an unprecedentedly large number of clowns, who mark again the triumph of Lao She's theatrical imagination. They are the true descendants of the buffoons and grotesques of *The Philosophy of Lao Zhang,* Lao She's first comic masterpiece. Opportunists, frauds, hypocrites, quacks, and impostors, they are now the *nouveaux riches* of the new regime, and they stage one chaos after another. In a novel full of patriotic speeches, conscience-stricken interior monologues, and tears and lamentations, the clowns' frequent appearances indeed furnish an ironic relief for the reader.

I have mentioned earlier that Lao She is assuming a different discursive law in describing his clowns. To be more specific, in giving a substantial shape to such a social circle, he harks back to the conventions of Late Qing exposé fiction: outraged by the clowns' moral bankruptcy, he is however taking a mock-sociological posture, studying their evil doings and collecting "inside stories" among them for his readers' reference. Lao She pokes fun at these clowns, especially when they are inventing ingenious plans to outwit each other. But however competent and imaginative, Lao She's traitors rarely reach the higher levels of power, such as policy-making or military planning. What they are good at—or what Lao She sees as their most dangerous moves—are gossiping, backbiting, buying and selling small bureaucratic positions, betraying family and friends, making small fortunes out of something illegal, and even chasing after good girls—all actions that threaten mostly individual and domestic values.

The thriving of the traitors in the novel also poses a serious question as to Lao She's changing interpretation of the war: who, *together with* the Japanese, are to be blamed for the war? While the Japanese undoubtedly play the role of archvillains, Lao She takes pains to suggest that traitors and meek, indifferent people are also responsible for what the country has endured. Just like *Cremation, Four Generations* contains no convincing depiction of the Japanese invaders; instead, it is crowded with Chinese traitors taking advantage of the Japanese invasion to exploit and torture their own compatriots. As Mr. Qian, Lao She's didactic voice, declares, the traitors "are not human beings but the worst disease of the Chinese people.... They are just as guilty as the Japanese and should all be killed."[49]

This fact indicates that Lao She is "domesticating" his anti-Japanese novel in two ways. He not only portrays international warfare in terms of family dynamics, as mentioned above, but also emphasizes that we *are* fighting enemies within ourselves: traitors in occupied areas, like those in *Cremation* and *Four Generations,* and bureaucratic opportunists in unoccupied areas, like those in *Unproblematic Problem,* are undermining the nation in a way that even the invaders fail to do. Suffice it to say that, the traitors, not the Japanese, personify the greatest fear in Lao She's patriotic thoughts.

Among the clowns in *Four Generations,* Mrs. Guan, nicknamed Big Red Melon, easily catches the reader's attention by her gaudy outlook and complete lack of moral qualms. She is the only female clown-villain ever fully treated by Lao She. "She behaved like the Imperial Dowager, and was more capable of cultivating social relations than her husband. She had the capacity of playing mahjong for forty-eight hours nonstop, while not losing a bit of her Dowager-like manners and pride."[50] A parody of the traditional stereotype of the *femme fatale,* Big Red Melon has, nevertheless, a special charm that draws men around her. With her husband's assistance, she designs and executes most of the wicked deeds in the first two parts of the novel. She is a workaholic, always in need of "sipping chicken broth from her three-pound thermos flask to keep herself in good shape. She worked hard because she was afraid that the war would end only too soon."[51]

By the middle of the novel, Big Red Melon has fittingly obtained herself a position as the inspector general of the bureau of prostitution affairs. She skillfully uses this position to squeeze money from the professional ladies. Those who want to pass their health check easily are advised to recognize Big Red Melon as their godmother: "once they establish a mother-daughter relationship, they naturally develop intimate feelings—as long as the girls pay a special 'mother recognition' fee and bring gifts on three major festivals."[52] As the patroness of all the prostitutes of Beijing, Big Red Melon is now organizing a bigger "family," and in so doing she essentially subverts the basic values of the family that Lao She has so appreciated. She has also been seen as the biggest exploiter of female virtues, especially threatening every girl's chastity. Even so, Big Red Melon is more amusing than threatening. Most of the time Lao She describes her as a monstrous gourmet, a gossipmonger, a shopping maniac, and a tasteless fashion designer. Few readers will forget how she "revives" Tang Dynasty costumes and hair styles, and making them the latest fashion in Beijing. "She was truly audacious, matching everything irreconcilable together. . . . Like the Great Wall, she was not pretty, but nevertheless awesome."[53]

In contrast to Big Red Melon's phenomenal success in every deal she enters into with the Japanese, Mr. Guan gains nothing by his attempts. Lao She actually injects more imagination into him than into Big Red Melon. Mr. Guan is not just a tired remake of a certain comic stereotype. His clowning contains meticulous references to the cultural codes of Beijing life as well as a trivialized image of the "Beijing gentleman." For Lao She, Mr. Guan personifies the worst that can happen when an erstwhile admirable character goes sour in the war. Courteous, suave, and presentable, Mr. Guan is the best product of the old Beijing culture. He lives in a leisurely manner which is composed of good food, rich acquaintances, pseudoscholarly get-togethers, theaters, and seasonal pastimes. Short of a real sense of nationality, Mr. Guan is the kind of person ready to bow down to whichever power has seized the political stage in Beijing. He most certainly should have been a rising star in the new Japanese regime.

But Mr. Guan fails again and again in seeking for a job in the puppet government, and it is in his failure that Lao She sees a strange type of tragicomedy happening in occupied Beijing. Mr. Guan is different from the rest of the clowns (including his wife) in that he has the aforementioned Beijing "style," and he is proud of this difference. Hypocrite that he is, he believes in playing his game with a touch of good taste. Thus, he tries to put on some poetic postures to impress the Japanese, assuming that they generally appreciate fine graces. He also works hard to find an euphemism for his wife's position: according to his wild etymological research, Big Red Melon should be called inspector general of Beijing's "weaving girls," not its "call girls." Noting the Japanese' superstitiousness about numbers, he always prepares three instead of four kinds of gift when visiting Japanese friends. He is even good at timing his friends' and family members' quarrels and appears at the best possible moment as an intermediary. Seeing himself as a "perfect" man,

Mr. Guan cannot understand why his wife and other vulgar traitors should gain more from the downfall of Beijing than himself. And it is at this point that Lao She's ambivalent nostalgia for Beijing takes a peculiar turn: as Beijing falls to the Japanese, even the "Beijing-style" bad guys lose their roots.

As it is, Mr. Guan is a petty clown suffering an existential crisis. "The harder he tries, the less he gains. . . . He feels this is unfair. His past experiences and good qualities have not helped him a bit but seemed to become a barrier for his advancement. . . . He has almost run out of self-confidence, worrying that he has lost control over his time and environment." His doubts lead him to surmise that "there must be something wrong with the Japanese occupation of Beijing. Otherwise, how come he could not find any job?"[54] Mr. Guan's untimely manners and frustrations make him one of the few "characters" in a novel peopled with stereotypes.

Though this was not Lao She's intention, Mr. Guan and the "Hamlet of Beijing," Qi Ruixuan, can be paired off as two of the most unhappy people in occupied Beijing. However different their ideals are, they are each conscious of the gap between what should happen and what is happening to them. In Qi Ruixuan's painful procrastination and Mr. Guan's mock Sisyphean pursuit of fame and fortune, Lao She finds the same kind of gratuitous expediency as a result of the irrational maneuvers of life or fate. While Qi Ruixuan finally joins an underground anti-Japanese campaign, Mr. Guan is trying his best to accommodate Japanese demands even on his last day of life. There is a cynicism looming large behind their characterizations, indicating that even melodramatic plotting and an all-too-clear patriotic theme cannot always allow things to work out as they should.

Throughout the novel, there is an invisible character to which Lao She devotes his most personal feelings, namely, Beijing. Lao She's love for Beijing overflows in the novel. Writing his novel in war-torn Chongqing or faraway America, he depicts with passionate detail the charm of Beijing in different seasons and recalls the smells and sights of the old city "with a tenderness that is not matched in any of his early works."[55] A novel about how Beijing has been deprived of her beauty, *Four Generations* serves nevertheless as an excellent source book on the city, detailing in retrospect all its festive scenes, preparations of seasonal food, social manners, easy life-styles, and so on. Because of the war, Beijing is defamiliarized and given a better-than-ever literary image in Lao She's imagination.

The lower-class people in the novel constitute wonderful *tableaux vivants* of the majority's life in Beijing. They include the families of a rickshaw puller, a barber, a home mover and funeral caretaker, a shower of street slides, a butler in the British consulate, a policeman, and so on. Growing up in poverty, Lao She was very familiar with these people's lives and describes them with full understanding and sympathy. They all suffer during the war, but if one recalls the life of Camel Xiangzi in *Camel Xiangzi* or of the old policeman's family in "This is My Life," one will wonder if life in Beijing was necessarily better before the war. Patriotism seems to have transcended the pains that were due to their own society's injustices. From this one can discern how Lao She uses the Japanese occupation as a viable cause, rather than just a reminder, of the unpleasant side of Beijing: its poverty-stricken lower class, sociopolitical turmoil, and moral inertia.

Besides coercion and persecution, the Japanese occupation also intensifies another formidable force that is shattering Beijing: time. Following the novel's logic, it is the Japanese who turn Beijing from the magical cultural capital of China, standing above the passage of time, into an old city disdained by history, a "City of Cats." Beijing is now a ghost town controlled by devils and demons. Not only have the gentry and middle classes lost their traditional prestige, even the poor seem to feel that they would rather live life as it was before the war, however horrible it might have been. By this, Lao She has evaded the issue he confronted in *Camel Xiangzi,* that Beijing's charm may have been reserved only for certain classes of people, and that life before the war did not promise only peace and fun. Given his strong nationalist motive, the past Lao She cultivates is a beautiful combination of nostalgia and propaganda, both subsuming history with myth.

To convey the destructive power of the war, Lao She chooses death as the most prominent image of the book. Never has Lao She been given a chance to explore the concept and variations of death as exhaustively as in *Four Generations.* By describing death, he indicates that people do not just die in a war; rather they die in different ways to validate the cruelty and chaos of war. Beyond this obvious purpose, there also lurks a much more personal motivation for his depiction of death. As indicated previously, Lao She's fiction has been underlain by an obsession with the sudden breakdown of decorum and sensibility, concepts in which he never invested much confidence anyway. This obsession has lent him an ambiguous viewpoint, allowing him to see social abuses and injustices as a mad circus of follies, and personal ideals as frail Quixotic daydreams. But Lao She sees the ultimate threat (or temptation?) in the form of death. The war merely sanctions him to enter fully into this personal darkness, and to name it as tangible reality.

In the novel, dozens of characters die from failed assassination attempts, from disease and starvation, from torture by Japanese soldiers' tortures, from suicide, bombs, or even mistaken identity. While people like Mr. Qian's second son and You Tongfang (Mr. Guan's concubine who later became a patriotic activist) die for their cause, most people simply lose their lives by chance. Yet chance *is* regularity in wartime. Lao She never hesitates to give this punishment, particularly to those who entertain themselves with the dream of living safely by living submissively, The Qi family's neighbors, Mr. Wen and his wife, a young, amiable, but politically callous Manchu couple, are bombed to death in a theater as they are happily staging a Beijing opera. Still, in the face of massive innocent suffering, Lao She is driven to make a Voltairean observation. In the third part of the novel, *Famine,* many Beijing citizens die from a man-made famine caused by a new food rationing policy. One of the dead is Xiaoniuzi, the great-granddaughter of Old Mr. Qi and daughter of Qi Ruixuan. She has been a little darling for everybody, and she too is made to die to bear witness to Lao She's pathos in face of the total insanity of human disasters.

Stunned by the senseless death of innocent or not too innocent people, one may find a paradoxical relief in watching how Lao She sends his villains to death. If the grand wheel of fortune has not worked favorably for the "good" people in the war, Lao She wants to make sure that villains, at least, will be repaid for what they did. Unless the bad guys are punished, a patriotic melodrama would have no closure. Switching back to comic discourse, Lao She is delighted to "invent" various kinds of deaths to suit his villains' outrageous but colorful lives. Here, wish-fulfillment and moral retribution prove to be two sides of the same coin. Big Red Melon is overthrown by her followers and put in jail, where she goes crazy and dies a most horrible death by scratching and tearing herself to death. Her usurper, Qi Ruifeng's former wife, is made a prostitute later on, and dies from syphilis in a low-class whorehouse on the eve of Japan's defeat. Qi Ruifeng is sold and put to death by one of his fellow traitors. Mr. Guan is buried alive, and his second daughter is strangled to death by her old lover. The most imaginative death goes to the biggest villain in *Famine*, Lan Dongyang, who runs away to Japan at the end of the war, only to be killed in Hiroshima by the atomic bomb.

Three of these death events deserve special attention. Mr. Guan does not die alone. At the end of his days, he contracts some contagious disease and is sent to a quarantine jail. Together with him is his neighbor, Sun Qi, a proud, hardworking barber now defeated by fate. Sun Qi looks down upon Mr. Guan, who is preaching to everybody the virtues of the Japanese even while faced with his impending death. At the order of the Japanese, Mr. Guan is finally buried alive by Sun Qi, who is himself buried the next moment. "In this way, our number one collaborator Guan Xiaohe, and our good neighbor, friend, and barber were all cleaned up."[56] A chilling scene of Japanese atrocity, it nevertheless clearly states Lao She's skeptical position that the fates of the good and the bad are always tangled together, subordinated to a higher and more sinister power.

The other death scene which raises a problem of moral ambiguity is the suicide of Qi Tianyou, Qi Ruixuan's father and the second generation of the Qi family. Qi Tianyou is an old-fashioned businessman. An honest and mild-mannered person, he plays only a secondary role in this story full of heroes, martyrs, and villains. After the Japanese occupation, his business shrinks; gradually he is forced to dismiss his employees, whom he has always treated kindly. Both his declining business and his struggle remind one of the nice businessman's tragedy in Lao She's early short story "Lao zihao" (An old brand). The final blow comes for Qi Tianyou when the Japanese, because of a mistake made by their own henchmen, charge him with being a profiteer. He is dragged to the street, forced to put on a jacket inscribed with the words "I am a profiteer" and ordered to shout to all passersby, "I am a profiteer."

This undeserved humiliation completely prostrates the businessman, who has always been proud of his uprightness and considerateness. To maintain his self-esteem, there seems only one way out:

> His mind was blank, his old father, his sick wife, his three sons, his daughter-in-law, his grandson and granddaughter, and his shop seemed all to have never existed. He saw only the moat and the lovely water, as though the water . . . beckoned to him. He nodded. His world was gone. He had to go to another world. In this other world his shame would be washed away . . . Floating, floating, floating, he was floating to the great ocean where he would have freedom—cool clean, and happy freedom, which would wash away the red letters on his breast. He would have become a big dark stain on his family and business, a dark stain which would dim the sunshine, make fresh flowers stink, turn justice into conspiracy, kindness into violence.[57]

In a novel which advocated personal strength in the fight against Japan, Qi Tianyou's suicide could have been criticized by Lao She. But compared with the execution of the innocent bathhouse owner in "Bath Slaves," Qi Tianyou's decision to end his own life quietly partakes of a sense of decency and self-respect.

Since Lao She drowned himself during the heyday of the Cultural Revolution in 1966, after he was mercilessly insulted and beaten by the Red Guards, Qi Tianyou's death in fiction ironically provides a prophetic insight into what will happen in reality, as scholars have noticed.[58] Biographical associations notwithstanding, Lao She had already developed this suicidal theme in his prewar fiction. In the novella "The Crescent Moon," the heroine jumps into Daming Lake in Jinan in order to end her pathetic life as a prostitute; Fortune, the kind-hearted prostitute and Xiangzi's confidante in *Camel Xiangzi* hangs herself when life has become too unbearable. Xiaoxie and his beloved in *The City of Cats* kill themselves at the fall of their country. Of course, one will not forget that the guerrilla leader Shi Lei in *Cremation* burns himself to death to achieve martyrdom. In different ways, Lao She weighs the conditions and results of suicide. His suicidal characters share a desperate attempt to "exploit" themselves to achieve their will. Heroic or not, the act of self-destruction has to be understood as their final gesture at proving their own power in a losing battle.

But even the slim tragic potential of suicide is deflated by Lao She in *Four Generations*. Qi Tianyou never floats to the sea of "cool, clean, happy freedom." His body is found "frozen and intertwined with ice floes, water-weeds, and tree roots on a river bank." A high-minded suicide-seeker like Qi Tianyou has to risk the unexpected disgrace and expediency that follows death. Once again, the pragmatic, cynical side of Lao She triumphs over his melodramatic side. The parallel between Qi Tianyou's and Lao She's "posthumous" fate has long been overlooked. As his son's recent memorial essay vividly recalls, Lao She's body was discovered, in just as miserable shape as Qi Tianyou's, on the second day after his suicide.[59] It will forever remain a question whether Lao She was rewarded with a clear, happy freedom.

The third death which should be noted is the death of the head of a Japanese family living in the same neighborhood as the Qis. Along with the other Japanese families, they move to Xiaoyangjuan after the Japanese take over Beijing. They are never fully treated in the first two parts of the novel, other than being seen as short, funny invaders of the residential compound. But in the middle of *Famine,* Lao She ventures to portray how Qi Ruixuan is moved by the deaths happening in the Japanese family.

> To his own embarrassment, [Ruixuan] found his eyes full of tears. He knew he should not pity enemies, who had killed thousands of Chinese, including his father and brother. But he also knew that it was no great mistake to feel sorrow for the dead; enemies are human beings.[60]

A passage like this suggests that Lao She has dramatically modified his attitude toward the war and is trying to see suffering and death from a more comprehensive angle. By the time he was writing this part of the novel, the war had long been ended. Lao She might well have benefited from this new political situation by working out a more forgiving account of the pains and sorrows brought by war. The amusing possibility exists that such compassionate thoughts, appropriately articulated by Qi Ruixuan, would not have withstood the fanatic campaigns of the first stage of the war, and might have even been debunked as irrelevant to the war in the debate over national resistance literature. But in its effort to embrace a broader historical scene and recognize the wide possibility of human conditions, *Famine* recapitulates the best part of the humanist strain in early modern Chinese realism.

We have so far not described Lao She's two unfinished novels. In 1938, Lao She wrote *Metamorphosis,* a novel dealing with some exiled students' anti-Japanese activities in a small town. These students leave home and school to fight the holy war, and, as the novel's title indicates, they will have completed an initiation rite by the end of the novel. In 1945, Lao She wrote *Democratic World,* in which he caricatures wartime life in unoccupied areas, bitterly satirizing bureaucratic corruption and social hypocrisy. From patriotic propaganda to cynical farce, these novels may well be used as two convenient landmarks, indicating Lao She's psychological and ideological pilgrimage during the eight years of the war. But judged from the bulk of Lao She's wartime fiction, it will be more appropriate to say that these two novels simply dramatize the dialogical tension continuously embedded in Lao She's mind.

Lao She's noble discourse—his "national resistance literature"—enacts a far more interesting story than do the surfaces of his works. One understands how a post–May Fourth writer tried to carry out the sociopolitical mandate of realist literature in a period of national crisis, and how such an effort brought forth ambiguous results that define a rather different reality. When he drafted the open letter attacking Liang Shiqiu in 1938, Lao She characterized himself as one of the forceful defenders of "national resistance literature," a literature formed "purely" for the sake of holy battle. Yet as the war developed, he felt compelled to write on subjects "irrelevant" to the war, so as to bear witness to what had been "really" happening to himself and to his country. Still, even if Lao She was aware of the inconsistency between his theory and his practice, could he have done anything else to escape from the imprisonment of ideology?

The drama of Lao She writing in the wartime period concludes with the image of the Beijing Hamlet, Qi Ruixuan. Lao She began as an earnest propagandist, only to end up being tangled in a socially and ideologically "unproblematic problem," in which, to quote Qi Ruixuan's words, "life and death, love and hate, patriotism and warfare, were all paired off like identical twins, keeping him from telling one from the another, or which was good and which was bad."[61] Paradoxically, this sense of ambiguity and indecision had become a distinctive mark of Lao She's estimate of war and life under war.

Chapter six

Critical Lyricism: The Boundary of the Real in the Fiction of Shen Congwen

The life and works of Shen Congwen (1902–1988) represent some of the most fascinating moments in modern Chinese literature. As a rebellious son from a West Hunan soldier's family, and then a teenage soldier in service to a warlord, Shen Congwen led an early life full of rustic experiences and rough-and-tumble adventures.[1] This rural and young soldier was as much enlightened by May Fourth causes as any urban youth, and in 1922 he made his way to Beijing to pursue a literary career. In Beijing, Shen Congwen first made the acquaintance of romantics like Yu Dafu, Xu Zhimo, Ding Ling and Hu Yepin.[2] He led a bohemian life with Ding Ling and Hu Yepin, and later got involved in Hu Yepin's arrest and execution in the so-called case of five martyrs.[3] Quite contrary to what might have been expected, Shen Congwen eventually became known, in the circle of belles lettristes, as an austere stylist and a sophisticated pacifist. Instead of putting on romantic poses or propagating "progressive" thought, he looked backward, aiming to recapture the landscape and lives of his provincial home; instead of shouting battlecries against social cannibalism or cultivating personal idiosyncrasies, he evoked a poetic vision of a rural China on the eve of a drastic transformation. By the mid-thirties, when his close friend Ding

Ling was finally converted to the cause of "literature for revolution's sake," Shen Congwen had established himself as a lyrical stylist, a vanguard regionalist, and a political conservative.

These three labels—a lyrical writer, a regional advocate, and a political conservative—might nevertheless prove misleading. They tend to simplify, if not obliterate, the liberal and even avant-garde sides of Shen Congwen's character and writing, turning him either into a quaint *raconteur* of local color, or into a Rousseauesque humanist yearning for a lost golden age. It is in reaction to these labels that this and the next chapter will examine the theoretical and formal dynamics underlying Shen Congwen's lyricism and regionalism. I suggest that, despite the tenderhearted, "nature"-oriented posture he seems to assume in most of his works, Shen Congwen wrote "radically" in response to the turbulent cultural/political scenes of the twenties and thirties, and that his works must be understood as a dialectical part of, rather than an exception to, post–May Fourth realism.

My reading of Shen Congwen against the backdrop of history means more than simply retrieving the lives and events his works reflect or pinning down the issues of his social/political criticism. Meticulous work has already been done along both these lines.[4] What concerns me instead are more "literary" questions: how Shen Congwen conjures up a historical vision by erasing or forgetting its immediate motivations—not only the social/political events but also the literary/linguistic medium; how he "naturalizes" subjects which would not have been considered "natural"; and how he either throws doubt on or leaves gaps in these efforts, thereby weaving his otherwise clear prose into an intricate web.

By raising these questions, I am at the same time taking issue with the usual critical polarities, such as country versus city; past versus present; tradition versus modernization; conservatism versus radicalism; innate rural virtues versus corrupt urban values; and all-embracing nature versus ever-changing culture. These dichotomies may constitute the thematic superstructure of Shen Congwen's works, but they are too obvious to account for his real charm. Shen has created neither an immaculate Nature nor a rural utopia in contrast with the fallen world that is the present. If a utopia does exist for him at all, it is already a damaged one. If modern society is criticized by him, it is done so ironically, in the light of its traditional counterpart. Shen Congwen's world is one full of polemical tension, investing gothic and vulgar themes with lyrical pathos, and finding in condemnable human follies a confirmation of life. In the following pages, I will try to circumscribe these tensions from the vantage point of Shen's much-acclaimed lyricism. My discussion will proceed in four sections, starting with a critical overview of Shen's concept of the lyrical mode of realism, followed by inquiries into his tendentious attempts at lyricizing the uncanny and the grotesque, his reinterpretation of the realist concept of time and its historical manifestations, and his aesthetic of Eros and Thanatos.

Critical Lyricism and Irony

Fans and critics of Shen Congwen often describe his works as "lyrical," because they patently possess features of poetic expression: a modulation of language that conveys a dreamlike "associational rhythm" (*Biancheng* [The border town]); a simultaneous perception of the world that brings the chronological flow of time to a halt ("Chun" [Spring]); the bracketing of an ephemeral experience with a personal epiphany or antiepiphany ("Jing" [Quiet]); the adoption of pastoral motifs and figures reminiscent of primitivist landscape ("Baizi" [Baizi], *Xiangxing sanji* [Random sketches on a trip to Hunan]); and a yearning for the ancient tribal condition of myth (*Fengzi* [Fengzi]). Through the conscious work of Shen's narrator, objective experience undergoes a process of metamorphosis, crystallizing into a constellation of sensuous pictures and musical patterns.[5]

Indeed, to write fiction that achieves the status of poetry represents the highest goal of literary creation for Shen Congwen. Time and again he mentions his indebtedness to poetry and to its rhetoric and imagery. In a lecture on the short story that he gave in 1941, Shen held that "all forms of art enable writers to express a feeling of poetry (*shide shuqing*), and there is no exception for short stories. Because of his obeisance to the form of poetry, a fiction writer will develop a special sensitivity to language, thereby producing patience in handling diction. He will acquire just the same kind of sensitivity to the varieties of humanity, clever or foolish, altruistic or self-seeking. In this way a fiction writer can touch on 'life' in ordinary circumstances of sadness and happiness. Above all, if a fiction writer can make a poet's pathos toward life his own impetus, he will assuredly increase the profundity of his works."[6]

Two questions enter one's mind at this juncture. First, if, as

Jaroslav Průšek pointed out many years ago, the overall tendency of modern Chinese literature is a movement of lyricization,[7] a turn toward the expression of writers' subjectivity and individual visions in the light of the classical Chinese poetic tradition, how can one sanction the lyrical quality of Shen Congwen at the expense of other writers' "lyrical" inclinations? Second, given Shen Congwen's convictions about writing fiction like poetry, how does he settle the paradox at the heart of his texts, a paradox which takes shape at the intersection of story telling (the hermeneutic mode) and the presentation of musical and pictorial patterns (the poetic mode)? What mediates between what Mikhail Bakhtin calls the dialogical confrontation between life and the autotelic, monolingual tendency of self-closure?[8]

Průšek's view that lyricism is the sign of modernity in modern Chinese literature reminds one of another Eastern European critic, Georg Lukács, who, with European literature in mind, considers romanticism the beginning of a lyricization of narrative which culminates in the modern novel.[9] But from the common starting point they share, the two critics reach apparently different conclusions. Whereas Průšek sees the lyrical expression of modern Chinese literature as "one of the symptoms of the emancipation of the individual from feudal traditions," Lukács suspects that this individualistic turn is a sign of the disintegration of the grand western narrative tradition that began with the epic.[10] The irony is that, for all the different historical subjects they deal with, the two critics are really not as far apart as they sound on the surface. In one way or another, they impose a nineteenth-century realist emplotment on their reading of the rise of the lyrical mode, treating it as a mimetic clue to the moral ethos reflected in a certain literary period. Lukács' theory of the novel has been widely discussed, so I would only enter a few more words here about Průšek's observation.

Průšek deserves full credit for demonstrating the direction of Chinese literature toward the subjective and individualistic mode at the turn of the century, but the way he describes modern writers' lyrical temperaments strangely reveals more their commitment to, rather than their emancipation from, the feudal literary tradition. From the writers' images as lonely scholars or romantic rebels to their discursive gestures of dissipation or indignation, melancholy or self-pity, Průšek draws a picture of modern Chinese literature where traces of the past are never erased but only slightly covered over by new strokes of the pen; such new strokes include the inauguration of vernacular narrative and the entry of western motifs. The individualism and subjectivity Průšek celebrates turn out to be conventional themes or poses repeatedly taken up by writers and poets, and thus can hardly be called modern. Ideological conviction notwithstanding, Průšek's survey simply reveals his nostalgia for the past traditions he means to overcome.

My comments should not be taken as a complete refutation of Průšek's observations. What I want to emphasize is that, if the lyrical or subjective mode does exist in modern Chinese literature, it has to be looked for somewhere other than the place Průšek and his followers have located. Shen Congwen's writing may well be one such locus.

The strength of Shen Congwen's lyrical discourse lies in the paradox that he rejects the self-indulgent pursuit of individualistic expression of his time by transgressing the lyrical conventions appreciated even by radical antitraditionalists. The seemingly spontaneous overflow of his lyrical style and the idyllic motifs prevailing in his stories constitute an equivocal sign, hinting not at a loosening up but at an intensifying of aesthetics, in both ideological and rhetorical terms. In view of his almost compulsive desire to combine pastoral motifs with horror and pain in reality, to salvage fantasies and dreams from the flux of historical chaos, and to sanction the power of love and desire through scenes of death and violence, one must recognize how Shen Congwen has radicalized the canons of lyricism as we understand them, how he has envisioned a world displaced from pure origin and the logic of opposition, and how, consequently, he abolishes the boundary between realism and lyricism.

In addition to utilizing the legacy of classical Chinese poetry, ranging from *Songs of the South* to the folk songs rooted firmly in his imagination, Shen Congwen takes up where May Fourth forerunners such as Lu Xun and Ye Shaojun leave off, in presenting tableaux of characters and impressionist sketches of scenery and mood. His immediate predecessors are writers like Zhou Zuoren and Fei Ming.[11] He discovers that Zhou Zuoren can use a "peaceful mind to feel all activities in nature, to see beauty otherwise ignored by ordinary eyes, and to approach all this with a slightly reserved attitude."[12] As for Fei Ming, his works are a "miracle" when describing "movements in quietness and in the beauty of placid humanity."[13] Fei Ming's sensitive manipulation of language is also highly appreciated by Shen Congwen. Western masters such as Turgenev and Chekhov acted as even richer examples for Shen Congwen.[14] Despite their differences in subject matter and style, both Russian writers are known for their sympathetic portrait of the minute aspects of life, and their skillful evocation, by understatement, of human psychology. Shen Congwen was particularly fond of Turgenev's *Sketches from A Hunter's Album*. He says that "Turgenev mixes prose travelogue and fictional narrative into a whole, thus foregrounding his characters and events amid the bright geographical surroundings characteristic of south western Russia. Everything still carries a sense of 'raw material,' which deserves our special notice. I had a similar intention when I wrote *Random Sketches on a Trip to Hunan* thirteen years ago."[15]

The intertextual network behind Shen Congwen's deceptively pure discourse leads one to the second question raised above, namely, how he faces up to the conflict between the lyrical demand of a monologized voice, free from historical and cognitive bonds, and the (realist) narrative paradigm of a polyphony that unfolds itself in the dense web of space and time. The conflict, of course, might well be seen as a false one, since, in spite of his lyrical rhetoric, Shen Congwen does have stories to tell; he by no means intends to do away with the rules of narrative. But I would rather point out the irony underneath the surface. Throughout his career, Shen Congwen endeavored to lay out guidelines for fiction in terms of poetry, the genre that is capable of rendering human experience in the purest form of language. Referring to his own vocation as a fiction writer rather than a poet, Shen once explained that the emotional involvement and formal demands of poetry were so intense that they might have driven him to madness, or even death, had he chosen that genre.[16]

Instead of smoothing out the conflicting interests of the lyrical and the realistic, of poetry and narrative, in his fiction, Shen Congwen invests them with a polemic of ambiguity. He opts for a revelation that brings to light "the divine" (*shenxing*) hidden in the world; but for the sake of sobriety and self-preservation, he can only do so by projecting the apocalyptic moment into the indefinite recess of a narrative sequence. He brings into play the poet's illusory effort to mute the gaps between sounds and signs and the fiction writer's self-consciousness of the difference between what is told and the telling of it, a proximity to music and a narrative inscribed in a hybridization of forms. Other than a dimension of metaphor that calls forth the sense of poetry, his fiction has a dimension of irony, irony that subverts the plenitude of his lyrical discourse and reminds one of the existence of the world of realist narrativity.

Northrop Frye once noted that lyrical poets share some connection with writers of irony, in that they (supposedly) turn their backs on their audiences in a rhetorical gesture and play with the literal and intended levels of meaning, with objects and their literary signs.[17] Altering this observation to our interest, we may say that Shen Congwen's emphasis on the lyrical quality of fiction and on the craft of language evokes a poetic performance of prose and a textual irony. This irony keeps the different levels of meaning from forming into a univocal whole; it also puts the aesthetic intentions of the text constantly at risk. Shen Congwen sees a danger of self-indulgence in both lyricism and irony. Whereas excessive lyrical expression invites narcissistic sentimentalism, excessive ironic discourse leads to a frivolous play with signifiers. The contradictory elements of the lyrical versus the ironical in Shen Congwen's fiction must be understood as something more complicated: they furnish not only a rhetorical gesture but also a critical attitude. The all-round, nonfinalized quality entailed by Shen Congwen's fiction is no more an innovative device than a signal of his conception of life that refuses to be confined by ideological or aesthetic closure.

The *interaction between the lyrical and the ironic* in Shen Congwen's fiction can further be discussed in the following three interrelated dimensions. First, by writing about what is apparently not available in the given historical context, or by embellishing reality with a seemingly inappropriate rhetoric, Shen Congwen may conceive a critical intention in his writing which can only be understood negatively. The distance between what should have been said and what is said creates a strong effect of irony in Shen Congwen's discourse. As his interpretation of *The Border Town* shows, Shen Congwen wants to introduce in his most lyrical narrative an ideal form of life that is "elegant, healthy, natural and in tune with humanity,"[18] as opposed to the chaotic, decadent status quo. He thus addresses the necessity of an ethical consciousness as figured by a harmonious human relation that cannot yet be lived or represented but only approximated in a rupture between the énoncé and its enunciation.[19]

While this view links Shen Congwen to the tradition of utopian writing, it tends to be reduced by wishful critics to the terms of their own mimetic theories. In the recent campaign to restore Shen Congwen to the mainstream of modern Chinese literary history, for example, mainland scholars have held that the lyrical aspects of Shen Congwen's fiction are but a "front," one that brings out the truth of reality in a negative way.[20] This cannot be altogether right, because it passes over the intricate lyrical dialectic in Shen Congwen's writing: it cannot explain why and how Shen Congwen touches us with a poetic ethos even when he confronts social and political abuses directly.

Second, Shen Congwen's narrative enables him to question not only the semantic and grammatical verisimilitudes of lyricism and realism but also their ideological bearings. At a time when most realist writers consider that words burdened with tears, indignation, and guilt are the only way to describe the insulted and injured, Shen Congwen's insistence on approaching the lower depths in terms of lyrical narrative is a double-edged critique. However inappropriate at first reading, it exposes the exclusiveness of the styles and subjects traditionally taken for granted; it also reveals that hard-core realism may reach its own limits in carrying out its mission. In the hands of post–May Fourth writers, hard-core realism may have become a reserved genre for humanitarian subjects, a codified way of seeing and talking about the lower classes, by self-righteous members of the elite. The realist narrative that at first enabled the writers to see the world clearly may prove to have its own blind spots, narrowing or even distorting the samples of reality. Shen Congwen's lyrical treatment of the insulted and the injured is thus an ironic and defiant move, eroding the autonomy both of the traditional lyrical mode and of the ongoing hard-core realist mode. More importantly, this calls attention to the fact that, besides pretending to reflect external verities, realist literature is a mode of discourse perpetually at variance with itself. Shen Congwen's erosive union of lyricism and realism has displaced the center from the system of events to the system of discourse that makes the events intelligible in a codified context. It then can serve as a formal index to Shen Congwen's liberalism.

The third view to be taken is that the irony in Shen Congwen's lyricism comes not only from a negative reading of reality, as suggested by the first view, nor just from a transgression of generic boundaries, as suggested by the second view, but also from his conscious play with the surface meaning of narrative. At stake here is Shen Congwen's use of irony as a self-reflexive rhetorical mode, which points not to the art of explanation or persuasion but to the essential figuration of all language. The surface structure of Shen's story often bids fair to become its deep structure, while at the same time remaining immune to the probings of interpretation because it is the surface. This possibility becomes clear as one rethinks Shen Congwen's philosophy of language and poetry.

Shen Congwen's belief in and "fear of" the pure form of language and its poetic performance should not be seen merely as a predilection for stylistic craftsmanship; rather, it must provide a key to his artist's vision of reality. His poetic (or lyrical) worldview demands that just as much attention be paid to the linguistic surface of a work as to the "deep" meanings behind it. An arguable "reality" does not represent itself, it is represented. If a literary presentation of life is substantially a rhetorical performance, a formal display of language rather than an outcome of logical prefiguration (such as the canons underlining hard-core realism), then the text can be liberated from the iron prisonhouse of referential determinism and can gain freedom to express its figurations of the real. Thus, emphasis on language and poetic expression is also confirmation of human choice in "figuring" out the world. At its peak, Shen Congwen's ironic view of text and world dissolves the distinction between realism and lyricism, between prose and poetry, and asserts the fundamentally figured—that is to say, poetic—nature of all language. This explains why Shen Congwen can still manage to transmit a sense of poetic composure even when he confronts a pathetic subject directly.

This special mode is not a Chinese strain of Mallarméan nihilism, nor does it leave its stories *mise en abîme,* as a poststructuralist might have done. Shen Congwen never makes irony a mode overpowering other modes, as, say, Lao She tends to do in his finest writings. One must always understand the deep moral concern behind Shen Congwen's mixed expression of lyricism and irony, however different his moral pose might look from that of other May Fourth writers. This moral bearing stems from the long Chinese tradition that stresses the ethical dimensions of rhetoric, and it is reenforced by Shen's own existential consciousness of human absurdity and his need to affirm choice against psychological and sociopolitical determinisms. In welding incongruities of rhetorical form and subject matter, Shen melds humanity's immensely complex emotional capacity to cope with the built-in contradictions of any ideal moral/political order. A discourse of lyricism enables him to emphasize the creative force of language and the freedom of human perception, while his sense of irony leads him to bracket, but not to do away with, any lyrical indulgence in life. Only through allowing both narrative modes to illuminate each other, putting one another "under erasure," as conventional critics would have it, can one appreciate that, in a most subtle way, Shen Congwen's art expresses the humanism of the May-Fourth Movement.

The Uncanny and the Grotesque

The first group of Shen Congwen's stories I would like to deal with can be classified as stories of the uncanny and the grotesque. In many cases, Shen Congwen touches on subjects hitherto thought to be impossible for lyrical presentation, in such a relentless way that he puzzles his readers, who would rather have seen him as a warm, gentle storyteller.

Decapitation is one of such subjects. Critics have hardly ever discussed why or how Shen Congwen wrote about this cruel form of capital punishment, to say nothing of its link with lyricism. The subject, nevertheless, merits attention, not only because it constitutes an important part of Shen's recollections of his childhood and military life but also because it serves as one of the best examples of his radical lyricism. More importantly, Shen Congwen's interest in beheading brings to mind some of Lu Xun's best short stories, which are equally haunted by a disconcerting imagery of headlessness and bodily mutilation. Placed side by side, these two writers' stories of decapitation form a dialogue, pointing to one of the major arguments in modern Chinese fiction, the argument as to the ethical and aesthetic limitations of a realist writing.

Shen Congwen's references to decapitation can be seen in "Wode jiaoyu" (My education, 1929); "Huanghun" (Twilight, 1934); "Xin yu jiu" (The old and new, 1935); "Qian xiaojing" (Little scene in Guizhou, 1931); "Sange nanren yu yige nüren" (Three men and one woman, 1930) *Congwen zizhuan* (Autobiography of Congwen, 1934); and *Xiangxi* (West Hunan, 1938). Decapitation is described as a common form of punishment used by rural authorities in late Qing and early Republican days, despite the fact that advanced penal technology was already accessible. In *Autobiography of Congwen,* Shen Congwen relates how the Miao aborigines were beheaded by the thousands after the failure of their rebellions in the late Qing period; how, on the eve of the Republican revolution, local agitators were arrested and put to death by chopping off their heads; and how this cruel form of execution still went on wherever warlords came to seize local power.[21] As a child, Shen Congwen saw thousands of heads hung out for display on the city wall, or simply dumped on the river bank before family members sorted them out. More appalling is his account of soldiers often arresting innocent peasants to fulfill their daily quota; after too many killings, they let their captives gamble their lives in a lottery-like religious ritual. The winners were set free, while the losers had to resign their lives to Fate.[22] Thus, it was not unusual to see an unlucky peasant bid farewell to his cellmates and ask them to settle things unfinished at home for him ("Twilight"); a sad child walking towards home on a mountain path, carrying baskets containing the heads of his father and his brother ("Little scene in Guizhou"), or even more gruesomely, dogs fighting for the decomposed bodies left on the river banks (*Autobiography of Congwen*).

Given the cruelty of public decapitation, one would have expected a post–May Fourth writer either to lash out at the backwardness of the Chinese penal system or to deplore the callousness of those who participate in such bloody spectacles. Lu Xun and Wang Luyan do both. In his short story, "Youzi" (Grapefruit), Wang Luyan bitterly criticizes the "shows" of public beheading in Hunan, and ridicules the onlookers as grapefruit buyers.[23] Shen Congwen must have witnessed many more scenes of decapitation than his peers, and he may well have been more qualified to testify to the injustice and inhumanity of the killings. But in the works under discussion, one gets a feeling that his attitude toward decapitation is ambiguous, if not meek. Besides his toned-down humanitarian comments, he always seems to have "something else" to say about the old form of capital punishments. In "Little Scene in Guizhou," the decapitation scene is like a vignette inserted into a broader picture that is itself an impressionistic slice of life in Guizhou. In "The Old and New," Shen displays a black humor by describing how a professional decapitator loses his sense of self-worth after the technique he has mastered so well is replaced by the introduction of a more modern method of execution. It is the decapitator, not the decapitated, who wins our sympathy. And in *Autobiography of Congwen* and *West Hunan,* for all the massive number of people killed on different occasions, Shen maintains a retrospective posture that combines both ironic curiosity and a sense of intellectual and emotional distance.

The best example that of Shen's unique view of decapitation is "Twilight." Lacking a clear plotline, "Twilight" tells of the daily routine of decapitation in a small town in the mid-Yangtze valley. It opens with an overview of the serene life of a shabby city at sunset: sunshine reflecting the last spectrum of colors in the darkening sky; smoke from cooking fires coming out of the chimneys; and children winding up their games before supper. As part of the late afternoon city scene, a decapitation is soon to be conducted in a detention center. Hearing soldiers' footsteps approaching, the prisoners start to become anxious. Names of those who will be executed are then announced, followed by sighs, cries, noises of feeble resistance, dragging, and beating. An old warden is standing by, watching the daily turmoil of his job. Moments ago, he was carried away by thinking of the gains and losses of his own life, necessary preparations for his own death, and the wanton adventures of his youth. He can do little with these innocent victims. Shortly, their heads will be cut off and scattered all over the execution site, becoming toys for children to kick around.

What baffles us here is Shen Congwen's narrator, who tells his story in an understated, familiar, casual tone. His use of the iterative style to describe the procedure of decapitation and its onlookers' responses especially risks dissolving the temporal and psychological urgency of the particular round of executions taking place at the moment. The narrator's voice also refuses to stay within the core of the narrative—the prisoners to be beheaded—and shifts from one consciousness to another. One will not forget the prisoner who, when asked about his last wishes, honestly desires his fellow villagers to pay on his behalf a small bill he owes to a painter, nor will one forget the execution supervisor who, while losing his temper at the delay of the daily routine because of a soldier's misdeed, thinks of the pot of braised pork already well-heated on his stove. By the end of the story, as the night finally falls, the narrator seems to subject himself to the embrace of the impending darkness. Human and nonhuman activities are thus gradually diffused into each other. What is important and what is not are no longer distinguishable in the glimmer of twilight.

One can of course point to Shen Congwen's ironic intention which reveals the absurdities of the real world by understating rather than exaggerating them. But I suspect that the real polemical problem with a story like "Twilight" lies in the fact that it draws readers' attention to it without any specific interest in the subject matter supposedly at issue, and without any necessary confidence that the work itself is a definitive treatment of anything. In conjuring up a story where things and creatures *seem* to exist in naked resistance to any interpretation, Shen Congwen must have learned a lot from Turgenev. Even his description of the prisoner's honest last wish, as mentioned above, reminds one of the farmer Maxim of "Death," in *Sketches from a Hunter's Album,* who asks his wife and friends to return money he owes to others, before his death from a logging accident.[24] However, since Shen Congwen is not bound to a conscious viewpoint like that of Turgenev's gentleman-hunter, he has more freedom to disorient his narratorial position, in exchange for an indefinite expansion of perspective. He removes and scatters the objects of his storyline, as it were; consequently, he offers his reader a mystically "graphic" construction of the scene of decapitation, in that the narrated "event" is literally described and that the "narrative" event, the language as displayed by Shen Congwen, demands equal attention.

Up to this point we have only described rather than investigated the question raised previously: why does Shen Congwen deal so lyrically with decapitation rather than with any of the other gruesome forms of death? To answer this question, we must turn back, for a while, to Lu Xun, the founding father of the discourse of modern Chinese realism. Most readers would consider Lu Xun to be a more appropriate candidate for the subject of decapitation, and he is indeed the first modern Chinese writer who endeavors to approach this subject and invest it with a system of meaning. For instance, his "Yao" (Medicine), reportedly motivated by the decapitation of the woman revolutionary Qiu Jin, points out the bloody costs of revolution and its gratuitous rewards. Yet the story also betrays Lu Xun's strange fascination with the macabre ritual and cannibalistic superstitions that accompany a beheading. Decapitation is one of the leitmotifs in another famous Lu Xun short story, "The True Story of Ah Q." Public beheading represents for Ah Q and his fellow villagers both a heroic way of death and the most thrilling form of entertainment. But the story culminates with the anticlimax of no decapitation, thereby striking the last blow to

Ah Q's logic of spiritual victory, and mocking his audience's nostalgia for the past. Stranger still is the story "Zhujian" (Forging swords), Lu Xun's rewriting of the classical tale about Mei Jianchi's revenge of his parents' murder by the Prince of Qin. In the story, beheading and self-beheading are depicted in such a way that they suggest not so much a necessary means of revenge as a decadent game participated in by both the heroes and villains, in search of sadomasochistic pain and pleasure.

But Lu Xun's most important presentation of the subject is to be found in his preface to his collection of short stories, *A Call to Arms*. He attributes the motivation for his writing of fiction to the traumatic experience of seeing a slide show about Chinese people watching one of their compatriots being beheaded by the Japanese in the Russo-Japanese War period of 1904–05. As Lu Xun puts it, the scene of decapitation made him realize that "the people of a weak, backward country, even though they may enjoy sturdy health, can only serve as the senseless material of and audience for public executions.... Our first task was surely to transform their spirit, and I thought at that time that literature could best meet the task of spiritual transformation. I then began to think about promoting literary activities."[25]

The moment of seeing a decapitation in the slide show thus triggers the most crucial turn of Lu Xun's life, changing him from a modern student of medicine into a traditional member of the literati. No longer would he try to adopt the viewpoint of a clinical anatomist when faced with a Chinese about to be beheaded. As a convert to the old way of literature, he sees in the body a representational organism of signs, voicing a complex of meanings about the Chinese character and society—showing them to be cowardly, selfish, callous, and cannibalistic.

As a matter of fact, the statement as Lu Xun presents it is itself already a figurative one, dramatizing his anxiety about the primordial loss of origin—meaning and life as symbolized by the head, loss as symbolized by the mutilated body. Critics such as Leo Lee have pointed out that, due to the fact that the traumatic slide could never be found, it is possible that Lu Xu made up the whole incident,[26] thereby giving an allegorical form to his abstract conception. Fiction and history might have been mixed up, at the (textual) beginning of modern Chinese (literary) history.

Besides criticizing the convict who is about to be decapitated, Lu

Xun is even more upset by those Chinese in the picture who stand round watching the execution. The audience are admitted to the scene literally to be taught a lesson, to be scared by the death of "one of them," but Lu Xun cannot but notice with resentment that the audience are equally excited by the rare spectacle, and that they share a secret sense of carnival! Literally and symbolically, modern China is a "head"-less country, crowded by spiritually decapitated people whose life is only intensified by watching beheadings or waiting to be beheaded.

Lu Xun declares that the task for intellectual reformers is to take over people's minds; the best way to accomplish this to inscribe in them a new consciousness in them, as if they were naked writing tablets. But judging by his decapitation complex, what really fascinates Lu Xun is the representational power of the body and the head. The new, sophisticated rhetorical power of literature in place of the ritual anatomy of torture and decapitation is, after all, derived from the politics of bodies and is to take effect on bodies. At its best, the mind serves as a surface for the submission of bodies to the control of ideas. Implied here is a theory of literature that emphasizes the representational link between body and language, referents and referentiality. The anguish Lu Xun suffers from seeing the scene of beheading is underlain by an imaginative encounter with a primordial emptiness. Decapitation, seen from this angle, must signal not only a barbaric form of punishment left by previous generations, and a powerful symbol of the Chinese people's state of spiritual dehumanization, but also the mutilated condition of the meaning system that makes Reality what it is not.

Lu Xun's anxiety over decapitation and headlessness serves as the secret fountainhead of his literary inspirations. Critics have repeatedly noticed that Lu Xun's most engaging works deal not with his concern over China's fate but with the "dark side" of his concern,[27] not with the coherent social and epistemological system in prospect or retrospect but with the ruptures of that system. When the representational order of the world he establishes for himself breaks loose, demons, superstitions, and macabre fantasies loom large. Strangely, it appears that, before he can exorcise these dark forces, he is first hopelessly taken in or even charmed by them. One can see this ambivalent adherence to the imagery of mutilation in the carnivalesque parade featuring the killing of Ah Q ("The True Story of Ah Q"); in the mysterious prescription of buns soaked with human blood ("Medicine"); and especially in the fantastic fight among three "heads" in the wok of the prince of Qin ("Forging swords"). Lu Xun's longing for the full-fledged representation of the real is ironically nurtured on the break of its chain of referentiality, which is emphatically symbolized by a beheaded body, a split personality ("Diary of a Madman"); a living dead ("Zai jiuloushang" [In the tavern]); and a "speaking" head whose body is already deformed ("Mujiewen" [Inscriptions on a tombstone], "Cong baicaoyuan dao sanwei shuwu" [From Baicao garden to Sanwei studio]).

Lu Xun would have agreed with Michel Foucault that classical punishments are often designed with a strong theatrical dimension.[28] Through performing corporal mutilation in public, the authorities not only impose torture and humiliation on the convicted victim but also extend their power to those who are watching the execution. But for Foucault, there always lurks a threat in the public show of bodily punishment. Besides fear, the bloody spectacle brings its audience an unexpected thrill, something that upsets the solemnity of the execution and may even threaten to turn it into a festive occasion. At its extreme, the audience's deviant response to public corporal punishment may endanger the authorities; such a response implies either an indifference to, or a rebellious consciousness of, the power displayed by the mutilated body.[29]

If one agrees with Foucault's reading of the mixed ideological and psychological outcomes of the public spectacle of punishment, one can then take note of the crisis involved in Lu Xun's treatment of decapitation. Insofar as he expects his readers to read the meaning of beheading more seriously than the witnesses of a decapitation, that is to say, to realize the tyrannical power at work behind the scene, he recapitulates the representational meaning imposed by the authorities on the body better than any other writer. Though conceptually against the authorities that legitimize the cruel decapitation, Lu Xun shares their moral and penal *episteme*. On the other hand, Lu Xun reveals his secret alliance with the cannibalistic audience he openly condemns when he indulges both his ironic fascination with the theatrical turmoil and spectacular bloodshed of public beheadings, and his cynical knowledge that whatever happens, things remain the same. Stretched between these two contradictory and complementary roles, Lu Xun may have found himself to be no better than poor Xianglin's wife in "The New-Year Sacrifice," who is haunted by the possibility of being dismembered by her two dead husbands in hell yet finds no plausible form of escape.

Shen Congwen differs from Lu Xun, in that he is far less worried about attaching any inherent meaning to the subject of decapitation and headlessness. Where Lu Xun sees in decapitation the stupidity and cannibalism of the Chinese mentality in decapitation, Shen Congwen finds in it a complex of coexisting human motives. In the decapitation scenes he narrates in "My Education," Shen Congwen is one of the heartless audience, as Lu Xun would have it, scared and thrilled by the bloody scenes. But Shen Congwen is also the young soldier dutifully observing daily routine as part of the war, and the young sensitive artist, saddened by the meaningless waste of human life. As shown by "Twilight," Shen Congwen's narrative manifests its lyrical rhythms by weaving varied sensory images from natural and human environments into a fabric and giving them correspondences to one another. The ever-changing colors in the darkening sky, mothers' dinner calls, a romantic flashback in an old prison warden's mind, prisoners' anguished cries, the smell of pork on the supervisor's stove, are all presented at the same level of narrative proportion, all calling for equal attention. Shen Congwen's lyrical imagination originates less in the metaphorical tie between the head and the body, or the individual and the society, than with the method of metonymic replacement, which provides a phantasmal connection between likes and unlikes, between existing phenomena of experience and absent objects of desire.

Let there be no misunderstanding that I am saying Shen Congwen lyricizes the horrors of decapitation at the cost of his social conscience. At the readerly level, when a lyrical tone is applied to a scene of cannibalism, or when legal injustice and bloody punishment are integrated with casual daily routines such as eating and sleeping, Shen Congwen's narrative is bound to drive us to question the moral consequences both of the political system that legitimizes decapitation and of a literary mode like lyricism being used to delineate such a political system. But this is not where the entire charm of Shen Congwen's art lies. What I am emphasizing is the rhetorical strategy with which Shen Congwen makes the urgent subject appear and disappear on the same surface of his narrative, and the way it renders a discordant harmony among things. In Shen Congwen's lyrical agenda, ugly things are neither erased nor reversed as an offset of the real, but only displaced, as it were, from their roots in order to evoke a dreamlike simulacrum. The most human part of his story (like decapitation) is rendered as the most literal, whereas the most insensible part may prove the most allegorical.

If one senses an irony here, the irony does not stem from Shen Congwen's reversal of the hierarchy of referents in reality: he never treats decapitation as something enjoyable. Rather the irony comes from his play with the recession and reversibility of language as a medium for representing the real. To write like a poet means to see the world with the third eye on the figurative basis of language itself, to rearrange linguistic codes in a tropological pattern. In his stories, Shen Congwen does not accord a transparent view to the sole subject of decapitation but, instead, invokes associative relations between what exists and what does not. The essential simultaneity embedded in his poetic presentation of the world demands that his reader almost take a multiple perspective, one that absorbs both the prisoners' cries and the old warden's daydreams, both the sounds of children lingering at the site of the decapitation and the smells of pork cooking on the supervisor's stove; the result is the fundamental "undecidability" at the heart of his story. But as previously mentioned, this *aporia* that opens up Shen's lyrical vision takes on a moral dimension, since it refuses to impose a new dogma on a Chinese society already overloaded with dogmatic voices, while revealing its own expression as an allegorical and therefore partial, culture-bound practice.

Shen Congwen's rewriting of decapitation in terms of a displaced lyricism thus proposes an alternative to Lu Xun's treatment, a treatment overloaded with guilty conscience and moral anxiety. The two writers share the same kind of repulsion against social/political abuses and feel the same pathos over the follies and cruelty of humanity. In search of an artistic expression of their feelings, they demonstrate different methods, however. Lu Xun is both horrified by and obsessed with the spectacle of decapitation; the severed body paradoxically embodies for him a world broken into pieces, while Shen Congwen, who has seen thousands more of decapitations than Lu Xun, is engaged not in what the beheading "means" in itself but in how it can be written about so as to let us remember and *re*-member the rest of the world. The modes of realism and lyricism are behind their respective narratives, serving not as an end but as a starting point for them to work out their own discursive format. The final irony is that, in the twenties and thirties, when most writers took Lu Xun's decapitation complex seriously and made him the "head" of modern Chinese literature, it was meek Shen Congwen who showed how to remove this "head" and break the spell of literary decapitation.

Critical Lyricism

As in his decapitation stories, Shen Congwen's radical lyricism can be illustrated by his tales of bizarre figures and unbelievable events. His homeland region—barbaric, mountainous West Hunan—and his legendary experience with the warlord troops, provide him with the best background for uncanny and gothic stories. As Shen Congwen's travelogues like *West Hunan* vividly relate, the Chu culture he is immersed in envisions a world in which ghosts, demons, and spirits thrive and interact with human creatures; it is a territory where shamanism and voodoo still exert their power over human fate. On the other hand, the Chu culture is also one enlivened by songs and dances, rituals and legends—a world rich in various forms of poetic imagination and ritualistic activity. When Shen Congwen looks around for fictional materials, it is only natural that the shadowy images of mountains and caves, ghostly figures, and inexplicable customs creep into his mind. Four cases, "Shangui" (Mountain ghost, 1928), "Shaobing" (Sentry, 1926), "Ye" (Night, 1930) and "Three Men and One Woman," will be discussed.

"Mountain Ghost" introduces a story of a madman. But the meaning of "madness" as conceived by consensus is exactly what Shen Congwen will not allow us to take for granted. Unlike Lu Xun who creates his madman after the images of the Mara poet and Nietzschean superman, Shen Congwen depicts this and other neurotic cases with both a clinical, Freudian sympathy and a mystical fascination rooted in his longing for the mysterious Chu culture. He takes pains to emphasize the thin line between insanity and sanity in the case of his mountain ghost. The madman, for example, is clean, quiet, and especially gifted with artistic talents in folksongs, puppet theater, and handicrafts. Even his strange behavior, such as running one whole day and night to see the peach blossoms in the next village, seems more romantic than neurotic. As a matter of fact, the story's title, "Mountain Ghost" is borrowed from one chapter of the *Songs of the South* by Qu Yuan, the unhappy poet of ancient Chu.[30]

"Madness," for Shen Congwen, will in fact be the term with which the natural attitude, the voice of poetic sensibility, will recuperate the transgression of consensual codes of decorum and sensibility. But "Mountain Ghost" is not a self-indulgent account of the blessed state of madmen and women as contrasted to that of ordinary people. Shen Congwen knows perfectly well that where public opinions and individualistic fixations part, a hiatus presents itself; he wants to approach this hiatus in terms of more sophisticated than reductive psychological categories. Realistic, mimetic narrative is not suitable for picturing this hiatus; instead, he finds in the lyrical voice a remote echo from the "other" world. In the middle of the story, the madman disappears mysteriously for days, only to return with a shabby, dispirited look. What happened to him during his absence? What is bothering him? Why cannot the language of the prosaic world express his pain?

Referring to Qu Yuan's original poems, one may guess that the madman might have fallen in love with a supernatural being. But evading the hermeneutic inquiry into the logical sequence of the narrative, Shen Congwen tries to deal with the madman's sadness and happiness in a speculative, pensive manner. The narrator looks at the madman through his young brother's and mother's wondering eyes, quietly describing their doubts and worries. Yet however strong his lyrical approximation to the world of the "mountain ghost" may be, Shen Congwen is aware that to cross the thin line between rationality and madness, reality and fiction, is more an epistemological or even mystical leap than simply a rhetorical renovation—and he is not ready for it. Pathos arises, therefore, not only where the madman's mother fails to understand her son but also where Shen Congwen's lyrical narrative comes to realize that the effort to recapture unspeakable encounters with beings of another world is in vain.

Shen Congwen also tries his hand at lyricizing the fiction of the fantastic. In "Sentry," a young soldier is assigned to standing the night watch. In spite of his wish to play tough before his companion, he is haunted by a fear of running into ghosts. Worse, he is soon left alone when his companion leaves for a small get-together with his buddies. Following the formula of ghost stories, Shen Congwen enjoys creating all sorts of irksome effects of horror and suspense. Be it an ill-formed shadow, a funny noise of a cat, or a small breeze, anything around the soldier is perceived and interpreted by him as something monstrous. There is little plot to discuss; what dominates the narrative is an edgy atmosphere just suitable for bizarre happenings. From here, Shen Congwen takes a decisive turn. Instead of pursuing the whereabouts of the ghosts like a common ghost story writer, he adopts an ironic pose and hints that the young soldier's way of projecting his sensory agitations can be seen in an aesthetic light. The alleged ghosts, of course, never appear in the story; what is left haunting the reader, however, is a fascinating portrait of a lonely young soldier's nocturnal journey though the realm of imagination. It is suggestive ghostly surroundings, not the possible ghosts sensed or conjured up by the soldier, that cast a spell on the readers.

For those who are familiar with Turgenev's works, "Sentry" may again prove Shen Congwen's indebtedness to the Russian master. One recalls that, in "Bezhin Lea" of *Sketches from A Hunter's Album*,[31] Turgenev takes just as indulging and ironic an attitude as Shen Congwen's in dealing with a group of peasant children who scare themselves by telling gruesome tales around a bonfire, in the weird atmosphere of a summer night. "Bezhin Lea" may also be compared to another Shen Congwen short story entitled "Night," in which a group of young soldiers take turns to tell tall tales one night in an old farmer's house, while their host quietly sits watching them. Shen Congwen lets each soldier relate a story that fits his personality and experience. The mood is high, but there is something unnatural about their hyperbolic manner of storytelling. As in "Bezhin Lea," as the night gets older, the stories told sound more daring and incredible. Shen Congwen then pushes his story in a direction reminiscent more of Maupassant than of Turgenev. As the soldiers have exhausted their imaginations, the old man is asked to tell his story. Without any story in his mind, the old man instead opens the door of a room, showing a dead, dry body lying in bed—his late wife. Everybody is horrified.

Neither Shen Congwen's design of a surprise ending nor his preference for the grotesque and the horrible is at issue here, but rather his ability to see in the disgusting scene an epiphanic revelation of an unspeakable sorrow in the human condition and in the mystical link of fate that bonds the young soldiers and the old couple together. In his horror, the young soldier-narrator comes to grips with the hidden apprehension in his and his fellow friends' otherwise frivolous tales. The ongoing war is dismal and the soldiers' futures remain unknown. The happy moment of story telling reveals nothing but their *carpe diem* mentality, already clouded by the awareness of the impending end of night and their furlough from war and death. The old man tells his story by saying nothing, but showing something totally in context; he transmits an almost oracular message to the young soldier and makes him a sadder but wiser man.

Shen Congwen's taste for the uncanny and grotesque finds its ultimate expression in the story "Three Men and One Woman."

Reportedly based on a personal experience, the story deals with a strange romance between a girl and her three suitors, a romance which leads to the horrors of suicide and necrophilia. The autobiographical part of the story will be discussed in the next chapter. Here we will focus only on Shen's ability to forge the most incongruous sentiments and subjects into a unified vision that salutes and at the same time undermines the verisimilitude of pastoral romance. The story starts with a romantic competition among three young men—two soldiers and one beancurd store proprietor—in pursuit of a pretty girl at a border town. While the two soldiers' fights for the girl's favor draw most of our attention, it is the beancurd store proprietor, always wearing an inscrutable smile, who turns out to be the girl's choice. Just as everything seems to be working out fine for the young couple, the girl commits suicide for no clear reason; soon after her funeral her body is found missing from the tomb. The thief is caught later—the beancurd store proprietor, who dug out the body, took it to a nearby cave, and for three days slept with it.

With its sensual quality and neurotic potential, the story could easily be made into an erotic thriller. But Shen Congwen is more ambitious than that. He takes advantage of the romantic fervor of the story only because he projects onto it a structure conducive to poetic reflection. This poetic reflection does not arise at the level of Shen Congwen's claim of biographical plausibility for his story, nor at the level of his reversal of idyllic figures and images, but at the level of its interlocutionary condition. The format of framed narrative merits special attention. As Shen puts it, the whole matter of story telling is caused by a rain shower, which temporarily keeps the storyteller and his ideal audience from their routine activities. Already at its very beginning, Shen's story inserts itself in a moment of indefinable suspension, and as the implied audience, we are also drawn into this enclosed condition.

Once the center narrative starts, Shen's first person narrator takes charge. He takes his readers to piece together the seemingly random, scattered images of the mountain town: the unending rain, the drudgery of soldiers' routines, the colorful patterns of local woman's aprons, the smile of the beancurd store proprietor, the dangling gold earrings of the girl, the splendid physiques of her two white dogs, and so on—all so sensuously described with moving lines and images as to constitute a picture.

But this impressionist picture of the idyllic is only a frontispiece. By introducing the arrival of the soldiers in the town at the beginning of the story, Shen Congwen has implanted into his narrative a seed of menace and uncertainty. The gaps between the soldiers and the townsfolk are gradually revealed. The simple, innocent mountain town seems to contain within itself a secret that appears so transparent yet tantalizingly inaccessible to an outsider. The two soldiers' pursuit of the girl first proceeds like an ordinary romantic game, only to be defiled or mocked by the girl's mysterious death and the beancurd store proprietor's necrophilic deed.

The narrator, who identifies himself as one of the two soldiers, continues his account in the manner of the dramatic monologue which strongly suggests an intersubjective pattern of dialogue between the narrator and his ideal audience. As the story develops, the reader finds that he or she seems forced into a transferential relationship with what he or she may or may not want to see or hear. Like the two soldiers, we too are intruders into a benign, pastoral world-in-text which finally refuses our further advances. But our frustration only reinforces our yearning for the world where love and death, insanity and ecstasy, bliss and curse, still take pure forms to supplement each other in a reversible way. By the end of the story, the narrator's obsession has become ours.

On the other hand, the narrator's dramatic monologue indicates that he is communicating just as eagerly with an objective listener as with himself. This self-reflexive manner is shown not only by the narrator's rationalization after his failure in the romantic competition and his discovery of the necrophilic act but especially by his lengthy descriptions of military life, which seem at first glance to add little to the story's plot. Yet it is only in the light of these long passages that we can see Shen Congwen's lyrical project, which takes the tedium of army life and the sheer irrationality of war, and parallels them to the uncanny romance. The narrator links two irrelevant worlds together, letting them form a new pattern in which war is defined by bizarre romance, and gothic horror is counterpointed to military boredom. This voice is the crucial magic that "turns the obscene into the divine."[32] Thus, we are told, when the girl's dead body is found, it is "completely naked on a stone ledge, with blue chrysanthemums scattered all over her body and on the ground."[33]

"Three Men and One Woman," therefore, can be considered as

Shen Congwen's self-forming treatise, through which he explores and breaks the limits of his understanding of the lyrical. Between autobiographical accounts and legendary anecdote, platonic love and necrophilic obsession, idyllic romance and gothic story, rationality and madness, Shen finds a rupture; there his kind of lyrical imagination is allowed to take charge, so much so that we are tempted to suspend our disbelief willingly and endorse his dreamlike world. With this in mind, we can now tentatively close this section by affirming that neither necrophilia nor decapitation is a barrier to the lyrical vision. Rather, it helps reveal where conventions have fallen short and what a modern lyricism might become. And it shows how firmly Shen Congwen remained in the avantgarde after the first waves of May Fourth antitraditionalism.

Lyricizing Time, War, and History

Because of its emphasis on an intensified expression of emotion, its tendency to juxtapose perceptual images with cognitive input, and its prefigured demand for an immediate, empathetic response from the audience, *lyricism* is often described as a narrative mode that presents an atemporal effect, "spatializing" the linear sequence of time in pursuit of an epiphanic look into the depth of life. This conceptual complex can conveniently be applied to a reading of Shen Congwen's works, as evidenced by existing criticism. But it also tends to simplify his discourse in terms of a series of dichotomies, such as poetic autonomy versus narrative referentiality, space versus time, myth versus history. I would offer a different view, by arguing that Shen Congwen's lyrical vision may obviate those apparent connections with time and history that are crucial to post–May Fourth realist writings, while at the same time it contains a critical dimension, which problematizes not only the binary oppositions mentioned above but also the historical assumptions held by established realists of the twenties and thirties such as Mao Dun.

In *The Odyssey of Shen Congwen*, Jeffrey Kinkley has proved that, contrary to general assumptions, Shen Congwen's works are intricately written in response to a historical era full of military and political turmoil.[34] Assuming Kinkley's analysis to be correct, one can take one more step and ask why Shen Congwen's delineation of history should be seen by many critics as unhistorical, and what the

Critical Lyricism

artistic and ideological motivations of his discourse on temporality might then be. Shen Congwen's persistent alliance with regionalism and nostalgia, two of the most prominent themes through which his concepts of time and history unfold, will be discussed at full length in the next chapter. Here I will touch on other dimensions of the question.

Let us begin with the chapter entitled "Yijiu sansi nian yiyue shiba" (January 18, 1934) in *Random Sketches*. With its specific reference to date and year in the title, the chapter has already manifested "meaningfulness" in a historiographical sense. But we will soon find out the date is meaningful not on the national but the personal level—it marks Shen Congwen's first return in sixteen years to Chenzhou, his second hometown. The ironic undertone implied in the title is further reinforced by Shen Congwen's way of selecting material to substantiate his narrative. Major and often negative forces that make history, such as war, violence, and death, are self-consciously repressed as extraneous to the main narrative; instead, marginal and aleatory incidents—boatmen's quarrels and oaths; a seventy-seven year old boat puller with the tough look and spirits "of a Tolstoy";[35] a happy reunion with a wild child; fleeting impressions of boats of big and small sizes; local merchandise, brothels, hillside foliage, and the Chen River—become crucial and liminal states or transitional processes.

Shen Congwen inserts into his narrative a voice that is aware of its own historical transitoriness. The subjunctive mood and the linguistic shifter "I" that begin the text ("as if I were called by an old acquaintance again and again, the voice lingers even after I have sobered up")[36] signal that Shen's position is a tentative, self-conscious one. The "voice" that wakes up Shen Congwen, we are told later, turns out to be the voice of the Chen River, which "speaks" in a continuously shifting moment that appears to be at a deceptive standstill. The voice of the river mimics the voice of time, of which the "I" is only a provisional register. Shen tries to make his narrative an echo of the river's soft incantation, awakening his reader from the slumberous routine of life to the immanence of time. But nothing can be spelled out obtrusively; like the "silent" river, Shen can narrate only in the most tacit way. "Watching the flow of the river, I suddenly had a feeling *as if* I understood life better; meanwhile, I *seemed* to have gained wisdom from this river" (italics mine).[37]

In recapturing the quotidian existence of these moments of being, Shen Congwen comes to sense a thrill of timelessness. Things may be changing outside the world, but "nothing" seems to have really happened to the town and people of Chenzhou. Thus, he writes:

> Seeing the pebbles and sands in the perennially flowing river, and the rotten grass and wood, broken pieces of boats drifting on the water, I am touched by a melancholy term. I come to think of history. Written history, besides telling us stories of mutual killing among certain groups of people in certain places on earth, will never sufficiently tell us what we should know. But this river has told me the sadness and happiness of some people in an era of time. The little gay fishing boats, . . . the half-naked, bending boat-pullers, walking on the pebble beach. These things have nothing to do with history, and they remain the same, in the last or the next hundred years. . . . History seems to have nothing to do with them at all, but when thinking of the unwritten history of this life of theirs that has not changed for thousands of years, I feel an unspeakable sorrow.[38]

The statement seemingly denounces conventional concepts of history in favor of the atemporal values by which these noble West Hunan savages have lived during hundreds and thousands of years. Behind Shen Congwen's transhistorical pose, there lurks a different kind of historical consciousness. The dimension of history emphasized by Shen Congwen's narrative is the microlevel of seemingly insignificant happenings, the empty space between the significant disruptions of historic events. The trivial, contingent events and figures may repeat one another in a meaningless way, but they may also manifest their historical significance by simply "being" there over a sizable period of time. Not without a sense of irony, Shen Congwen feels this is where the real history happens, a history that refuses to be interrupted by the "plotting" of wishful historians, one that asserts its own autonomy in a repetitive temporality. As far as its traits of chronological obscurity and indefinitely expandable focus are concerned, Shen Congwen's style reminds one of the historical accounts by French *Annaliste* scholars, in particular Braudel's study of the Mediterranean in the epoch of Philippe II.[39]

While Shen Congwen's existential status provides a reassuring definition of the roundness of time itself, it may also imply a sense of the terrifying blankness which expands and deflates the plenitude of Shen Congwen's autonomous view of time and history from the inside. The voice of the river may be an empty echo of the eternal void, signifying nothing. Or, the voice may be the projection of Shen Congwen's own changing perceptions. Can West Hunan really continue on its own way, out of the flux of history as defined by the outside world? Does its seemingly eternal quietness represent only a sign of its inertia? Does what Shen Congwen sees reflect only what he *wants* to see? Oscillating between the different readings of historical contingency, Shen no longer feels sure of his ground: "I feel a little worried, the place may not have changed. Maybe I have changed too much."[40] This internal self-erosion of meaningfulness is perceived as a more threatening force than the invasion of a linear history from the outside world. It brings the real pain and anxiety to *Random Sketches,* and works such as *The Border Town* and *Long River.*

The interplay between time and space, between the diachronic and synchronic, is even more subtly presented in another story, "Jing" (Quiet, 1932). A story that strictly follows the lyrical design of spatialization, "Quiet" focuses on a fourteen-year-old girl's idle experience of looking around on a late spring morning, from the shaky terrace of a bungalow where she and her family take shelter from a war. Through the girl Yuemin's "gaze," scenes such as clouds floating in the sky; a kite fallen on the roof next door; dim noises from a boat-building house; quarrels between a ferryman and one of his passengers; melodies of a wedding procession; a little nun washing clothes along the river are all absorbed together to form an idyllic picture. The only major "action" is staged by Yuemin's five-year-old nephew, Beisheng, who goes peevishly up and down stairs.

Thus situated in the terrace, Yuemin's gaze drives home Shen Congwen's attraction to vision and space. The visual and spatial positions are foregrounded, as opposed to the murky flow of historical realities which takes place downstairs. A war is going on. Yuemin and her family members, all female except for Beisheng, are stuck on their trip to a safer place, short of money and of news from her father and brother. Even worse is that her mother is getting sicker and sicker. Yuemin also has her own personal worries. At fourteen, she has been left all alone to face a still mysterious stage of adolescent desire and fear. Only at the brief moments of looking out from the terrace, will she set her imagination free and see the scenery as well as her own future, whether that future be good or bad. In his attempt to make the girl's visual presence into the readers' surrogate, Shen Congwen evokes a style completely hers. Yuemin's ascension of the poorly maintained terrace seems full of symbolism in binary form, such as upstairs/downstairs, vision/reality, peace/war, life/death, waking/dream, sexual fantasy/religious abstinence (wedding procession/lonely little nun), and lyricism/realism.

However, a closer reading will reveal that these binary oppositions may actually be dualities, and that a scheme of time is at work behind the quiet, sculpturesque display of life. When Yuemin is upstairs, her gaze is not a prolonged, self-contained action; rather, it is repeatedly interrupted by her own and her nephew's movements of going upward and downward between the two stories. The different segments of time spent upstairs are so tentatively bracketed as to give rise to an illusion of immobilization. But in a larger temporal context, the life downstairs proceeds no less as a suspension of the normal course of history and reality than does the life upstairs: Yuemin and her family are stranded in a foreign place, out of touch with either end of their journey. What Yuemin does each time after going back to the terrace is not idle browsing; it is a literal *and imaginative* "displacement" of what she has seen and felt downstairs just moments before. Insofar as the world down below is itself put into a temporary bracketing, images perceived by Yuemin in the terrace constitute not opposites but dreamlike counterparts, or *re*-visions, of the world down below. The movements of going upstairs and downstairs serve therefore as the reminder of the contiguity between these two worlds that only look different, a reminder of the spiral procession of time linking the diachronic and the synchronic.

The story's ending complicates Shen Congwen's subtle game with time and space. In this scene, Yuemin goes back to the terrace after seeing her mother for a short time. Except for the precocious maid who is "stealthily applying Peerless Brand toothpowder to her face as if it were facial powder,"[41] the family has fallen asleep. Minutes before, hearing somebody knock at a neighbor's door, Yuemin was excited by the wishful thought that her father might have suddenly come home. But "everything soon lapsed into silence. Yuemin smiled aimlessly. Under the slanting sun a part of the wall and the laundry are spread on the floor of the courtyard just as elsewhere a paper flag casts its shadow on the tomb of the man the women here are expecting—the father of Yuemin."[42] This final message of death gives a tangible form to the dark force which has all along haunted the world of both downstairs and upstairs, unifying them by asserting their "likeness" in front of the unknown, while it also reminds the reader of the narrator's ghostly presence throughout the story. As if situated in a different time zone, the narrator's vision of Yuemin innocently gazing brings the reader a foreknowledge of what has happened yet remains unavailable to her and her family, producing an ironic cognitive effect which can best be described as *anti-epiphany*. Vacillating between various temporal and epistemological dimensions, Shen's method of narration thus amounts to a subversive force, undermining the firm ground of the Real on which most realist writers believe they stand.

The story's little drama about time extends even to its extra-textual level. Readers might often overlook the short authorial statement immediately after the end of the text: "related by my sister Ming, in memory of our elder sister's dead son, Beisheng."[43] The dead in the real world is the child, not the father. This autobiographical entry adds a yet more subtle turn to the story's meditation on time and history; it not only upsets the text's boundary at another level, twice blurring the boundaries between fiction with reality, but also stages the reversibility of dream and reality, life and death on the "narrative" plane.

Looking around at the unstable balcony, Yuemin's posture parallels the simultaneously relaxed and intense tempos followed by the story. Beyond contrasts such as those between upstairs and downstairs, indoors and outdoors, Shen Congwen sees his lyricism arise as a result of an unexpected convergence of conflicting perceptions, a phantasmal expression of the real which is itself already palpable. The transformative power of vision and space is affirmed, but only on the verge of an apprehensive insight of ghostly simulacra, incipient calamity, and the changing forms of time and reality. Historical contingencies and psychological vicissitudes continually cross over and mediate each other's domains, questioning and reversing the reader's (and characters') perception of life, to the point where the death both disrupts and confirms the lyrical plenitude.

Shen Congwen finds another expression for his view of time in "Sheng" (Life, 1933), a story about an old mummer in Beijing. The old man's show features a special prop made of two life-size puppets attached to each other. By putting on one puppet's body and the other's legs, the mummer moves around as if he were wrestling with an opponent. The two puppets are respectively named Wang Jiu and Zhao Si, and, however tough the fight, the assumed wrestling always ends with Wang Jiu's victory. The reader is not informed till the end that the old mummer does not perform simply to make a living. The two puppets' wrestling game refers to a fight ten years before, a fight which cost the life of the old man's only son, Wang Jiu.

The old man entertains his audience by enacting a family history. In his show, he does not just revive his own son in his mimicry; he also reverses the fatal result of the real fight. But his theatrical triumph over death is undercut by another irony of time. As the story's ending relates, "Wang Jiu has been dead for ten years, and the old guy has played Wang Jiu defeating Zhao Si around Beijing for ten years, too. As for the Zhao Si of real life, he died from liver cancer as far back as five years ago."[44] This "random" statement does not provide the reader with a belated poetic justice so much as cast a chilly overview on the fragile human condition in its journey to death. The old mummer, in order to revenge his son's death and to redirect the course of history, has to bring back to life both his son and his son's deadly enemy. He plays not only his son's part but also his son's murderer. His will to revenge thus partakes of an unexpected dimension of mercy: both son and murderer are resurrected from the dead, to live on in the old murmur's drama. The ethical and temporal ambiguities he wishes to do away with accompany every show he puts on.

The ritualistic effect of the old man's show is primarily transmitted by the use of the *iterative mode,* a narrative mode that occurs in most of Shen Congwen's writings. The iterative mode refers to "a single narrative utterance" that "takes upon itself several occurrences together of the same event."[45] It condenses recurrent events over a period of time into a single narrative and thus renders a synchronic overlay of the diachronicity of events. In the case of the old man's wrestling show, the seeming fixation of his daily routine is described in such a way that it highlights his repetitive attempt to halt time as well as the death of his son; the reader comes to realize the existence of temporality only from a retrospective view, as indicated by the summary ending about what happened in reality. Accordingly, there arises a parallel between the old man's wrestling with his past and the wrestling between the iterative mode and the linear mode of the past tense. The story's grammar mimics its action.

I will reserve the rest of this section for a study of Shen Congwen's treatment of one of the major themes of historical narrative: war and lives under war. Even if Shen Congwen takes up the events such as war, violence, and death, that make history sensible to us in public terms, he tends to dilute war's intensity, and renders us a view very different that of conventional war narratives. Thanks to his adolescent experiences in warlord armies, Shen Congwen is able to deal with army lives in a way inaccessible to general writers, and to provide a special interpretation of Chinese rural society from the vantage point of a soldier. The routine drudgery of lower ranking soldiers ("Ruwuhou" [After entering the ranks, 1927]); their romantic adventures ("Lianzhang" [Captain, 1927]); bloody killings ("Heiye" [Dark night, 1932]); fatal missions ("Guolingzhe" [Those who cross over the mountains, 1934]); and gratuitous sacrifice ("Zaoshang—yiduitu, yigebing" [Morning, a soldier on a mound of earth, 1933]) constitute a view of life that is both excitingly adventurous and dreadfully contingent, a life whose content and rhythm form its own ethics, such that any surface assessments or accusations become simplifications.

One of the most remarkable traits of Shen Congwen's stories about army life is the apparent lack of a context which justifies both the necessity of an action and the narrative format relating the action. In the gap between the irrationality and contingency of army life and the imposed (ideological and cultural) conventions as to the "right" kind of war narrative, Shen proffers a lyrical discourse as a substitute. Take a story such as "My Education" as an example. At first it appears to be a biographical report about Shen's life during the time when he was stationing with a troop of seventy soldiers in Huaihua. In the form of journal entries, Shen's narrative is composed of twenty-four discrete sections, covering a variety of activities ranging from routine reviews and errands, visits to a steel plant, watching the decapitation of bandits, chasing after runaways, to gambling and daydreaming. These activities never evolve into anything more than a series of discontinuous incidents, followed by structural disruptions whose emptiness Shen Congwen never fills with sufficient reflections. Since he has no obligation to sort out the relevant from the irrelevant, everything crowds into the narrator's consciousness with all the force of immediate confusion. What is implied behind the confusion, however, is an acute sense of disorientation and a highly ironic presentation of a life experience that affects the consciousness of a young soldier-writer, as if the misery of thousands were the price of maturing an artist. Similarly, one can read *Autobiography of Congwen* as an expanded version of "My Education," because it too recapitulates national history on the personal level through the artistry of confusion.

Short of discernible ideological underpinnings, army lives and actions in Shen's stories appear like fragmented emotional and psychic impressions without the focus a conscious recognition would have brought. In "Dark Night," two young soldiers swim and walk across the enemy's fire zone to deliver a message. In spite of the danger around them, they undertake the mission as if it were a hypnotic game. Running or swimming, talking or swearing, every deadly move is made to appear more like a gesture than an action. Even when they stumble over the worm-ridden body of a fellow soldier, killed in the same kind of mission they are assigned to, or when one of the two finally dies while covering for his companion on the way to their destination, one does not feel the sensations of war or violence one would have expected from such a subject. Shen Congwen's style is drastically different from conventional war narratives that blame or justify the excesses of war. Concepts like courage versus cowardice, betrayal versus martyrdom, maneuvering versus outmaneuvering seem dissolved into the background in his narrative context.

This ambiguity is further demonstrated in "Morning, A Soldier on a Mound of Earth," a short story allegedly written in memory of the Shanghai Resistance to Japan in 1932.[46] The way Shen Congwen deals with the war seems to unsettle rather than sanction the meaning of the war. A veteran soldier and his young companion are the focus of the story, yet the reader does not know for sure what they are fighting for and how they are going to fight. What we perceive is not a conventional battle scene but the loss of any framework capable of informing the scene with significance. The short exchange of words between the old and young soldier point to nowhere, and before they get to know each other better, the young one is killed. The soldiers seem so consumed by a battle in the act of manifesting itself as to make them indistinguishable from what they perceive around them. There is little hinted that this sporadic incident of the sacrifice of a young, inexperienced soldier constitutes part of a battle that will eventually be inscribed as a monumental event. There is also a break in voice and viewpoint on the narrative level. While the thrilling impressions of battle are delivered as if from a perspective full of curiosity and confusion, the overall tone of narration is cool and somewhat cynical. Both characters and readers are absorbed not in a war narrative but in its loss—the disappearance of what places a picture in a significant frame of reference.

Even more noticeable is the case of "Those Who Cross over the Mountains," a story also describing messengers who journey at the risk of enemy gunfire. Apparently owing to the sensitive subject it describes, Shen Congwen deletes from his text all realist data such as time, place, names, content of campaigns, etc., using "X's" instead. These marks, together with the extensive use of ellipses, constitute a graphic sign in the text, erasing and revealing at the same time what cannot be seen or read. While such a conspicuous display of omission may be taken as a method to get around political censorship, it is just as likely to be Shen Congwen's triumph over conventional war narratives with their defensive armory of quantitative fact.

In this story devoid of specific context, the center of consciousness is a middle-aged soldier, who is sent to hide in a mountain cave as a mediator for messengers. For nine days, he has waited, meeting young soldiers, exchanging messages and chit-chatting with them, offering them food, and even seeing some of them get killed before or after their mission is complete. Left alone in the damp, muddy cave, waiting for good and bad news, the middle-aged soldier seems isolated from the war of which he is a part. At seeing yet another, recently met, young messenger shot dead on a hill, the middle-aged soldier is drawn into his own recollections of the war he has been fighting:

> X X X X X, X X X X X.
> ... besiege, night ambush, public rallies in the five thousands, crude executions, meetings on food rations, the crackdown of the X X division, besiege again, night ambush ... big knives, crazy throwing grenades filled with T.N.T, pistols, manual machine-guns, shoot like crazy, pa ... one down, pu ... a mound of soil shoots up, an arm, a piece of flesh hung on the wall. Rally again, food distribution again ... and Order No. 71 issued by the Transportation Committee, Xiong Xi to be appointed X X of the 9th Liaison Center of the 7th District, find out his mission by going to X X X X first.
> X X X X, X X X X X, X X X, X X X, X X X X X X, X X X X X X![47]

In this passage of narrated interior monologue, each image pops up with a suddenness whose intensity is unmediated by a context capable of either subduing or containing it. Not only do the individual chance impressions fail to modify one another, the phrases and sentences in which they appear also clash and collapse into the ambiguity of cross marks and ellipses. Instead of settling into a narrative in which a figure is clearly contextualized upon a stable ground and in which a coherent picture can arise, these bare impressions flash out as if in defiance of an unspoken order to move into focus.

The dismissal of a coherent perspective, of course, functions as a new kind of perspective. From the examples we have discussed, we find a voice that emphatically makes audible Shen Congwen's muted political comment, a sensed alienation from the scene he describes, faded adolescent adventures, and a rather idiosyncratic entry into the margins of war and history. Moreover, when carefully listened to, this voice fabricates a reality able to invest a past with a naturalist sense of immediacy, but an immediacy carrying with itself an irony that questions any realist effort to resurrect the past from the realm of irretrievable "pastness." History, after all, utters its voice through Shen Congwen's lyrical narrative, only in a rather inflected tone.

With this in mind, we can then understand better the sense of gratuitousness and condescending forgiveness in Shen's relatively light-hearted treatment of soldiers' life in wartime, such as "Captain," in which a captain falls helplessly in love with a widow in a town where he is temporarily stationed, so much so that he does away with the scheduled plan of moving his troops to the next military point; and "Huiming" (Huiming, 1929) in which the naive, tenderhearted army cook Huiming finds a new meaning of life in raising chickens, waiting for a real battle which never comes. Both stories domesticate the war by resorting to romantic or pastoral motifs. By displacing the war into something incompatible, these stories offer a paradoxical *raison d'être* for the war.

Eros, Thanatos, and Their Poetic Manifestations

Shen Congwen once commented, "readers may appreciate the vividness of my writing, but they often neglect the passion hidden beneath it; they may appreciate the naturalness of my language, but they neglect the pathos beneath it."[48] Muffled cries of passion and pathos can indeed be heard beneath the formal reticence of his narrative, especially in the case of his romantic stories. As a nonconformist celebrating liberation from ethical bondage, a regionalist calling for the return to Nature, and a Freudian explorer of human psychology,[49] Shen Congwen cherishes the power of love and sexuality, which symbolize a healthy and beautiful form of life, as opposed to social mores. But Shen Congwen is neither a naive Rousseauist nor a fanatic pansexualist. He knows only too well that violence is a condition of vitality, and that Eros revels only in the shadows cast by Thanatos.

Shen Congwen's portraiture of love and passion always implies a tendentious wish for transgression, a wish that drives his characters not only to go beyond the limits of ordinary ethical assumptions but also sometimes turn against themselves. In his best romantic stories, Eros often manifests itself in a childlike naiveté, while conceiving a subliminal force connected with irrationality and violence. At its extreme, this defiant side of passion amounts to the threatening power of (self)destruction and death. Shen Congwen's legendary accounts of the Miao tribes such as Long Zhu (Long Zhu, 1929) and "Shenwu zhi ai" (A shaman's love, 1929), cannot be fully appreciated until connected with his gruesome stories about love-suicide ("Meijin, Baozi, yu nayang" [Meijin, Baozi, and the white kid, 1929]) and bloody massacre ("Qige yeren yu zuihou yige yingchunjie" [Seven savages and the last spring festival, 1929]). The romantic accounts of prostitutes and boatmen (as illustrated by "Baizi" [Baizi, 1928] and "Zhangfu" [Husband, 1930]) must be juxtaposed with descriptions of their disease and accidental death ("Xiaozhai" [Xiaozhai, 1937, *The Border Town*); and idyllic portraits of adolescent affairs are unfailingly marked by forced separation and violence ("Guisheng" [Guisheng, 1937], "Qiaoxiu yu Dongsheng" [Qiaoxiu and Dongsheng, 1947]), death ("Sansan" [Sansan, 1931]), or madness ("A Hei xiaoshi" [The story of A Hei, 1933]).

Shen Congwen's dialectic of love and death, the desire to live and reproduce and the desire to die, is most emphatically indicated by his Miao tribal romances. Take his blatantly romantic stories, "Long Zhu" and "The Shaman's Love," as well as the unfinished novella *Fengzi* (Fengzi, 1933). In these works, Shen Congwen deals with the genuine love between a young man and woman as a grace of deities, an apocalyptic encounter with the divine in person. Both "Long Zhu" and "The Shaman's Love" introduce Miao girls who consummate their desire by coupling with representatives of gods—Long Zhu the most handsome man of the tribe, or the Shaman. At the climax of "The Shaman's Love," the Shaman finds that, of all the girls the most appealing one is a mute, thus bespeaking Shen Congwen's idea that the power of true passion is beyond words. The unfinished novella *Fengzi* features an urban youth's search for love in the barbarous region of West Hunan, and culminates in a religious celebration where primitive desires are stylistically expressed in singing, dancing, and ritualistic formalities.

The other sides of these stories are seen in a work such as "Fenghuang," the penultimate chapter of Shen's travelogue *West Hunan*. In "Fenghuang," Shen Congwen singles out a kind of romantic ecstasy with symptoms of possession that cause madness, voodooism, and mysterious death. The account is gothic in flavor, contrasting sharply to the pastoral simplicity characteristic of stories like "Long Zhu" or "The Shaman's Love." Immersed in a demonic atmosphere of superstition and macabre fantasy, Fenghuang, nevertheless, serves as the frontier of Shen Congwen's landscape of desire, where the primordial conflict of Eros and Thanatos is enacted. It is the territory where love-ridden woman can speak her ecstasy in a trance, uttering what is forbidden by the discourse of the decent and rational. This also characterizes Shen Congwen's interest in cases of madness. When Shen Congwen writes about Wuming's loss of his mind after A Hei is forced to marry somebody else, in "The Story of A Hei", about Guisheng's burning down the house of the master who stole away his beloved Jinfeng, in "Guisheng," or about the young tofu proprietor's necrophilic love on the stone bed strewn with chrysanthemums, in "Three Men and One Woman," he sees in these transgressions an impossible desire to own what is denied by reality or by realist writing, to reunite a world that has been partitioned into these signifiers. Pathos arises, not just as a result of Shen Congwen's compassionate look at the repressed expressions of human desire but also as a result of his lyrical contemplation of the fate of yearning as inscribed in realistic discourse.

While more about "Fenghuang" will be said in the next chapter, what concerns me here is the latent parallel between the two kinds of romantic works. For Shen Congwen, a description of passion or possession may be regarded as unrealistic, but they constitute "still a reality that transcends common limits."[50] Whether it is expressed in the form of pure eroticism or of bodily sensuality, the power of Eros intensifies to the point where the temptation of Thanatos, the total denial of being, looms large. The forces at work in the dark realm of the unconscious can be simulated only through the similarly symbolic process of poetic language. Beyond tears and pain, one finds in scenes of madness, death, and suicide an evocative call for poetic appreciation. Lyrical rhetoric is inaugurated to depict this divine/demonic experience. Lyricism is seen as a mode that attempts to capture, to possess and be possessed by, what otherwise is severed by a realist presentation of the world.

Fine examples can be found in the love-suicide episodes in "Meijin, Baozi, and the White Kid" and *The Border Town*. Rationalizations based on social or ethical canons are given to these suicides. In the first case, Meijin kills herself out of pride and indignation when her lover Baozi fails to appear at their rendezvous, not knowing that he is late because he wants to bring her the best possible sheep as a gift. Similarly, Cuicui's parents commit suicide for the sake of honor and love. But judged by the highly stylized manner in which both pair of lovers commit suicide as if confronting a predestinated fate, one suspects that, beyond any rationalization, there lurks in the death scenes something else that resists any ethical explanation. Both cases suggest that the basis of passion is the negation of the self in the embrace of the beloved.

The ambiguous link between Eros and Thanatos is further illustrated by "Lüdian" (The inn, 1929), in which the love between a widowed proprietress of an inn and a travelling merchant is consummated with the merchant's sudden death, while the widow finds herself already pregnant; and by "Shuo gushi ren de gushi" (The tale of a storyteller, 1929), in which the narrator's fellow-soldier friend is so enticed by a pretty woman robber under arrest that he not only has sex with her right in the jail but also plans to run away with her—only at the cost of both their lives. The other version of "The Tale of A Storyteller" appears in *Autobiography of Congwen,* as "Dawang" (A bandit king); the title refers to this daring soldier's original identity. In these stories, love or desire is seen as governed by both childlike innocence and sensual intoxication, whose purity can only be made known through the cruel atonement of violence and death. One loses oneself in something other than oneself in order to gain access to the desired object.

Coherent narrative cannot account for the mystical agenda in this experience; one may approximate it, nevertheless, either through the contrived detour of poetry or, paradoxically, though the statement of one's scattered impressions. Shen Congwen's deceptively clear and noncommittal style can thus be understood as a lyrical strategy with which to utter the unspeakable. But evidence shows that from time to time he refuses to essentialize his stories into pure romance. Irony is apparent whenever his narrative indicates an awareness of its referential context. As the young narrator in "The Tale of A Storyteller" says, at the sight of the pretty girl robber, "I could not say anything I wanted to say, but *put on* an honest smile for her, and in the meantime, I gave her my sympathetic look, *showing* that I was on her side" (my italics).[51]

Even in descriptions of the social and communal persecutions of men or women who have sexually transgressed, Shen Congwen's pathos stems not so much from humanitarian indignation as from a deep knowledge of the libidinous forces working behind one's own and society's rational face. In "Fufu" (The Lovers, 1929), for example, a man and woman are caught making love in a field of the countryside where the I-narrator, an urban intellectual, is taking a vacation. Angry country folk tie up the couple and are about to punish them. Their indignation, however, is mitigated when the I-narrator intervenes and finds out that the man and woman are actually a married couple. What was deemed as licence is immediately turned into a much smaller case of indecency. Though a marginal figure, the I-narrator actually plays the *deux ex machina* of the story, deriving his authority from his social and intellectual status. The paradox is, despite the narrator's sympathy for the couple's immense passion, he can only justify their sexual deed in terms of the ethical mores he means to denounce.

It is with this recognition of the pathos and irony involved in the expression of passion that we can now see Shen Congwen's relatively warm-hearted romantic stories more clearly. These stories have been his most popular; one of the most acclaimed short stories, "Baizi," will serve as example. Dealing with a sailor's short visit to the familiar prostitute on a rainy night, the story is almost plotless. What we see are fragments of scenes such as flirtatious talk, bodily contact, and bawdy jokes and songs between two rustic West Hunanese. Shen Congwen pieces together these fragments in such a way as to work out a vivacious and touching one-night romance. The story can be characterized as lyrical because it captures in a trivial moment of life a brief but intense expression of happy or sad feelings. It also integrates seemingly irrelevant sensuous experiences—a hug, a wink, wet footprints in the glare of big red lanterns, a lullaby a boatwoman hums while feeding her baby—into a unified picture of nightlife in a harbor town. Moreover, it features two unforgettable figures whose naiveté and life force seem to have transcended all moral qualms. The implied author conceals his subjectivity within an anonymous, all-embracing narrator's voice, thus twice intensifying the emotional charge throughout the narrative.

Sketchy as it may be, a reading like this is at least illustrative of the kind of lyricism readers expect (or even are expected) to find in "Baizi." But if the story's lyrical discourse celebrated only a simple life as yet undisturbed by civilization, or the good-hearted, childlike nature of country folk, it would mean no more than the boatwoman's cradlesong at the end of story that lulls readers into a state of forgetfulness and complacency. I would suggest that Shen Congwen's lyrical narrative disturbs just as much as it mesmerizes the reader. This does not have to mean that Shen writes to convey tongue-in-cheek social criticism. It is just too easy to argue that neither the sailor nor the prostitute could be so happy in reality, or that Shen attempts to question the moral domain of modern society by describing the unlikely happiness of lower-class people.

One way to explain the complexity of the story is to distinguish the idea of *nature,* which people usually take for granted when reading Shen's lyrical narratives, from *naturalization,* which represents his rhetorical and conceptual strategy in depicting the real. Whereas "nature" refers to an unpolluted ideal origin, "naturalization" indicates a process of removing things and ideas from historical contingencies and fitting them into a cultural/ideological pattern as if they had always been there. Instead of seeing the two poles as unjoinable entities, Shen Congwen suggests that all the oppositions implied therein are already removed from a simple origin and implicated in its doubling. In the case of "Baizi," the romance between the sailor and the prostitute can be accepted as such only when it is refracted through the lens of lyricism under an *as if* condition. When the endeavor of naturalization appears in the guise of the natural, or when nature is revealed merely as the premise of ongoing historical consciousness, Shen's lyrical discourse is on the brink of exhausting its binding forms and turning itself into irony.

Let us take another look at "Baizi." Shen Congwen's penchant for innocent human relations and earthy mannerisms is well illustrated by the story. But these elements do not constitute the lyricism of the story. What has been erased from the surface of the text operates just as vigorously in bringing forth the intended poetic effect. It requires a master to leave a few traces as reminders of that erasure, foregrounding, paradoxically indeed, the literal inscription of naturalness in narrative. Whereas Baizi pays a high price (a whole month's salary) to venture into the prostitute's arms—the land of forgetfulness—Shen Congwen writes "casually," from the outset, in order to register on his hero's behalf what he has chosen to forget: the natural dangers on the river, hardships at work, meager wages, etc.

The blessed moment of lyricism arises not solely from the consummation of Baizi's passion for his lover, but from the hiatus between what the narrator selectively remembers and what his hero has chosen to leave behind. Our delight or pathos in reading the story stems partly from our awareness, not ignorance, of what the hero and heroine have come to be, and how they manage to deflect a self-awareness of what that reality is. Neither Baizi nor the prostitute, nor Shen Congwen, therefore, can be seen simply as engaged in a totally carefree mood. Instead of reciprocal spontaneity, one finds in his lyrical discourse a complicity shared between characters, and between characters and narrator.

Shen Congwen's strategy of lyrical wish-fulfillment is more subtly indicated in "Husband," a story about an embarrassing visit a prostitute's husband pays to his wife's workplace. In his characteristic iterative voice, Shen Congwen describes in the first part of the story how, for economic reasons, young husbands in a place named Huangzhuang usually allow their wives to leave home and do "business" along the harbor area. Husbands may visit their wives occasionally, only to find that their women have adopted decadent manners on their way to eternal downfall. Given this foreknowledge of the pathetic fate shared by most of the young couples he is describing, Shen Congwen sets about rewriting the fate of one of them. The nameless husband in the second part of the story visits his wife on a boat, hoping to spend one night with her. Despite the few intimate moments he shares with his wife in the midst of her business activities, his hope is continuously disturbed by her busy schedule, her customers' untimely visits, and his own thwarted pride.

Critics have tended to see this story as Shen Congwen's effort to reveal the moral corruption and inertia of rural people in a modern era.[52] Accordingly, both the husband and wife in the story are seen as hopelessly weak-minded and unable to care for themselves. This reading ignores Shen Congwen's unique concept of love, making the story simply a morality play. It is not Shen Congwen's purpose to condemn the local custom or the husband's and wife's vanity. He may intend to criticize sexual transactions, but it is the ambiguity of the ethical codes applied to them that concerns him the most. The husband does not feel entirely frustrated that his wife is a prostitute; he "is well aware of the benefits of this business, he understands the woman still belongs to him, her children will belong to him, and part of her income will belong to him, too."[53] What bothers him is the sense of estrangement and disorientation any countryman might feel in a foreign place, a sense only intensified by his wife's preoccupation with her job. Sex, as it is treated by Shen Congwen, is both the primary sign pointing to the private domain of social life and, paradoxically, the last factor censored by the characters' conscience. This explains the characters' and their narrator's apparent tolerance of the sexual activities throughout the story as well as the lyrical ambiguity arising therein.

Shen Congwen takes a sympathetically ironic attitude in narrating how the husband is so bored by his lonely stay that he pours out his mind to his wife's "godfather," a local figure who protects the prostitutes in exchange for their bodies; how the husband and wife forget their awkward relation for a short moment by playing the new Chinese fiddle she had bought him and singing with the others on the boat; and, of course, how they easily reach a reconciliation and leave town the second morning. In these episodes, Shen Congwen tries to assert the fantastic possibilities in the pathetic moments of the human condition, not because he is a naive humanitarian daydreamer but because he believes in the immense capacity of human desires to gratify themselves in real or putative terms, despite any predetermined fate. For this reason one can appreciate scenes such as the husband developing a feeling of brotherhood with his wife's "godfather"; he and his wife unwittingly assuming the roles of patron and performer when they play the Chinese fiddle; and their running away from "home" like a romantic hero and heroine. Individual desires and ethical qualms are reconciled in these moments—as they frequently are in reality—and give rise to passages best demonstrating Shen Congwen's lyrical imagination. Refusing to patronize the underprivileged with the sympathetic eye of hard-core realism, Shen Congwen restores to his characters such games and dreams, however humble and indecent, as they would have had in reality. In so doing, he has implicitly expanded the horizon of human reality into areas that his opponents want to exclude for ideological reasons.

I will conclude my discussion of Shen Congwen's approach to romantic subjects by a comparative reading of the popular story "Xiaoxiao" (Xiaoxiao, 1930) and the relatively less well known trilogy of short stories entitled *Jieyu cangao* (Fragments of a manuscript surviving the holocaust, 1947, hereafter referred to as Fragments), a cycle about a mother and her daughter who both transgress the law of marriage, at the cost not only of their own lives or welfare but also of the lives and fortunes of the community. Whereas Shen Congwen is determined to make Xiaoxiao's story a pastoral triumph over actual hypocrisy and prudery, he invests the trilogy of *Fragments* with just as much poetic ethos, this time, however, presenting a story about a hysterical desire for love and death so strong that it would overwhelm lighthearted readers. Both works refuse to subordinate the subject of passion to the rhetoric of hard-core realism, and because of the opposite romantic visions they project, they best demonstrate the two sides of Shen Congwen's dialectic of *desire* and *transgression* in lyrical form.

In "Xiaoxiao," the farm girl Xiaoxiao is found pregnant before she is formally married to the husband who is nine years younger than she. According to local rules, an adulterous woman like her should either be sold to somebody else or drowned. But nobody in the family seems really eager to carry out these rules; since Xiaoxiao gives birth to a baby boy, she is more than welcome to stay, and she eventually marries her young husband. The surprise turn of the story hinges on Shen Congwen's conviction that the moral codes of a community should not be predicated on preestablished grounds but should evolve as a result of the harmonious association of things in their phenomenal state. The life force embodied by Xiaoxiao makes her an earth mother figure toward the end of the story, when she holds her new "legitimate" baby and supervises the wedding of her "illegitimate" son with a girl much older than he is.

In a matter-of-fact style, Shen Congwen relates the whole event as if it were happening the way it ought. His narrative fascinates by its apparently innocent attitude toward life. Xiaoxiao's husband is only three years old when he gets married, and the couple grow up together like sister and brother. They see the world from a child's viewpoint because they are children. Even after Xiaoxiao enters puberty and is impregnated by Spotty Dog, she and her husband cover up the crisis as if they did only something naughty. Shen Congwen indulges Xiaoxiao, unwilling to see her suffer for what she does; this indulgent attitude expands in his narrative, to the point that even the villagers are described like a group of children, who are reluctant to face up to the moral consequences of "adult" institutions. One senses a strong irony here, of course, given Shen Congwen's indication of what might happen to Xiaoxiao under normal conditions. But the reader is willingly invited by Shen Congwen to see how "fantastic" (rather than disastrous) a result an adultery can lead to. Between ideal pastoral romance and dismal accounts of reality, the world Xiaoxiao and her villagers live in is one in which the laws of society exist, only to be observed and interpreted by its inhabitants with an infantile imaginativeness.

The crucial image bringing out Xiaoxiao's desire is that of the "coed," as conceived by her grandfather-in-law one summer night. To the old man, coeds are strange creatures: "they wore clothes without regard to the weather; they ate whether they were hungry or full; they didn't go to sleep until late at night; during the day they worked at nothing at all, but sang and played ball or read books from abroad."[54] More unthinkable are the "facts" that "boys and girls go to class together, and when they get acquainted, the girls sleep overnight with the boys, with no thought of a go-between or a matchmaker, or even a dowry. This is what they call being 'free.'"[55] The grandfather's talk about the coeds may well be erroneous and silly, but to an attentive audience like Xiaoxiao, they sound like an incantation that initiates her into an occult knowledge of being free. The old man's crude babble is turned into a poetic chant, manifesting its own special figurative pattern. It is to this process of transformation that Shen Congwen would call the reader's attention. The grandfather's way of seeing and narrating a world with which he is not totally familiar soon develops into the basic tonality of the whole story. Shen Congwen usurps the grandfather's voice and narrates the whole story in a wishful manner after the old man's style. Not unlike Xiaoxiao, the reader is the willing audience of Shen Congwen's fantastic story about a country girl's initiation into the realm of desire upon hearing her grandfather-in-law's story.

As mentioned above, the innocence and simplicity in "Xiaoxiao" must be regarded as a rhetorical gesture of Shen Congwen's lyrical discourse, strongly demanding an audience committed to the rule of encoding and decoding with poetic sophistication. Behind his childlike narrative, Shen Congwen knows only too well the pain and horror any free-play of childish instinct can bring. As if subverting the complacent neatness of "Xiaoxiao," Shen Congwen tells in "Qiaoxiu and Dongsheng," part two of *Fragments,* another girl's adventure, one that costs hundreds of deaths. In the story, Qiaoxiu falls in love with a horn player from a neighboring village, despite her engagement to another man. Qiaoxiu's history is not a simple one; her mother committed adultery many years earlier and was stripped naked and drowned by the community leader, leaving Qiaoxiu to grow up an orphan. What Shen Congwen wants to convey is not so much the sadistic persecution of women in a male-centered ethical world, as the power of passion that rejuvenates itself generation after generation in spite of social and ethical repression. And it is in describing young men and women who fervently meet their fate, for all their sufferings, that Shen Congwen sees a domain of humanity beyond the reach of ordinary realistic discourse.

The deepest threat in "Xiaoxiao," the old punishment of drowning an adulterous woman, is the climax of the story. The scene where Qiaoxiu's mother is stripped of all her clothes and tied to a big rock for drowning conveys a seductive beauty amidst its horror, not only because she shows a tragic calmness in the face of humiliation and punishment, but also because her exploiters share with her the secret yearning for violence and destruction through the sadistic ritual penalty. On hearing the story, the narrator relates,

> In fancy I saw myself sitting at one end of that little boat as it was rowed to Long Lake, saw the woman pitched overboard, after which the boat turned back. . . . Then everything calmed down, and that was the end of it all. Nothing is really enduring. The one thing that will last for ever is the tender peaceful twilight and the reflection of clouds and stars in the water stirred up by two oars seen by the bright, mild, all-forgiving eyes of the twenty-three-old widow who so loved life, yet who was robbed of her love by society. Half a month had passed since Qiaoxiu's flight, sixteen years since her mother sank, a millstone round her neck, into Long Lake.[56]

Qiaoxiu's romance results in a disastrous war between two villages and costs hundreds of lives. Insofar as her romance invites violence and death, and her baby is born after the death of her lover, Qiaoxiu shares with her mother a fate prefigured in a mythical cycle. This mythical cycle, nevertheless, has be to be recognized as the same one of which Xiaoxiao is a part. Reproduction and death condition the immortal renewal of life. As the ending of "Qiaoxiu and Dongsheng" puts it, "but nothing had ended, this was only a start."[57] It is this immense mystery of human desire to love and die, desire to transgress and defy, that leads Shen Congwen to ponder in his romantic works how little we have known of passion and pathos in terms of rationality; and it is only by means of thematic and stylistic transgression, that he can bring us a glimpse of that mysterious world. Lyrical discourse is not only a rhetorician's critique of an ailing society; it is not just an extension of narrative frontlines across the borders of poetry. Lyrical discourse is a tropological move that fills in those human territories still mapped as *terra incognita* on the charts of realism and rationality.

Chapter seven

Imaginary Nostalgia: Shen Congwen and Native Soil Fiction

Because of the numerous fictional and nonfictional accounts of his home region of West Hunan, Shen Congwen has long been regarded as one of the most important native soil writers in modern Chinese fiction. Although Shen also wrote a considerable number of works on city life, it was the travelogues, biographical sketches, and stories about the manners and morals, legends and figures, of West Hunan that caught the heart of thousands of readers. Yet Shen Congwen is neither a romantic, yearning for a lost paradise, nor a utopian, allegorizing the lacks of the given political condition. Romantic and utopian elements play an important part in Shen Congwen's writing, but he has a much more intricate vision of a homeland in mind. The homeland he reconstructs must not be regarded merely as a geographical wonderland but also a topographical locus, a textual coordinate that demands multiple readings that lay out its contours.

At the center of Shen Congwen's discourse of his home is the conflicting image that it projects into history. West Hunan is an area historically best known for its mountainous land, tribal riots, voodoo customs, banditry and poverty—a barbarous country to people living in the "Middle Kingdom." But West Hunan also provides the landscape that allegedly inspired two great masterpieces of classical Chinese literature: Qu Yuan's *Songs of the South* and Tao Qian's "Taohuayuan ji" (Peach blossom spring).[1] Whereas *Songs of the South* represents both an intricate political allegory and a literary recapitulation of the cultural/mythical heritage of the marginal South, as opposed to the tradition emblemized in *Shijing* (The book of poetry), "Peach Blossom Spring" has been lauded as one of the most prominent sources of Chinese utopian imagination. Both works are politically and historically motivated, but beyond the level of immediate exegesis, they evoke a forgotten past and the ignored culture of the other, the disappearing homeland that enchants and tantalizes.

Shen Congwen is quite conscious that he is writing within the tradition of *Songs of the South* and "Peach Blossom Spring."[2] But he writes about his homeland with a dialogical intention. A native of West Hunan, he knows only too well that his homeland is not as immaculate as it is depicted in those ancient works; wars, riots, ignorance, and poverty are the reality that has existed all along. As the latest practitioner of the great *Songs of the South* and "Peach Blossom Spring" tradition, he knows that his impressions and inscriptions of his homeland, for good or for ill, cannot do away with the impact of Qu Yuan and Tao Qian. His nostalgia for West Hunan stems not only from a personal attachment to his birthplace but also from an imaginative tie to the literary place. From these two ties, Shen Congwen develops a unique interpretation of the past and of his native soil. At a time when most Chinese writers write about wars, famines, and social injustice, Shen Congwen proceeds to create an idyllic country of his own, as exemplified in a novel such as *The Border Town*. But Shen's textual utopia reveals its imaginary quality, because it is encased in a menacing reality that is anything but utopian, and because, after all, it is only a reinscription of the ancient desire for Home and Origin.

Beneath Shen Congwen's seemingly soft, smooth writing about West Hunan, one therefore finds a radical melancholy. He writes to project a view of Chinese reality and of writing about reality, but he is aware that any attempt has invoked self-irony. If there is an ideal West Hunan that has fallen into the present and the real, reconstituting it yields to an aesthetic of residuality and incompleteness: his homeland tour, actual or textual, must betray its imaginary roots. Nostalgia refers not so much to a representational effort to enliven the irretrievable past as to a creation of an imaginary past on behalf of the present. In this chapter I will try to propose a reading of Shen Congwen's native soil fiction in terms of this poetics of *imaginary nostalgia*. I may raise more questions than I can answer, but I hope that my discussion will open up perspectives on Shen Congwen's fictive native land.

Towards a Poetics of Imaginary Nostalgia

Xiangtu xiaoshuo (native soil fiction) has been one of the most popular genres in modern Chinese fiction. When a genealogy of native soil fiction of the past seven decades is mapped out, Lu Xun (again) must be treated as one of its initiators.[3] Lu Xun wrote many short stories about his home, Shaoxing, making it a literary locus rich in symbolism; he was also one of the earliest critics to attempt to circumscribe the themes and structures of native soil literature. Of the twenty-five stories Lu Xun wrote, at least three, "My Old Home," "The New Year Sacrifice," and "In the Tavern" deal with different facets of his hometown complex. For all their thematic and stylistic differences, these stories spotlight a cluster of motifs and images which will be elaborated by writers in the next seventy years: the passage of time; the clash between old and new values; yearning for the lost days of innocence or childhood; (re)encounters with quaint, backward country figures; observations of customs, anxieties about impending change; and mixed feelings of homesickness and fear of going home—all part of the bittersweet experience called nostalgia.

Lu Xun was also a critical pioneer in using the term "native soil fiction" to describe the kind of short stories written by writers such as Wang Luyan and Xu Qinwen. In these writers' works, Chinese rural life is depicted so as to show the invasion of new political/economic forces into the old agricultural society, and the inevitable breakdown of the ethical/cultural structure that had prescribed human relations in that society. In his introduction to an anthology of modern Chinese fiction, Lu Xun gave his opinions about the burgeoning trend of native soil literature:

> Jian Xian'ai writes about Guizhou, Pei Wenzhong is concerned about Yuguan. Those who stay in Beijing and write down their feelings about [their homelands], either subjectively or objectively, as

they claim, actually are producing native soil literature . . . Although these writers live in a place other than their homeland (qiaoyu), their writings are not about the place they currently live in. Therefore, what emerges is a feeling of nostalgia, rather than an exoticism that might either open up readers' minds or expose them to the writer's experience. . . Before a writer [like Xu Qinwen] sets out to write native soil literature, he finds himself already exiled from his home, driven by life to a strange place. What can he do but recall his father's garden, a garden which does not exist any more? It is more comfortable and self-consoling to recall things at home which do not exist any more than things which still exist yet are inaccessible.[4]

Lu Xun notices a new literary trend that is taking shape in the early twenties and he tries to describe the paradoxical position a native soil writer assumes. Native soil literature, as the term indicates, is nurtured on a writer's deep-rooted concern with his home region, but this concern can be acutely felt only after the author is uprooted from the soil he cherishes so much, and, more ironically, has been denied any possibility of savouring or understanding its actuality. But Lu Xun reveals his attachment to the ontological impulse beneath native soil fiction, an impulse he set out to question, when he contrasts nostalgia with exoticism. Lu Xun holds that nostalgia appears only in writings about a loss of something one is already familiar with, while exoticism indicates an effect coming from perceiving something totally strange or foreign. This contrast is less clear-cut than it sounds; when all questions of imagination and textuality are introduced, there must be a recalculation of the boundaries of nostalgia.

Taking one step beyond Lu Xun's observations, I would like to argue that native soil literature is literally and rhetorically a rootless literature, a kind of literature whose meaning hinges on the simultaneous (re)discovery and erasure of the treasured image of the homeland. Native soil writers come forth to write out what they fail to experience in reality. Their imagination plays just as important a role as their lived experience, and their gesture of remembering is no less important than the things remembered. Insofar as the lost past can only be regained through the act of writing, the form of remembrance may become itself the content of what is to be remembered. It is from here we can explore the verisimilar norms to which native soil literature adheres, and the dialects of realism it speaks. Having no illusion of exhausting these issues, I would like to circumscribe my discussion in certain ways before proceeding to Shen Congwen's work in the mode of regionalism.

To begin with, native soil fiction is characterized by its accounts of rustic figures, provincial customs, peculiar linguistic codes, festive conventions, rituals, and so on, traits constituting the so-called effect of *local color*. Native soil writers may claim that they derive the local color of their works from the objects and moments with which they are or were most familiar, but in rendering these objects and moments they are engaged in a task of defamiliarization, a task that allows them to assume an outsider's viewpoint and see things on a contrastive basis. Not unlike a tour guide who cashes in on his knowledge by emphasizing the qualities of a locale that are exotic to its visitors, a native soil writer takes a double view of the image of his homeland. We may thus reach a different conclusion from Lu Xun's with regard to the nostalgia/exoticism dichotomy. Describing the homeland as a both familiar and foreign place, taking objects seen and experienced as ordinary in their own land and making them strange, writers of native soil fiction entertain a secret alliance with exoticism.

Accordingly, the framing of temporal and spatial schemes in native soil literature is more complicated than we usually think it to be. Dealing with conventional themes such as the contrast between the new and old, the loss of childhood or youth, and the effort to remember things past, native soil writers always have to refer to an inevitable passage of time. Time plays a crucial role in the discourse of native soil literature. Beyond the linear concept of temporality, native soil writers try hard to recapture the lost times by reorienting the order of time. Through the ritual of memory, imagination, or writing, they twist, multiply, and even transform what has happened and what is happening. They tentatively bring together the past and present, defining or undercutting the meaning of one at the expense of the other. They reconstruct the past in terms of the present; and they see in the present a residue of the past. Time is reorganized or "anachronized," so to speak, in native soil literature, in the service of the liberation or repression of writers' and readers' regressive nostalgia.

Just as the idea of anachronism works behind the temporal scheme of native soil fiction, so the idea of displacement can be adopted to describe its spatial scheme. I have referred to Lu Xun's ironic observation that a writer's reminiscences of his native soil presuppose his own dislocation. Actually, displacement does not point merely to a writer's physical dislocation from his homeland; rather it indicates a relocation of his social status and intellectual/emotional capacity. A writer feels homesick not just because of his separation from his homeland but also because of his loss of the aura of the homeland he believes himself to have had. Moreover, in mythological and psychological terms, displacement points to a narrative device or psychic mechanism that makes possible the (re)definition of something either irretrievable or unspeakable, and to the eternally regressive state of such a narrative and psychological quest.[5] Displacement, therefore, implies the condition in which a native soil writer is situated, the method he employs in search of a lost time and place, and the result he obtains in words. As long as the meaning of the lost time and place can be regained only in a mediated, hence displaced and incomplete, form, nostalgia is equatable to the insatiable desire for more narrative and more memory.

The reassessment of the spatial/temporal scheme may lead us to the following two observations. First, as a literary convention, the image of native soil or homeland suggests not so much a geographically verifiable place, which bears exclusive significance to a writer born there or growing up there, as a topographical system of coordinates—a *chronotope,* in Bakhtin terminology[6]—which lends itself to anyone wanting to locate the origins of a text. Sites, like texts, are essential loci of remembrance, bounded spaces in which the complexity of human nature and experience are concentrated. More than just his birthplace, Shen Congwen's West Hunan is a textual locus where his discourse about the homeland has germinated, and through which he transports his social/political ideas. In its textual transcription, West Hunan is as much a homeland for Shen Congwen as it is for his readers, wherever their actual homelands are.

Second, the above argument calls into question the realistic project underlying native soil literature. Native soil writers may start their literary journey with a sense of clear perspectives: overcoming the power of time by recalling figures, events, and values from the realm of oblivion, and making sense of the present by resorting to an original meaning which is identifiable with the vision of the homeland or native soil. What is at stake here is a firm belief in the trans-temporal and trans-spatial power of literary representation. Both literally and symbolically, this quest is doomed to end with the recognition of gaps between the words and the world, between memory and desire, between history and originary being.

Native soil literature does not simply present stories of the vain seeking of lost childhoods or inaccessible homelands. The genre itself enacts the split of representation and the incongruity of what realist literature proposes to do and what it can do. While the homeland in reality never looks as it did in memory, especially as a native soil writer would have it remembered, a realist text always takes the risk of betraying the arguable reality it once set out to recover.

Instead of nostalgia, therefore, it is more interesting to posit *imaginary nostalgia* as the fundamental theme of native soil literature. Imaginary, in the sense that nostalgia is something that comes not as the effect but as the absent cause of native soil literature, and that nostalgia is as much a spontaneous overflow of personal feeling as a convention of writing overdetermined by literary and non-literary factors. Insofar as the real native soil and homeland can only be recapitulated in the form of continuous regression, native soil literature always appears as a belated form of writing, nurtured ironically on the imagination of loss that calls itself nostalgia. In this, I do not deny the individual experiences each native soil writer might have undergone. But I would question the psychological and ideological mandate by which we might have equated the whereabouts of native soil and homeland with the origin of time, history, and writing. Imaginary nostalgia, therefore, questions the ontological assumption often associated with the concept of nostalgia, and refers us to the intra- and intertextual dynamic that configures the yearning for home.

Random Sketches on A Trip to Hunan and *West Hunan*

In 1917, Shen Congwen moved with his family out of their native region of Fenghuang. For financial and other reasons, he decided to join the warlord army in August and stepped out into a brave new world. In the next five years, he followed his troops from place to place in the area around Hunan, Szechuan, and Guizhou. His experiences with the army were "unthinkably painful and horrifying"; little did he know that they would provide him with a rich treasure of materials to write about in the future. Shen Congwen arrived Beijing in 1922 and did not return to his home region till 1934. He later made another short return visit in 1937, on the way to southwestern China.⁷ The two homecoming experiences gave Shen Congwen mixed feelings. He was stunned by the haunting beauty of the landscape once so familiar to him, but he was saddened by the obvious incompatibility between the old and new values, an incompatibility manifested by people's life-styles. While local legends and anecdotes still fascinated him, he could not help noticing how the legendary region of Peach Blossom Spring was undergoing a rapid deterioration, due to military, political, economic, and cultural invasions from the outside world.

The results of the two homecoming trips were two novels, *The Border Town* (1934) and *Changhe* (Long river, 1943); two travelogues, *Random Sketches on a Trip to Hunan* (1936) and *Xiangxi* (West Hunan, 1938), and some other short stories and essays. *The Border Town* and *Long River* have long been celebrated as showcases of modern Chinese native soil literature. But any reading of the two novels would be incomplete without a reference to the two travelogues, *Random Sketches on a Trip to Hunan* (hereafter cited as *Random Sketches*) and *West Hunan*. Critics have traditionally treated the two travelogues as writing in a different generic category. But given the fact that Shen Congwen embellishes them with narrative formats ranging from gazetteers, biographical accounts, anecdotes, and legends, to lyrical prose, and that he wrote them in parallel with his fiction, one should pay close attention to the intertextual relation formed between the travelogues and novels. They supplement as much as undercut one another's statements, and make Shen's vision of the native soil genuinely complex.

With an accumulation of data—natural and human scenery, detailed biographical information—and an intention of revealing the true image of West Hunan behind the veil of myth and misunderstanding, *Random Sketches* and *West Hunan* showcase the ideally transparent writing of realism. But close reading reveals that the two works contain a dramatic intertextual play, prolonging and parodying the literary tradition of homecoming within which Shen Congwen is writing. To begin with, *Random Sketches* calls for a reading parallel to Tao Qian's "Peach Blossom Spring," the ultimate Chinese utopian text. Shen Congwen's homecoming trip is subtly counterpointed to the ancient fisherman's explorations along the river leading to Peach Blossom Spring, and his cultural/

geographical (re)discovery is supplemented by a hermeneutic of the literary myth. What results is Shen Congwen's ironic recognition of the disappearance of utopia, in personal nostalgia as in literary nostalgia; he endeavors to discover a new entry to it.

Random Sketches opens with Shen Congwen's reunion with an old friend on his 1934 homecoming trip, a man who always wears a beaver fur hat. This friend enjoys a dubious local reputation, for his scoundrel-like personality, his charm for women, and ironically, his penchant for curios and classical painting. For Shen Congwen, the friend "may as well be called a 'fisherman', because he is wearing a beaver fur hat worth forty-eight dollars, which helps him catch women's attention whenever he goes by."[8] The "Peach Blossom Spring" the friend with a beaver fur hat is "good at" discovering is not amid remote mountains but amid the bodies of women, as the friend's vulgar joke says at the end of the chapter. Travelling with such a friend, a "fisherman" of the 1930's, to famous Taoyuan county, Shen can not but feel amused when thinking of the way "the high school students all over China diligently study Tao Qian's 'Peach Blossom Spring.'"[9]

Shen demythifies the ancient utopian story by vulgarizing the crucial lines of Tao Qian's original. In his eyes, the current Taoyuan is anything but a blessed land. It is a place dominated by opium smugglers, sailors, small warlords, corrupt bureaucrats, and prostitutes. Signs of military threat, power struggle, and social injustice can be seen everywhere. "The local residents have never thought they themselves might be descendants of the previous dynasty or gods; nor have they ever met any descendants of the previous dynasty or gods."[10] The name "Taoyuan" or Peach Blossom Spring rings a bell only to those visiting literati, who come, often with a collection of Tao Qian's works, to pay homage to the alleged grove; they compose cliché-ridden poems, and complete their pilgrimages by spending a night with a prostitute at bargain prices. It's not that Taoyuan is a place which "had never even heard of the Han, let alone its successors the Wei and the Jin."[11] Inscriptions of history can be read everywhere. The sad songs of Qu Yuan, the "frenzied, exiled minister of the Chu"[12]; local riots endlessly followed by massacres; a recent rebellion of five miners against army officers, etc., bear witness to social and political turmoil.

Shen Congwen's mockery actually extends to himself. If his friend with the beaver fur hat is to be identified with the fisherman of "Peach Blossom Spring," to whom is Shen Congwen comparable? The prefect of Wuling County and the hermit Liu Ziji in Tao Qian's original account, both in vain trying to find the entry to the Peach Blossom Spring, immediately come to mind. Yet is Shen really comparable with the prefect or Liu Ziji? One still recalls how "Peach Blossom Spring" ends: "the learned and virtuous hermit Liu Ziji heard the story and went off elated to find the place. But he had no success, and died after a long sickness. Since that time there have been no further seekers of the ford."[13] Shen Congwen must have felt the double edge of his parodies of modern "seekers of the ford," since no matter how ironical an attitude he assumes, he too is making a trip based on the mythical path of the ancient story. His trip is doomed to end with disappointment from the outset, as it has already been inscribed by Tao Qian hundreds of years before.

The irony implied in *Random Sketches* takes on yet another dimension. Shen Congwen's homeland is located in West Hunan, and he was accordingly once a resident of "Peach Blossom Spring." Seventeen years after he left his homeland, he is now making a journey back to where he grew up, only to find that the things he used to appreciate are no longer there. He has become a native son denied the right to reenter the mysterious utopia. "I have come back to the environment of my stories. I am a little enchanted. The surroundings seem very familiar to me, while in fact everything is different and strange."[14] Shen tries hard to draw our attention to the beauty of the landscape, the divine quality hidden in the rustic people. Still, his glorification of the Hunan countryside betrays a certain degree of alienation from the environment to which he is emotionally attached. As Leo Lee has pointed out, Shen Congwen's "immersion in his familiar landscape is not so complete as he may have wished, for after years of absence he has become something of an outsider."[15] He has become a passive onlooker, unable to exert a personal impact on his environment. There are at least half a dozen occasions on which Shen intends to approach his characters, either offering help or articulating protest on their behalves. But, "in silence, I have learned the bitterness of 'life . . . ' I feel their desire and sadness are sacred, and I am not supposed to intervene in their fate with money or anything else, thus disturbing the predestined happiness and sadness in their life."[16]

Instead of recapitulating a full, coherent image of the homeland region as it was or should be, what Shen Congwen best manages to present are but "random sketches," fragments, of what he sees and hears. He can only spot lingering traces of the golden past in one scene or one person he happens to pass by. In the alleged geographical site of Peach Blossom Spring, he therefore launches a new quest, and his chance to re-locate the mythical utopia is no better than that of Tao Qian's fisherman.

Besides the sounds and sights of the rural landscape of West Hunan, Shen Congwen find it most enjoyable to portray people from the lower classes: a young boatman who against all odds is carrying on a love affair with a "married" prostitute; an old soldier friend who dedicates his whole life to a girl Shen Congwen once favored; a "wild child" who failed Shen Congwen's plan of civilizing him in Shanghai and regained his vigor back in his homeland; a seventy-year-old boat-puller with a tough look and spirit that reminds Shen Congwen of Tolstoy; and a coal miner who organized rebellions against local warlord troops and died a heroic death. One can easily sense Shen Congwen's admiration for these characters and his efforts to endorse their virtues. But, by ordinary standards, these people are not habitants of Peach Blossom Spring. To appreciate their "sacred" quality, as Shen would have it, a writer or reader needs a special sensibility to see what one normally does not see, and feel what one normally does not feel. At a time when Peach Blossom Spring is lost, it is the surviving elements of the noble savages, residual remembrances of the golden time, or lingering impressions of the landscape that one must learn to capture and decipher so as to reconstruct things past.

What figures here is an aesthetic of the residue or the fragment, an aesthetic crucial not only to *Random Sketches* but to native soil fiction in general.[17] The fragmentary image serves as a synecdoche, suggesting what the missing whole might have been as well as the impossibility of restoring it. Thus, as he turns to the individual scenes, characters, or moments for an intense reflection of his ideal homeland, Shen Congwen tends to exercise a special kind of connoisseurship that calls for an imaginary configuration of what is to be seen and felt. However trivial they may be, the fragments or traces can be turned into autonomous signs, vindicating not so much the outside world of which they are part as the landscape envisioned by the writer by and for himself. At this point, the fragment becomes nothing more than a prop with which the writer's imagination can occupy center stage.

Imaginary Nostalgia

Nevertheless, although they trigger ruminations about the lost utopia, the random sketches after all remain parts of a whole which can no longer be pieced together. The harder Shen Congwen works to sort out the precious traces of the past from the lump of present affairs, the more strongly he feels the sadness of incompleteness. While each sketch may be interesting or beautiful in its own right, it serves all the more poignantly as an index of absences, absences of the golden time, of innocence, of order, and of the plenitude of meaning. The two tendencies form a paradoxical logic that both evokes and denies the yearning for "Peach Blossom Spring," yet drives home the verisimilar rule that substantiates the discourse of native soil literature.

Going back to my parallel reading of *Random Sketches* and "Peach Blossom Spring," I would therefore suggest that, for all his rhetoric of parody, Shen Congwen prolongs Tao Qian's quest for, through words, the ideal utopia. As yet another dialogical response to "Peach Blossom Spring," *Random Sketches* remains appropriately open at both ends, attached to both the ancient story which is itself a postscript or afterword of what has already happened, and to many more like-minded writings to come. Shen lays bare the historical condition that makes it impossible for Peach Blossom Spring to (re)appear in reality, but, in so doing, he advocates the priority of imagination and writing over actual perception and experience, thus tacitly reconfirming Tao Qian's project of writing down his utopia sixteen hundred years before. What he does best in *Random Sketches*, accordingly, is the inscription of personal sensibilities and impressions in terms of the fragments of a supposedly lost world, and the fantastic substitution of what should be for what is.

Shen Congwen wrote *West Hunan* with a clear purpose in mind: to tell the "truth" about West Hunan, how the local people lived and thought, and what problems they were now faced with. A collection of gazetteer-like essays, the work bears some resemblances to *Random Sketches* in terms of its lack of apparent coherent structure and its inclination to articulate what might be bypassed in the official accounts of the place. But there is a distinct difference between the two works. Whereas *Random Sketches* tells of an implicit drama about the return of a native son and his deploring of the changes in his native region, *West Hunan* sounds more like an adventure story, aimed at unraveling the mystery that haunts both outsiders and

Shen Congwen himself. Despite the fact that *West Hunan* is often read not as a fiction but as a chronicle of the historical and geographical specialities of Shen Congwen's homeland area, one can find in the work a very interesting project concerning the formation of a realist discourse. If *Random Sketches* is written to prolong the quest for the lost Peach Blossom Spring, *West Hunan* represents an attempt to enter the "heart of darkness."

In the prologue of *West Hunan,* Shen Congwen sarcastically lists the general prejudices outsiders might hold about the region. "West Hunan is an area inhabited by Miao tribes and bandits. Women are good at voodoo, and men are bloodthirsty."[18] With its bad road conditions, treacherous landscapes, and barbarous residents, West Hunan is a place suitable only for explorers to seek adventures. But West Hunan is not all lacking in tourist attractions: Taoyuan is the homeland of the legendary "Peach Blossom Spring," where one is supposed to run into the hospitable descendants of the pre-Han dynasty, and, on the other hand, Chenzhou is famous for mercury, voodoo posters, and walking zombies. "If you are lucky, you might even see with your own eyes zombies walking in the midst of cars on the highway, as ignorant of traffic safety as local residents!"[19] In conclusion, "West Hunan is an area poor in both soil and culture; its people are savage and stupid."[20]

Shen Congwen vows to argue in the rest of the book that these impressions are wrong; that they are accounts based on traditional misunderstanding and ignorance. To prove his points, he will serve as our guide, taking us into the mysterious region and interpreting all its "bizarre" manners and morals from a rational perspective. Our trip starts with Changde, the big port city on the Yuan River and the gateway leading to the vast area of West Hunan, then follows the river upward and enters such branch rivers as the You River and the Chen River. Along the river(s), we are to stop by harbor towns and villages, learn their geographical locations and products, and review their past through literary and historical references; we will also come to know the local people, their customs, and even their gossip. Above all, we ought to share with Shen Congwen an admiration for the natural beauty of West Hunan and a deep concern about its rapid degradation resulting from civil wars, riots, and the threats of modern civilization.

The rhetorical strategy Shen Congwen employs here is the old realist device of "laying bare." Shen Congwen succeeds in creating a sense of accuracy and immediacy by providing us with an excess of information. Names, dates, historical events, anecdotes, personal comments, are poured out without any obvious link with each other. They are not meant to make any specific point but just to exist and state in a mute way that they are there—one of the most powerful ways to achieve the effect of the real. By just taking a quick look at the titles of some chapters, like "Changde de chuan" (The boats of Changde), "Chenxi de mei" (The coal mines of Chenxi), "Yuanling de ren" (The people of Yuanling), and "Baihe liuyu jige matou" (Harbors on the Bai River), we can already know that Shen means to deal with everything as it is. No longer is he the lonely traveller of *Random Sketches,* returning home after an absence of eighteen years and anxiously looking for the traces of the lost golden days. However strong his feeling for West Hunan, Shen is now taking the narrative viewpoint of an earnest tour guide, a sympathetic outsider.

Unlike his attitude in *Random Sketches,* Shen Congwen shows a strong restraint in *West Hunan* about dramatizing scenes, figures and anecdotes from a personal perspective. Take, for example, two stories in "The People of Yuanling." In one story, a girl is abducted by the head of a group of armed soldiers. Afraid of being killed by the head of the band, and impressed by his handsome looks and gentle manners, she agrees to marry him. The marriage turns out to be a perfect match for both the girl and her family. In its happy ending, the only person left to suffer is the girl's fiancé, a mediocre apprentice tailor. In another story, a pretty widow falls in love with a pious young monk. Her love never gets a response, though for twenty years she visits him at his steep mountain temple. As the widow's son grows up, he detects his mother's secret. But instead of taking issue with her, he hires workers to build a safe shortcut for his mother, and then leaves home forever. In spite of their melodramatic potentials, Shen Congwen does not make his stories into sensational romances, they are rendered no more obtrusively than other sketches of local figures, and qualified with only a mild ironic reflection on the complex motives and peculiar moral codes experienced by people of a different region such as West Hunan. Neither too involved in, nor too detached from his subjects, he carefully modulates his middle distance, and thus makes his stories quaint yet still intelligible to his readers. Together with the boats, the coal mines, the ancient historical sites, the colorful foliage and vegetation of

West Hunan, these characters contribute to Shen Congwen's local color style.

But by describing the discourse of *West Hunan* as realist, one can only "assume" that Shen Congwen has provided a transparent look at the mysterious area. In his effort to make his homeland region more accessible and therefore more real to outsiders, one might ask, has not Shen Congwen imposed a new set of values and verisimilar laws on his subjects? In the name of conveying a sensible report of the real West Hunan, has he not also explained away many things whose "real" mystic charm he sets out to protect? Can he avoid any temptation to plot by claiming to describe rather than narrate what he sees and knows? Is not his narrative itself already a violation of the ban on the unspeakable? By these questions, I do not mean to deny the valuable pictures of West Hunan that Shen Congwen brings before our eyes, nor do I mean that he fails to do justice to his homeland region. At stake is the textual dilemma any writer of realism will have to face. I suggest that because Shen Congwen does not always solve the problems mentioned above, he makes his sketches all the more fascinating.

To complicate this matter a little more, one should pay attention to a very interesting phenomenon in the narrative stream of *West Hunan*. As many as seven times, Shen Congwen describes a place by quoting passages at considerable length from his other works. He refers to *The Border Town* twice in introducing the Bai River and towns along it.[21] Half of the space of the chapter "Luxi, Pushi, Xiangziyan" (Luxi, Pushi, Xiangziyan) is filled in by passages from *Random Sketches*,[22] and the chapters "The Coal Mines of Chenxi" and "Fenghuang" begin respectively with long quotations from *Random Sketches* and the novella *Fengzi*.[23]

We are in no position to guess why Shen Congwen used quotations so often, but the fact leads us to ponder the validity of the truth claims underlying *West Hunan*. As he refers to what he has already said, he serves as his own source, thus betraying the tautological circle of his realist project. Even though he aspires to impartial interpretation and just remembrance, he ascribes his own impressions and concerns to his subjects. Considering that both *Fengzi* and *The Border Town* are fiction in the vein of idyllic romance, by quoting from them, Shen Congwen must beg the question of how a narrative once written for fiction can now serve to illustrate a "real" scene. When history and story, facts and remembrances of facts,

Imaginary Nostalgia

"real" and "fictive" statements merge in *West Hunan,* what is finally written is an intertextual fabric that is indeterminately fictive and real.

Just like the numerous historical sites, ruins, remnants, and scenic spots referred to in his narrative, Shen Congwen's self-quotations demand a "place," a space, on his literary tour in West Hunan. When we pay our visit to the pre-historical woodchests left in the caves on the Yuan river; to the old shrine in honor of the general Ma Yuan of the Eastern Han dynasty; to the Ming dynasty statue of Buddha destroyed by the local people of Fenghuang in the name of reform; to the deserted mansion of a warlord whose assassination brought to an end his life as landowner, gentleman, bandit king, and plutocrat, we are motivated to unravel the secret meanings, to listen to the muffled cries buried in the eternal muteness of these relics. We are engaged in historian's work, trying to make sense to ourselves out of what has happened and what is happening. Now works like *The Border Town, Fengzi,* and *Random Sketches* also make their presence amid the ancient sites and shrines, broken sculptures, and ruined mansions, demanding that their voices be heard by the generations of visitors/readers to come. It is from here that we discern the change in Shen Congwen's historic mission. He wants to annotate, to decipher the mysterious past of West Hunan, in such a way that he makes his annotations just as important as the past under discussion. In fact, by giving expression to what has been muted and forgotten, *West Hunan* has made itself a historical account of its best kind, and the most important scene in the landscape of West Hunan.

Fenghuang is the destination of Shen Congwen's literary tour. A small, provincial town at the center of West Hunan, Fenghuang is where Shen Congwen's family came from; it is the source of his creative imagination. Traditionally settled by the ethnic tribes of Miaos and Tujias, the mountainous areas of Fenghuang provide a suitable backdrop to Shen Congwen's tribal romances such as "Yuexia xiaojing" (Under moonlight, 1933), "Long Zhu" and "The Shaman's Love." But the place is also considered the origin of much of the myth and mystery of West Hunan, in terms of tribal conflict, banditry, superstition, voodoo, and many other bizarre customs. In terms of the narrative layout of *West Hunan,* Fenghuang marks the "heart of darkness" where the phantasmal scenarios of Shen Congwen's memory take their first shape, the desired locus that he feels obliged to illuminate at the end of his trip:

> The legend of Miao tribal voodoo originates here. Practitioners of Chenzhou voodoo posters come here to try out their magical power. Thanks to the traditional system of soldier settlers, Fenghuang still nurtures the authentic spirit of knight-errantry that characterizes the children of Chu. There are many peculiar things to say about the local religious rituals, while people's belief in religions or superstitions is so fanatic as to go far beyond imagination.[24]

The outer frontier of the legendary South, Fenghuang is culturally and politically foreign to the "Middle Kingdom." Not only have the majority of residents inherited a mixed blood of Han and Miao peoples, they have also lived by a unique set of morals and manners for hundreds of years. It is the place where the present repeats the past, where gods and demons meet and where the power of pantheistic spirits nurtures endless legend and superstition. It is the site where the repressed energies of the human body and psyche are unleashed to form a spectacular horizon of mores and manners, challenging the codes of decorum and propriety of the Middle Kingdom and questioning the borderline between the real and fantastic.

Particularly noticeable are the power of shamanism over women and the code of brutal virility shared by men. Shen Congwen takes pains to detail how women of different ages are victims caught by the numerous local gods, spirits and demons. They become either voodooists, witches, or psychotics obsessed by the "love" of gods or demons. Shen Congwen's play with the fascination and repulsion of these hysterical cases suggests again that his homeland (as well as woman's body) entertains a libidinous force hitherto ignored or marginalized, and that its release in displaced forms of taboo, ritual and psychotic symptom calls for careful study. While the lives of the possessed women may end up pathetically, their bizarre actions and fantasies bear witness to the vigor of romantic passion, thereby furnishing the repertoire of Shen's numerous love stories between young men and women. Fenghuang may well deserve to be the imaginary backdrop for stories such as "Three Men and one Woman," "Mountain Ghost," and "Night."

On the other hand, the libidinous carnival expressed by the women under possession is juxtaposed to the men's obsessive adherence

Imaginary Nostalgia

to social mores. Shen salutes those men who dedicate their lives to the codes of heroism and machismo. In the name of honor, they chop at each other in duels, till one party dies; in service to chastity, they kill their beloveds for the smallest suspicion of dishonor. Barbarous and bloodthirsty as they may be, they are the last descendants of classical knight-errantry. At a time when the codes of honor, brotherhood, and self-sacrifice have gradually faded away, these men make themselves a group of Don Quixotes, fighting for an ideal that is no longer there. But there is a hysterical element lurking within the men's social behavior that amounts to a counterpart of the women's neuroses. Men in Fenghuang dedicate themselves to the codes of virility as fervently as women let themselves be enchanted by the power of passion.

By all standards, "Fenghuang" represents one of Shen Congwen's most fascinating studies of southwestern Chinese regionalism. Paradoxically, he manages this only by allowing himself a self-contradictory narrative stance. The romantic native son who shares a passion for the unknown with the people of Fenghuang, Shen is also the realist chronicler who writes to demythify the land and its culture. In his approach to those women empowered by shamanism, for instance, he is not content with simply describing the erotic fear and ecstasy they experience and the occult hallucinations they claim to witness; rather, he proposes a diagnosis in terms of psychopathology and anthropology. Shen Congwen tries to make historical sense of the men's chivalric fervor; he notices the relationship between those possessed women's symptoms and their menstrual periods; he even offers a prescription for those young ladies troubled by sexual hallucinations—get a husband.

But one question remains: as Shen Congwen lays bare the "real" picture of Fenghuang, he risks explaining away the mystical charm of the ancient Chu culture he originally meant to recollect. Madness, Voodooism, and moral fanaticism represent the ghosts of the mysterious past, which the realist impulse have excluded from the text, and which, as a primitive scene of the unspeakable, are hauntingly searching for readmission to discourse. The uncanny elements shrouding the town must be expelled, so that one can see a clearer image of it. Yet we have also been told again and again that Fenghuang is the last homeland of the ghosts and spirits in Qu Yuan's *Songs of the South*. "The imagination of the ancient Chu people must be nurtured on the land so as to give rise to touching poetry; if we want to preserve [the imagination and the poetry], we cannot do away with the environment."25

This apparent contradiction brings us to the final drama of Shen Congwen's account of his homeland. Given his rationalization that the rituals of shamanism and the codes of chivalry are results of religious superstitions and moral fanaticism, one surmises that the ghosts and demons may never go away. They are so described only to indicate the limits of the realist effort to demythify. While trying to exorcise Fenghuang (the residents will hold on to what they believe to be "real" anyhow), Shen Congwen himself may want to save a secret place for the supernatural and the uncanny—not in the apparently realist reportage of Fenghuang, but in the dark realm of the imaginary nostalgia about Fenghuang that subsumes the text. Floating around and haunting Shen Congwen's memory, the supernatural powers and ancient morals are the essential elements that distinguish Fenghuang and West Hunan from Shanghai or Beijing and constitute the Chu culture. More importantly, they form the fantastic landscape, tempting Shen Congwen's desire to recapture the lost homeland yet always evading his realist snares. "Fenghuang" represents the last stage in unraveling the obscure fabric of historical West Hunan; it is also the beginning point for Shen's rewoven tapestry of mythical West Hunan.

The Border Town and *Long River*

By comparing *The Border Town* and *Long River* one can easily demonstrate Shen Congwen's different attitudes towards his homeland and his use of different narrative strategies in giving shape to those attitudes. *The Border Town* impresses with its author's determined recourse to idyll and its melancholy contemplation of the mythic human cycle. In *The Border Town,* serene mountains and rivers, good-natured country folk, legendary romances, and ancient festive rituals are so introduced as to constitute a seemingly enclosed, self-sufficient world whose historical background remains comfortably vague. By contrast, *Long River* brings one from a pastoral paradise back to the flux of time. Although still flavored with "a touch of pastoral romance,"26 as Shen Congwen admits, *Long River* betrays his anxiety about the inevitable downfall of his homeland at the time of an impending Japanese invasion. Even the titles of the two novels seem to carry subtle hints of Shen Congwen's differing attitudes: the "border town" points to a mythical utopia which stands outside time and change, whereas the "long river" might indicate national or human struggles in the stream of history.

But this contrastive reading evades the nuances of Shen Congwen's imaginary nostalgia, making him appear a simple-minded native soil writer juggling two discrete themes of paradise found and paradise lost. I would argue that the contrast exists not only between the two novels but also *within* each of them, and therefore confronts the reader with the endless interplay between myth and history, dream and reality.

The Border Town appears first as a composite portrait of epiphanic experiences. As Shen Congwen admits, almost in a Proustian manner, the novel was triggered by a couple of contingent moments of life which crystallized the vision of his homeland for him. Whereas the overall ambiance of *The Border Town* was motivated by the sight of wood ferry boats on his mission from Baojing to eastern Szechuan in his soldier days,[27] Cuicui, the novel's heroine, was inspired by a young girl in a grocery store whom Shen Congwen encountered on his 1934 homecoming trip.[28] In his essay "Water Cloud," written years after the publication of *The Border Town,* Shen Congwen mentions that he derived the novel's raw material from imagining the life of a young country widow he met in Qingdao, Shandong province, and that his own wife, Zhang Zhaohe, served as his model for his heroine's character.[29] What is interesting here is not whether these sources are consistent with each other but how Shen Congwen draws on a wide range of experiences, some of which did not even take place in West Hunan, and how he transcribes them into a coherent narrative about an ever present homeland.

The location of *The Border Town* is suggestive in this regard. Shen Congwen makes it clear in the novel's preface that.

> The purpose of writing the novel is to represent a form of life that is graceful, healthy, spontaneous, and in tune with humanity. I do not intend to take my readers on a tour to Peach Blossom Spring, but to deal with how a couple of ordinary people, living in a small town *seven hundred lis upward of Taoyuan,* along the You River, are involved in a common human problem, and how they express their destined sadness and happiness, thereby serving as an appropriate example for the ideal of love of human beings. . . . Even if this world may have

been ruined, it will survive in my story. Even if this world has never existed, it will not affect the validity of my story. [italics mine][30]

The statement is striking in that, while Shen Congwen consciously follows the steps of Tao Qian by establishing a more "real" world outside fiction, hence criticizing the sociopolitical context in which he is writing, he does not want to make Taoyuan, the alleged site of Peach Blossom Spring, the locale of his ideal homeland. As *Random Sketches* indicates, since the legendary place of Peach Blossom Spring has been contaminated and degraded into part of an ongoing reality, the ideal native soil, the new Peach Blossom Spring, has to be found somewhere else. No longer can a modern reader enter Taoyuan county and retrieve the old path to the old mysterious grove; instead, he or she has to go another hundred *lis* and try a different place named Chadong, "the last harbor town on the border of West Hunan."[31]

The Border Town is thus a book full from the outset of ironic undertones. Written to displace and replace in words the brutal and corrupt external world, it subverts the old utopian myth from which it first draws inspiration. Can Peach Blossom Spring, once lost, be duplicated in another place, and in another text? Can the people of the modern Peach Blossom Spring really lead a carefree life? Will not Chadong undergo the same threat of downfall someday as Tao Qian's Peach Blossom Spring has undergone in the twentieth century?

Shen Congwen must have sensed these questions in writing *The Border Town*, despite his own much brighter comments quoted above, and despite the critics' forthcoming praise for it as a masterpiece of Chinese pastoral romance, a book that "proves the prevalent goodness in humanity," or a "poem . . . a love song."[32] He confesses in the essay "Water Cloud" that the novel helped him write out all the repressed pains and struggles he had felt as a country man; by idealizing West Hunan in terms of the idyllic, he registered both his skepticism about and confidence in China.[33] He asks, with *The Border Town* in mind, "what is the real meaning of life? Is it restraint or licence? Is it reserve or madness? Is it fiction or fact?"[34] Indeed, a careful reading shows that, given the spontaneous rhythm and lyrical tempo that prevail, the novel is subsumed by an all too acute awareness of the ominous forces of misunderstanding, deferral, desperate passion, and destruction.

Imaginary Nostalgia

The Border Town opens with the following paragraph:

> The highway running east from Szechuan to Hunan comes, just west of the border, to Chadong, a small town in the hills. Nearby, a stream flows past a small pagoda, at the foot of which lives a solitary household: an old man, a girl and a dog.[35]

Notice how the element of time is deliberately omitted in this paragraph. Although ample examples of this device may be found in classical travelogues (as illustrated, say, by Liu Zongyuan) and in vernacular Chinese fiction, one must still pay close attention to the utopian intention conceived by Shen Congwen. The extensive use of the spatial indicator "there is" ("you" in Chinese) seems to function as a textual frame, one that locates the continuum of human conditions and declares its form of permanence.[36] As if assuming a divine position, Shen gives form and order to a place.

Descriptions of the old ferryman and his granddaughter Cuicui's daily life follow. "Aged seventy today, the ferryman has stayed since the age of twenty besides this stream, ferrying in those fifty years who knows how many passengers across it."[37] While generalizing the vast span of time the ferryman has spent on his job, Shen Congwen, on the other hand, zeroes in on the ferryman's routine job, not to highlight his work of a particular day but to transmit a life that has always been led like this: how people slip a specially designed hoop over the hawser spanning the stream, and pull themselves slowly to the other side; how the ferryman turns down passengers' money or uses it to buy tobacco and tea as gifts for them; how Cuicui takes over her grandfather's job whenever he falls asleep on the big rock next to the stream.

Despite the narrative's swift shuttling back and forth between the ferryman's lifelong activities and his daily chores, it manages to avoid using any proper names, personal pronouns, or temporal indicators. The seemingly "tenseless" narration helps the reader synthesize or even dissolve different time zones at the grammatical and semantic level, whereas the careful omission of personal pronouns disorients the otherwise well-manipulated relation between the narrator and his characters and readers, and diffuses their positions into a bracketed state of intersubjectivity.

If this explanation of Shen Congwen's narrative features sounds familiar, it might be partially due to Gérard Genette, who has neatly described the *iterative mode* as one of the most important styles used by realist writers, a style evoking a single narrative utterance taking upon itself several occurrences together of the same event.[38] As one can see in the second chapter of *The Border Town,* Shen Congwen extends the iterative mode of narrative even to his observation of people's unchanging life style in Chadong: quaint households amid peach blossoms; old soldiers whiling away their time by practicing on the bugle; housewives in starched blue cotton clothes and floral-patterned aprons chatting to each other; travellers flirting with the female proprietor of a small tavern; prostitutes expressing bittersweet love for young boatmen. Time seems to have come a halt. The iterative style brings out a mythical cycle of life in which every inhabitant participates.

> Peace reigns supreme and the townsfolk spend all their days in an unspoiled solitude hard to imagine. Tranquility makes them reflect more deeply on life, makes them dream more. Naturally every soul in this little town in his allocated span of days has his private hopes and is torn by love and hate.[39]

"Dream" is the key word here. The border town is a dream world from which nobody wakes up, a world wherein anything can happen, even if only in the form of phantasmal images. Thus, when her beloved fails to come back, a prostitute either "dreams of his boat putting in to shore and sees him bound down the gangway to run to her side," or "dreams of him singing to another woman, forgetting her."[40] In despair, she would commit suicide or carry out a cruel revenge—desperate action conducted, nevertheless, only "in dreams."

Both the narrative mode and the rhetoric of the first two chapters of *The Border Town* are crucial for the reader's understanding of Shen Congwen's brand of utopia, in that they give form to a geographical closure dominated by myth and dream and that they recommend to the implied reader an attitude of acquiescence to what is happening in the world. At the best of his plan, even pain, death, and other forms of unhappiness are supposed to be seen as built-in ingredients, existing only to complete the cycle of human experiences. One can thus talk about a stylized quality in Shen Congwen's rural picture, in that nothing amounts to tangible bliss or threats except as artistic reflections of them.

But this is of course only part of Shen's vision of the border town. A realist, Shen Congwen knows only too well that, though isolated from "the unhappy struggles going on elsewhere in the country,"[41] Chadong is itself undergoing a process of self-erosion. As the novel unfolds, Shen Congwen encounters moments in which even the divine plan cannot sufficiently rationalize the gratuitous sufferings falling on his characters; it is to no avail that he will try to ward off the insidious elements nurtured *within* his ideal country. It is these accidental events and miscalculated actions that blur the thin line between idyllic predestination and realistic uncertainty, and thus suggest the imperfection of his utopia. His "writing" of a modern Peach Blossom Spring can best tell a story of the impossibility of that writing.

As mentioned above, if *The Border Town* is concerned with the possible existence of paradise, it pays just as much attention to the chance happening or contingency always threatening to disintegrate that paradise. Contingency makes itself felt most poignantly as Shen Congwen relates the numerous occasions in which his characters misunderstand or misinterpret each other, or are simply left in a position of deferral and waiting. We remember how the old ferryman is determined to find his granddaughter the best husband, only to be trapped in a series of misjudgments that culminates in the death of Tianbao. We also remember how Cuicui shies away from every chance of expressing herself either to her grandfather or to Nuosong, thus deepening the misunderstanding among characters. One of the best examples is the first encounter between Cuicui and Nuosong.

In this scene, Cuicui is waiting anxiously to go home with her grandfather. Earlier that day, she had come to town with her grandfather to watch the annual dragonboat race, but the old man sneaked away to look for a drink in the middle of the race and has since disappeared. As the sky gets darker, the fear in Cuicui's mind looms larger. She asks herself, "Can grandpa already be dead?" Next to where she stands are two boatmen telling bawdy jokes about a prostitute, whose father, according to them, was "murdered seven years ago on Cotton Hill, slashed with seventeen knives."[42] It is at this moment that Nuosong appears and offers to take Cuicui to his home to wait for her grandfather. But he only manages to offend Cuicui, since she misunderstands his "home" for the brothel nearby, and mistakes his good intent for a seduction attempt.

The episode presents the first meeting between Cuicui and Nuosong as a mixture of pastoral naïveté and natural menace. Their romance does not begin simply as love at first sight, rather it happens in the midst of Cuicui's deep apprehension of her grandfather's possible death; the flirtation between the prostitute and the boatmen; the gossip about the murder of the prostitute's father; and Nuosong's apparently sexual advances. A moment of initiation into adolescent life, the encounter is described as both tender and vicious, innocent and erotic. Cuicui learns the first lesson of love as something linked with expectation and excitement, which are nevertheless subsumed by error, violence, and death. Cuicui is situated at a juncture where bliss and torture meet; her parents committed love-suicide for unknown reasons after she was born out of wedlock, and she is indirectly responsible both for the drowning of Nuosong's brother, Tianbao, and for the death of her grandfather. Shen Congwen intends to describe love in its purest form, yet he finds it impossible not to touch on the maculate conditions in which love first germinates. Be it called contingency or predestination, the unwelcome element in Shen's idyllic romance amounts to an evil force, that breaks the closure of the tranquil, defers the completion of human relations, and subverts the narrative's attempt at autonomous performance.

In their efforts to demythify the utopian world of *The Border Town,* critics from mainland China have tried to emphasize the uncrossable economic barrier between Cuicui and Nuosong.[43] In contrast to the local lieutenant Wang's daughter, who gets herself a brand-new watermill as a dowry, Cuicui understands well that she has nothing to offer but the broken ferryboat. Throughout the novel, the ferryboat and the watermill are referred to by Nuosong, Tianbao, and the townsfolk as metaphors of conflicting social and economic status. Moreover, it has been suspected that even the suicide of Cuicui's parents was due to the intervention of feudalist customs. There may be grounds for the critics to enumerate the social/economic factors that prefigure the characters' fates in the novel, but in so doing, they tend to be lured into yet another brand of determinism—socioeconomic fatalism—and therefore are not too far away from the predestined idyll they claim to attack.

Insofar as *The Border Town* attempts to circumscribe an ideal locus that escapes temporal and historical forces, the ultimate factor endangering its autonomy has to be defined as time—time that changes, prolongs, and defers variegation in the human condition. I have previously mentioned how Shen Congwen plays with the iterative narrative mode to evoke a mythical rhythm of the idyllic, and how he tries, however fruitlessly, to fit the factor of contingency into the framework of fate. These issues can now be joined and discussed in the context of time. The border town Chadong is meant to be a Peach Blossom Spring, whose inhabitants "have been cut off from the outside world . . . They had never even heard of Han, let alone its successors."[44] The passage of time is observed simply by the annual dragonboat race and other festivities. Life, growth, and death form a biological cycle that is not to be measured by the historical sequence of the external world.

But given this apparently tranquil state of timelessness, something is bothering the old ferryman and Cuicui as their story develops. For the old man, the tragic past of his daughter's and her lover's suicide has long seeded his mind with worry over his granddaughter's future. For the young girl, the mysterious experience of growing up has brought her both fear and expectation. Once Cuicui and her grandfather venture to deal with the problems of puberty and aging as well as their correlated consequences, time manifests a course that is more than just a cycle. As the narrator predicts, "everything must undergo some changes along with time. The peace of their uneventful life was soon to be irrevocably shattered."[45] Coincidentally, the old ferryman's visit to the new watermill, the townsfolks' gossip about Cuicui's socioeconomic background, and the appearance of a go-between all converge at this juncture.

Another important incident is of course the two brothers' deal that they take turns to sing love songs across the stream at night, and leave Cuicui to decide on the winner. The competition is never carried out; on hearing his younger brother singing, Tianbao realizes his inferiority and quits, despite his brother's offer to sing on his behalf so as to carry out the contest. Shen Congwen had good reason to make this scene the turning point of his plot, since he had long cherished a tremendous attachment to the custom of singing matches in West Hunan. Through love songs, young men and women are brought together and become couples; and through love songs, his vision of pastoral romance consummates its poetic climax. If Shen Congwen's ideal of the idyllic is crystallized by the ritualistic serenades of young men to young women in the moonlight, the scene where Tianbao and Nuosong are supposed to sing against each other is an aborted contest, a frustrated attempt at "singing away" problems in reality. Just as pastoral songs will no longer settle the trouble Cuicui and the two brothers encounter in the flow of time, so poetry gives way to realistic narrative.

The penultimate paragraph of the novel relates that, "when winter comes the new pagoda is complete. But the young man whose serenading in the moonlight made Cuicui's heart soar up lightly in her dreams has not come back to Chadong."[46] When the songs and dreams of the idyllic fade away, one can do nothing but wait, in a state of suspense. Hence the tantalizing conclusion of the novel: he "may never come back. Or he may come back tomorrow."[47]

No longer does her daily routine as a ferrygirl indicate the self-sufficiency of work; rather it represents an infinitely tentative position, one awaiting final redemption. Cuicui ferries back and forth across the stream of time, neither ascending nor descending, and so choosing anticipation and nostalgia. While her waiting may be taken to mean an excuse for Shen Congwen to obviate the reality of human imperfections, or China's uncertain position in the shadow of forthcoming history, as critics have indicated, it may also reflect the paradox of Shen Congwen's native soil fiction. Not unlike Cuicui's waiting, writing (not singing), prose (not poetry), is the uncertain craft Shen Congwen has been condemned to exercise. It is this task of writing (waiting, in Cuicui's case) in the absence of a certain object, place, or person to be written about (waited for), that Shen Congwen has inherited.

Beneath the deceptively smooth narrative of *The Border Town,* we thus discern Shen Congwen's deep melancholy. The novel is touching, not simply because Shen Congwen successfully tells a pastoral romance set against the landscape of West Hunan but also because he cannot do so without referring to the other side of the romance. The nostalgia he entertains here is threefold. First, as long as the ideal vision of the homeland is always already lost, Shen Congwen's desperate attempt to re-present it will produce only a simulacrum, an imaginary replacement and displacement of the original, which is associated more with dream-like textuality than with reality. Echoing to the magic word of dream so frequently appearing in the novel, one might say *The Border Town* is itself a dream work.

Second, the novel sheds light on the condition of (realistic) writing. As its iterative tense is gradually replaced by a linear sequential tense, as its framework of collective exemplars is reduced to an individual case, one sees how the novel's lyrical mode, together with its thematic assumptions, yields to the realistic mode, and how myth evolves to meet history. Nostalgia, accordingly, means a sadness for Shen Congwen, not just about paradise lost but about the disappearance of a primal writing that might have brought back ontological plenitude.

Finally, if the ideal West Hunan is a landscape that only exists in Shen Congwen's imagination, to deplore its loss risks becoming a self-serving gesture. In other words, nostalgia might function both as means and end in Shen Congwen's native soil literature. What the reader is fascinated with is really his or her own action of reading about the lost homeland rather than the homeland itself. What might have never existed is exactly what we are looking forward to. When anticipation and nostalgia are intertwined, it is imaginary nostalgia, not nostalgia, that weaves the spell of *The Border Town*.

Shen Congwen wrote *Long River* at the turn of the forties, the heyday of the second Sino-Japanese war. Like *West Hunan, Long River* is historically motivated. Shen Congwen wants to "use a small harbortown on the Chen River as backdrop, and familiar things and people as raw material, to write about the 'changes' and 'continuities' of the region as well as the joys and sorrows of the people."[48] For fear that his readers might be upset by the painful pictures he displays, Shen Congwen deliberately adds "a flavor of the idyllic" to his otherwise realist attempt.[49] The result is a strange mixture of styles reminiscent of the surface complacency of *The Border Town* on the one hand and the historical uncertainty of *West Hunan* on the other.

Long River takes place in a small town on the Chen River, Lüjiaping. Just as in the first two chapters of *Border Town,* Shen Congwen presents an overview of the town before he narrows down his focus to a small group of its inhabitants. He picks up the iterative mode characteristic of the beginning of *The Border Town* as he generalizes life in Lüjiaping. But there is a remarkable difference between the two beginnings. Whereas Chadong first appears "like" a modern Peach Blossom Spring situated in a tranquil atmosphere of timelessness, Lüjiaping is a town already experiencing the bittersweet winds of social/political change. The iterative style that once evoked the atmosphere of perennial tranquility of the border town is now employed to multiply the mutations of West Hunan within a given timespan. In so doing, Shen Congwen has tacitly demoted the se-

Imaginary Nostalgia

mantic input of the style, depriving it of the privilege of registering a cycle of mythic time, and making it instead an indicator of the massive plurality of actions carried on in real time.

Entitled "People and Land," the first chapter also shares the historical concern of *West Hunan*. As Shen Congwen puts it, "everything is changing in this world. In the unpredictable course of change, coincidences and contingencies, laughter and tears, each develops in its own special form."[50] If they manage to survive the tests of the river, boatmen now have a chance of starting their own enterprises on shore. Those who are especially lucky can make money by shipping merchandise up and down the river and by running farms on the land. They can then build their own estates, make themselves members of the gentry, and send their children to schools for the new education. The younger generation, inspired by progressive thought, soon become both the pride and the burden of their parents. They might not have learned anything by graduation, but in appearance, they are intellectuals, reformers, and liberators. They fight for freedom of marriage, but never turn down the dowries or betrothals coming to them; they look down on their feudalist parents, but always keep in mind their inheritances. They will eventually either take local office and become celebrities, or go off to join a revolution and end up being arrested and executed, thus returning to the soil. While Shen Congwen ridicules these new youth, he takes just as many pains to criticize the peasants and the gentry, whose stubbornness and provincialism have formed a conservative force that keeps progress from happening.

In terms of characters and plot, *Long River* does bear resemblance to *The Border Town*. Characters of *The Border Town* such as the old ferryman and Cuicui, Nuosong and his father find their replicas here, too. At the center of the story are Manman, an old retired sailor taking shelter in the Teng family shrine, after experiencing all the ups and downs appropriate to his profession, and Yaoyao, the youngest daughter of Teng Changshun, an honest veteran sailor now running his own small shipping enterprise. Just like Cuiui and her grandfather, Yaoyao and the old sailor cherish a special emotional tie. Unlike his counterpart, however, the old sailor does not worry about Yaoyao's marriage, since she has been betrothed to a young student studying in another city. But there is something even larger and vaguer distressing him—the future of the town and the river. Life is carefree for Yaoyao, apart from the occasional bother of a petty bureaucrat or a soldier. In spite of the surrounding sociopolitical uncertainties, all is well.

Long River was never finished. According to Shen Congwen's original plan, the novel was to contain four volumes; its current version represents only the end of volume one.[51] What happens to Yaoyao, the old sailor, and the town of Lüjiaping will forever remain an unanswered question, though incidental references all point to one possibility, that the novel would end with disasters befalling Lüjiaping.

Why did Shen Congwen never finish the novel? While the instability of wartime life must have served as a direct interruption to Shen Congwen's plans, some other possibilities exist. Allegedly exposing the moral and socioeconomic degradation of rural China under the KMT regime, the novel was never welcome among the censors; a considerable number of words and lines were actually expunged when it was first published in 1943. On the other hand, the ominous vision of West Hunan's future may have proved an unbearable strain for Shen Congwen at the time and disabled him from writing and personally fulfilling its doom. Leaving *Long River* unfinished, therefore, might have meant for Shen Congwen both a political gesture, "saying" in silence what was unsayable in a policed literature, and a psychological self-censorship, blocking the textual manifestation of a unbearable trauma.

Amid these circumstantial factors, however, it is equally significant to base the novel's incompleteness in the working out of imaginary nostalgia. As will be recalled, Shen Congwen's fiction had long had a record of resisting completion, in the sense not of technical defect but of aesthetic and ideological determination. Examples can always be found, from the ending of *The Border Town,* where Cuicui waits interminably for the return of her beloved, to the ending of "Xiaoxiao," where Xiaoxiao finishes the cycle of her role as mother/wife at the expense of her wish to be a "girl student." The problem can be approached in two aspects. On the one hand, always obsessed with the lost homeland, Shen Congwen's native soil fiction may well be an attempt to fill in what is missing in reality and to enrich what is impoverished in memory. Left on its own, this fiction will call attention to its mediative position and thus will reveal its insufficiency at re-membering its lost home. On the other hand, it contains no less a desire for incompleteness, a strong wish to defer and thereby to question the formal closure of a narrative sequence or moral/historical mechanism.

The two aspects are again two sides of one coin, laying out in a special way the dialectic of Shen Congwen's writing about his native soil and his nostalgia. Insofar as West Hunan is no more a geographical locus than a dreamland composed of phantom images and languages, Shen Congwen's yearning to return home evokes an endless chain of desire and despair. He cannot complete his trip; perhaps he does not even want to. In any case, the power of nostalgia hinges on the eternal regression to home and origin. Incompleteness has become an important trope, indicating both the condition and the strategy of Shen Congwen's nativism.

It is in this sense that we may regard the current unfinished form of *Long River* as a result of both historical contingency and aesthetic necessity. I am not, of course, trying to find an excuse for the artistic defects of *Long River*. I am just suggesting that the reasons for Shen Congwen's leaving the novel unfinished may be far more complicated than has been previously thought, given the aesthetic and ideological bearings of his nostalgic discourse. As a matter of fact, because of its incomplete form, *Long River* ironically reveals one of the most tendentious sides of Shen Congwen's native soil fiction: that his nostalgia may have always already been there, even before the loss of his homeland. I will call this syndrome *anticipatory nostalgia,* in the sense that one "looks forward to" missing what one now has.

Anticipatory nostalgia situates itself at the heart of Shen Congwen's imaginary landscape of nostalgia, because it indicates more than any other form of nostalgia the primal sense of loss and incompleteness, and because it manifests itself by resorting more to the play of imagination. In *Long River,* Shen Congwen the narrator is not the only one to suffer foretastes of the sad downfall of Lüjiaping. The old sailor Manman may also know the fate of his town. The most dramatic scene in this regard is, of course, the sailor's talk with other country fellows about the arrival of the New Life movement.

A superb one act comedy, the scene begins with chit-chat between the old sailor and another man and woman. Gossiping about unthinkable recent events, they are soon caught up in the rumor that the Xin Shenghuo (the New Life movement) is coming.[52] Totally ignorant of the new political campaign, they take it for the name of a powerful creature. As their talk continues, the image of the Xin Shenghuo amplifies from a general, an ideologue, a commander-in-chief, to an enormous monster. Armed with guns, cannons, artillery and gimmicks seen only in chivalric romances, the Xin Shenghuo runs fast and sees far. "He" is on a mysterious mission, but most likely he is heading toward Yunnan Province to fight the well-known Melon Spirit. It is unknown yet what the Xin Shenghuo will do here in Lüjiaping, yet one thing is for sure, that farmers are going to lose their pigs, local gentry are going to have to donate money, and our old sailor might lose his job as janitor of the Teng family shrine.

The comic episode is rife with political overtones. By hilarious guessing and bawdy jokes, it laughs away the serious claims of the New Life movement, a movement designed to reform Chinese people's cultural as well political assumptions. It also dramatizes how country folk incorporate new things into their reality by means of what they are already familiar with. They draw superstitions, clichés, old wisdom, and hearsay from their dictionary of idées fixes, in such a relentless way as to conjure up something truly nonsensical. But there is something else hidden in the episode. In a lighthearted way, it transmits the inscrutable but formidable power that ever lurks in the town mind. Be it called the unknown, the other, or history in absence, or the New Life movement, this power leads people to a foreknowledge of impending changes and the consequent loss of what they now possess. And thereby they come to appreciate a current life which otherwise may not be all that enjoyable. The pain of anticipatory nostalgia is not felt on account of missing what is already lost but of missing what will be lost.

Thus Shen Congwen relates, at the end of chapter two, "Like the man of Ji [in the ancient fable, who can never stop worrying about the sky falling], the old sailor was somewhat upset by thoughts of the arrival of the 'Xin Shenghuo', that was bound to change everything here." But at the same time, he sees "Yaoyao and her sister play at the edge of boat, trying to grab the vines and leaves on the water in an extremely leisurely manner."[53] The old man is greatly saddened by this innocent and serene picture. Indeed, the old sailor's ominous feeling becomes a leitmotif of the novel, always lingering nearby to cast a shadow on what is happening. He is an unwitting prophet, knowing and feeling too much about what is going to happen; but at times he is also an unconscious decadent artist, whose sense of beauty blooms only at seeing how his world shines just moments before its decay.

On the other hand, Shen Congwen spares no effort to call attention to the vicious force that will soon threaten the peace of Lüjiaping. The middle part of the novel deals with a group of military officers and local bureaucrats who continue to bother Yaoyao and her family under the pretext of buying tangerines or raising money. Compared with *The Border Town,* which emphasizes an alienating factor growing within the community and finally bringing it to its downfall, *Long River* tends to highlight the external forces that infiltrate step by step into the territory of Lüjiaping, in the forms of military troops, greedy governmental officials, modern educators, and, above all, the New Life movement. And judged by what has been said in the novel so far, Shen Congwen might have had more to say about the clash between old and new values, the invasion of more soldiers and political campaigns; the hardship of rural life on the eve of the second Sino-Japanese war; and the violation of Yaoyao, the embodiment of purity and innocence in Lüjiaping.

The mounting crises come to a sudden halt in the penultimate chapter of *Long River,* where Yaoyao's brother Sanheizi makes a timely appearance and interrupts three police investigators' advances to Yaoyao. The last chapter, entitled "Shexi" (Community theater), redirects the plotline by concentrating on how people prepare the annual theatrical performance. Like the dragonboat race in *The Border Town,* the six-day theatrical festival means both an entertainment for the town and a festive occasion full of religious implications. Shen Congwen takes great interest in detailing how the local residents put on their best clothes and carry their own stools to attend the theater; how the local gentry and officers preside over rituals in honor of deities before the performance starts; how the audience watches plays while busy laughing, chitchatting, debating, eating and drinking, walking around, doing small house chores, and even looking for a place to empty themselves. Time stops. Soldiers and villagers find themselves sitting together enjoying the same play; the audience are so drawn to the stage that they feel they are actually part of the ongoing melodrama. Everybody seems lost in a mesmerizing atmosphere from which they hate to be awakened. At least for a while, the chapter reminds us of the mythical scenes of the idyllic marking the beginning of *The Border Town.*

But both the old sailor and Yaoyao leave the theater early. When we see them later, they are on a boat talking about a spectacular wildfire burning in the distant hills. The sky looks all red, and the boat moves smoothly, while laughter comes from afar from the village. Moved by the scene, Yaoyao says, "whatever is beautiful should last forever."⁵⁴ The old sailor, however, disagrees, saying, "whatever is beautiful will not last long. Good bowels easily break down, pretty flowers easily freeze to death—honest people do not live long."⁵⁵ It is from this that we discern again the philosophy of anticipatory nostalgia. Beautiful things merit twice our appreciation, especially when we know they will not last long. The old man and the young girl soon forget their disagreement and, now joined by Sanheizi, indulge themselves in another round of idle speculation: "What if Sanheizi became Governor someday?" "What would I do if I became Governor?" "Why not forget all that and go hunt wild duck eggs, which city people might buy at a price as high as swan fairy eggs?" The novel, or volume one of the novel, ends with Yaoyao's request, "Don't ever forget to appoint Manman River Affairs Officer, third brother, if you make Governor someday!"⁵⁶

What really happens on that "someday," of course, remains unknown, since *Long River* was never finished. Yet it is noteworthy that the novel culminates in a subjunctive narrative mode. However impossible the fantasies are, their results are yet to come and so will sustain our hopes. By leaving *Long River* the way it is, Shen Congwen has suspended the present of his story, thereby anticipating an endless hypothetical game. This conclusion neatly presents the paradox embedded in the discourse of anticipatory nostalgia. As long as anticipatory nostalgia dwells on a prescient sadness about the disappearing present, the best way to savor the sadness is not to cancel, but to *prolong* the *disappearing present*. In sharp contrast to the conventional theme of nostalgia, which presupposes the loss of the homeland or the beloved, anticipatory nostalgia works only so long as its endearing object still lingers on, contained in the hypothetical "if."

Imagination, not experiential data, is required to carry out anticipatory nostalgia, which is elegant proof of how fiction constitutes our perception of the real. Unlike *The Border Town*, in which Cuicui is thrown into the stream of time to wait for the return of the person who is already gone, *Long River* ends in a moment of speculation. Given the novel's current form, the loss of Lüjiaping will be deferred forever. The incompleteness of the novel thus contains a strange sense of relief rather than a sense of melancholy. It is in this way that Shen Congwen turns the implicit eschatology of the novel into an aesthetic investment; in so doing, he elevates art over history, fiction (myth) over reality, imaginary nostalgia over nostalgia.

The Art of Remembrance of Things Past

The art of remembering and writing is the last issue I will address in relation to imaginary nostalgia. In numerous essays and interviews, Shen Congwen reiterated the importance of the art, as opposed to sheer memory, that substantiated his native soil writings. He points out how he was consciously influenced by Chinese and Western literature when conjuring up his vision of West Hunan. Nineteenth-century writers such as Maupassant and Chekhov are often mentioned by Shen Congwen with regard to his "Western learning,"[57] while Turgenev is undoubtedly the figure influencing him the most, as I have tried to illustrate in the previous chapter. As late as in an interview in 1980, he made it clear that Turgenev's *Sketches from A Hunter's Album* inspired his native soil writings, in terms of its understatement, local color, and gallery of peasant characters.[58]

Shen Congwen's indebtedness to the treasury of classical Chinese literature is even more intricate to trace. According to him, he enjoyed reading a variety of classics ranging from *Songs of the South,* the *Shiji,* Cao Zhi's poetry, *Liaozhai zhiyi* (Strange stories from the Leisure Studio) and *Jingu qiguan* (Wonders of the past and the present), to folk songs.[59] Scholars have also noticed that his literary gazetteers and travelogues can be appreciated in the light of Liu Zongyuan's sketches and Li Daoyuan's *Shuijing zhu* (A commentary to the classic of the waterways),[60] that his description of the land and people of West Hunan recapitulates the grand tradition of the South represented by such masterpieces as Qu Yuan's *Songs of the South, Shanhaijing* (The classic of the mountains and seas), and the *Zhuangzi,*[61] and that he might owe his rhetorical simplicity and humor to the style of Song dynasty vernacular stories and theater.[62]

The list, of course, can be expanded further. But what I am concerned with here is not how Shen Congwen was inspired by a certain Chinese or Western writer but how he wrote and recreated West Hunan in the light of a large Chinese repertory of conventions and images. In this sense, West Hunan is no more a geographical locus, registering Shen Congwen's personal experiences in the past, than Peach Blossom Spring is a fictional landscape, projecting Tao Qian's daydreams. The vast territory of southwestern China must be regarded as a chronotope, referring as much to a physical juncture of time and place in the course of history as to a position in the fabric of rhetorical expressions, a position that foregrounds a writer's literary as well as cultural/ideological imaginations vis-à-vis the environment in which he writes. Therefore, the place of West Hunan can be appreciated only because it triggers a cluster of images: rural China, peasantry, homeland, memory of the past, nostalgia.

Four cases can be used to illustrate the interplay between the art of writing and the art of remembering: *Autobiography of Congwen* and "Yige chuanqi de benshi" (Material for a legend, 1947), "Three Men and One Woman," and "Deng" (The lamp, 1930). Each case shows a different aspect of Shen Congwen's efforts to come to terms with the problem of memory and writing.

Autobiography of Congwen describes Shen Congwen's first twenty years of life, starting with his childhood and culminating in his arrival in Beijing, ambitious to become an intellectual writer. A seminal work containing lots of material that will be developed into individual works later, the autobiography impresses with its lyrical renderings of the various stages of Shen's early years: the military background of his family; the ethnic color of his homeland; school days rife with records of cutting classes and schoolboy mischief; the Republican revolution followed by riots and massacres; initial experiences as an adolescent soldier; wars and aftermath of wars, encounters with figures from different social strata; first love and so on. Life was never easy for the young Shen Congwen, but when put in words, that life fascinates with its picaresque experiences and fantastic adventures. It has become a simulation of the real that can be dreamed.

Nevertheless, as an autobiography, the book cannot avoid the verisimilar irony that underlines the genre in general. It apparently provides firsthand material about the author's past, including psychological nuances that would otherwise be unavailable. Who else could understand Shen Congwen's past better than himself? But when a man sets out to deal with his own past, what he does is more than just to record whatever comes to his mind from the dark realm of memory. He has to reorganize his memory, make speculations, leave out painful and embarrassing moments, and fill in "unforgettable" moments, so that he can endow the materials with coherence and intelligibility. Autobiography is a kind of fiction-making.

Autobiography of Congwen also merits attention in that it is written by a writer as a record of how he has come to be a writer. We are supposed to see how the image of West Hunan expands parallel to the unfolding of the narrative and the growth of the young Shen Congwen. Writing and life are set side by side and then overlaid in a richer total pattern. As far as the theme of nostalgia for the native soil is concerned, one finds another layer of irony: just as Shen Congwen has to grow up to appreciate the meaning of childhood, so the young writer cannot write about his home till he leaves it. The autobiography ends as Shen Congwen arrives in a shabby inn in Beijing and puts down his name: "Shen Congwen aged twenty native of Fenghuang county Hunan Province."[63] It is actually a historical moment in Shen's life, registering the beginning of his adulthood and, not coincidentally, of his writing. Writing makes him feel the pain of being severed from the past, homeland, and childhood; yet at the same time writing enables him to inscribe memory under conditions of imaginary nostalgia. The autobiography starts where it ends. It is the book itself that contains all other native soil writings by Shen Congwen. A final point: insofar as *Autobiography of Congwen* is strangely loaded with recollections of deaths, from disease, war, riot, decapitation, and passion, Shen Congwen's book indicates another kind of triumph over the threat of the irrational and the contingent. To write means to revivify and so overcome the past.

Shen Congwen also wrote a biographical account of the family of an artist, Huang Yushu. Entitled "Material for a Legend," the work is an even more dramatic testimony to the intricate relations between art, memory, and time. The work is meant to be an introduction to the young artist Huang Yongyu's woodcuts, but it barely mentions Huang's works. Instead, Shen dedicates most of his space to the sad life of an artist named Huang Yushu with whom he had lived in Changde twenty-seven years before. Huang Yushu was poor, yet his Bohemian life-style and his romantic temperament eventually won him a wife, who was also an art student. But his dreams of becoming rich and famous never came true. Years later, Shen Congwen learned that he had died from disease, after a petty existence as school teacher, army clerk, supervisor of a wharf loading station, and father of five children. The disillusioned artist, Huang Yushu, was Shen Congwen's counsin, and was in fact the father of the young woodcut-maker Huang Yongyu.

In an afterword added in 1979, Shen Congwen explains that though "Material for a Legend" may at first look like mere random recollections of Huang Yongyu's father, it was written in such way as to evoke a much broader retrospect of "the historical development and tragic conditions of his home region."[64] What enabled him to do this were the woodcuts mailed to him by Huang Yongyu, who at that time Shen had never met. The artworks thus serve as an intermediary, giving form to family as well as to social histories. They lead Shen Congwen to his and his dead friend's past, while allowing him an anticipatory glimpse of the young printmaker's future. Huang Yongyu did eventually become one of the most important painters and sculptors in the People's Republic of China.

Shen Congwen wrote the essay in 1947, when his own career was under a severe test, due to sociopolitical changes. Looking back at where he came from, in the light of Huang Yushu's case, he was saddened by the road he had taken and the road he might have taken. Huang Yongyu's woodcuts must have recalled the life he had experienced before he arrived in Beijing. His nostalgia, nevertheless, must be expressed as art. A remake of what has happened, the past remembered does not hold true in the present: it must be no more or less than an artwork, or a "legend," as the title of the biographical account suggests. Like the woodcuts by Huang Yongyu, Shen Congwen's essay now bears the inscriptions of the past and speaks to its readers, thereby reinforcing his recurrent association of writing with survival and life.

Nostalgia is also related to the artistic form of repetition. If the past is like a Chinese box, with layers of boxes inside, a writer's hermeneutic search for original meaning will soon become a burden, even a curse. He unpacks those memories, trying again and again to bring the narrative to a different conclusion, but always finds the story broken off, interrupted, forcing him to write it once again. The most obvious example of this may be the story "Three Men and One Woman." I dealt with this story of mysterious death and necrophilia in the last chapter, in terms of its lyricism of grotesquery and violence. What I am concerned about now is the fact that the story was related by Shen Congwen at least four different times. It is retold in "Yisheng" (Doctor, 1931). In that version, a doctor is abducted by a young man to a mountain cave, where he is asked to resurrect a pretty young woman, who has obviously been dead for quite a while. More to the doctor's dismay, the dead body still has fresh soil all over the clothes, a sign that she might have been dug out of her grave and brought here by the young man. Ten days later, the doctor manages to run back to the town and tell his story. "On the following day, the whole town knew the doctor's story, and concluded that he must have encountered a ghost."[65]

In *West Hunan,* Shen Congwen generalizes the story in an understated manner, using it to illustrate the local people's crazy passions, "which have disappeared in recent years."[66] In *Autobiography of Congwen,* by contrast, he exposes his own part in the event. As a junior soldier stationed in a small town called Yushuwan, Shen actually witnessed the execution of the young man, a beancurd vendor. Although sentenced to death, the young man showed no sign of fear and quietly awaited his fate. Shen even asked him, "Why did you do it?" In response, the young beancurd vendor "smiled, casting a glance at me as if I were too young to understand the meaning of love. . . . But later on, he murmured to himself, 'Beautiful, beautiful.'"[67] Shen remembers that smile, "which has maintained a very clear impression for the past ten years in my mind."[68]

In different narrative styles and voices, Shen Congwen endeavors to find the perfect form of narrative which he hopes will redeem him from repetition. The story in discussion appears to the reader as a local anecdote (in *West Hunan*), a biographical incident (in *Autobiography of Congwen*), a gruesome adventure (in "Doctor"), and a gothic romance (in "Three Men and One Woman"); each account invites a different interpretation. Was the young man a lunatic or a Romeo? Which of Shen Congwen's voices is more convincing? What really did happen? As for the answer to these questions, Shen Congwen might feel as anxious as his readers. Caught in the net of memory, Shen Congwen writes only to multiply his struggle to escape.

At the end of "Three Men and One Woman," Shen Congwen writes,

> I am forever restless because the past returns to haunt me often. To each his own destiny: this I know. Some things of the past perpetually gnaw the inside of me. When I talk about them you would

Imaginary Nostalgia

think they were only stories. Nobody can understand how a person feels who lives day after day under the weight of hundreds of stories like this one.[69]

To narrate, or, to write, is the translation of memory into art, an effort to re-member the pieces of the past in determinate form. But in the case of Shen Congwen, writing (narrating) is not only a ritual of exorcism, trying to expel demons, but also a form of incantation, taking one again and again into the cavern of memory, throwing different lights on its sunken passages. In the exploratory art of writing, recovery of the past may bring new pain and pleasure, not just catharsis and banishment.

Not coincidentally, it is in a story like "Three Men and One Woman" that Shen Congwen lays bares his philosophy of storytelling. The desire to emplot realist events becomes more than just an entertainment; repetition indicates a continued attempt to articulate a master-plot under repression. Shen Congwen is thus the storyteller who is condemned to tell stories which are true to his own life. Just like Coleridge's Ancient Mariner, Melville's Ishmael, and Conrad's Marlow, Shen Congwen (and his I-narrator) has to tell his story over again, to ease the burden in his mind. To tell the story is a vicarious form of exorcism, an effort to solve the riddle of the myths of youth and homeland. Any future telling of Shen Congwen's biographical experience will have to be narrative in nature because there is no way to locate its center directly; it can only be approached metonymically, through plottings and story tellings. The meaning of "homeland" will never lie in the definition but only in the transmission: in the passing-on of the horror or the beauty of the homeland, the lives and deaths of the townsfolk, the faded image of home is refigured.

My last example is "The Lamp." "The Lamp" is presented in the form of a story within a story. The frame of the story opens with a scene where a girl in green asks the young writer about an old kerosene lamp on the table. The inquiry motivates the young writer to enter the inner narrative of the story, which is about his relationship with an old soldier. An old serving-man to the young writer's father, the soldier has lost contact with his troops in a war and is looking for a place to settle down. His arrival pleases the writer, since he would make "an ideal companion, a companion I had been hoping for, day and night, for a long time."[70] To the young man, the old soldier seems like a living embodiment of the past. His age and appearance represent modern Chinese history for the young writer, from "the Boxer Rebellion of 1900, the revolution of 1911 . . . [and] an untold number of battles."[71] His talk and movement represents "so many of his rural fellow-countrymen, all uneducated, but at the same time all so very good and honest." Even his cooking "brought forth a strong nostalgia for [the young writer's] old army life." The young man's memory is stimulated even more, when the old man tells stories of his past experiences in the village and in the army. Under the dim light of a kerosene lamp provided by the soldier, "we talked, and so the magic of a familiar voice and atmosphere lured me into losing myself in reverie over an old world in which everything called to me and moved me."[72]

On the surface, "The Lamp" deals with the way a young writer successfully captures a female visitor's heart by telling her a story about a kerosene lamp. But a closer look will lead one to a theory about how fiction is fabricated in such a way as to embrace reality, how the past figures forth in memory and writing to redefine the present, and how the desire for the myth of native soil engages both a writer and his reader in the endless yarn of imaginary nostalgia. The tale within the tale does not contain meaning, but rather brings it out as a surrounding medium, acting itself as a virtual source of illumination which must be perceived in that which, outside itself, it illuminates. If one asks what a meaning that is outside rather than inside the narrative might be, what status it might have, one is forced to the conclusion that the truth of Shen Congwen's narrative must be in what his listeners can do with it. Perhaps the most important dramatization of such interlocution comes at the ending of the story.

As storyteller and audience, the old and young men indulge in an almost sensuous pleasure of looking backward. The lamp has become an instrument enlightening the darkness of the past which promises dreams never to be realized in the present. "This kerosene lamp, and the soldier's face under the lamplight, and his slightly stooped shoulders that expressed so very well the classical style of life that typified my old home: I would forget the days' frustrations and fatigue, forget the chaos in front of me."[73] The young writer has fallen victim to the old man's narrative. He consumes the old soldier's stories ferociously, so much so that he loses any interest in routine business. But as his desire for the past is consummated in the old man's yarns, ironically, he finds himself powerless to write his own homeland stories.

Nowhere else in Shen Congwen's works can we see such a vivid revelation of the magic of storytelling, a magic that he himself perfects by subjugating his readers to the textual mirage of West Hunan and soliciting from them a yearning for home and the past. Yet nowhere else either can we see such an emphatic display of the power struggle between the addresser and the addressee, between past and present, between narrative and reality. As the story continues, the old man is fed with so much desire to narrate, to have a say, that he no longer feels content with retelling the past but attempts to plot the young man's future as a completion of that past. He plans how the young writer will approach and marry a girl in blue. At this point, a traditional reading might have ended up celebrating the old soldier's honesty and naiveté. My reading, however, suggests that the old man has now been caught in the imaginary snare of his own recollections. He wants things to happen as they "should have" happened, only to expose himself as a victim of his own nostalgia. As his young master never marries the expected "girl in blue," his ideal story must remain incomplete, and his own disappearance becomes a plot necessity.

As if the inner story were not complicated enough, Shen Congwen now gives the young writer and the girl in green another round of telling and listening to stories in their frame narrative. In her desire to know more about the old soldier's and the writer's past, the girl in green has unwittingly allowed herself to be implicated in a chain of storytelling situations. Two things should be noticed here. The young writer is not merely telling the girl an old soldier's story. He shows her the situation in which the storytelling took place: "he told her where the old soldier used to stand and how he looked when he talked, and in the old soldier's hands how sparkling the glass chimney of the lamp always looked, against such a messy desk strewn with books and paper."[74] And for the girl in green, listening to the story is not enough; she hopes to meet the old soldier and join in his narrative as a character. On the next meeting, she changes her green dress into blue so as to play out the rule of fantasy, in honor of the lamp.

But the story has another twist. Asked by the girl about the whereabouts of the now-missing lamp, the young writer slips up and indicates that the whole inner story might have been a fabrication of his. The old soldier might not exist and the lamp might belong to the landlady. Nothing is for sure. But does it really matter? The girl in green is not upset by the writer's lie. In fact, by the end of the story, the young couple's desire to relive the past has been replaced by the romance they have engendered in the process of storytelling. The old soldier's wish (if there had been an old soldier) to unite his young master with the girl in blue is somehow carried out, but in a form that suspends him in order to succeed. "The Lamp," therefore, is a story of the seduction of a young woman by a young writer telling an old tale, the tale of an old soldier who imagines a young woman for a young writer who cannot write. The inner narrative, which turns out to be fictional, is a verbal movement toward the young man's unnameable desire for the past and home, but the thrust of this desire is played out in the frame story where the man and the woman reenact, upon every rereading, Shen Congwen's own desire.

I can find no better way to conclude my discussion of Shen Congwen's native soil fiction and his play with imaginary nostalgia than to reiterate the lesson one might learn from the four stories I have discussed. In his autobiographical accounts, Shen Congwen neatly weaves a tapestry of personal and family pasts, and emphasizes how the artist is born to bear witness to past things. In the repetitive rewriting of legendary events that happened to him in youth, personal experience and fictional fantasy meet to reinterpret the past, which, after all, amounts to a tremendous burden upon memory. For remembrance, the story-teller who tells is more important than the story told, because remembrance includes the told in the telling. Shen Congwen's native soil fiction is not about a revelation of the past so much as about a romance between him and his readers set off by the fiction of West Hunan. By eternally postponing the union with the remembered, Shen Congwen's stories open themselves to the reinscription of joy in separation, and to imaginary nostalgia.

Chapter eight

Conclusion

I have discussed Mao Dun, Lao She, and Shen Congwen as the three writers who opened the polychrome horizon of modern Chinese realistic fiction. My discussion treated modern Chinese realism not as a unified movement, dominated by a set of rigid rules of seeing and writing the world, but as a *narrative domain*. Within a narrative domain, generic tropes and conventions cross-reference each other, indexing the spatiotemporal substance of their context. In the thirties and forties, historiography and melodrama, lyric and farce, had become configured in the formal parameters by which writers could depict the real China, yet in the meantime they were being reformed by the same historical forces which had once conferred authenticity upon them and incorporated them as variables into a hermeneutic of the real.

With Mao Dun, Lao She, and Shen Congwen as examples, I suggested that modern Chinese realism manifested itself in *at least* six major narrative modes from this domain: the historical/political novel, the melodramatic/farcical novel, and the lyrical/nativist novel. These six modes point to six forms of representation (forms that in fact predate the rise of nineteenth-century European as well as twentieth-century Chinese realism); they also arise from *and* circumscribe epistemological or ideological territories in which realist writers located the issues of their own time. In contrast to the conventional wisdom that modern Chinese fiction is dominated by a unanimous discourse of critical realism, I have argued that writers were far more imaginative about invoking the real, and that critical intent did not imply a single form of realistic expression. In too narrowly defining the expected boundary of the real, some modern-day critics of Chinese realism have been more conservative than the actual writers of the post–May Fourth era.

Even at the end of the twentieth century, the specific impact of the three writers, to say nothing of the verisimilitudes to which they submitted themselves in order to write, can still be discerned everywhere in China. Their versions of realism still dominate late twentieth-century Chinese intuitions of reality. To conclude this book, therefore, I would like to turn to contemporary Chinese fiction, taking a preliminary look at what writers of the seventies and eighties have done with the achievements of these three writers of the thirties. My concern is not influence and reception but rather *reciprocal invocation:* discovering the eighties in the thirties and the thirties in the eighties. In the manner of a Foucauldian genealogy, I would like to follow certain late twentieth-century writers along pathways toward realism which were first traced out for Mao Dun, Lao She, and Shen Congwen. These paths are: choosing the future via a (re)writing of history; distancing the present with radical laughter; discovering the past by means of "imaginary" nostalgia. Needless to say, the three paths intersect.

The Politics of (Re)writing History in Mainland Chinese Fiction

One of the most remarkable phenomena in contemporary Chinese literature is the resurgence of historical fiction. As if responding to the political situations which have arisen since the late seventies, writers on both sides of China have raised questions about the genre's paradoxical nature: how do fiction writers claim a historical validity in their fictional retailing of bygone events, what valorizes the verisimilitude of a historical narrative, who legitimizes the "voice of history." As the demarcation line between history and fiction becomes more and more dubious, historical fiction can no longer be regarded as a rigid genre, with codified features drawn from nineteenth-century European or classical Chinese historical novels; rather it must refer to a field which encompasses traditional forms of the historical novel as well as such subgenres as reportage and biographical accounts.

My discussion of Mao Dun's realist fiction has shown that modern Chinese historical novels have been closely and constantly bound up with immediate political and moral demands. Particularly pertinent to my current concern are leftist novelists' experiences over the past several decades. Whereas the young Mao Dun in the 1930s—a period relatively more open to dialogues on history—committed the historical novel to registering "reality" when official historiography allegedly failed to do so, a converted Ding Ling, after Mao's talks on literature and the arts in Yanan, produced the novel *Taiyang zhaozai Sangganhe shang* (The sunshine over the Sangan River, 1948), only to submit to Marxist historical myth at the expense of tangible fact.

As I-tsi Feuerwerker forcefully argues, insofar as traditional historiography and Communist fiction share the notion that truth is what is consensual or officially sanctioned, "it is tempting to see the Marxist novel's claim to be contemporary history as a return, albeit with difference, to the Chinese narrative tradition in which historiography served as the central model of narration."[1] Two decades after Mao Dun and his peers launched their attacks on the metaphysical absolutism embedded in traditional historical and historiographical assumptions, the old belief that official historiography is approximate "reality" has sneaked back in Communist guise, with more severe demands than ever that fiction should be an approximation not of history but of the "official" account of History. The chilling fact must also be taken into account that the fickle modern party line might reclassify an erstwhile "authentic" historical fiction as a distortion of the "updated" version of history, and that a writer might be forced to give up or repeatedly revise his work at the latest party command. For writers such as Ouyang Shan (*Yidai fengliu* [One generation of noble souls], 1959–1984), and Yao Xueyin (*Li Zicheng* [Li Zicheng], 1963–1978), who lived through two decades of governmental interventions before their epic novels were completed, history and (re)writing about history have become too intermingled to be distinguished from each other.

Contemporary PRC writers' interest in historical fiction is thus revived on two terms: while it recapitulates a time-honored tradition of the historical novel, it also opens a new plateau of the politics of fiction. It has been all too well remembered that a novel (and drama) can easily be turned into a political "event," fulfilling a "historical" function with regard to what should have happened and what did happen. The brutal incident in Tian'anmen Square televised live before audiences all over the world, followed by the Communist government's denial of any bloodshed in the massacre, has raised such pointed questions as: how is official "history" sanctioned? and how does a conscientious writer deal with such a "history"?

I shall lay out four trends which have preoccupied contemporary Chinese writers while writing about history. These trends demonstrate what Mao Dun and his peers managed or failed to do with the genre more than half a century ago. The first trend, represented by novels like Dai Houying's *Ren ah, ren!* (Man ah, man!, 1981) and *Shiren zhisi* (Death of a poet, 1982), nurtures itself on a narrative format first set up by Mao Dun, one that delineates ordinary people's changing consciousness and behavioral patterns over a tumultuous timespan. But it surpasses Mao Dun's verisimilar norm by inquiring more openly into the nature of what is history.

Man ah, Man! is a historical novel not simply because it traces a group of intellectuals' mistaken historical judgment, blind faith, cowardice and betrayal, and painful reawakening from the Anti-Rightist movement to the Cultural Revolution—a subject which is only too commonly shared by writers since 1978 under the banner of *"shanghen wenxue"* (literature of the wounded). It excels other fiction of the same kind by its claim to rethink history itself in ideological and philosophical terms. Dai Houying's questions are simple yet powerful: if history, according to Mao and Marx, is a prewritten holy text, leading toward a socialist paradise, how are we going to justify the mistaken development in the past three decades? Is it a painful but necessary detour before the great turn comes? Is it a miscalculation on the part of the leadership? Or was it just a bad joke from the beginning? "History! We have all been made fools by you!"[2] sighs one character in the novel.

Dai Houying merits applause simply for raising these questions. But stunning as her skepticism concerning the official definition of history may first appear, her answers turn out to be very weak. This is, however, due not so much to visible censorship as to her own unwitting endorsement of a theoretical framework she set out to demolish. At the core of the novel lurks a dilemma she can hardly solve: whether history is a composite of lived experiences, directed toward a teleological end—Marxist Humanism, for instance—or but an individual interpretation of the real in flux, subject to revisable ideological and perceptual assumptions. Dai Houying must have relished the possibility of a pluralized vision of history, as indicated by the caption for the novel's first part: "every human being has a history stored up in his mind and it is active in many diverse ways."[3] Yet as her theory of Marxist Humanism is gradually given shape, she harks back to, rather than gets rid of (as might have been expected), a total Idea that calls for a reconciliation between past and Future, individual and Mass, history and History.

Dai Houying's *Death of a Poet* again manages to inspire its readers with something other than mere reportage of betrayals, physical and intellectual abuses, and injustices. Describing the persecution and eventual suicide of a poet during the Cultural Revolution, the novel raises the question of the eternal strain between writing and reality, between poetry (literature) and historiography.

The poet is persecuted because he wrote a poem about those "unmentionable" aspects of the past, which had cost his wife's suicide and their children's disgrace. Instead of giving up or revising the manuscript at the "People's" demand, he continues to write and expand it, while the search for the manuscript on the party's side simply amounts to an obsession, leading from one purge to another. Ironically enough, for all the disputes over history, the hero and villains share a common conviction of the immanence of History as well as Writing about History. In fact, one of the most important motifs in the novel is writing: almost everybody is busy writing secret confessions, self-criticisms, family histories, overheard secrets, conspiratorial strategies, ideological conversions and reconversions, indictments and verdicts. Writing itself, however, either as graphic text charged with information or as act of communication, never becomes a problem for either the Party or the poet.

It is from here that we discern a revival of Mao Dun's and other early leftist writers' conviction that literature (poetry) is obligated to fulfill a duty of telling the historical truth when official historiography is untrustworthy. Yet the irony indicated here is only too clear: Mao Dun and his peers were writing in anticipation of the eventual coherence of literary and historical texts in a new Communist era.

Conclusion

How is it that, forty years after Mao's rule, the gap between the poet's fictitious yarn and the government's story has still remained unbridgeable? In this sense, Dai Houying's novel presents an intriguing paradox. She sets out to describe a poet who wants to write a "superpoem," a poem subsuming all other literature and transcending all linguistic and ideological barriers, in a historical context where writing in all forms has proven to be just as vulnerable as it is unreliable. But she ends up writing only a story about the impossibility of writing.

The second and third tendencies of historical fiction can be discussed in the light of Feng Jicai's two kinds of fiction. Though not among the most outstanding writers of the Post-Mao era, Feng leads the second tendency with a series of novels on late Qing political events; his intention is to dig out the roots of the problems modern China has suffered from. He contributes to the third tendency by compiling in fictional form individual interviews and confessions on the Cultural Revolution. While the first type is written in a way reminiscent of Mao Dun's rewriting of historical events, the second, with its accumulation of personal accounts, has its roots in Mao Dun's reportage, *One Day in China: May 21, 1936*.

Feng Jicai's *Yihequan* (The boxers, 1977), cowritten with Li Dingxing, is a historical novel in the most traditional sense, telling of the uprising and failure of the Boxers from 1898 to 1900. But despite the fact that the authors use correct names, dates, and other verifiable details, the novel is no more than an amateur costume drama, put on only to entertain some ideological formula. Abiding by Chinese Communist interpretations,[4] the writers work hard to justify the Boxers' campaign as a heroic deed, a historical necessity, and a "victory" to be proven by the unfolding of time.

Chinese Communist fiction and drama have a long genealogy of reading and writing about classical figures and events in order to transmit a certain political message. Mao Dun's "The Great Marsh District" and "Stone Tablet," Tian Han's *Xie Yaohuan* (Xie Yaohuan, 1961), Wu Han's *Hairui Baguan* (Hairui resigns office, 1961), and Yao Xueyin's *Li Zicheng* are only the most prominent examples, to say nothing of Lao She's *Shenquan* (The magical boxers, 1963), a play on the Boxer Rebellion. While some works succeeded in making interesting juxtaposition of past and present, the ghosts of the past, once called back to life, may in their turn set a suspicious reflection on the present, causing the writers endless trouble. The cases of Lao She and Tian Han are still fresh in our memory.

Feng Jicai is working in this tradition, and thus has to share with his predecessors the same potential to elicit threatening historical parallels. Faced with incompatibilities between historical sources and ideological constraint, Feng Jicai and Li Dingxing have a lot of holes to fill in and contradictions to even out; it is never dull to observe how they emplot history to serve a specific purpose. Precisely because censorship calls for fiction's "correct" interpretation of history, writers' imaginations are in just as high demand as proper ideology. Feng Jicai and his partner derive their inspiration mainly from such classical Chinese novels as the *Shuihu zhuan* (The water margin,).[5] Ideological motivation notwithstanding, at stake is the paradox that as the "historical fact" about the Boxer Rebellion is uncovered, it sounds more and more like a remake of a classic of historical fiction.

What adds more twists to our survey is the historical context in which Feng Jicai and Li Dingxing were writing their novel. By telling the story of the Boxer Rebellion from the Boxers' side, Feng Jicai and Li Dingxing might or might not have succeeded in turning the tables, depending on the degree to which readers were convinced by their version. But they have surely left a door open for those who would see the novel in a broader historical light—PRC literary criticism itself has taught us all too well how to read a text against the ever-changing political context. Published amid the aftermath of the Cultural Revolution, the novel does not salvage the images of the Boxers so much as set up a very ambiguous analogy between the past and present. Who are, after all, most comparable to the Boxers, if not certain participants in the Cultural Revolution? And in what ways—especially those emphasized by erasure—are they all too like the Boxers?

Feng Jicai is also known for the unfinished book *Yibaigeren de shinian* (One decade, one hundred people, 1987). It represents one of the recent examples of combining the genres of reportage literature and historical fiction. As the title suggests, *One Decade, One Hundred People* is a "novel" composed of one hundred short stories on the most painful decade in PRC history. For Feng Jicai, the Cultural Revolution is so complicated a subject that it takes not one but at

Conclusion

least one hundred accounts and viewpoints to deal with it. The project may be associated with exposés done by writers/reporters such as Liu Binyan, but it is particularly comparable with Zhang Xinxin's (with Sang Ye) book of reportage, *Beijing ren* (People in Beijing, 1984), which also collects one hundred interviews with individuals from different social strata and age groups. Mao Dun's stupendous work, *One Day in China: May 21, 1936,* is, of course, the origin of this kind of literature.[6]

That editors and writers of reportage literature can eliminate themselves completely from their text is an old realist myth long ago devalued by modern critics and writers. Compare Liu Binyan's, Zhang Xinxin's and Feng Jicai's work, and one finds that how they conduct interviews, what they expect their contributors to talk about, and how they render the results do lead to different versions of the manners and morals of the same Chinese people from the same social ambience. Liu Binyan is at his best when he describes his case stories from an impartial, public stance.[7] Literature works just like a social indictment for him, lashing out at those corrupt bureaucrats and villains who benefitted from the Cultural Revolution. Zhang Xinxin succeeds in transmitting a verisimilitude of storytelling by making her contributors blurt out just what they had on their minds at the moment of the interview. Memories of the Cultural Revolution loom, but it is the present that concerns her interviewees the most.

Feng Jicai goes further. He sets out to solicit his contributors to remember the past (i.e. the Cultural Revolution), especially those experiences people normally prefer to forget due either to shame or to guilty consciences. Instead of the good-hearted *tableaux vivants* that characterize Zhang Xinxin's book, Feng Jicai makes his a sullen ritualistic attempt at exorcism. Only by forcing witnesses into the forbidden traumatic realm can one learn the hard lessons inscribed in history. If Feng Jicai's stories make more sense than the bulk of the literature of the wounded, it is because they reveal more than just the persecution and pain—they also reveal the fanaticism, cruelty and irrationality *shared* by people in the Cultural Revolution.[8] A historical sense is thus evoked, as Feng Jicai's narrators, through their remembrance of things past, gradually come to realize how much their way of life and their understanding of human relationships, as well as their attitude toward politics, have been drastically changed over the crucial last ten years.

Conclusion

The fourth tendency of contemporary historical fiction is represented by writers such as A Cheng, Han Shaogong, and Yu Hua. My choice may raise some doubts, because A Cheng and Han Shaogong are normally related to the *"xun'gen"* (search for roots) movement, while Yu Hua is often considered to be an experimentalist novelist. Though their works might not be strictly defined as historical fiction, these writers do produce unique concepts of history which, in my view, have crossed over the horizon first opened by Mao Dun, and point to yet another possible direction for PRC writers working in the genre.

A Cheng won fame for his three "king" novellas, *Qiwang, Shuwang, Haiziwang* (Chess king, Tree king, Child king, 1984). Beyond an immediate concern with political struggles or individual troubles, he draws historical inspiration from rethinking conventional wisdom. As evinced by his most celebrated "Chess King," his fiction elicits the quasi-philosophical parallel of man's condition with a game. In the novella, A Cheng elaborates a philosophy of chess playing which turns out to be a no less subtle interpretation of history. A Cheng, of course, is not the first Chinese writer inspired by the analogy. Liu E made a similar association in his preface to *Lao Can youji* (The travels of Lao Can) as early as in 1904, and Zhang Xiguo, a contemporary overseas writer, even wrote a novel with the same title as A Cheng's. However, A Cheng surpasses his predecessors by providing a synchronic vision in which past and present, historical turmoils and trivial games, military maneuvers and chessboard moves, are all summoned together, staging in their own ways a story which is both familiar yet strange. A Cheng *localizes* the past in the form of a chess game, subverting the grandiose scale of historical accounts.

With novellas like "Bababa" (Papapa, 1986) and "Nününü" (Woman woman woman, 1986), Han Shaogong invests the temporal sequence of his narrative with a dimension of mythical recurrence *and* hiatus, and thus sheds light on problems other novels have not faced. With the Cultural Revolution in mind, Han manages nevertheless to avoid immediate historical exegesis, yielding to a visionary yearning for the lost Chu culture, a culture rife with spellbinding mysticism and passionate romance. Making an allegorical landscape of his hometown region, he observes the chaos of a Chinese society on the brink of total disintegration ("Papapa"), and the moral and intellectual degeneration of the Chinese people living in that society ("Woman Woman Woman"). Starting with grotesque realism, Han develops his fiction into a narrative mixing Gothic charm and Lu Xunesque cannibalistic horror. Chronicling the last days of a civilization, Han's fiction approximates an eschatological myth, with a touch of lyrical pathos.

Yu Hua's historical fiction is even more radical. Not only does he throw doubt upon the epistemological basis of traditional historical writing, he questions the very linguistic medium with which history makes itself intelligible. His fictions such as "Yijiu baliu nian" (Nineteen eighty-six, 1987), "Shishi ruyan" (The past is like smoke, 1987) and "Wangshi yu xingfa" (Past and punishment, 1990) subvert the conventional narrative from the level of language and style. Facing up to the past and endowing it with meaning is no longer seen as a rational endeavor but as a schizophrenic *cum* paranoiac desire disguised as reason and humanity. Thus in "Nineteen Eighty-Six," the novel of a year with "no" significance, the Chinese people's fractured memories of the Cultural Revolution find yet another manifestation, in a madman's fancies of bodily mutilation and dismemberment. Even the most innocent people are burdened with sins; to be a survivor of the revolution indicates voluntary suppression of memory and therefore an ironic complicity with the menace of history. In "The Past is like Smoke," history is treated as a disoriented genealogy, full of forced erasures and illogical ruptures. And in "The Past and Punishment," history is embodied as a vulgar figure or a mysterious machine of punishment, playing dirty tricks on anyone who dares question its authority. The good realist writing that Dai Houying and Feng Jicai have posted on the wall of history is defaced in Yu Hua's world by unpleasant grafitti.

In dramatizing the existential sentiment of one's own, or, rather, one nation's, encounter with a historical abyss, these three writers recapitulate Mao Dun's anxiety and confusion after the failure of the first Chinese Communist revolution. Their attempt to demythify History is not unlike Mao Dun's when he started to write his first novel *Eclipse*. But writing after the Great Cultural Revolution, these writers emplot history in a way more radical and self-reflexive than that of Mao Dun. History is seen less as a linear procession toward a telos than as a break in which all sorts of possibilities are left in disorder. History can not have promised a periodical restoration of just the "right" elements of tradition, nor has it run short of examples of abrupt and irreparable disappearance and loss. There are too many things that, once abolished or destroyed, will not be restored by a magic turn of the wheel.

The existence of these four tendencies of historical fiction in modern Chinese literature suggests the plural possibilities of historical interpretation in the post-Mao era. By this observation on the plurality of interpretation, however, I am not granting a transhistorical prestige to my own argument. What I do suggest is that, considering what they have produced, contemporary writers, especially those of the fourth group, are better prepared to combine their moral integrity with an intellectual shrewdness. Their statements about the past direct themselves more openly to questions about the (present) criteria for believing that such statements have been meaningful. Perhaps only a demystification of History can allow us to gain the lucidity and the freedom to deal with the confusions and atrocities that history has thrust upon us.

Radical Laughter from Taiwan

In an essay published in 1979, Joseph Lau commented that modern Chinese writers had been so "obsessed" with China's fate that they wrote their fiction as if in the midst of "snivelling and tears."[9] Self-righteous outcries and bitter sentiments seem to be the basic mood of modern Chinese fiction. This phenomenon, however, has undergone a change in recent years; at least in Taiwan, some writers have been taking a different approach to subject matter that might otherwise have produced sentimental tearjerkers. These writers share a sense of keen humor and sarcasm that enables them to bring to modern Chinese fiction a species of laughter rarely encountered since the generation of Lao She, Zhang Tianyi, and Qian Zhongshu. More significantly, through reading them, our perspective on the comic narrative of the last generation has been altered.

With Lao She as my point of reference, I shall introduce five representative writers: Wang Wenxing, Wang Zhenhe, Huang Fan, Lin Shuangbu, and Li Qiao. Each of these five writers conjures up a comic/farcical vision that is far more coherent and spectacular than Lao She's, possibly indicating that they are more aware of the imaginary basis of all fictional modes and therefore more willing to abide by the aesthetic norms of a mode that is as "unrealistic" as farce.

Of the five writers, Wang Zhenhe most readily evokes a kinship with Lao She, since both are masters of parodying the classical tradition of storytelling, and both like to poke fun at provincial lives and trivial characters as they are caught between contradictory values at times of drastic cultural and economic changes. In *Meigui, meigui, woaini* (Rose, Rose, I love you, 1984), a novel about the boom of Hualian's prostitution business in the late 1960s when legions of American soldiers were coming for vacation from Vietnam, we witness for the first time a complete Chinese version of carnivalesque comedy. Pimps, whores, petty politicians, and opportunists turn the city topsy-turvy, while featuring in a parade of extremely absurd scenes. The language used in telling the story is a composite of Taiwanese slang, Mandarin clichés, pidgin English, and broken Japanese. All these rhetorical confusions constitute a cacophonous discourse that not only ridicules the promiscuous nature of Taiwan's culture but also reinforces the novel's nonconformist bent against the orthodox monophonic system of fiction writing.

Wang Zhenhe never lets the social/political criticism embedded in the novel overshadow its festive mood. Like Lao She at his funniest, he insinuates his most biting jokes into the most sensitive topics. Readers will forget neither the city parliamentary election debate, which is turned into a stripping contest between (male) candidates, nor the pimps' seminar in which serious study is given to girls' sizes, skills and even menstrual regularities. Wang's hero Dong Siwen (literally meaning 'understanding decorum') is astonishingly similar to Lao Zhang in *The Philosophy of Lao Zhang*. Both are unscrupulous opportunists who seek every possible way to make money, and both are versatile instigators who turn every occasion they preside over into a hilarious disaster. Like Lao She, Wang Zhenhe well understands the danger a clown like Dong Siwen poses to a normal society, but his ambivalent feelings for him keep him from allowing his downfall.

Whereas Wang Zhenhe presents a world full of obscene jokes, slapstick routines and vulgarized cartoon figures, Huang Fan cultivates in his novel *Fanduizhe* (The opponent, 1984) a vein of black humor derived from Kafka's tradition. *The Opponent* is a political novel in intention, recording how a college professor is involved in a campus sex scandal that eventually evolves into a case of political persecution. But Huang Fan makes the novel only *seem* to carry profound messages. When all the pompous characters and grim events reveal themselves as possible jokes, we grasp the author's subversively comic strategy in operation.

Conclusion

Far from living out the nuances of human sensibilities, Huang Fan's characters are mere robots, farcical puppets set in motion by empty ambition, who in their turn set in motion machines of persecution and scandal whose relentless march they are unable to stop. In this sense, the novel reminds one of Lao She's *The Biography of Niu Tianci,* in that both writers see behind the flux of assorted events a monstrous machine dominating individual will in terms of money or power. Tear off the mask of cultural/political ideals, and one finds sordid bargains and deals. Especially notable is the fact that both novels introduce a meek, amiable protagonist who, for all his misbehavior, nonetheless wins the reader's sympathy. But if we applaud Niu Tianci's initiation into society, or the final acquittal of Huang Fan's protagonist, our moral standard has become shaky. Neither "happy ending" indicates a return to poetic justice, only a successful enterprise of the political/commercial machine to which these heroes have chosen to conform.

Unlike *The Opponent,* which exposes the absurdities of ongoing political conflicts in society, Wang Wenxing's *Beihai de ren* (The man with his back to the sea, 1981) focuses on a single character's psychological state after he retreats into an isolated environment. In the form of an interior monologue which lasts for one night, the novel represents one of the most ambitious attempts in contemporary Chinese fiction to reconstitute a man's inner activities. But Wang Wenxing enjoys a self-deconstructive pleasure by continuously parodying and undercutting the conventions and models from which his novel is derived. To accommodate his epistemological and stylistic circus, Wang Wenxing even works out a playfully obscure style that will easily irritate a carefree reader.

The novel can be roughly divided into three parts. Opening with a cluster of thirty-one swear words in various dialects, the first part reads like an exhaustive exhibition of our nameless hero's perverse knowledge and social criticism. His topics range from philosophy to pornography, all rendered in such a way as to be confused with one another, forming a mock encyclopedia. The novel's middle section introduces a mysterious, nearly forgotten governmental office. By all standards, this section contains one of the most imaginative portraits of bureaucratic life in modern Chinese fiction. Besides influences from Kafka's *Castle,* Lao She's *Divorce* and part of *Four Generations under One Roof,* come to mind.

The most radical and controversial part of the novel comes in the last forty pages, where the protagonist describes his four brothel adventures. With startlingly imaginative vigor, Wang Wenxing manages to include every detail, and to invent some that flabbergast the imagination. Rather than bypass physical processes, he indulges them, pushing the genre of farce toward its limits. Mingling sardonic with outrageous detail, mock-erotic behavior with comic violence, Wang's vision of pornography seems to salute and parody simultaneously the long tradition of *ars erotica*. It also serves as a triumphant moment in a farcical attack on realism, which claimed to represent life in full. This last section culminates in an orgiastic battle between the hero and a happy prostitute, a rare example in modern Chinese fiction of a female trickster. She consistently outmaneuvers the cynical protagonist, toys with his expectations, tightens and relaxes the tension, building an otherwise predictable sequence into a prelude and fugue of baroque follies. She uses laughter rather than tears to redeem the misery and unhappiness of life. In Wang Wenxing's own words, this exuberant whore "is a saint."[10]

Li Qiao's "Kongnanzheng" (Phallophobia, 1985), though only a short story, contains a farcical vision whose vulgarity and topicality deserve attention. The story deals with a woman who, after being forced to quit her job because of her recent marriage, suffers from a phobia of the male sexual organ. Li Qiao inserts biological jokes in places least appropriate for erotic associations. Everything this poor lady sees and touches turns into a phallus. The final catastrophe comes when the heroine hallucinates falling into a deep valley in which thousands of excited phalluses stand ready to attack her. In panic, she takes refuge in first a temple and then a church, only to find there the figures of Buddha and Christ exposing themselves to her.

Just as in Wang Zhenhe's and Wang Wenxing's novels, sacrilege and profanity are two weapons used by Li Qiao to subvert solemn and pompous institutions. But in the light of works written before and after "Phallophobia," we have a good reason to surmise that Li Qiao might have wanted to write not only a farce about feminism and sexual oppression but also a political allegory. After all, feminism, with its orientation to women's physical/psychological experiences, is a movement calling for ideological commitment. *Phallophobia,* while serving as proof of a male society's threatening power over women, symbolizes a tension that has long bothered dissidents, outsiders and the oppressed. Moreover, Li Qiao unwittingly betrays his condescending and ambiguous attitude toward women while lavishly proving his heroine's predicament. Vacillating between phobia and mania, fear and desire, the laughter he evokes deserves ironic investigation.

The same kind of radical laughter can also be heard in Lin Shuangbu's novel, *Juezhan xingqiwu* (The final combat on Friday, 1986). A well-known dissident writer, Lin sets out to chronicle the political transformation of Taiwan in the mid-eighties. Instead of confronting sensitive subject matter directly, he resorts to the form of allegory which is an almost transparent veneer for his real intent. The novel takes place in a co-ed high school dominated by a mainlander principal and his cohorts. Of the many methods these "villains" use to control and penalize disobedient students, the most outrageous one is the denial of their right to relieve themselves.

The result is a hilarious mixture of styles and smells. Blending political discontent, dissident outcry and feminist protest with the pain of constipation, *The Final Combat on Friday* lashes out at the social/political status quo in excremental terms, and makes itself one of the most imaginative political novels of the eighties. The crisis finally breaks out when the principal refuses to build additional restrooms for the female students and faculty despite their urgent need. A mock-epic war is thus declared. Lin wants to make his hero a respectable fighter. But shouting and fighting in the midst of the stinking environment, the hero comes across less an idealistic leader than a filth-stained, hysterical twit. In a world where the high and the low, the fragrant and the stinking mingle, nobody has clean hands. Still, *The Final Combat on Friday* contains a tendentious and aggressive momentum not seen in other works under discussion.

Wang Zhenhe once said, "Maybe because I have seen too many heartbreaking things in my life, I have always hoped to produce in my fiction a little more laughter, as long as I can afford to."[11] Wang Zhenhe was not alone. Half a century ago Lao She commented, "I hate bad guys, but they are not without virtues; I like good guys, but they have their own foibles . . . I used to look at the world with a mixed feeling of disgust and laughter."[12] In the midst of the sighs and groans provided by most modern Chinese fiction, it is refreshing to read something that makes us laugh. But the laughter evoked by Lao She and Wang Zhenhe is a result of various impulses and motivations. It leads us to the following observations, observations which are consciously apologetic and serious, like those of Lao She and Wang Zhenhe.

First, sighing and groaning should not be regarded as the only permissible states of mind for modern Chinese fiction. This means not only that writers are obliged to try out a wider range of subject matter and fictional styles but also that readers and critics are encouraged to explore more possibilities of reading. As Leo Lee has suggested, compared with East European and Latin American literature, the bulk of modern Chinese fiction is simply too conservative in its practice of literary imagination. Humor and laughter might serve as alternatives to work on in reading and writing Chinese fiction.[13]

Second, laughter, especially farcical laughter, demands a more conscious modulation of its aesthetic conventions and distance, and therefore serves as an effective method to demythify most writers' and readers' obsession with the representational power of realism. In the name of rendering the truth in life, realism has been unquestionably believed and practiced by Chinese writers for more than half a century. In contrast to the tenets of mimesis, farce, with all its hilarity and outrage, lays bare again the fact that art is art and not an amalgam of reality. Farcical laughter disappears and gives way to dull sobriety if we look at it in strictly mimetic and moral terms.

Third, a comical/farcical view enables us to see the history of modern Chinese fiction in a new light. Besides Lao She's early fiction, we may well want to reexamine works by writers such as Zhang Tianyi and Qian Zhongshu. Moreover, the corpus of late Qing exposé fiction stands as a rich treasury prefiguring these writers' comic/farcical attempts.

Fourth, because it sets out to challenge readers' intellectual and emotional faculties at the same time as it attempts to challenge governmental censorship, comic/farcical fiction is by nature a polemical and risky genre. When he gave up laughter in favor of snivelling and tears in the forties, Lao She actually chose a relatively more cowardly way to confront social/political problems. Radical laughter not only attacks but also achieves a fantasy triumph and a triumph of fantasy; it may well be argued that the five Taiwan writers started where Lao She and his peers left off.

While the new period of mainland literature has subsided for political reasons, readers and writers in Taiwan have been *learning* to laugh at and with the comical/farcical works discussed in this section. Does this result from different governmental policies concerning the allowed latitude of creativity? Does this simply indicate a divergence of literary mentality? How much laughter can Taiwan readers tolerate when serious issues are under discussion? Will suppressed laughter be heard in fiction from the mainland in the near future? These are topics for literary historians, who are willing to speculate on the intricate relations between politics and literature in the last decade of the twentieth century, on both sides of the Taiwan Strait.

Imaginary Nostalgia: Scenes from the Two Chinas

Along with all the political turmoils after 1949, native soil fiction bifurcated into two traditions, each carrying on its own formal and ideological evolution. In Taiwan, while the lost homeland has always been a popular theme among novelists, the locus of the homeland underwent a significant change. Since the mid-fifties, native soil fiction has been best handled by writers from the mainland, especially those who were exiled to Taiwan with the military forces, such as Sima Zhongyuan and Zhu Xining. They associate their homelands with the lost mainland, and often describe the Communist revolt and consequent success as the trauma that broke away the present from the past, the island from the mainland. Personal nostalgia and national humiliation are closely related, so much so that the loss of the past and homeland has almost become an original sin, one that can never be remitted through the ritual of writing.

Native Taiwanese writers such as Huang Chunming and Wang Zhenhe started to draw attention to themselves in the mid-sixties, with a series of writings about Taiwan, their own land, and their own people. Their works soon proved to be more than just literary masterpieces; they were in effect dramatized manifestos for the validity of a Taiwan consciousness that had been downplayed under governmental hegemony. Much has been said about the artistic merit and social/political impact of Taiwanese native-soil writers. What I would like to point out is that the shift in location of the *homeland* in these writings, from, say, Hunan Province on the mainland to Tainan County on Taiwan, threw doubt upon the homeland myths cherished by the ruling powers, in politics and in criticism. As the (Taiwanese) native soil movement grew in the seventies, a conscientious reader had to come to terms with the fact that he had not one, but two, homelands to deal with—each either real or phantasmic, depending on the play of rhetoric.

One of the most dramatic testimonies to this phenomenon can be seen in the changing style of Sima Zhongyuan, one of the best postfifties' native soil writers writing about the lost mainland. Using a pen name literally meaning "riding a horse in the Middle Kingdom," Sima Zhongyuan wrote a series of narratives about his home region in northern Jiangsu, whose desolate land, quaint customs, and military turmoil constitute an epic landscape for heroic actions. Sima Zhongyuan maintained his popularity even in the midst of the Taiwanese native soil movement, a rare thing among his peers. Yet he no longer told realistic tales with historical substance as in earlier days but ghost stories, bizarre accounts against the now remote backdrop of mainland China. His change may indicate only a writer's personal choice, but we might well take it as signalling the fate of mainland-oriented native soil fiction in a period of radical regionalism.

Shen Congwen's kind of native soil fiction was suppressed for political reasons, in mainland China, for more than three decades; it was too sentimental, and too elitist to suit the new national ethos. Instead, it was the discourse of peasant literature, prefigured by Mao's Yanan talks and perfected by writers such as Zhao Shuli of the forties and Liu Qing of the fifties, that was praised. Given continuously changing party lines and literary policies, mainland peasant literature evolved without substantial formal change for more than three decades. Dealing with tests of comradeship among the peasants in their struggles against natural and man-made adversities, its personalities are types, and its plots are largely predictable. It was not until the eighties that such peasant literature finally gave way to the search for roots movement.

Seen in this light, mainland peasant fiction of the fifties and sixties may at first seem an exception to the criteria for native soil literature discussed in the previous chapter, since, besides playing with local color, it sets out to tone down nostalgia and to propagate an optimistic expectation of reform and revolution in the future. The fact is, however, that mainland peasant fiction reverses but never subverts the formula of conventional native soil literature. Substituting foreknowledge of what should happen in the future for the remembrance of what must have happened in the past, the new for the old, and the vision of progress for the vision of regress, it actually embraces the verisimilar codes of conventional native soil literature. It shares with this literature the same enthusiasm to (re)discover a lost utopia, be it located in the past or the future, and the same belief in the mythical power of time. What is hidden beneath peasant fiction as well as beneath native soil literature, one may argue accordingly, is the paradox of nostalgic anticipation.

As of the late seventies, Shen Congwen was deliberately ignored by scholars on the mainland, who claimed he lacked political awareness; he remained at best only an underground celebrity among literature lovers in Taiwan, who admired him for having stayed on the mainland and therefore being politically significant. Apart from the case of Wang Zengqi, Shen Congwen's former student and best imitator in terms of literary style and philosophy, any attempt to highlight the superficial affinity between a particular contemporary writer and Shen Congwen risks the danger of all self-serving parallelisms. The more significant questions to ask, therefore, are: how the vision of native soil established by Shen Congwen half a century before has undergone various stages of transformation; how contemporary writers employ the image of a homeland to convey different concepts, and more importantly, how in so doing these writers have responded to, clarified, or even amended Shen Congwen's formulation of imaginary nostalgia.

To my mind, three writers of the eighties deserve attention, each demonstrating a new direction in the wake of the discourse of imaginary nostalgia first initiated by Shen Congwen. They are Song Zelai, one of the last vanguards of the Taiwan native-soil movement, Mo Yan, the mainland search for roots writer acclaimed for his fantastic family-cycles, and Li Yongping, an overseas Chinese (now settled in Taiwan) who has fascinated readers by presenting a native soil landscape as a pastiche of literary images, conventions, and clichés about one's home town. These writers may not write "like" Shen Congwen, yet the way they elaborate the aesthetic and conceptual motivations of imaginary nostalgia radicalizes native soil literature and brings to light an aspect of Shen Congwen's fiction hitherto unnoticed by critics.

Song Zelai was a latecomer to Taiwan's native soil literature movement which bloomed in the early seventies. When his series of short stories entitled *Daniunan cun* (Daniunan village, 1978) first won critical acclaim, it was already the spring of 1978. By that time, well known native soil writers had either turned their attention to other subjects (such as Wang Zhenhe), or temporarily quit writing (such as Huang Chunming), or committed themselves to political activity (such as Wang Tuo and Yang Qingchu). The vehement debate over the essence of a native soil movement, which involved literati from the extreme right to the extreme left and resulted in an extensive writers' war over ideological convictions, had ended the previous year. In spring 1978, Taiwan was yet to encounter such economic and political storms as the U.S. recognition of the PRC and the Gaoxiong mass riots.

Writing at this historical juncture, Song Zelai had to face up to dilemmas his predecessors had not been obliged to deal with. Considering that veteran writers had already done so much and so well with native soil themes, could Song Zelai come up with anything new and provocative while maintaining the charm of an established discourse? Seeing that radical peers had turned the Taiwan native soil movement into a political campaign, should Song Zelai keep describing impoverished country life, decorated with quaint customs and good-natured rustic figures, or should he propagate activism at the expense of writing itself? Song Zelai has never been able to fully solve these dilemmas. But because of these dilemmas, I would argue, Song Zelai expresses in his best stories a strange nostalgia, nostalgia not so much about the loss of simple village life in an increasingly Philistine society—a common theme shared by almost all native soil writers—as about the loss of the simple style and environment his predecessors were privileged to dwell in and write about.

Song Zelai's biggest contribution to the tradition of Taiwan native soil fiction lies in his collection of short stories entitled *Penglai zhiyi* (Bizarre stories about Formosa, 1988). In the name of protesting against social injustice and against the pathetic lot of lower-class Taiwanese, Song Zelai actually tells a series of bizarre stories (zhiyi), as the title of his book suggests, whose charm consists in nothing but the mythical coincidences of human interaction and the inscrutable mechanism of the Wheel of Fortune. His naturalist landscape is haunted by ghostly figures, hushed scandals, and buried secrets. In these stories Song Zelai invests his regionalism with a unique imagination and thus fashions a nativist aesthetic that is his own.

Stylistically, *Bizarre Stories about Formosa* is characterized by Song Zelai's extensive use of framing. More often than not, Song's stories begin with the narrator's/character's visit to a town or village, where he is first lured by a strange figure or event and then (over)hears a story about that figure or event. Given the stories' limited length and simple plot, the design of story-within-a-story looks clumsy and obsolete. The people and the land are like figures in a shadow theater in his framed accounts, registering an age so remote that it evades definition. Compared with the native soil writers at the turn of the seventies, such as Huang Chunming or Wang Zenhe, Song Zelai seems simply unable to present the past, bitter or sweet, personal or communal, in its full immediacy and intimacy.

The way Song Zelai narrates his story naturally reminds us of Shen Congwen, who is also apt to retail stories in a framed structure, as illustrated by stories such as "Three Men and One Woman," and "Lamp." But Song Zelai's pose as a passive auditor and incompetent transcriber pits itself against Shen Congwen's earnest but troubled narratorial voice, which engages us with him in exploring the mysterious past, however regressive the resolution. Shen Congwen has a basic skepticism about the function of storytelling in channelling a haunted past, yet he persists, so as to articulate the unfulfilled desire to piece together memory. Song Zelai has an opposite problem. He fully believes the narrative medium is the way to link present with past, but the ambiance of his stories only confirms that there is no viable means of visiting the past again, even if the past poses as something palpable and retrievable.

Written in the late seventies when the legitimacy of Taiwan's economic, political, and historical position was faced with a tremendous challenge from within and without, Song Zelai's native soil fiction can no longer capitalize on the existing native soil discourse that, even when condemning social/political abuses, arouses our desire to go back to the shabby hometown under description. The days for Huang Chunming's kind, earthy prostitute or stubborn, old-fashioned farmer making their presence in words, are over. Song Zelai's nostalgia has doubled the nostalgia of Huang Chunming's period: it is derived from a yearning not just for the old Taiwan before it fell into the menacing web of History, but also for the simple, immaculate form of storytelling that renders that Taiwan in imagination. Song Zelai can neither go back to the old world where naiveté and simplicity shine, nor can he conjure up a world in the discourse where he actually lives. When the supposedly direct, genuine native soil experience has become unavailable in the given cultural and literary context, what remains is but a story of stories about a legendary past, nostalgia over the original (imaginary) nostalgia.

By all standards, the rise of search for roots fiction should be considered one of the mainland's most sophisticated trends of the past decade. Returning to the customs and morals of local regions, this fiction first appeared as a modest reaction against the increasingly formulaic literature of the wounded. But at a time when the whole nation of the PRC was "looking forward," the search for roots writers' insistence on looking backward, downward, and even inward must take on a polemical dimension.

Although Shen Congwen never plays a visible role in the search for roots movement, he is one of the firm roots, if we trace the genealogical tree of the young writers' native soil imaginations. Wang Zengqi, Shen Congwen's student in the forties, has written dozens of stories since 1981 with the intention of recapturing the old master's style;[14] A Cheng, forerunner of the search for roots movement, has expressed his indebtedness to Shen Congwen;[15] Jia Pingwa, the writer famous for his series of stories on Shangzhou, Shanxi, may well have had Shen Congwen's *Random Sketches* in mind when he created *Shangzhou chulu* (Preliminary accounts of Shangzhou, 1984); to say nothing of writers of the Hunan school such as Han Shaogong, Gu Hua, He Liwei, etc., who inherit Shen Congwen's deep feeling for the same region. But when one thinks of the magnitude and complexity of Shen Congwen's imaginary nostalgia, the Shandong writer Mo Yan comes to mind, rather than the Hunan writers.

By this comparison, I do not mean that Mo Yan writes like Shen Congwen in any palpable way. What I want to argue is that Mo Yan succeeds more than any of his peers in turning familiar hometown scenes into a fantastic landscape, and in creating a unique axiological system for that new territory—merits first achieved in modern Chinese tradition by Shen Congwen. Take Mo Yan's *Honggaoliang jiazu* (The red sorghum family, 1987) as example. The novel chronicles the sufferings, romances, and heroic deeds of peasants of northeastern Shandong over a period from 1923 to 1976. On the one hand, Mo Yan sees his family members as larger-than-life, judging them not by what they do but how they carry out their deeds. On the other hand, he minimizes them, so to speak, by hurling them into the huge torrents of national disaster, showing how little individual efforts count against immense historical forces. The image of his hometown vacillates between being the center of personal memory and being a negligible corner of official history, to the point where the line separating memory from history finally becomes indiscernible.

Mo Yan relies on the magic power of memory and language to enliven the legend about his homeland and ancestors, while he knows only too well that memory and language can lead nostalgia into a fragile, closed world that crumbles whenever reality intervenes. In another group of native soil fiction, such as "Baozha" (Explosion, 1985), "Baigou qiuqianjia" (White dog and swing, 1986), and *Tiantang suantai zhige* (Garlic-song in Paradise City, 1988), Mo Yan either lays bare the conventions of native soil writings of the thirties—nostalgic pathos mixed with self-derogatory social criticism—or parodies the folksy style and plot of the peasant fiction sanctioned by Mao Zedong and perfected by writers such as Zhao Shuli in the forties. He reinforces the stasis of the present by subverting the past.

In Mo Yan's own words, his homeland "northeastern Gaomi (in Shandong province) is undoubtedly the prettiest and the ugliest, the most unworldly and the most mundane, the holiest and the most vulgar, the most heroic and the rottenest, the most drunken and the most romantic place on earth."[16] In a way, Mo Yan is responding to the Shen Congwen who juxtaposed two hometown visions drawn respectively from *The Border Town* and *Long River* half a century ago. Mo Yan's vision of northeastern Gaomi may have nothing to do with Shen Congwen's West Hunan, but both writers show in their narrative the same ability to radicalize their nostalgia. They invest their nostalgia either with utopian fantasy or with heroic grandeur, then problematize it with realist references, ending up by exposing its fundamental complicity with illusion. Paradoxically, Mo Yan's distinct stylistic difference from Shen Congwen brings to the fore a belief in personal vision and a power of storytelling Shen Congwen would have endorsed.

The last writer I would like to call attention to is Li Yongping, whose novel, *Jiling chunqiu* (Jiling chronicles, 1986), represents yet another contemporary writer's radical attempt to rewrite the discourse of native soil fiction. Born and brought up in Brunei, Li Yongping went to Taiwan for his advanced high school education.

Conclusion

After college, he pursued graduate work in the United States and received a Ph. D. degree in comparative literature. He is currently a professional writer living in Taiwan. Contrary to public perception, Li Yongping's early overseas experience clearly did not cripple his sensitivity to Chinese language and literature. Of the three writers under discussion, Li Yongping is in fact the most austere stylist, whose narrative continuously surprises the reader by showing just how concise and lively the Chinese language can be. On the other hand, his training in foreign literature must have had a direct impact on him, especially in terms of plot and structure.

Li Yongping's best known work is *Jiling Chronicles,* a novel composed of twelve interrelated short stories. Dealing with a rape incident and its disastrous consequences for a rural town, *Jiling Chronicles* is rich in stereotypical figures, familiar scenarios, conventional themes, all catering to the reader's taste for a particular past era. Yet these ingredients are so shuffled together that we can no longer be sure where, when, and even how the story happened. The town's landscape and weather conditions, the townsfolks' linguistic registers and cultural habits suggest not only southern and northern China, but also Southeastern Asia! Despite a few historical references, Jiling is a town without past and future. Always floating somewhere one step beyond our reach, it exists like a mirage. The question is, if Jiling is such a phantom place, where does the effect of nostalgia come from? How do we define such a nostalgia with regard to those native writers who write about their real homelands?

In my discussion of Song Zelai's and Mo Yan's fiction, I have tried to call attention to their conscious play with the concept of a homeland and their renovations of the conventions of native soil fiction. Especially in the case of Mo Yan, home has been turned into a vast stage where fantasy and reality conflict and converge in a flagrantly dramatic fashion. But no matter how wild their imaginations, the two writers resort to a general impression of their real life homelands of southern Taiwan and northeastern Shandong. Li Yongping questions the very soil of native soil fiction. With his phantom town called Jiling, he seems to suggest that home can be a construction of literary images and that nostalgia may come less from our yearning for what we have lost than our desire for what we can never have had.[17] Stripping it of its temporal and spatial connections, one finds nostalgia nakedly tied to imagination.

Here one may notice a hidden paradox in Li Yongping's novel.

Because of his rootless background, he may be less qualified than a Mo Yan or a Song Zelai to recapitulate his authentic past in his native land; at the same time he may gain freedom to seek those roots at will, to bring imaginary nostalgia to life. As if reflecting his personal condition, his Jiling has no ontology; the town is already fallen at the beginning of the novel and may always have been so. An extravagant word play, the existence of Jiling denies the necessity that a homeland has to be firmly grounded in history and reality. If Jiling exists out of the closure of a prefigured moral or political agenda, it may be less important, if not irrelevant, to talk about its moral degeneration, as most critics have done.

I would therefore suggest that *Jiling Chronicles* is an important native soil novel of the eighties, not so much because it renders a moral vision we have been familiar with as because it represents a literary *tour de force,* showing what a writer can do once he has mastered the rules of the game. In contrast to Lu Xun's Luzhen, which symbolizes the total moral stagnation of a traditional Chinese community, we find in Jiling a decadent utopia, a fallen Peach Blossom Spring, pointing less to its writer's moral reflections on the outside world than his aesthetic self-extension. From Li Yongping's self-indulgent play with the conventions of nostalgia, we discern that his rootlessness is not an original sin he wants to overcome through native soil writing but a fortunate state of which he has taken advantage.

Li Yongping's *Jiling Chronicles* thus brings us a full circle to the point where we started our discussion of Shen Congwen. Though Shen Congwen looked at first like a conventional realist, his discourse planted all the seeds of Mo Yan's, Song Zelai's, and Li Yongping's radical harvest of nativism. These writers have taken up where Shen Congwen left off, demonstrating that nostalgia is something more than a yearning for the past. In fictional history, one tries to come to terms with the genealogy of nostalgia. Song Zelai vacillates between a longing for the lost native soil and a longing for the lost verisimilitude of native soil writing; Mo Yan brings time and history into question through a fantastic rendering of personal and national past; and Li Yongping reveals the utterly imaginary grounds of nostalgia by creating a homeland out of other texts. They see into neglected regions of the landscape remembered by Shen Congwen, and once again open up the borders of the real.

Notes

1. Introduction: After Lu Xun

1. By myth, I mean a narrative and/or behavioral manifestation that crystallizes in a figurative way the beliefs and disbeliefs, desires and fears of a society in a given historical moment. Myth substantiates seemingly atemporal truth claims in a social/cultural/political praxis, while its existence and erosion always point to built-in factors of historicity and narrativity. See Barthes, *Mythologies,* 109–159; Derrida, "White Mythology," 5–74. The mythical power of Lu Xun is specially related to modern Chinese politics. In the last forty years, Nationalist and Communist literary bureaucrats have respectively regarded Lu Xun either as the totem or as the taboo of cultural institutions; this Lu Xun paranoia/mania reached its peak in the Cultural Revolution. See Goldman, "The Political Use of Lu Xun," in *Lu Xun and His Legacy,* ed. Lee, 187–192. For the recent attempts at demythifying Lu Xun and his works, see, for example, Lee, *Voices from the Iron House.*

2. Yü-sheng Lin, *The Crisis of Chinese Consciousness,* 26–55.

3. Liang Qichao, "Lun xiaoshuo yu qunzhi zhi guanxi" (On the relations between fiction and ruling the people) *Wanqing wenxue congchao: xiaoshuo xiqu yanjiujuan* (Compendium of late Qing literature), ed. A Ying, 12–15; Chen Duxiu, "Wenxue geming lun" (On literary revolution), in *Duxiu wencun,* (Writings of Chen Duxiu), 1:135–140; Hu Shi, "Jianshe de wenxue geminglun" (Constructive revolution in Chinese literature), 289–306; Lu Xun, preface to *Nahan* (A call to arms), *Lu Xun quanji* (Complete works of Lu Xun, hereafter

Notes, Chapter 1

cited as *LXQJ*), 1:417. See also Wen Rumin, *Xinwenxue xianshi zhuyi de liubian* (Changes of realism), 3–29.

4. One of the most thorough discussions of the historical and theoretical mutations of post–May Fourth literature can be found in Hou Jian, *Cong wenxue geming dao geming wenxue* (Literary revolution to revolutionary literature); See also Anderson's cogent approach in *Limits of Realism*.

5. I am referring mainly to the Russian formalists' effort to redefine realism and realist "effect." See Jakobson, "On Realism in Art," in *Readings in Russian Poetics*, ed. Matejka and Pomorska; following his argument, realism may indicate the aspiration and intent of the author: "a work is understood to be realistic if is conceived by its author as a display of verisimilitude as true to life" (p. 38). Similarly, realism can also refer to a work which the reader perceives as true to life; nineteenth-century European realism is in effect a subdivision of the above definitions, pointing to "the sum total of the features characteristic of one specific artistic current of the nineteenth century" (p. 39). Jakobson thus implies that realism is a polemical illusion and what the author and audience recognize and enjoy may not be the reality but the artifice itself. For a different formal approach, see, for example, Levin, *Gates of Horn*, esp. 34–36.

6. Hanan, "The Technique of Lu Xun's Fiction," 53–96; Semanov, *Lu Hsun and Predecessors*.

7. Anderson, *Limits of Realism*, 8–26.

8. For recent reassessment of the theory and practice of mimesis, see Prendergast, *Order of Mimesis*, 1–82. For more discussion on the concept of verisimilitude, see Genette, "Vraisemblance et motivation," 6; Todorov, "Introduction to Verisimilitude," in *Poetics of Prose*, 82–83; Lucente, *Narrative of Realism and Myth*, 2–25.

9. See Genette's observation, "mimesis in words can only be mimesis of words. Other than that, all we have and can have is degree of diegesis." Genette, *Narrative Discourse*, 134; see also Burke's criticism, that "though man is typically the symbol using animal, he clings to a kind of naive verbal realism that refuses to realize the full extent of the role played by symbolicity in his notion of reality." Burke, *Language as Symbolic Action*, 5.

10. Anderson, "The Morality of Form: Lu Xun and the Modern Chinese Short Story," in Lee, ed., *Lu Xun and his Legacy*, 32–53.

11. Genette, *Narrative Discourse*, 199n, 212–214,

12. "Mara" is a buddhist term, referring to the devil. Lu Xun uses the term to describe writers endowed with a romantic rebellious spirit. See Lu Xun, "Moluo shili shuo" (On the poetic power of the Mara poet), in *LXQJ*, 1:63–115.

13. Foucault, *Madness and Civilization*. See also Lentricchia, *Ariel and the Police*, 29–69.

14. Lu Xun, "Kuangren riji" (Diary of a madman), in *LXQJ*, 1: 423.

15. T. A. Hsia, *Gate of Darkness*, 146–162.

16. Mao Dun, *Wozouguo de daolu* (Road I have taken), 2: 195–236.

17. Mao Dun, "Du *Ni Huanzhi*" (Reading *Ni Huanzhi*), *Mao Dun wenyi zalunji* (Miscellaneous essays), ed. Shanghai wenyi chubanshe, 2:228.

18. Mao Dun, "Chuangzuo yu ticai" (Creation and subject matter), *Mao Dun wenyi zalunji* (Miscellaneous essays), ed. Shanghai wenyi chubanshe, l:347.

19. Lau, *Tilei piaoling de xiandai wenxue* (Modern Chinese literature), 1–8.

20. Lao She, "Wo zenyangxie *Zhao Ziyue*" (How I wrote *Zhao Ziyue*), in *Lao She shenghuo yu chuangzuo zishu* (Lao She's accounts), ed. Hu Jieqing, 14.

21. I am referring to Peter Brooks's definition that the "moral occult" is "the repository of the fragmentary and desacralized remnants of sacred myth. It bears comparison to the unconscious mind, for it is a sphere of being where our most basic desires and interdictions lie, a realm which in quotidian existence may appear closed off from us, but which we must accede to since it is the realm of meaning and value." See Brooks, *The Melodramatic Imagination*, 5.

22. See Lu Xun, introduction to *Zhongguo xiandai wenxue daxi* (Compendium), ed. Zhao Jiabi, 2:9.

23. Shen Congwen, "Xue Lu Xun" (Study Lu Xun), in *Shen Congwen wenji* (Works of Shen Congwen, hereafter cited as *SCWJ*), 11:233. The essay was first published in 1947.

24. See, for example, Ling Yu, *Cong biancheng zouxiang shijie* (March from the border town), 295–310.

25. Shen Congwen, "Duanpian xiaoshuo" (On short story), in *SCWJ*, 12:123.

26. See Shen Congwen, preface to *Congwen xiaoshuo xizuoxuan* (Selected exercises from Congwen's fiction writing), in *SCWJ*, 11:44–45.

27. Shen Congwen, preface to *Shen Congwen xiaoshuo xuanji* (A Selection of fiction by Shen Congwen), in *SCWJ*, 11:67.

28. Shen Congwen, "Lamp," trans. Kai-yu Hsu, in *Modern Chinese Stories and Novellas*, ed. Lau, C. T. Hsia, Lee, 265.

2. Fictive History: Mao Dun's Historical Fiction

1. See Zhu Defa, A Yan, Zhai Deyao, *Mao Dun qianqi wenxue sixiang sanlun* (Mao Dun's early literary thoughts); Gálik, *Mao Dun*.

2. Mao Dun, *Wo zouguo de daolu* (Road I have taken), 2:1–23.

3. For contemporary criticism on *Shi*, see, for example, Qian Xingcun, "Mao Dun yu xianshi" (Mao Dun and reality), in *Mao Dun pingzhuan* (Critical and biographical essays), ed. Fu Zhiying, 159–216.

4. The Nationalist Party, or the *Kuomintang*, has traditionally been abbreviated as the KMT. The two terms will be used interchangeably in the following discussion.

5. See Wang Jialiang, "Lun Mao Dun xiaoshuo de shehui biannianshi tezheng" (On the characteristics of social chronicle in Mao Dun's fiction), in *Mao Dun jiushi danchen jinian lunwenji* (Essays), ed. Zhongguo Mao Dun yanjiu xiehui, 335–349.

6. See Kellner, *Language and Historical Representation*, 1–74; White, *Metahistory* 2–20; LaCapra, *History and Criticism; History, Politics and the Novel*, 1–14; Momigliano, *Ancient and Modern Historiography;* Ricoeur, *Time and Narrative*, vol. 1.

7. Plaks, "Critical Theory of Chinese Narrative," in *Chinese Narrative*, ed.

Plaks, 311; Y. W. Ma, "The Chinese Historical Novel," 278; Průšek, "History and Epic," 17–34.

8. John C. Y. Wang, "Early Chinese Narrative," in *Chinese Narrative,* ed. Plaks, 3–20; Egan, "Narrative in the *Tso-chuan,*" 325–353.

9. See Yu, 221–255; David Der-wei Wang, "Fictional History/Historical Fiction," 68–70.

10. Plaks, *Chinese Narrative,* 312–313.

11. Zeng Pu, letter to Hu Shi, in *Niehaihua* (A Flower in the sea of sins), app. 2, 18–19.

12. For more discussion of Zeng Pu's historical perspectives, see David Der-wei Wang, "Nonconformism as Narrative Strategy," 66–70.

13. Lukács, *The Historical Novel,* 42.

14. Mao Dun's own memoirs remain extremely vague about his loss of contact with the Chinese Communist Party after the 1927 revolution. In recent years, scholars have tried to offer explanations for the gap in Mao Dun's life. See, for example, Li Guangde, "Shilun Shen Yanbing zaoqi yu dang de guanxi" (On Shen Yanbing's relations with the Communist Party in his early years), in *Mao Dun yanjiu lunwen xuanji* (Anthology), ed. Quanguo Mao Dun yanjiu xiehui 2:752–766.

15. Průšek, "Mao Dun and Yu Dafu," in *The Lyrical and the Epic,* ed. Lee, 121.

16. Yu-shih Chen, *Realism and Allegory.*

17. Mao Dun, "Cong Guling dao Donjing" (From Guling to Tokyo), in *Mao Dun pingzhuan* (Critical and biographical essays), ed. Fu Zhiying, 341–342.

18. C. T. Hsia, *History,* 533–554.

19. Lucente, *Narrative of Realism,* 20.

20. Tolstoy, *War and Peace,* 258.

21. Mao Dun, "Cong Guling dao Dongjing" (From Guling to Tokyo), in *Mao Dun pingzhuan* (Critical and biographical essays), ed. Fu Zhiying, 345.

22. See Yu-shih Chen, *Realism and Allegory,* 51–75.

23. Mao Dun, "Cong Guling dao Dongjing" (From Guling to Tokyo), *Mao Dun pingzhuan* (Critical and biographical essays), ed. Fu Zhiying, 342.

24. Mao Dun, *Shi* (Eclipse), 165.

25. C. T. Hsia, *History,* 148.

26. Qian Xingcun, "Mao Dun yu xianshi," (Mao Dun and reality), in *Mao Dun Pingzhuan* (Critical and biographical essays), ed. Fu Zhiying, 159–200.

27. Mao Dun himself also calls attention to the symbolism of the opening scene of *Rainbow.* See, Mao Dun, *Wo zouguo de daolu* (Road I have taken), 2:34.

28. Mao Dun, *Hong* (Rainbow), 118.

29. Chan, *Problematics of Modern Chinese Realism,* 142.

30. According to Mao Dun's plan, *Rainbow* should have a sequel entitled *Xia* (Morning sunshine); this was never written. See, Mao Dun, *Wo zouguo de daolu* (Road I have taken), 2:32–36.

31. See Duan Bailing, "Mao Dun yu zhongguo baogao wenxue" (Mao Dun

and Chinese reportage literature), in *Mao Dun yanjiu lunwen xuanji* (Anthology), ed. Quanguo Mao Dun yanjiu xiehui, 2:371–384; Zhao Xiaqiu, *Zhongguo xiandai baogao wenxueshi* (Modern Chinese reportage literature), 105–139, 148–156.

32. See Mao Dun's own description of sketches and reportage literature, "Guanyu baogao wenxue" (On reportage literature), *Mao Dun wenyi zalunji* (Miscellaneous essays), ed. Shaghai wenyi chubanshe, 639–642.

33. See, Mao Dun, *One Day in China,* trans. and. ed. Cochran, Hsieh, xiv–xv. See also, Zhao Xiaqiu, *Zhongguo xiandai baogao wenxueshi* (Modern Chinese reportage literature), 146–158.

34. Mao Dun, "Guanyu bianji *Zhongguo de yiri* de jingguo" (On the process of editing *One Day in China, May 21, 1936*), *Mao Dun wenyi zalun ji* (Miscellaneous essays), ed. Shanghai wenyi chubanshe, 599–606; see also Zhao Xiaqiu, *Xiandai zhongguo baogao wenxueshi* (Modern Chinese reportage literature), 147.

35. Mao Dun, "An Announcement of Calling for Essays," *One Day in China,* app. A, 267.

36. Yu-shih Chen, *Realism and Allegory,* 161–166. See also Zhu Defa, A Yan, Zhai Deyao, "Mao Dun Lishi xiaoshuo de chuangzuo tese" (Characteristics of Mao Dun's historical fiction), in *Mao Dun qianqi wenxue sixiang sanlun* (Mao Dun's early literary thoughts), 296–310; Zhang Ping, "Ping jipian lishi xiaoshuo" (On several historical stories), in *Mao Dun yanjiu lunji* (Research articles), ed. Zhuang Zhongqing, 304–305.

37. Mao Dun, "Ziran zhuyi yu zhongguo xiandai xiaoshuo" (Naturalism and modern Chinese fiction), *Mao Dun wenyi zalunji* (Miscellaneous essays), ed. Shanghai wenyi chubanshe, 98.

38. Mao Dun, *Wo zouguo de daolu* (Road I have taken), 2:82–131.

39. I am referring to the term as used by Mikhail Bakhtin. "Chronotope" means a narrative's way of conceptualizing and representing the interrelations of time and space. In the chronotopes of literary narratives, according to Bakhtin, "spatial and temporal indicators are fused into one carefully thought-out, concrete whole. Time, as it were, thickens, takes on flesh, becomes artistically visible; likewise, space becomes charged and responsive to the movements of time, plot and history. This intersection of axes and fusion of indicators characterizes the artistic chronotope . . . The chronotope as a formally constitutive category determines to a significant degree the image of man in literature as well. The image of man is always intrinsically chronotopic." See Bakhtin, *Dialogic Imagination,* 84–85.

40. Mao Dun, *Wo zouguo de daolu* (Road I have taken), 2:111.

41. C. T. Hsia, *History,* 163.

42. Mao Dun, *Mao Dun quanji* (Complete works of Mao Dun, hereafter cited as *MDQJ*), 8:368.

43. For more detailed discussion on the irony in "Spring Silkworms," see M. A. Abbas and Tak-wai Wong, "Mao Dun's 'Spring Silkworms': Rhetoric and Ideology," in *Chinese Text,* ed. Zhou Yingxiong, 191–207.

Notes, Chapter 2

44. Li Shangyin, "Wuti" (To the unnamed), in *Jade Mountain,* trans. Witter Bynner (New York: Knopf, 1957), 81.

45. See, for example, LaCapra, *Soundings,* 155–181.

46. See, for example, Zhuang Zhongqing, "Mao Dun de nongcun sanbuqu de dutexing jiqi pingjia" (The chrarcteristics of Mao Dun's *Village Trilogy* and assessment of it), in *Xiandai wenxue lunji* (Critical essays on modern Chinese literature), ed. Shehui kexue zhanxian (Jilin: Renmin chubanshe, 1980), 11–24; He Jiahuai, "Mao Dun de 'Chuncan'," (Mao Dun's "Spring Silkworms"), 30–31; 18–19; Luo Fu, "Ping 'Chun Can'" (A criticism on "Spring Silkworms"), in *Mao Dun yanjiu lunwenji* (Anthology), ed. Quanguo Mao Dun yanjiu xiehui, 273–280; Feng Wu, "Guanyu 'fengshouzai' de zuopin" (Works on the "harvest disaster"), 290–292; Quanlin and Ge Qin, "'Candong' fenxi" (An analysis of "Winter Ruins"), 293–296.

47. Bi Shutang, "Duojiao guanxi" (On *Multifaceted Relations*), *Mao Dun yanjiu lunji* (Research articles), ed. Zhuang Zhongqing, 243–245.

48. Mao Dun, *Duojiao guanxi* (Multifaceted relations), *MDQJ,* 4:114.

49. Mao Dun, *Wo zouguo de daolu* (Road I have taken), 2:118.

50. Ibid., 82–97.

51. Critics have also compared *Midnight* with novels on the grand scale, such as *War and Peace.* See, for example, Lin Hai, "Ziye yu zhanzheng yu heping" (*Midnight* and *War and Peace*), in *Mao Dun yanjiu lunji* (Research articles), ed. Zhuang Zhongqing, 235–242.

52. See, for example, Qu Qiubai, "Ziye yu guohuonian" (Midnight and the year of national products), in *Mao Dun yanjiu ziliao* (Research materials), ed. Sun Zhongtian and Zha Guohua, 2:224–227. Gálik, *Milestones,* 90–93. Mao Dun's denial can be seen in *Wo zouguo de daolu* (Road I have taken), 2:104.

53. Mao Dun, *Midnight,* 9.

54. See Chingqiu Stephen Chan's and Gálik's discussion of the opening paragraph of *Midnight;* in Chan, *Problematics of Modern Chinese Realism,* 212–216, Gálik, *Milestones,* 88.

55. Gálik, *Milestones,* 88.

56. For discussions on the character of Wu Sunfu, see, for example, Luo Zongyi, "Wu Sunfu shilun" (A tentative discussion of Wu Sunfu), *Zhongguo xiandai wenxue yanjiu congkan* (Compendium of research on modern Chinese literature), (1980) 4:254–256; Chen Shijing, "Lun Wu Sunfu" (On Wu Sunfu), 61–74.

57. The term is borrowed from Dembo, *Detotalized Totalities,* 91. Dembo, however, uses it to describe Sartre's literary career from 1938 to 1940.

58. Gálik, *Milestones,* 97–99.

3. Plotted Revolutions: Mao Dun's Politics of the Novel

1. Shao Bozhou, *Mao Dun pingzhuan* (Critical biography), 62–63; Hu Yaobang, "Zai Shen Yanbing tongzhi zhuidaohui shang Hu Yaobang tongzhi zhi daoci" (Speech at the memorial service in honor of Mao Dun), in *Mao Dun zhuanji* (Critical anthology), ed. Fujian renmin chubanshe, 1:6–9.

Notes, Chapter 3

2. See Desan et al., *Literature and Social Practice;* Arac, *Postmodernism and Politics;* Barker et al., *Literature, Politics and Theory;* Jameson, *The Political Unconscious.*

3. Leo Lowenthal, "Sociology of Literature in Retrospect," in *Literature and Social Practice,* ed. Desan et al., 11–25. Arac, "Introduction," *Postmodernism and Politics,* ix–xxxix.

4. Howe, *Politics and the Novel,* 17–26.

5. Liang Qichao, "Lun xiaoshuo yu qunzhi zhi guanxi" (On the relationship between fiction and ruling the people), in *Wanqing wenxue congchao: sixoshuo xiqu yanjiujuan* (Compendium of late Qing literature), ed. A Ying, 12–15.

6. C. T. Hsia, "Yen Fu and Liang Ch'i-ch'ao as Advocates of New Fiction," in *Chinese Approaches to Literature,* ed. Rickett, 222–223, 236–237; Doleželová-Velingerová, "Introduction," in *Chinese Novel,* 8. Also see Liang Qichao, "Benguan fuyin shuobu yuanqi" (Announcing our policy to print a supplementary fiction section), in *Wanqing wenxue congchao: xiaoshuo xiqu yanjiujuan* (Compendium of Late Qing literature), ed., A Ying, 21–27.

7. Lu Xun, "Moluo shili shuo" (On the poetic power of the Mara poet), in *LXQJ,* 1:63–115.

8. Lu Xun, preface to *Nahan* (A call to arms), in *LXQJ,* 1:415–420.

9. Mao Dun, "Dazhuanbian de shiqi heshi laine?" (When will the period of great transformation come?), in *Mao Dun wenyi zalunji* (Miscellaneous essays), ed. Shanghai wenyi chubanshe, 1:160.

10. Mao Dun, "Cong Guling dao Dongjing" (From Guling to Tokyo), in *Mao Dun pingzhuan* (Critical and biographical essays), ed. Fu Zhiying, 314. Mao Dun made his remarks in response to the English critic Havelock Ellis' statement that Zola went to gather social experience for the sake of writing fiction, while Tolstoy came to writing fiction after he had experienced much about life. See Gálik, *Milestones,* 74–75.

11. Gálik, *Mao Dun,* 21.

12. For more information about the Chinese reception of Western literary theories in the May Fourth era, see, McDougall, *Introduction of Western Literary Theories,* 54–83.

13. Pei Wei (Mao Dun), "Xiaoshuo xinchaolan xuanyan" (Manifesto of the column of the "new tide of fiction"), in *Mao Dun wenyi zalunji* (Miscellaneous essays), ed. Shanghai wenyi chubanshe, 1:6–11.

14. Schwartz, *Search of Wealth and Power,* 239.

15. Zhou Zuoren is one of the most noticeable voices in propagating the concept of "rende wenxue" (human[e] literature). See Zhou Zuoren, "Rende wenxue" (human[e] literature), in *Zhou Zuoren lunwenji* (Collection), ed. Huang Zhiqing, 11–30. Just like the double meaning implied by the essay's title, Zhou Zuoren's theory of literature intertwines both the biological and ethical concepts of Social Darwinism; his image of man is that of a mixture of body and spirit. Since humanity is continuously moving upward on a Darwinian biological and ethical ladder, the literature created should also proceed from the inhuman(e) to the human(e) level.

Notes, Chapter 3

16. Wellek, *History of Modern Criticism*, 383.
17. Tolstoy, *What is Art?*, 35.
18. Yanbing (Mao Dun), "Tuoersitai yu jinri zhi Eluosi" (Tolstoy and today's Russia), p. 47.
19. Mao Dun, "Jinian Fuloubaier bainian shengri" (Remembering Flaubert's one hundredth birthday), in *Xiaoshuo yuebao* (Short story monthly), 12, 12:1–4.
20. Shen Yanbing (Mao Dun), "Ziranzhuyi yu Zhongguo xiandai xiaoshuo" (Naturalism and modern Chinese fiction), in *Mao Dun wenyi zalun-ji* (Miscellaneous essays), ed. Shanghai wenyi chubanshe, 92–93.
21. Ibid.
22. See Mao Dun, "Zuola zhuyi de weixianxing" (The danger of Zolaism), in *Mao Dun wenyi zalunji* (Miscellaneous essays), ed. Shanghai wenyi chubanshe she, 109.
23. Ibid., 817.
24. Ibid.
25. Ibid.
26. Ibid.
27. Lucente, *Narrative of Realism and Myth*, 22–23.
28. Mao Dun, "Zuola zhuyi de weixianxing" (The danger of Zolaism), in *Mao Dun wenyi zalunji* (Miscellaneous Essays), ed. Shanghai wenyi chubanshe, 109.
29. As J. H. Matthews notices, for all the differences between "Zolaism" and Marxist canons, Zola's works remain favorite subjects for Marxist critics. Novels such as *L'Argent*, *L'Assommoir*, and *Germinal* have been repeatedly referred to by leftist critics who, though impressed by Zola's incomparable ability to portray social abuses and injustices, cannot help deploring the fact that Zola's talent is crippled by his bourgeois ideology. See Matthews, "Zola and the Marxists," 262–272.
30. Lukács, *Studies in European Realism*, 87.
31. Ibid., 135.
32. Lenin, "Tolstoy," in *Marxists on Literature*, ed. Craig, 32.
33. See Mao Dun, *Wo zouguo de daolu* (Road I have taken), 1:148–168; For Lu Xun's influence on Mao Dun in terms of a Marxist view of art, see Gálik, *Mao Dun*, 94; for Mao Dun's reception of Marxism, see Gálik, *Mao Dun*, 83–110.
34. See, for example, Mao Dun, "Lun wuchan jieji yishu" (On proletarian art), *Mao Dun wenyi zalunji* (Miscellaneous essays), ed. Shanghai wenyi chubanshe, 182–199; "Wenxuezhe de xinshiming" (The new mission of literati), ibid., 217–219; "Wenxue yu zhengzhi shehui" (Literature and politics and society), ibid., 115–117.
35. Meisner, *Li Ta-chao*, 154. For a general background of the introduction of Marxist literary thought to China, see, Pickowicz, *Marxist Literary Thought in China*.
36. Mao Dun, "Du *Ni Huanzhi*" (Reading *Ni Huanzhi*), *Mao Dun wenyi zalunji* (Miscellaneous essays), ed. Shanghai wenyi chubanshe, 291–293.

Notes, Chapter 3

37. Mao Dun, "Cong Guling dao Dongjing" (From Guling to Tokyo), in *Mao Dun pingzhuan* (Critical and biographical essays), ed. Fu Zhiying, 364–366.
38. Mao Dun, "Du *Ni Huanzhi*" (Reading *Ni Huanzhi*), in *Mao Dun wenyi zalunji* (Miscellaneous essays), ed. Shanghai wenyi chubanshe, 293.
39. Yü-sheng Lin, *Crisis of Chinese Consciousness*, 26–29.
40. Ibid.
41. C. T. Hsia, *History*, 165.
42. David Der-wei Wang, "Xunzhao nüzhujiao de nanzuojia" (Male writers in search of heroines), *Cong Liu E dao Wang Zhenhe: Zhongguo xiandai xieshi xiaoshuo sanlun* (Liu E to Wang Zhenhe), 183–188.
43. Besides fictional writings with women as central figures, Mao Dun wrote a considerable number of essays in support of women's liberation. The majority of these essays now appear in *Mao Dun quanji* (Complete works), 14. See, for example, "Funü yundong de yiyi yu yaoqiou" (The meaning and demands of the women's movement), 14:158–163; "Jiefang de funü yu funü de jiefang" (Liberated women and women's liberation), 14:63–69; "Funü jingji duli taolun" (A discussion on women's economic independence), 14:244–246. See also Zha Guohua, "Lun Mao Dun zaoqi de funüguan ji qita" (On Mao Dun's concept on women in his early period and other subjects), in *Mao Dun jiushi danchen jinian lunwenji* (Essays), ed. Zhongguo Mao Dun yanjiu xiehui, 335–349.
44. See Siebers, *Ethics of Criticism*, 194–198.
45. Yu-shih Chen, *Realism and Allegory*, 139–143.
46. I am referring to Fredric Jameson's use of the term *ressentiment*. See Jameson, *Political Unconscious*, 200–205.
47. Yu-shih Chen, *Realism and Allegory*, 155.
48. Mao Dun, *Wo Zouguo de daolu* (Road I have taken), 2:32.
49. C. T. Hsia, *History*, 152–153.
50. Mao Dun, *Hong* (Rainbow), 237.
51. Ibid.
52. Ibid., 243. Also see Lin Hsiu-ling, "Zhongguo geming he nüxing jiefang: Mao Dun xiaoshuo zhong de liangda zhuti" (Chinese revolution and women's liberation: two major themes in Mao Dun's fiction), 117–151.
53. See Sedgwick, *Between Men*, 83–96.
54. Mao Dun, *Midnight*, 17.
55. Ibid., 21.
56. Mao Dun, *Midnight*, 7.
57. My description of Shanghai stock market is derived from Prendergast's description of the Galeries-de-bois in Balzac's fiction, *Illusions perdues*. See Prendergast, *Order of Mimesis*, 90.
58. Ibid.
59. For more discussion of the dance scene, see Gálik, *Milestones*, 90–91.
60. See Chan, *Problematics of Modern Chinese Realism*, 145.
61. Mao Dun's familiarity with Zola's *Nana* has been pointed out by Marián Gálik. See Gálik, *Milestones*, 81.

Notes, Chapter 3

62. For more discussion about the character of Sai Jinhua, see David Derwei Wang, "Nonconformism as Narrative Strategy," 67–69.

63. See, for example, Qian Xingcun, "Mao Dun yu xianshi" (Mao Dun and reality), in *Mao Dun pingzhuan* (Critical and biographical essays), ed. Fu Zhiying, 159–216; Pulushi, "Mao Dun sanbuqu xiaoping" (A comment on Mao Dun's trilogy), ibid., 107–109,

64. Mao Dun, "Cong Guling dao Dongjing" (From Guling to Tokyo), ibid., 362–364.

65. Ibid., 361.

66. Ibid., 362.

67. For Mao Dun's reception of Russian models, see Ng, *Russian Hero in Modern Chinese Fiction,* 137–154.

68. Mao Dun, *Shi* (Eclipse), 19.

69. The phrasing of the argument is derived from Prendergast, *Order of Mimesis,* 92.

70. Mao Dun, "Cong Guling Dao Dongjing" (From Guling to Tokyo), *Mao Dun pingzhuan* (Critical and biographical essays), ed. Fu Zhiying, 352.

71. C. T. Hsia, *History,* 144.

72. Mao Dun, *Shi* (Eclipse), 172.

73. Wu Woyao, *Ershinian mudu zhi guaixianzhuang* (Strange Things), 3.

74. Mao Dun, *Fushi* (Putrefaction), in *MDQJ,* 5:5.

75. Ibid.

76. Ibid.

77. Hu Yaobang, "Zai Shen Yanbing tongzhi zhuidaohui shang Hu Yaobang tongzhi zhi daoci" (Speech at the memorial service in honor of Mao Dun), *Mao Dun zhuanji* (Critical anthology), ed. Fujian renmin chubanshe, 8.

78. Sun Zhongtian, *Lun Mao Dun de shenghuo yu chuangzuo* (Mao Dun's life and works), 175; ibid., 179.

79. Yu-shih Chen, *Realism and Allegory,* 35–50.

80. Mao Dun, *Guling zhiqiu* (Autumn in Guling), 64.

81. Hu Yaobang, "Zai Shen Yanbing tongzhi zhuidaohui shang Hu Yaobang tongzhi zhi daoci" (Speech at the memorial service in honor of Mao Dun), *Mao Dun zhuanji* (Critical anthology), ed. Fujian renmin chubanshe, 8.

82. Mao Dun, "Shuizaoxing" (Story of marsh hay), in *MDQJ,* 9:299.

83. Ibid., 9:305.

84. Gálik, *Milestones,* 78; ibid., 81.

85. See Anderson, *Limits of Realism,* 125–127.

4. Melancholy Laughter: Farce and Melodrama in Lao She's Fiction

1. C. T. Hsia, *History,* 187.

2. For Lao She's family background, see Hu Jinquan, *Lao She he tade zuopin* (Lao She and his works), 7–24; At least two of Lao She's fictions contain a considerable amount of his early experiences: *Zhenghongqi xia* (Under the red banner), published posthumously in 1979, reprint, in *Lao She shenghuo yu*

chuangzuo zishu (Lao She's accounts), ed. Hu Jieqing, 179–350; and *Xiaorenwu zishu* (A trivial figure's autobiographical account), originally published in 1937, reprint. in *Shiyue* (October), (1986)43:248–255.

3. Lao She, "*Shenquan* houji" (Afterword to *Magical Boxers*) (Beijing: Zhongguo xiju chubanshe, 1963), reprint, in *Lao She shenghuo yu chuangzuo zishu* (Lao She's accounts), ed. Hu Jieqing, 175.

4. See, for example, Lao She, *Zhenghongqi xia* (Under the red banner).

5. Lao She, "Wozenyang xie *Lao Zhang de zhexue*" (How I wrote *The Philosophy of Lao Zhang*), in *Lao She shenghuo yu chuangzuo zishu* (Lao She's accounts), ed. Hu Jieqing, 6–7.

6. See Hu Jinquan, *Lao She he tade zuopin* (Lao She and his works), 29–53; Ning Encheng, "Lao She zai yingguo" (Lao She in England), in *Lao She yanjiu ziliao* (Research materials), ed. Zeng Guangcan and Wu Huaibin, 1:273–281.

7. Lao She, "Wo zenyang xie *Zhao Ziyue*" (How I wrote *Zhao Ziyue*), in *Lao She Shenghuo yu chuangzuo zishu* (Lao She's accounts), ed. Hu Jieqing, 19.

8. Lao She was honored "People's Artist" by Peng Zhen, Mayor of Beijing, on behalf of the Beijing city government, on 23 December 1951, for the success of his play *Longxu gou* (Dragon-beard ditch). See *Lao She yanjiu ziliao* (Research materials), ed. Zeng Guancan and Wu Huaibin, 1:77.

9. For Lao She's suicide, see Shu Yi, "Lao She zuihou de liangtian" (Last two days of Lao She's life), in Shu Yi, *Lao She zuihou de liangtian* (Last two days), 219–238; and Paul Bady, "Death and the Novel: on Lao She's 'Suicide'," in *Two Writers and the Cultural Revolution,* ed. Kao, 5–14.

10. Lao She, "Wo zenyang xie *Lihun*" (How I wrote *Divorce*), in *Lao She shenghuo yu chuangzuo zishu* (Lao She's accounts), ed. Hu Jieqing, 44–45.

11. Lao She, "Wo zenyang xie *Lao Zhang de zhexue*" (How I wrote *The Philosophy of Lao Zhang*), *Lao She shenghuo yu chuangzuo zishu* (Lao She's accounts), ed. Hu Jieqing, 5. See Song Yongyi's extensive discussion on the influence of Western litcrature on Lao She, in *Lao She yu zhongguo wenhua guannian* (Lao She and Chinese culture), 41–79; and Hao Changhai, "Lao She yu waiguo wenxue" (Lao She and foreign literature), in *Lao She yanjiu ziliao* (Research materials), ed. Zeng Guangcan and Wu Huaibin, 2:1000–1025.

12. Lao She, "Wo zenyang xie *Lao Zhang de zhexue*" (How I wrote *The Philosophy of Lao Zhang*), in *Lao She shenghuo yu chuangzuo zishu* (Lao She's accounts), ed. Hu Jieqing, 5.

13. Lao She's love for Chinese performing arts from Beijing opera to *xiangsheng* is well described by his son Shu Yi, in "Lao She de aihao" (Lao She's hobbies), in *Lao She zuihou de liangtian* (Last two days), 8–31. See also Liang Shiqiu, "Yi Lao She" (Remembering Lao She), originally published in *Kanyunji* (Seeing clouds), reprint, in *Lao She Yanju ziliao* (Research materials), ed. Zeng Guangcan and Wu Huaibin, 1:281–284.

14. Jaroslav Průšek, "Basic Problems of the History of Modern Chinese Literature and C T. Hsia, *A History of Modern Chinese Fiction,"* in *The Lyrical and the Epic,* ed. Lee, 222.

15. Lao She's indebtedness to the classical Chinese satirical novel and the

late Qing exposé fiction was noticed by Zhu Ziqing as early as 1929. See Zhu Ziqing, "*Lao Zhang de zhexue* yu *Zhao Ziyue*" (*The Philosophy of Lao Zhang* and *Zhao Ziyue*), in *Lao She yanjiu ziliao* (Research materials), ed. Zeng Guangcan and Wu Huaibin, 2:727–733.

16. Lao She, *Lao Zhang de zhexue* (Philosophy), 1.

17. Ralph Nickleby is a stingy moneylender who exploits young Nicholas; Mr. Squeers is the cruel, deformed school master of Dotheboys Hall. The latter's fight with Nicholas, which results in the young hero's running away, is suggestive of Lao Zhang's fight with his student Wang De, who later leaves the school.

18. See, for example, Richard Barickman, "The Comedy of Survival in Dickens' Novels," *Novel* (1972) 3:128; Williams, *English Novel*, 32–33; and Van Ghent, *English Novel*, 126.

19. For a more thorough definition of farce as a literary mode and its relation to comedy and humor, see Eric Bentley, "Farce," in *Comedy: Meaning and Form*, ed. Corrigan, 295; Gurewitch, *Comedy: The Irrational Vision*, 9; and Bermel, *Farce: Aristophanes to Woody Allen*. See also Kern, *Absolute Comic*; and Bakhtin, *Rabelais*.

20. Bakhtin, *Rabelais*, 11.

21. For more discussion on the ambiguity of farcical laughter, see Charles Baudelaire, "On the Essence of Laughter," trans. Jonathan Mayne, in *Comedy: Meaning and Form*, ed. Corrigan, 453; Sigmund Freud, "Humor," in *Standard Edition of the Complete Psychological Works of Sigmund Freud*, trans. and ed. James Strachey, (London: Hogarth Press, 1927), 21: 159–166.

22. Doleželová-Velingerová, "Typology of Plot Structures in Late Qing Novels," in *Chinese Novel at Turn of Century*, ed. Doleželová-Velingerová, 38–56.

23. Lao She, *Lao Zhang de zhexue* (Philosophy), 4.

24. David Der-wei Wang, "Storytelling Context in Chinese Fiction," 133–150. See also Miller, *Form of Victorian Fiction*, 76–78. Using *Oliver Twist* as his example, Miller contends that the novel is the expression of a "juxtaposition of two minds: the mind of the narrator and the mind of the protagonist." Since the narrator is "in no danger of finding himself in Oliver's position, he can make arch jokes about the hero's experiences. These function partly as an ironic rhetorical device to generate by negation the outraged sympathy of the reader, but the disproportion between Oliver's inarticulate sufferings and the narrator's ornate style maintains firmly the narrator's detachment from events and experiences he describes."

25. Bentley, *The Life of the Drama*, 195–218; Rosenberg, "Melodrama," in *Context and Craft of Drama*, ed. Corrigan and Rosenberg, 168–185; Heilman, *Tragedy and Melodrama*; Smith, *Melodrama*; Brooks, *Melodramatic Imagination*.

26. Brooks, *Melodramatic Imagination*, 5.

27. Not only do Lao She's caricatures deviate from Dickensian stereotypes, his use of melodrama also turns out to be a parody of the English master's. What Dickens writes, according to Northrop Frye, are "fairy tales in the low mimetic displacement." Todorov also notices that Dickens is playing with two

Notes, Chapter 4

typological orders in his novels: "All through the book it is the external order, the order of life, which dominates the actions of the characters; in the conclusion a miracle occurs, some wealthy character is suddenly revealed as a generous being and makes possible the instalment of a new order which exists, obviously in the book for he who triumphs after denouement." The plot of melodrama and the sentimentalism it entails are important not only because they function as a wish-fulfillment mechanism for both readers and Dickens himself but also because they facilitate the master's mythical vision of plenitude in which human experience, be it happy or wretched, is sublimated and bracketed by a continuous appearance of wonders. Therefore, even a pathetic scene like Little Nell's death in *The Old Curiosity Shop* is emotionally so luxurious that "it provides a kind of muted festivity for the conclusion, or what Joyce in *Finnegans Wake* calls a 'funferall'," as Frye puts it. Lao She's manipulation of melodramatic plot, however, always reveals the writer's reluctance to conform to the Dickensian miraculous denouement. The multiplot structure of Lao She's novels is also based on the interplay between what Todorov calls the two orders of life and fantasy. But Lao She simply reverses the typology, letting cruel, downbeat, realistic factors undercut the fantastic ones. More often than not, his miracles or *deus ex machina* episodes prove useless in salvaging situations. As a result, there is a tendency for Lao She's novels to become a critique of Dickensian melodrama. See Frye, "Dickens and the Comedy of Humors," in *Victorian Novel,* ed. Watt, 47; ibid.,51; Todorov, "The Categories of Literary Narrative," *PLL,* (1980)2: 36.

28. Lao She, *Lao Zhang de zhexue* (Philosophy), 252.

29. C. T. Hsia, *History,* 170.

30. Lao She, "Wo zenyang xie *Erma*" (How I wrote *The Two Mas*), and "Wo zenyang xie *Lihun*" (How I wrote *Divorce*), in *Lao She shenghuo yu chuangzuo zishu* (Lao She's accounts), ed. Hu Jieqing, 15–21; ibid., 41–45.

31. C. T. Hsia observes the parallel between the two Mas and Leopold Bloom and Stephen Daedalus. While it is a little too far-fetched to compare the elder Ma with Bloom (because the former is never given a chance to show the kind of psychological and behavioral versatility of the latter), the similarity between Ma Wei and Stephen Daedalus is suggestive. Both have an artist's quality, both are treated amusingly *and* sympathetically by their creators, and both flee to France (though for different reasons). See *History,* p. 172.

32. Lao She, *Erma* (The two Mas), 142.

33. C. T. Hsia, *History,* 171–172.

34. Frye also defines the *alazon* as "a deceiving or self-deceived character in fiction, normally an object of ridicule in comedy or satire, but often the hero of a tragedy. In comedy he most frequently takes the form of a *miles gloriosus* or a pedant." Frye points out that characters like Tartuffe, Madame Bovary, Lord Jim, Othello, Faustus, and Hamlet all share the attributes of the *alazon* because their action combines both theatricality and obsession and makes readers find it difficult to judge them by the rigid rules of either comic or tragic stereotypes. See Frye, *Anatomy of Criticism,* 39–40; ibid. 226–228; ibid. 365.

35. Frye, *Anatomy of Criticism,* 172.

Notes, Chapter 4

36. Lao She, "Xin hanmuliede" (New Hamlet), in *Hezao ji* (Clams and seaweeds), 157.
37. Ibid., 158.
38. Lao She, "Xianhua wode qige xiju" (Idle talks on my seven plays), in *Lao She shenghuo yu chuangzuo zishu* (Lao She's accounts), ed. Hu Jieqing, 118.
39. Lao She, *Erma* (The two Mas), 1–2.
40. Lao She expresses in "Wo zenyang xie *Erma*" (How I wrote *Erma*) that he owes the novel's narrative format of "beginning with the ending" to Joseph Conrad. For him, Conrad is not only a serious writer of psychological realism but also a most competent "storyteller." See *Lao She shenghuo yu chuangzuo zishu* (Lao She's accounts), ed. Hu Jieqing, 15–16.
41. Lao She, *Hezaoji* (Clams and seaweeds), 181.
42. Birch, "Lao She: The Humorist in his Humor," *China Quarterly*, 152.
43. Lao She, *Lihun* (Divorce), 160.
44. Ibid., 106.
45. Lao She, *Lihun* (Divorce), 1.
46. Ibid., p. 283
47. Helena Kuo, *The Quest for Love of Lao Lee* (New York: Reynal and Hitchcock, 1948).
48. Shu Yu (Lao She), "Tang's Love Stories," originally published in *Yanjing shuyuan xuekan* (Journal of Yanjing college, 1932), quoted by Song Yongyi in *Lao She yu zhongguo wenhua guannian* (Lao She and Chinese culture), 85.
49. Lao She, *Wenxue gailun jiangyi* (Outlines of a general introduction to literature) (Beijing: Beijing Chubanshe, 1984), 126.
50. Lao She, "Wo zenyang xie *Daming hu*" (How I wrote *Daming Lake*), *Lao She shenghuo yu chuangzuo zishu* (Lao She's accounts), ed. Hu Jieqing, 32.
51. Song Yongyi, *Lao She yu zhongguo wenhua guannian* (Lao She and Chinese culture), 80–108.
52. The law was published on 6 December 1930 and put into practice on 5 May 1931. See Song Yongyi, *Lao She yu zhongguo wenhua guannian* (Lao She and Chinese culture), 84.
53. The name Ma Ketong, a parody of Marx (Ma Kesi), also betrays Lao She's critical attitude toward Chinese Marxism.
54. Lao She, *Lihun* (Divorce), 281.
55. Lao She deeply admires Joseph Conrad's fiction, especially those dealing with the absurdist moments in man's struggle for meaning and order. In an essay on Conrad, Lao She writes, "'Nothing' often becomes the ending of Conrad's fiction. No matter how much will and vitality a man has, no matter how good or bad his personality is, once he steps into this realm of 'Nothing,' he is unable to free himself from the curse." See Lao She, "Wo zuijingai de zuojia—Kang Lade" (Conrad—my most favorite writer), in *Lao She wenyi pinglun ji*, (Collection of Lao She's literary criticisms), ed. Anhui renmin chubanshe, 9.
56. Ibid., 241.
57. Lao She, "Wo zenyang xie *Maocheng ji*" (How I wrote *The City of Cats*),

in *Lao She shenghuo yu chuangzuo zishu* (Lao She's accounts), ed. Hu Jieqing, 39.

58. Hao Changhai, "Lao She yu waiguo wenxue," *Lao She yanjiu ziliao* (Research materials), ed. Zeng Guangcan and Wu Huaibin, 2:1010. Hao Changhai also holds that Lao She may have been influenced by such foreign satires as Aristophanes' *Birds,* Rabelais' *Gargantua and Pantagruel,* and arguably Dante's *Divine Comedy.*

59. Bermel, *Farce: from Aristophanes to Woody Allen,* 224–235.

60. For a comparative reading of *The City of Cats* and Lu Xun's "The True Story of Ah Q," see Wang Shuming, "*Maocheng ji* shuping" (A review of *The City of Cats*), in *Lao She yanjiu ziliao* (Research materials), ed. Zeng Guangcan and Wu Huaibin, 2:745.

61. Lao She, *Maocheng ji* (The city of cats), 60

62. Ibid., 61.

63. Ibid., 60.

64. Ibid., 96.

65. Ibid.

66. Ibid., 26.

67. Ibid., 173.

68. Lao She, *Niu Tianci zhuan* (The biography of Niu Tianci), 1.

69. C. T. Hsia, *History,* 180.

70. Bi Shutang, "*Niu Tianci zhuan* shuping" (A review of *The Biography of Niu Tianci*), in *Lao She yanjiu ziliao* (Research materials), ed. Zeng Guangcan and Wu Huaibin, 2:764–765.

71. Lao She, *Niu Tianci zhuan* (The biography of Niu Tianci), 26.

72. Ibid.

73. Ibid., 179.

74. Ibid., 8.

75. Ibid.

76. C. T. Hsia, *History,* 206.

77. Lau, "Naturalism in Modern Chinese Fiction," 148–160.

78. Ibid., 150.

79. See Henri Bergson, "Laughter," in *Comedy,* (New York: Doubleday, 1956), 84.

80. Lao She, *Camel Xiangzi,* 18.

81. See, for example, Jameson, "Literary Innovation and Modes of Production: A Commentary," 67–72.

82. Lao She, "Lian" (Predilection), in *Lao She wenji* (Works of Lao She, hereafter cited as *LSWJ*), 9:28.

83. C. T. Hsia, *History,* 182.

84. Lao She, *Camel Xiangzi,* 179.

85. Ibid., 182.

86. Ibid., 146.

87. Ibid., 9.

88. Lao She, "Duanhun qiang" (Soul-shattering spear), in *Hezao ji* (Clams and seaweeds), 11.

Notes, Chapter 4

89. Ibid., 147.
90. The description is left out in the revised version of *Luotuo Xiangzi*. Lao She, *Luotuo Xiangzi* (Camel Xiangzi), 288.
91. Lao She, *Camel Xiangzi*, 193.
92. Ibid., 243.
93. See Shi Chengjun, "Shilun jiefanghou Lao She dui *Luotuo Xiangzi* de xiugai" (On Lao She's revision of *Camel Xiangzi* after the liberation), 278–288; Xu Lin, "Lun *Luotuo Xiangzi* de jiewei ji qita" (On the ending of *Camel Xiangzi* and other revisions), 255–269. Shi Chengjun concludes that Lao She's deletion of the last chapter of *Camel Xiangzi* is a success. In contrast to Shi Chengjun's opinion, Xu Lin holds that Lao She's revision has affected the novel's artistic and conceptual coherence.
94. Lao She, *Luotuo Xiangzi*, 298.
95. Ibid., 299.
96. Ibid., 302.
97. Ibid., 308.
98. C. T. Hsia, *History*, 185.

5. "I Love My Country, Does My Country Love Me?"

1. Lao She, *Chaguan* (Tea house), 72. The original statement can also be translated as "I love my country, but *who* loves me?" The "who" (shei) bespeaks even more poignantly Lao She's ontological skepticism. Since the current chapter discusses only one aspect of Lao She's skepticism—his uncertainty about patriotism, I have translated the "shei" or "who" into "country"—in order to make the statement more pertinent to my argument.
2. Lao She, "Bafang fengyu" (Hard times), in *Lao She shenghuo yu chuangzuo zishu* (Lao She's accounts), ed. Hu Jieqing, 430–437.
3. Ibid., 434.
4. Xiao Boqing, "Lao She zai Wuhan Chongqing" (Lao She in Wuhan and Chongqing," 138–146.
5. Wang Huiyun and Su Qingchang, *Lao She pingzhuan* (Critical biography of Lao She), 184–205.
6. Lao She, "Xianhua wuode qige xiju" (Idle talks on my seven plays), in *Lao She shenghuo yu chuangzuo zishu* (Lao She's accounts), ed. Hu Jieqing, 110–122. For Lao She's activities during the wartime period, see Ma Xiaomi, "Shitan Lao She dui kangzhan wenyi de gongxian" (On Lao She's contributions to the literature of national resistance), in *Lao She yanjiu lunwenji* (Critical essays), ed. Meng Guanglai, 60–72.
7. During his stay in the States, Lao She also wrote the novel *Gushu yiren* (The drumsingers), which was translated into English by Helena Kuo. The Chinese manuscript was, however, lost. Just like the last part of *Four Generations*, the novel was translated back into Chinese sometime before 1981 by Ma Xiaomi. In recent years, some of Lao She's wartime publications have been rediscovered, such as *Xiaorenwu zishu* (A trivial figure's autobiographical account). See the republication of the work in *Shiyue* (October), (1986) 1:218;

ibid, 248–254. The work is presumably an early version of *Zhenghongqi xia* (Under the red banner).

8. See, for example, C. T. Hsia's comment, in *History*, 374–382.

9. Vicente L. Rafael, "Nationalism, Imagery, and the Filipino Intelligentsia in the Nineteenth Century," *Critical Inquiry*, (1990) 16: 592.

10. I am borrowing Benedict Anderson's idea that nationalism is a cultural artifact. To see nationalism (and patriotism) as a cultural artifact is to argue against attempts at essentializing it; such a view is especially suggestive in the light of Lao She's apparently unconditional patriotic rhetoric and implied skepticism. See Anderson, *Imagined Communities*, 11–15. See also Homi Bhabha, "DissemiNation: time, narrative, and the margins of the modern nation," in *Nation and Narration*, ed. Bhabha, 291–322.

11. Liang Shiqiu, "Bianzhe dehua" (Editor's words), in literary supplement, *Zhongyang ribao* (Central daily news), 1 December 1938. Reprint, in *Wenxue yundong shiliaoxuan* (Literary movements), ed. Department of Chinese Literature, Beijing University, et al., 4:243.

12. See, for example, Luo Sun, "Yu kangzhan wuguan" (On literature irrelevant to the resistance war), ibid., 244–245; Song Zhidi, "Tan kangzhan bagu" (on Eight-legged resistance war literature), ibid., 248–249; Zhang Tianyi, "Lun wuguan kangzhan de ticai" (On subjects which have nothing to do with the resistance war), ibid., 261–270.

13. Lao She, "Gei Zhongyang ribao de gongkaixin" (An open letter to the Central Daily News), in *Lao She yanjiu ziliao* (Research materials), ed. Zeng Guangcan and Wu Huaibin, 1:444–445. The letter was never published in print, due to the mediation of Zhang Daofan and others. It was put in print as late as in 1961, as part of Luo Sun's *Kangzhan wenyi huiyiduan* (Fragmentary recollections).

14. Quoted from "Zhonghua quanguo wenyijie kangdi xiehui xuanyan" (Manifesto of the Chinese writer's anti-Japanese aggression association), in Liu Shousong, *Zhongguo xinwenxueshi chugao* (Modern Chinese literature), 2:12–13.

15. See, for example, Leo Ou-fan Lee's description, in Lee, *Voices from the Iron House*, 173–189.

16. Hou Jian, "Liang Shiqiu xiansheng renwen sixiang de laiyuan" (Sources of Mr. Liang Shiqiu's humanist thoughts), 38–43.

17. Vohra, *Lao She and the Chinese Revolution*, 139.

18. Lao She, *Zhao Ziyu* (Zhao Ziyue), 41. The passage is translated by C. T. Hsia, in *History*, 171.

19. Lao She, "Wo zenyang xie *Zhao Ziyue*" (How I wrote *Zhao Ziyue*), in *Lao She shenghuo yu chuangzuo zishu* (Lao She's accounts), ed. Hu Jieqing, 12.

20. Lao She, "Wo zenyang xie *Er Ma*" (How I wrote *The Two Mas*), ibid., 20.

21. Lao She, *Maocheng ji* (The city of cats), 181–182.

22. Lao She, *Chaguan* (Tea house), 72.

23. Shu Yi, *Lao She zuihou de liangtian* (Last two days), 221.

24. Ibid., 222.

Notes, Chapter 5

25. See, for example, Yin Xueman, *Kangzhan shiqi de xiandai xiaoshuo* (Modern Chinese fiction), 45–58. Also see Lao She "Wo zenyang xie *Huozang*" (How I wrote *Cremation*), in *Lao She shenghuo yu chuangzuo zishu* (Lao She's accounts), ed. Hu Jieqing, 81–83.

26. Lao She, "Wo zenyang xie *Huozang*" (How I wrote *Cremation*), ibid., 86.

27. Ibid., 86–87.

28. Ibid.

29. See both Lu Xun's introduction and afterword to his translation of *The Rout*, in *LXQJ*, 18:265–274; ibid., 603–613.

30. Even Lao She himself admits that he is not comfortable in dealing with female characters. See, "Wo zenyang xie *Zhao Ziyue*" (How I wrote *Zhao Ziyue*), in *Lao She Shenghuo yu chuangzuo zishu* (Lao She's accounts), ed. Hu Jieqing, 14.

31. Yin Xueman, "Kangzhan shiqi de xiandai xiaoshuo" (Modern Chinese fiction), 53.

32. See, for example, Lao She, *Huozang* (Cremation), 216.

33. Ibid., 217–218.

34. Ibid., 216.

35. Ibid., 225.

36. Lao She, "Wo zheyibeizi" (This is my life), in *LSWJ*, 9: 82.

37. Lao She's cousin Fuhai may well be one of the models for the characterization of the old policeman. See Lao She, *Zhenghongqi xia* (Under the red banner), in *Lao She shenghuo yu chuangzuo zishu* (Lao She's accounts), ed. Hu Jieqing, 213–221.

38. Lao She, "Bafang fengyu" (Hard times), 434.

39. Lao She, "Huoche" (Train), in *LSWJ,* 9:10

40. Ibid., 12–13.

41. Ibid., 13.

42. Lao She, "Yunu" (Bath slaves), in *LSWJ*, 9:29.

43. Lao She's praise for *War and Peace* can be seen in "Wuo zenyang xie *Huozang*" (How I wrote *Cremation*), in *Lao She shenghuo yu chuangzuo zishu* (Lao She's accounts), ed. Hu Jieqing, 87.

44. Shu Yi, "Lao She zuopinzhongde beijingcheng" (Beijing in Lao She's works), in *Lao She yanjiu lunwenji* (Critical essays), ed. Meng Guanglai et al., 156–157.

45. Vohra, *Lao She and the Chinese Revolution*, 142.

46. Lao She, *Tousheng* (Ignoble life), part 2 of *Sishi tongtang* (Four generations), 232.

47. Lao She, "Xianhua wode qige xiju" (Idle talks on my seven plays), in *Lao She shenghuo yu chuangzuo zishu,* ed. Hu Jieqing, 118.

48. Lao She, *Tousheng* (Ignoble life), 355–356.

49. Ibid., 265.

50. Lao She, *Huanghuo* (Bewilderment), part 1 of *Sishi tongtang* (Four generations), 348.

51. Ibid., 406.

52. Ibid.
53. Lao She, *Tousheng* (Ignoble life), 35.
54. Ibid., 37.
55. Vohra, *Lao She and the Chinese Revolution*, 143.
56. Lao She, *Jihuang* (Famine), part 3 of *Sishi tongtang* (Four generations), 163.
57. Lao She, *Tousheng* (Ignoble life), 419
58. See Paul Bady, "Death and the Novel: On Lao She's Suicide," in *Two Writers and the Cultural Revolution*, ed. Kao, 5–14.
59. Shu Yi also notices the parallel between Qi Tianyou's and Lao She's death. See *Lao She zuihou de liangtian* (Last two days), 234.
60. Lao She, *Jihuang* (Famine), 173
61. Ibid.

6. Critical Lyricism: The Boundary of the Real in the Fiction of Shen Congwen

1. For Shen Congwen's early experiences, see Shen Congwen, *Congwen zizhuan* (Autobiography of Congwen), in *SCWJ*, 9:100–225; Kinkley, *Odyssey of Shen Congwen*, 8–66; Ling Yu, *Shen Congwen zhuan* (Biography), 41–92.

2. For Shen Congwen's acquaintance with Yu Dafu and Xu Zhimo, see Ling Yu, *Shen Congwen zhuan* (Biography), 194–201; Kinkley, *Odyssey of Shen Congwen*, 66–70; ibid., 82–85. For Shen Congwen's friendship with Ding Ling and Hu Yepin, the best reference is Shen Congwen's *Ji Ding Ling* (Remembering Ding Ling).

3. On February 7, 1931, five young Communist writers—Rou Shi, Hu Yepin, Feng Keng, Li Weisen, and Yin Fu—along with eighteen other party members were executed in Longhua, Jiangsu Province, on charges of conspiracy against the Nationalist government. Though they were all writers of small talent, they have been assured posthumous honor in Chinese Communist literary history as the Five Martyrs. See T. A. Hsia, *Gate of Darkness*, 163–233. For Shen Congwen's involvement in the incident, see Shen Congwen, *Ji Ding Ling* (Remembering Ding Ling); "Ji Hu Yepin" (Remembering Hu Yepin), *SCWJ*, 9:52–98; Kinkley, *Odyssey of Shen Congwen*, 202–209; Ling Yu, *Shen Congwen zhuan* (Biography), 287–297.

4. The best English study on Shen Congwen's life and works to date is Kinkley's *Odyssey of Shen Congwen*. See also Ling Yu's *Shen Congwen zhuan* (Biography).

5. For a definition of lyrical novel, see Freedman, *Lyrical Novel*, 1–32. Shen Congwen's own definition of lyricism can be seen in "Cong Xu Zhimo zuopin xuexi shuqing" (Learn lyricism from Xu Zhimo's works), *SCWJ*, 11:211. For the lyrical traits of Shen Congwen's fiction, see Ling Yu, "Zhongguo xiandai shuqing xiaoshuo de fazhan guiji jiqi rensheng neirong de shenmei xuanze" (Modern Chinese lyrical fiction), 229–246; Liang Bingjun, "Zhongguo xiandai wenxuezhong de shuqing xiaoshuo," in *Xiandai zhongguo wenxue xin-*

Notes, Chapter 6

mao (New facets), ed. Chen Bingliang, 117–138. See also Jaroslav Průšek, "Subjectivism and Individualism in Modern Chinese Literature," in *The Lyrical and the Epic,* ed. Lee, 1–28.

6. Shen Congwen, "Duanpian xiaoshuo" (On Short Stories), *SCWJ,* 12:126. See also Shen Congwen, "Chouxiang de shuqing" (Abstract lyricism), in *Changhe liubujin: huainian Shen Congwen xiansheng* (Remembering Mr. Shen Congwen), ed. Jishou daxue Shen Congwen yanjiushi, 1–9.

7. Průšek, "Subjectivism and Individualism in Modern Chinese Literature," in *The Lyrical and the Epic,* ed. Lee, 1–28.

8. Bakhtin contrasts novel with poetry in terms of dialogism and monologism. See Bakhtin, *Dialogic Imagination,* 287–297. This contrast, however, has been seriously challenged by scholars. See, for example, Paul DeMan, "Dialogue and Dialogism," in *Rethinking Bakhtin,* ed. Morson and Emerson, 105–114. Also see Morson and Emerson, *Mikhail Bakhtin,* 319–325.

9. Lukács, *Theory of Novel,* 112–113.

10. Ibid. See also Tilottama Rajan, "Romanticism and the Death of Lyric Consciousness," in *Lyric Poetry,* ed. Hosek and Parker, 194–207.

11. Shen Congwen, "Lun Feng Wenbing" (On Feng Wenbing [Fei Ming]), in *SCWJ,* 11:96–112. Ling Yu, "Zhongguo xiandai shuqing xiaoshuo de fazhan guiji jiqi rensheng neirong de shenmei xuanze" (Modern Chinese lyrical fiction), 229–246.

12. Shen Congwen, "Lun Feng Wenbing" (On Feng Wenbing [Fei Ming]) in *SCWJ,* 11:96–97.

13. Ibid., 97.

14. See Ling Yu's interview with Shen Congwen, "Shen Congwen tan zijide chuangzuo" (Shen Congwen's talk), 320; Shen Congwen, "*Shen Congwen xiaoshuo xuanji* tiji" (Preface to *A Collection of Shen Congwen's Selected Fiction*), in *SCWJ,* 11:69.

15. Shen Congwen, "Xin feiyou cundi, 23" ("New" letters never mailed, no. 23), in *SCWJ,* 12:67–68.

16. Shen Congwen, "Xin feiyou cundi, 21" ("New" letters never mailed, no. 21), ibid, 61.

17. Frye, *Anatomy of Criticism,* 321–324; 271–272; 285–289. See Jonathan Culler, "Changes in the Study of the Lyric," in *Lyric Poetry,* ed. Hosek and Parker, 38–54.

18. Shen Congwen, "*Congwen xiaoshuo xizuoxuan* daixu" (In lieu of a preface for *Selected Exercises from Congwen's Fiction Writing*), in *SCWJ,* 11:45.

19. Shen Congwen, "*Biancheng* tiji" (Preface to *The Border Town*), in *SCWJ,* 6:70–72.

20. See, for example, Ling Yu, *Cong Biancheng zouxiang shijie* (March from the border town), 295–310.

21. Shen Congwen, *Congwen zizhuan* (Autobiography), 121–169.

22. Ibid., 126.

23. Wang Luyan, "Youzi" (Grapefruit), in *Youzi* (Grapefruit) (Shanghai: Liangyou, 1947).

Notes, Chapter 6

24. Turgenev, *Sketches from A Hunter's Album*, 129–144.
25. Lu Xun, Preface to *Nahan* (A Call to Arms), in *LXQJ*, 1:417.
26. Lee, *Voices from the Iron House*, 18.
27. T. A. Hsia, *Gate of Darkness*, 146–162.
28. Foucault, *Discipline and Punish*, 24–95.
29. Ibid. For detailed discussion of Foucault's concept of discipline and punish, see, for example, Lentricchia, *Ariel and the Police*, 29–102.
30. The ninth chapter of Qu Yuan's *Jiuge* is entitled "Shangui" (Mountain ghost). In Qu Yuan's text, "Shangui," nevertheless, refers to the female spirit living in the mountains.
31. Turgenev, *Sketches from a Hunter's Album*, 50–75.
32.. Shen Congwen, "Three Men and One Woman," trans. Kai-yu Hsu, in *Modern Chinese Stories and Novellas*, ed. Lau, C. T. Hsia, and Lee, 265.
33. Ibid.
34. Kinkley, *Odyssey of Shen Congwen*, esp. chs. 1, 2, 4, and 7.
35.. Shen Congwen, "Yiju sansi nian yiyue shiba" (January 18, 1934), in *SCWJ*, 9:252.
36. Ibid., 250.
37. Ibid., 254.
38. Ibid.
39. Kellner, *Language and Historical Representation*, 153–187.
40. Shen Congwen, "Yijiu sansi nian yiyue shiba" (Janunary 18, 1934), in *SCWJ*, 9:254.
41. Shen Congwen, "Quiet," trans. Wai-lim Yip and C. T. Hsia, in *Modern Chinese Stories and Novellas*, ed. Lau, C. T. Hsia, and Lee, 252.
42. Ibid.
43. Shen Congwen, "Jing" (Quiet), in *SCWJ*, 4:256. The note is omitted in Yip and C. T. Hsia's translation.
44. Shen Congwen, "Sheng"(Life), in *SCWJ*, 5:310.
45. Genette, *Narrative Discourse*, 116.
46. Kinkley, *Odyssey of Shen Congwen*, 258, 360–361.
47. Shen Congwen, "Guolingzhe" (Those who cross over the mountains), in *SCWJ*, 6:207.
48. Shen Congwen, "*Congwen xiaoshuo xizuoxuan* daixu" (In lieu of a preface for *Selected Exercises from Congwen's Fiction Writing*), in *SCWJ*, 11:44.
49. For Shen Congwen's reception of Freudian theory, see, Kinkley, *Odyssey of Shen Congwen*, 215–219.
50. Shen Congwen, "Fenghuang" (Fenghuang), in *SCWJ*, 9:403.
51. Shen Congwen, "Shuo gushi ren de gushi" (The tale of a storyteller), in *SCWJ*, 2:428.
52. See, for example, Wu Lichang, review of "Zhangfu," in *Shen Congwen*, ed. Wu Lichang, 74.
53. Shen Congwen, "Zhangfu" (husband), in *SCWJ*, 4:5.
54.. Shen Congwen, "Hsiao-hsiao [Xiaoxiao]," trans. Eugene Ouyang, in *Modern Chinese Stories and Novellas*, ed. Lau. C. T. Hsia, and Lee, 229.

Notes, Chapter 6

55. Ibid.
56. Shen Congwen, "Qiaoxiu and Dongsheng," in *Recollections of West Hunan,* trans. Gladys Yang (Beijing: Panda Books, 1982), 164.
57. Ibid.

7. Imaginary Nostalgia: Shen Congwen And Native Soil Fiction

1. See, for example, Shen Congwen, "Taoyuan yu Chenzhou" (Taoyuan and Chenzhou), in *SCWJ,* 9:234–236. The whereabouts of "Taohuayuan" has long been a controversial issue. For recent discussion on the subject, see, for example, Lu Yaodong, "Hechu shi taoyuan" (Where is Taoyuan), in *Qiezuo shenzhou xioushou ren* (May as well be an idle onlooker in the sacred kingdom), 85–100.
2. Shen Congwen, *Xiangxing sanji* (Random sketches), in *SCWJ,* 9:227; ibid., 234–241, 281; *Xiangxi* (West Hunan), ibid., 351, 363, 398.
3. Yang Yi, *Zhongguo xiandai xiaoshuoshi* (History of modern Chinese fiction), 1:414–430. Xu Zhiying and Ni Tingting, "Zhongguo nongcun de mianying: ershi niandai xiangtu wenxue guankui" (Survey of native soil fiction), 72–82; Huang Wanhua, "Xiangtu wenxue yu xiandai yishi" (Native soil literature), 152–166. See also Shen Congwen, "Xue Lu Xun" (Study Lu Xun), in *SCWJ,* 11:233. On the other hand, the popular movement that prevailed among Beijing's academic circles, under the aegis of scholars such as Gu Jiegang, Liu Bannong, Zhou Zuoren, and Chang Hui, should not be overlooked. Clear evidence of Shen Congwen's relation to this movement is yet to be found. But even if Shen Congwen developed his writings on folk tales, local traditions, and provincial lives on his own, his endeavor can still be gauged in terms of a contemporary intellectual's zeal of "going to the people." See Kinkley, *Odyssey of Shen Congwen,* 112–129, Hung Chang-tai, *Going to the People.*
4. Lu Xun, introduction to *Xiandai zhongguo wenxue daxi* (Compendium), ed. Zhao Jiabi, 2:9.
5. See Gay, ed., *The Freud Reader,* 155–157, 648–649.
6. Bakhtin, *Dialogic Imagination,* 84–85.
7. Ling Yu, *Shen Congwen zhuan* (Biography), 309–319, 357–368.
8. Shen Congwen, "Yige dai shuitapi maozi de pengyou" (A Friend in an otterskin hat), in *SCWJ,* 9:226.
9. Ibid., 227.
10. Shen Congwen, "Taoyuan yu Chenzhou" (Taoyuan and Chenzhou), in *SCWJ,* 231.
11. Ibid.
12. Ibid., 235.
13. Tao Qian (T'ao Ch'ien), "Peach Blossom Spring," trans. Cyril Birch, *Anthology of Chinese Literature,* ed. Cyril Birch (New York: Grove Press, 1965), 167–168.
14. Shen Congwen, "Taoyuan yu Chenzhou" (Taoyuan and Chenzhou), in *SCWJ,* 9:324.

Notes, Chapter 7

15. Lee, "The Solitary Traveler: Images of the Self in Modern Chinese Literature," in *Expression of Self in Chinese Literature,* ed. Hegel and Hessney, 296.

16. Shen Congwen, "Yige duoqing shuishou yu yige duoqing furen" (A hot-blooded boatman and an amorous woman), in *SCWJ,* 9:269.

17. My concept of the aesthetics of residue and fragment is partially derived from Stephen Owen's discussion on classical Chinese poetry. See Stephen Owen, *Remembrances,* esp. 66–79. See also Liao Binghui, "Xiangwang, fangzhu, kuique: 'Taohuayuanshi bing ji' de meigan jiegou" (Desire, exile, and lack: the aesthetic structure of the poem and text of 'Peach Blossom Spring'," in *Jiegou piping lunji* (Critical essays on deconstructionism), 21–38.

18. Shen Congwen, "Yinzi" to *Xiangxi* (Prologue to *West Hunan*), in *SCWJ,* 9:337.

19. Ibid.

20. Ibid.

21. Shen Congwen, "Baihe liuyu jige matou" (Harbors on the Bai river), in *SCWJ,* 9:364, 368–370.

22. Shen Congwen, "Luxi, Pushi, Xiangziyan" (Luxi, Pushi, Xiangziyan), in *SCWJ,* 9:372, 376.

23. Shen Congwen, "Chenxi de mei" (Coal mines in Chenxi), in *SCWJ,* 9:381–382; "Fenghuang" (Fenhuang), ibid., 397–398.

24. Shen Congwen, "Fenghuang" (Fenhuang), in *SCWJ,* 9:398.

25. Shen Congwen, "Yuanling de ren" (People of Yuanling), in *SCWJ,* 9:363.

26. Shen Congwen, preface to *Xiangxi* (West Hunan), in *SCWJ,* 9:6.

27. Shen Congwen, *Congwen zizhuan* (Autobiography), in *SCWJ,* 9:202.

28. Shen Congwen, "Laoban" (Old companion), in *SCWJ,* 9:297.

29. Shen Congwen, "Shuiyun" (Water cloud), in *SCWJ,* 10:280.

30. Shen Congwen, "*Congwen xiaoshuo xizuoxuan* daixu" (Preface to *Selected Exercises of Congwen's Fiction Writing*), in *SCWJ,* 11:45.

31. Shen Congwen, *Biancheng* (The Border town), in *SCWJ,* 6:73.

32. Liu Xiwei, "Lun *Biancheng* yu 'Bajuntu'" (On *The Border Town* and "The Portrait of Eight Steeds"), quoted from Ling Yu, *Cong biancheng zouxiang shijie* (March from the border town), 237.

33. Shen Congwen, "Shuiyun" (Water cloud), in *SCWJ,* 10:279.

34. Ibid., 282.

35. Shen Congwen, *The Border Town,* 5.

36. Chan, *Problematics of Modern Chinese Realism,* 285.

37. Shen Congwen, *The Border Town,* 6.

38. Genette, *Narrative Discourse,* 116. David Der-wei Wang, "Chulun Shen Congwen" (A Preliminary Study of Shen Congwen), in *Zhongsheng xuanhua* (Heteroglossia), 119–120. See also Chan, *Problematics of Modern Chinese Literature,* 291.

39. Shen Congwen, *The Border Town,* 12.

40. Ibid., 15.

Notes, Chapter 7

41. Ibid., 18.
42. Ibid., 52.
43. See, for example, Sun Changxi and Liu Xipu, "Lun *Biancheng* de sixiang qingxiang" (Conceptual tendency), 152–163; Ling Yu, *Cong biancheng zouxiang shijie* (March from the border town), 240–243.
44. Tao Qian, "Peach Blossom Spring," 168.
45. Shen Congwen, *Biancheng* (The border town), *in SCWJ*, 6:126. My translation.
46. Shen Congwen, *The Border Town*, 101.
47. Ibid.
48. Shen Congwen, "*Changhe* tiji" (Preface to *Long River*), in *SCWJ*, 7:4.
49. Ibid., p. 6.
50. Ibid.
51. Shen Congwen, "*Changhe* tiji," (Preface to *Long River*), in *SCWJ*, 7:8.
52. Kinkley, *Odyssey of Shen Congwen*, 172–173, 208–209, 246–247.
53. Shen Congwen, *Changhe* (Long river), in *SCWJ*, 7:38.
54. Ibid., 171.
55. Ibid.
56. Ibid., 172.
57. See Ling Yu's interview with Shen Congwen, "Shen Congwen tan ziji de chaungzuo" (Shen Congwen's talk), 315–20; Shen Congwen, "*Congwen xiaoshuo xuanji* tiji" (Preface to *A Collection of Congwen's Selected Fiction*), in *SCWJ*, 11:69.
58. Ibid.
59. Shen Congwen, "*Congwen xiaoshuo xuanji* tiji" (Preface to *A Collection of Congwen's Selected Fiction*), in *SCWJ*, 11:69.
60. Wang Zengqi, "Shen Congwen de jimo" (Shen Congwen's loneliness), 145; Ling Yu, *Cong biancheng zouxiang shijie* (March from the border town), 397.
61. Ling Yu, *Cong biancheng zouxiang shijie* (March from the border town), 408–410. See also Shen Congwen, "Tan xie youji" (On writing travelogues), in *SCWJ*, 12:143.
62. See Shen Congwen, "Songren xiequ" (The humor of Song dynasty people), in *SCWJ*, 12:246–265; "Songren yanju de fengcixing" (The satirical element in the Song dynasty theater), ibid., 266–278.
63. Shen Congwen, *Congwen zizhuan* (Autobiography), in *SCWJ*, 9:224.
64. Shen Congwen, afterword to "Yige chuanqi de benshi" (Material for a legend), in *SCWJ*, 12:162.
65. Shen Congwen, "Yisheng" (Doctor), in *SCWJ*, 4:201.
66. Shen Congwen, "Yuanshui shangyou jige xianfen" (Counties in the upper valley of the Yuan River), in *SCWJ*, 9:389.
67. Shen Congwen, *Congwen zizhuan* (Autobiography), *SCWJ*, 9:159–160
68. Ibid.
69. Shen Congwen, "Three Men and One Woman," trans. Kai-yu Hsu, in *Modern Chinese Stories and Novellas,* ed. Lau, C. T. Hsia, and Lee, 265.

70. Shen Congwen, "The Lamp," trans. Kai-yu Hsu, in *Modern Chinese Stories and Novellas,* ed. Lau, C. T. Hsia, and Lee, 237.
71. Ibid., 238.
72. Ibid., 239.
73. Ibid., 239–240.
74. Ibid., 246.

8. Conclusion

1. Feuerwerker, *Ding Ling's Fiction,* 129.
2. Dai Houying, *Ren a, ren!* (Man ah, man!), 54.
3. Ibid., 5.
4. See, for example, Jin Jiarui, *Yihetuan yundong* (The Boxer Rebellion movement).
5. The analogy between *The Water Margin* and *The Boxers* also brings to mind the "gang of four's" campaign against *The Water Margin* in the mid-seventies. A reading of *The Boxers* in terms of the classic thus adds another twist, however unintentionally, to the political and ideological ambiguity underlying Feng Jicai and Li Dingxing's work.
6. In my interview with her, Zhang Xinxin indicated that, though aware of the existence of Mao Dun's *One Day in China: May 21, 1936,* she never used it as a model for *People in Beijing.* Rather it is the American writer Studs Terkel's reportage that inspired her project.
7. See Michael Duke, *Blooming and Contending,* 98–122.
8. See Shi Shuqing's interview with Feng Jicai, in *Duitanlu* (Conversations), 204–208.
9. See Joseph Lau, *Tilei piaoling de xiandai wenxue* (Modern Chinese literature), 1–8.
10. My interview with Wang Wenxing, November 20, 1985.
11. Wang Zenhe, *Meigui, Meigui, Woaini* (Rose, Rose, I love you), 269.
12. Lao She, "Wo zenyan xie *Lao Zhang de zhexue,*" (How I wrote *The Philosophy of Lao Zhang*), in *Lao She shenghuo yu chuangzuo zishu* (Lao She's accounts), ed. Hu Jieqing, 7.
13. Lee, "Shijie wenxue de liangge jianzheng" (Two showcases in world literature), 8–17.
14. See Shi Shuqing's interview with Wang Zengqi, in Shi Shuqing, *Duitanlu* (Conversations), 164–180; also see Wang Zengqi, "Shen Congwen xiansheng zai xinanlianda" (Mr. Shen Congwen), 160–164.
15. See, for example, Shi Shuqing's interview with A Cheng, in *Duitanlu* (Conversations), 110.
16. Mo Yan, *Honggaoliang jiazu* (The red sorghum family), 2.
17. See Lau, "The Tropics Mythopoetized," 1–26.

Glossary

A Cheng	阿城
A Hei xiaoshi	阿黑小史
A Q zhengzhuan	阿Q正傳
Aiguo	愛國
Bababa	爸爸爸
Ba Jin	巴金
Baigou qiuqianjia	白狗鞦韆架
Baihe liuyu jige matou	白河流域幾個碼頭
Baizi	柏子
Baosun	抱孫
Baozitou Lin Chung	豹子頭林沖
Bataiye	八太爺
Bayue de xiangcun	八月的鄉村
Beihai de ren	背海的人
Beijing ren	北京人
Biancheng	邊城
Bucheng wenti de wenti	不成問題的問題
Candong	殘冬
Cao Zhi	曹植
Changhe	長河
Chende de chuan	常德的船

Glossary

Chaguan	茶館
Chen Duxiu	陳獨秀
Chenlun	沉淪
Chenxi de mei	辰溪的煤
Chu	楚
Chuci	楚辭
Chun	春
Chuncan	春蠶
Chuangzao	創造
Cong Baicaoyuan dao Sanwei shuwu	從百草園到三味書屋
Congwen zizhuan	從文自傳
Dabeisi wai	大悲寺外
Dai Houying	戴厚英
Daniunan cun	打牛湳村
Dawang	大王
Dazexiang	大澤鄉
Deng	燈
Ding Ling	丁玲
Dongxi	東西
Dongyao	動搖
Duanhun qiang	斷魂鎗
Duanlian	鍛鍊
Duojiao guanxi	多角關係
Erma	二馬
Ershinian mudu zhi guaixianzhuang	二十年目睹之怪現狀
Fandui zhe	反對者
Fei Ming	廢名
Feizao	肥皂
Feng Jicai	馮驥才
Fenghuang	鳳凰
Fengzi	鳳子
Fufu	夫婦
Fuqin de bing	父親的病
Fushi	腐蝕
Gu Hua	古華
Guanchang xianxing ji	官場現形記
Gudu	故鄉
Gudu zhe	孤獨者
Guiqu laixi	歸去來兮

Glossary

Guisheng	貴生
Guling zhiqiu	牯嶺之秋
Guoling zhe	過嶺者
Gushi xinbian	故事新編
Guxiang	故鄉
Guxiang zaji	故鄉雜記
Hairui baguan	海瑞罷官
Haizi wang	孩子王
Han Shaogong	韓少功
He Liwei	何立偉
Heibai Li	黑白李
Heiye	黑夜
Hong	虹
Honggaoliang jiazu	紅高粱家族
Hunui	虎妞
Hu Shi	胡適
Hu Yepin	胡也頻
Hu Yaobang	胡耀邦
Huang Chunming	黃春明
Huang Fan	黃凡
Huanghun	黃昏
Huiming	會明
Huoche ji	火車集
Huozang	火葬
Jia	家
Jia Pingwa	賈平凹
Jian Xian'ai	蹇先艾
Jiehou shiyi	劫後拾遺
Jieyu cangao	劫餘殘稿
Jihuang	饑荒
Jiling chunqiu	吉陵春秋
Jingu qiguan	今古奇觀
Jiusi yisheng	九死一生
Juezhan xingqiwu	決戰星期五
Kaishi daji	開市大吉
Kangzhan wenyi	抗戰文藝
Kongnan zheng	恐男症
Kuangren riji	狂人日記
Lao She	老舍
Lao Zhang de zhexue	老張的哲學

Laozihao	老字號
Li Baojia	李寶嘉
Li Daoyuan	酈道元
Li Dingxing	李定興
Li Lisan	李立三
Li Qiao	李喬
Li Shangyin	李商隱
Li Yongping	李永平
Li Zicheng	李自成
Lian	戀
Liang Qichao	梁啓超
Lianzhang	連長
Liang Shiqiu	梁實秋
Liaozhai zhiyi	聊齋誌異
Lihun	離婚
Lijiao	禮教
Lin Shuangbu	林雙不
Linjia puzi	林家鋪子
Liu Zongyuan	柳宗元
Liucun de	柳邨的
Long Zhu	龍朱
Lu Xun	魯迅
Ludian	旅店
Lun xiaoshou yu qunzhi zhiguanxi	論小說與羣治之關係
Luotuo Xiangzi	駱駝祥子
Luxi, Pushi, Xiangziyan	瀘溪，浦市，箱子岩
Maocheng ji	貓城記
Mao Dun	茅盾
Meigui, meigui, woaini	玫瑰，玫瑰，我愛你
Meijin, Baozi, yunayang	媚金，豹子，與那羊
Mianzi wenti	面子問題
Minzhu shijie	民主世界
Miye	迷葉
Mo Yan	莫言
Mujiewen	墓碣文
Nahan	吶喊
Niehaihua	孽海花
Niu Tianci zhuan	牛天賜傳
Nununu	女女女
Ouyang Shan	歐陽山

Pei Wenzhong	裴文中
Penglai zhiyi	蓬萊誌異
Pinxie ji	貧血集
Qige yeren yu zuihou yige yingchunjie	七個野人與最後一個迎春節
Qianxiaojing	黔小景
Qian Xingcun	錢杏邨
Qiaoxiu yu Dongsheng	巧秀與冬生
Qiaoyu	僑寓
Qiu Jin	秋瑾
Qiushou	秋收
Qu Yuan	屈原
Ren A! Ren	人啊！人
Rentong cixin	人同此心
Ruwuhou	入伍後
Sang Ye	桑曄
Sange nanren yu yige nuren	三個男人與一個女人
Sansan	三三
Shagou	殺狗
Shanghai danianye	上海大年夜
Shanghen wenxue	傷痕文學
Shangui	山鬼
Shangzhou chulu	商州初錄
Shen Congwen	沈從文
Shen Yanbing	沈雁冰
Sheng	生
Shenquan	神拳
Shenwu zhiai	神巫之愛
Shenxing	神性
Sheyu	舍予
Shi	蝕
Shi de shuqing	詩的抒情
Shi yu sanwen	詩與散文
Shiji	史記
Shijie	石碣
Shiren zhisi	詩人之死
Shu Qingchun	舒慶春
Shu Yi	舒乙
Shuangye hongci eryuehua	霜葉紅似二月花
Shuijing zhu	水經注

Glossary

Shuizao xing	水藻行
Shuo gushi ren de gushi	說故事人的故事
Sima Zhongyuan	司馬中原
Sishi tongtang	四世同堂
Song Zelai	宋澤萊
Taiyang zhaozai Sangganhe shang	太陽照在桑乾河上
Tan	曇
Taohuayuan ji	桃花源記
Tao Qian	陶潛
Tian Han	田漢
Tiantang suantai zhige	天堂蒜臺之歌
Tieniu yu bingya	鐵牛與病鴨
Tousheng	偷生
Tu	兔
Tui	蛻
Wang Jingwei	汪精衞
Wang Luyan	王魯彥
Wang Tuo	王拓
Wang Wenxing	王文興
Wang Zengqi	汪曾祺
Wang Zhenhe	王禎和
Wangshi yu xingfa	往事與刑罰
Weishen	微神
Wode jiaoyu	我的教育
Wo zhe yibeizi	我這一輩子
Wu Han	吳晗
Wu Woyao	吳沃堯
Xiangtu xiaoshuo	鄉土小說
Xiangxi	湘西
Xiangxing sanji	湘行散記
Xiao mutouren	小木頭人
Xiaopo de shengri	小坡的生日
Xiaoxiao	蕭蕭
Xiaozhai	小寨
Xie Yaohuan	謝瑤環
Xin Hanmuliede	新韓穆列德
Xin yu jiu	新與舊
Xinshenghuo	新生活
Xinshidai de jiubeiju	新時代的舊悲劇

Xu Qinwen   許欽文
Xungen   尋根

Yan Fu   嚴復
Yang Qingchu   楊青矗
Yao   藥
Yao Xueyin   姚雪垠
Ye   夜
Ye Shaojun   葉紹鈞
Yeqiangwei   野薔薇
Yeshi sanjiao   也是三角
Yibai genren de shinian   一百個人的十年
Yidai fengliu   一代風流
Yifeng jiaxin   一封家信
Yihequan   義和拳
Yijiubaliu nian   一九八六年
Yijiusansi nian yiyue shiba   一九三四年一月十八日
Yige chuanqi de benshi   一個傳奇的本事
Yige nuxing   一個女性
Yikuai zhugan   一塊豬肝
Yisheng   醫生
Yu Dafu   郁達夫
Yu Hua   余華
Yuanling de ren   沅凌的人
Yuexia xiaojing   月下小景
Yueyaer   月牙兒
Yunu   浴奴

Zai Jiuloushang   在酒樓上
Zaoshang, yiduitu, yigebing   早上，一堆土，一個兵
Zeng Pu   曾樸
Zhangfu   丈夫
Zhang Tianyi   張天翼
Zhang Xinxin   張辛欣
Zhao Shuli   趙樹理
Zhao Ziyue   趙子曰
Zhenghongqi xia   正紅旗下
Zhong   忠
Zhongyang ribao   中央日報
Zhongguo de yiri, yijiusanliu nian wuyue ershiyi   中國的一日，一九三六年五月二十一

Glossary

Zhou Zuoren	周作人
Zhu Xining	朱西寧
Zhuangzi	莊子
Zhufu	祝福
Zhuiqiu	追求
Zhuizi	墜子
Zhujian	鑄劍
Zisha	自殺
Ziye	子夜
Zuozhuan	左傳

Selected Bibliography

A Cheng. *Qiwang, Shuwang, Haiziwang* (Chess king, tree king, child king). Taipei: Xindi chubanshe, 1987.

A Ying (Qian Xingcun), ed. *Wanqing wenxue congchao: xiaoshuo xiqu yanjiujuan* (A compendium of late Qing literature: volume of fiction and drama), Beijing: Zhonghua shuju, 1960.

Anderson, Benedict. *Imagined Communities: Reflections of the Origin and Spread of Nationalism.* London: Verso Editions, 1983.

Anderson, Marston. *The Limits of Realism: Chinese Fiction in the Revolutionary Period.* Berkeley: University of California Press, 1990.

Arac, Jonathan, ed. *Postmodernism and Politics.* Minneapolis: University of Minnesota Press, 1986.

Bhabha, K. Homi, ed. *Nation and Narration.* New York: Routledge, 1990.

Barker, Francis, Peter Hulme, Margaret Iversen, and Diana Loxley, eds. *Literature, Politics and Theory.* London: Methuen, 1986.

Bakhtin, Mikhail. *Rabelais and His World,* Helen Iswolsky, trans. Cambridge: MIT Press, 1968.

———. *Dialogic Imagination,* Caryl Emerson and Michael Holquist, trans. Austin: University of Texas Press, 1983.

Barthes, Roland. *Mythologies.* Annette Lavers, trans. New York: Hill & Wang, 1972.

Bentley, Eric. *The Life of the Drama.* New York: Atheneum, 1964.

Bermel, Albert. *Farce: A History from Aristophanes to Woody Allen.* New York: Simon & Schuster, 1982.

Birch, Cyril. "Lao She: The Humorist in his Humor." *China Quarterly*, (1961) 8:51–55.
Brooks, Peter. *The Melodramatic Imagination: Balzac, James, Melodrama, and the Mode of Excess*. New York: Columbia University Press, 1985.
Burke, Kenneth. *Language as Symbolic Action: Essays on Life, Literature, and Method*. Berkeley: University of California Press, 1966.
Chan, Chingkiu Stephen. *The Problematics of Modern Chinese Realism: Mao Dun and His Contemporaries (1919–1937)*. Unpublished doctoral dissertation, University of California at San Diego, 1986.
Chen Bingliang, ed. *Xiandai zhongguo wenxue xinmao* (New facets of modern Chinese literature). Taipei: Xuesheng shuju, 1990.
Chen Duxiu. *Duxiu wencun* (Writings of Chen Duxiu). Shanghai: Yadong tushuguan, 1922.
Chen Jiying. *Sanshi niandai zuojia zhijie yinxiangji* (Personal impressions of writers of the thirties). Taipei: Taiwan shangwu yinshuguan, 1986.
Chen Shijing. "Lun Wu Sunfu" (On Wu Sunfu). *Zhongguo xiandai wenxue yanjiu congkan* (Compendium of research on modern Chinese literature), (1981) 4:61–74.
Chen, Yu-shih. *Realism and Allegory in the Early Fiction of Mao Dun*. Bloomington: Indiana University Press, 1986.
Corrigan, Robert W., ed. *Comedy: Meaning and Form*. San Francisco: Chandler, 1965.
Corrigan, Robert W. and James L. Rosenberg, eds. *The Context and Craft of Drama*. San Francisco: Chandler, 1964.
Craig, David, ed. *Marxists on Literature*. Baltimore: Penguin, 1975.
Dai Houying. *Ren a, ren!* (Man ah, Man!). Guangzhou: Renmin chubanshe, 1981.
Dembo, L. S. *Detotalized Totalities: Synthesis and Disintegration in Naturalist, Existential, and Socialist Fiction*. Madison: University of Wisconsin Press, 1989.
Department of Chinese Literature, Beijing University, et al., eds. *Wenxue yundong shiliaoxuan* (Anthology of historical documents on literary movements), 4 vols. Shanghai: Shanghai jiaoyu chubanshe, 1980.
Derrida, Jacques. "White Mythology." *New Literary History*, (1974) 6:5–74.
Desan, Philippe, Priscilla Parkhurst Ferguson, and Wendy Griswold, eds. *Literature and Social Practice*. Chicago: University of Chicago Press, 1989.
Dolčzelová Velingerová, Milena, ed. *The Chinese Novel at the Turn of the Century*. Toronto: University of Toronto Press, 1980.
Duke, Michael. *Blooming and Contending: Chinese Literature in the Post-Mao Era*. Bloomington: Indiana University Press, 1985.
Egan, Ronald. "Narrative in the *Tso-chuan*." *Harvard Journal of Asiatic Studies*, (1977) 37:325–353.
Feng Jicai and Li Dingxing. *Yihequan* (The Boxers). Beijing: Renmin wenxue chubanshe, 1977.
Feuerwerker, Yi-tsi Mei. *Ding Ling's Fiction*. Cambridge: Harvard University Press, 1982.

Foucault, Michel. *Madness and Civilization*. Richard Howard, trans. New York: Random House, 1973.

———. *Discipline and Punish: The Birth of the Prison*. Alan Sheridan, trans. New York: Pantheon, 1977.

Freedman, Ralph. *The Lyrical Novel: Studies in Herman Hesse, André Gide, and Virginia Woolf.* Princeton: Princeton University Press, 1966.

Frye, Northrop. *Anatomy of Criticism*. New York: Atheneum, 1968.

Fu Zhiying, ed. *Mao Dun pingzhuan* (Critical and biographical essays on Mao Dun). Shanghai: Xiandai shuju, 1931.

Gálik, Marián. *Mao Dun and Modern Chinese Literary Criticism*. Wiesbaden: Franz Steiner Verlag, 1969.

———. *Milestones in Sino-Western Literary Confrontation (1898–1979)*. Wiesbaden: Otto Harrassowitz, 1986.

Gay, Peter, ed. *The Freud Reader*. New York: Norton, 1989.

Genette, Gérard. "Vraisemblance et motivation," *Communications,* (1968) 11:6–10.

———. *Narrative Discourse*. Jane E. Lewin, trans. Ithaca: Cornell University Press, 1980.

Gurewitch, Morton. *Comedy: The Irrational Vision*. Ithaca: Cornell University Press, 1976.

Hanan, Patrick. "The Technique of Lu Xun's Fiction." *Harvard Journal of Asiatic Studies,* (1974) 34:53–96.

He Jiahuai. "Mao Dun de 'Chuncan,' 'Qiushou,' he 'Candong'" (Mao Dun's "Spring silkworms," "Autumn harvest," and "Winter ruins"). *Wenxue zhishi* (Literary knowledge), (1959) 1:18–31.

Hegel, Robert and Richard C. Hessney, eds. *Expressions of Self in Chinese Literature*. New York: Columbia University Press, 1985.

Heilman, Robert B. *Tragedy and Melodrama: Versions of Experience*. Seattle: University of Washington Press, 1968.

Hosek, Chaviva and Patricia Parker, eds. *Lyric Poetry: Beyond New Criticism*. Ithaca: Cornell University Press, 1985.

Hou Jian. *Cong wenxue geming dao geming wenxue* (From literary revolution to revolutionary literature). Taipei: Zhongwai wenxue chubanshe, 1971.

———. "Liang Shiqiu xiansheng renwen sixiang de laiyuan" (The sources of Mr. Liang Shiqiu's humanist thoughts). *Lianhe wenxue* (Unitas), (1987) 31:38–43.

Howe, Irving. *Politics and the Novel*. New York: Avon, 1967.

Hu Jieqing and Shu Yi. *Sanji Lao She* (Essays on Lao She). Beijing: Shiyue wenyi chubanshe, 1986.

Huang Fan. *Fanduizhe* (The opponent). Taipei: Zili chubanshe, 1984.

Hsia, C. T. *A History of Modern Chinese Fiction*. New Haven: Yale University Press, 1961.

Hsia, T. A. *The Gate of Darkness*. Seattle: University of Washington Press, 1968.

Hu Jinquan. *Lao She he tade zuopin* (Lao She and his works). Hong Kong: Wenhua shenghuo chubanshe, 1977.

Bibliography

Hu Shi. "Jianshe de wenxue geminglun" (On a constructive revolution in Chinese literature). *Xin qingnian* (New youth), (1918) 4, 4: 289–306.

Huang Wanhua. "Xiangtu wenxue yu xiandai yishi" (Native soil literature and modern consciousness). *Zhongguo xiandai wenxue yanjiu congkan* (Compendium of research on modern Chinese literature), (1988) 2:152–166.

Hung, Chang-tai. *Going to the People: Chinese Intellectuals and Folk Literature: 1918–1937.* Cambridge: Council on East Asian Studies, Harvard University, 1985.

Jameson, Fredric. *The Political Unconscious: Narrative as a Socially Symbolic Act.* Ithaca: Cornell University Press, 1981.

———. "Literary Innovation and Modes of Production: A Commentary." *Modern Chinese Literature,* (1984) 1:67–72.

Jin Jiarui. *Yihetuan yundong* (The Boxer rebellion movement). Shanghai: Renmin chubanshe, 1962.

Jishou daxue Shen Congwen yanjiushi, ed. *Changhe liubujin: huainian Shen Congwen xiansheng* (Endlessly flows the long river: remembering Mr. Shen Congwen). Changsha: Hunan wenyi chubanshe, 1989.

Kao, George, ed. *Two Writers and the Cultural Revolution.* Hong Kong: The Chinese University Press, 1980.

Kellner, Hans. *Language and Historical Representation: Getting the Story Crooked.* Madison: The University of Wisconsin Press, 1989.

Kern, Edith. *The Absolute Comic.* New York: Columbia University Press, 1980.

Kinkley, Jeffrey C. "Shen Congwen and the Use of Regionalism in Modern Chinese Literature." *Modern Chinese Literature,* (1985) 1, 2:157–183.

———., ed. *After Mao: Chinese Literature and Society 1978–1981.* Cambridge: Harvard University Press, 1985.

———. *The Odyssey of Shen Congwen.* Stanford: Stanford University Press, 1987.

LaCapra, Dominick. *History and Criticism.* Ithaca: Cornell University Press, 1985.

———. *History, Politics and the Novel.* Ithaca: Cornell University Press, 1987.

———. *Soundings in Critical Theory.* Ithaca: Cornell University Press 1989.

Lao She. *Lao Zhang de zhexue* (The philosophy of Lao Zhang). Shanghai: Shangwu yinshuguan, 1928. Reprint, Hong Kong: Huitong shudian, 1976.

———. *Zhao Ziyue* (Zhao Ziyue). Shanghai: Shangwu yinshuguan, 1928.

———. *Erma* (The two Mas). Shanghai: Shangwu yinshuguan, 1931. Reprint, Shanghai: Chenguang, 1948.

———. *Lihun* (Divorce). Shanghai: Liangyou tushu gongsi, 1933. Reprint, Hong Kong: Nanguo chubanshe, 1975.

———. *Maocheng ji* (The city of cats). Shanghai: Xiandai shuju, 1933. Reprint. Shanghai: Chenguang wenxue, 1947.

———. *Hezao ji* (Clams and seaweeds). Shanghai: Kaiming shudian, 1936.

———. *Niu Tianci zhuan* (The biography of Niu Tianci). Shanghai: Renjian shuwu, 1936. Reprint, Hong Kong: Nanguo chubanshe, 1976.

———. *Luotuo Xiangzi* (Camel Xiangzi). Shanghai: Renjian shuwu, 1939. Reprint, Hong Kong: Nanhua shudian, 1976.

———. *Huozang* (Cremation). Shanghai: Chenguang gongsi, 1944. Reprint, Hong Kong: Huitong shuju, 1975.

———. *Tousheng* (Ignoble life), part 2 of *Sishi tongtang*. Shanghai: Chenguang chubanshe, 1946. Reprint, Hong Kong: Huitong shuju, 1979.

———. *Chaguan* (Tea House). Beijing: Zhongguo xiju chubanshe, 1958. Reprint, Chengdu: Sichuan renmin chubanshe, 1980.

———. *Lao She Shenghuo yu chuangzuo zishu* (Lao She's accounts of his life and works). Hu Jieqing, ed. Hong Kong: Sanlian shudian, 1980.

———. *Camel Xiangzi*. trans. Shi Xiaoqing. Bloomington: Indiana University Press, in association with Beijing: Foreign Language Press, 1981.

———. *Lao She wenyi pinglunji* (Collection of Lao She's literary criticisms). Hefei: Anhui renmin chubanshe, 1982.

———. *Lao She wenji* (Works of Lao She). 9 vols. Beijing: Renmin wenxue chubanshe, 1986.

Lau, Joseph. "Naturalism in Modern Chinese Fiction." *Literature East and West*, (1970) 2:148–160.

———. *Tilei piaoling de xiandai wenxue* (Modern Chinese literature in snivelling and tears). Taipei: Yuanjing chubanshe, 1980.

———. "The Tropics Mythopoetized: The Extraterritorial Writing of Li Yung-p'ing in the Context of Hsiang-t'u Movement." *Tamkang Review*, (1981) 3:1–26.

Lau, Joseph, C. T. Hsia, and Leo Ou-fan Lee, eds. *Modern Chinese Stories and Novellas: 1919–1949*. New York: Columbia University Press, 1981.

Lee, Leo Ou-fan, ed. *Lu Xun and His Legacy*. Berkeley: University of California Press 1985.

———. "Shijie wenxue de liangge jianzheng" (Two showcases in world literature). *Lianhe wenxue* (Unitas), (1985) 11:8–17.

———. *Voices from the Iron House: A Study of Lu Xun*. Bloomington: Indiana University Press, 1987.

Lentricchia, Frank. *Ariel and the Police*. Madison: University of Wisconsin Press, 1988.

Levin, Harry. *The Gates of Horn*. New York: Oxford University Press, 1964.

Li Qingxi. "Xungen: huidao shiwu de benshen" (Search for roots: back to the essence of things). *Wenxue pinglun* (Literary criticism), (1988) 4:14–23.

Li Yongping. *Jiling chunqiu* (Jiling chronicles). Taipei: Hongfan shudian, 1986.

Liang Shiqiu. *Kanyunji* (Seeing clouds). Taipei: Zhiwen chubanshe, 1974.

Liao Binghui. *Jiegou piping lunji* (Critical essays on deconstructionism). Taipei: Dongda tushu, 1985.

Lin Hsiu-ling. "Zhongguo geming he nüxing jiefang: Mao Dun xiaoshuo zhong de liangda zhuti" (Chinese revolution and women's liberation: two major themes in Mao Dun's fiction). *Zhongwai wenxue* (Zhongwai [Chungwai] literary monthly), (1988) 18, 5:117–151.

Bibliography

Lin, Yü-sheng. *The Crisis of Chinese Consciousness*. Madison: University of Wisconsin Press, 1979.

Ling Yu. "Shen Congwen tan zijide chuangzuo" (Shen Congwen's talk on his own creative writing). *Zhongguo xiandai wenxue yanjiu congkan* (Compendium of research on modern Chinese literature), (1980) 4:319–321.

———. "Zhongguo xiandai shuqing xiaoshuo de fazhan guiji jiqi rensheng neirong de shenmei xuanze" (The course of development of modern Chinese lyrical fiction and its aesthetic approach to the content of life). *Zhongguo xiandai wenxue yanjiu congkan* (Compendium of research on modern Chinese literature), (1983) 2:229–246.

———. *Cong biancheng zouxiang shijie* (March from the border town to the world). Taipei: Luotuo chubanshe, 1987.

———. *Shen Congwen zhuan* (A biography of Shen Congwen). Beijing: Shiyue wenyi chubanshe, 1988.

Liu Shousong. *Zhongguo xinwenxueshi chugao* (A draft of the history of modern Chinese literature), 2 vols. Beijing: Zuojia chubanshe, 1957.

Lu Xun. *Lu Xun quanji* (Complete Works of Lu Xun). 16 vols. Beijing: Renmin chubanshe, 1981.

Lu Yaodong. *Qiezuo shenzhou xioushou ren* (May as well be an idle onlooker in the sacred kingdom). Taipei: Yunchen wenhua, 1989.

Lucente, Gregory L. *The Narrative of Realism and Myth: Verga, Lawrence, Faulkner, Pavese*. Baltimore: Johns Hopkins University Press, 1979.

Lukács, Georg. *The Historical Novel*. Hannah & Stanley Mitchell, trans. London: Merlin, 1962.

———. *The Theory of the Novel*. Anna Bostock, trans. Cambridge: MIT Press, 1972.

———. *Studies in European Realism*. New York: Grosset and Dunlap, 1972.

Luo Sun. *Kangzhan wenyi huiyiduan* (Fragmentary recollections of the national resistance literature). Shanghai: Shanghai wenyishe, 1961.

Ma, Y. W. "The Chinese Historical Novel: An Outline of Themes and Contents." *Journal of Asian Studies*, (1975) 34, 2:277–294.

Mao Dun. *Shi* (Eclipse). Shanghai: Kaiming shudian, 1930.

———. *Hong* (Rainbow). Shanghai: Kaiming shudian, 1930.

———. *Guling zhiqiu* (The autumn in Guling). Shanghai: Wenhua shenghuo chubanshe, 1937.

———. *Midnight*. Xu Mengxiong and A. C. Barnes, trans. Beijing: Foreign Language Press, 1957.

———. *Mao Dun wenyi zalunji* (Mao Dun's miscellaneous essays on literature). 2 vols. Shanghai wenyi chubanshe, ed. Shanghai: Wenyi chubanshe, 1981.

———. *Mao Dun zhuanji* (A critical anthology on Mao Dun). 2 vols. Fujian renmin chubanshe, ed. Fuzhou: Fujian renmin chubanshe, 1983.

———. *One Day in China: May 21, 1936*. Sherman Cochran and Andrew C. K. Hsieh with Janis Cochran, trans. and eds. New Haven: Yale University Press, 1983.

———. *Wozouguo de daolu* (The road I have taken). 2 vols. Hong Kong: Sanlian shudian, 1981, 1984.

Bibliography

———. *Mao Dun quanji* (Complete works of Mao Dun), 14 vols. Beijing: Renmin wenxue chubanshe, 1985.
Matejka. L, and K. Pomorska, eds. *Readings in Russian Poetics.* Cambridge: MIT Press 1971.
Matthews, J. H. "Zola and the Marxists." *Symposium,* (1957) 11, 1:262–272.
McDougall, Bonnie. *The Introduction of Western Literary Theories into Modern China, 1919–1925.* Tokyo: Centre for East Asian Cultural Studies, 1971.
Meisner, Maurice. *Li Ta-chao and the Origins of Chinese Marxism.* New York: Atheneum, 1977.
Miller, J. Hillis. *The Form of Victorian Fiction.* London: University of Notre Dame Press, 1968.
Mo Yan. *Honggaoliang jiazu* (The red sorghum family). Beijing: Jiefangjun wenyi chubanshe, 1988.
Momigliano, Arnaldo. *Essays in Ancient and Modern Historiography.* Oxford: Basil Blackwell, 1977.
Morson, Gary Saul and Caryl Emerson, eds. *Rethinking Bakhtin: Extensions and Challenges.* Evanston: Northwestern University, 1989.
———. *Mikhail Bakhtin: Creation of a Prosaics.* Stanford: Stanford University Press, 1990.
Ng, Mau-sang. *The Russian Hero in Modern Chinese Fiction.* Hong Kong: The Chinese University Press; New York: State University of New York Press, 1988.
Nieh, Hua-ling. *Shen Ts'ung-wen.* New York: Twayne, 1972.
Owen, Stephen. *Remembrances: The Experience of the Past in Classical Chinese Poetry.* Cambridge: Harvard University Press, 1986.
Pickowicz, Paul. *Marxist Literary Thought in China: A Conceptual Framework.* Berkeley: Center for Chinese Studies, University of California, 1980.
Plaks, Andrew, ed. *Chinese Narrative: Critical and Theoretical Essays.* Princeton: Princeton University Press, 1977.
Prendergast, Christopher. *The Order of Mimesis.* Cambridge: Cambridge University Press, 1986.
Průšek, Jaroslav. "History and Epic in China and the West." *Chinese History and Literature.* Prague, 1970.
———. *The Lyrical and the Epic: Studies of Modern Chinese Literature.* Leo Ou-fan Lee, ed. Bloomington: Indiana University Press, 1980.
Pruyn, Carolyn S. "Humanism in Post-Mao Mainland Chinese Literature: The Case of *Ren A, Ren!* by Dai Houying." *Asian Culture Quarterly,* (1985) 13, 3:15–34.
Quanguo Mao Dun yanjiu xiehui, ed. *Mao Dun yanjiu lunwen xuanji* (Anthology of critical essays on Mao Dun). 2 vols. Changsha: Hunan renmin chubanshe, 1983.
Rickett, Adele Austin, ed. *Chinese Approaches to Literature from Confucius to Liang Ch'i-ch'ao.* Princeton: Princeton University Press, 1978.
Ricoeur, Paul. *Time and Narrative,* vol. 1. Kathleen Maclaughlin and David Pellauer, trans. Chicago: University of Chicago Press, 1984.
Rosenberg, William G. and Marilyn B. Young. *Transforming Russia and China:*

Revolutionary Struggle in the Twentieth Century. New York: Oxford University Press, 1982.

Schwartz, Benjamin. *Chinese Communism and the Rise of Mao*. Cambridge: Harvard University Press, 1951.

Sedgwick, Eve Kosofsky. *Between Men: English Literature and Male Social Desire*. New York: Columbia University Press, 1985.

Semanov, V. I. *Lu Hsun and His Predecessors*. Charles J. Alber, trans. New York: M. E. Sharpe, 1980.

Shao Bozhou. *Mao Dun pingzhuan* (A critical biography of Mao Dun). Chengdu: Sichuan wenyi chubanshe, 1987.

Shen Congwen. *Ji Ding Ling* (Remembering Ding Ling). Shanghai: Liangyou, 1935.

———. *The Border Town and Other Stories*. trans. Gladys Yang. Beijing: Panda, 1981.

———. *Shen Congwen wenji* (The Works of Shen Congwen). eds. Shao Huaqiang and Ling Yu. 12 vols. Hong Kong: Sanlian shudian and Guangzhou: Huacheng chubanshe, 1984.

Shi Chengjun. "Shilun jiefanghou Lao She dui *Luotuo Xiangzi* de xiugai" (On Lao She's revision of *Camel Xiangzi* after the liberation). *Zhongguo xiandai wenxue yanjiu congkan* (Compendium of research on modern Chinese literature), (1980) 4:278–288;

Shi Shuqing. *Duitanlu: miandui dangdai dalu wenxue xinling* (Conversations: facing the literary minds of contemporary mainland China). Taipei: Shibao chuban gongsi, 1989.

Shu Yi. *Lao She zuihou de liangtian* (The last two days of Lao She's life). Guangzhou: Huacheng chubanshe, 1987.

Shehui kexue zhanxian, ed. *Xiandai wenxue lunji* (Critical essays on modern Chinese literature). Jilin: Renmin chubanshe, 1980.

Siebers, Tobin. *The Ethics of Criticism*. Ithaca: Cornell University Press, 1988.

Smith, James L. *Melodrama: The Critical Idiom*. London: Methuen, 1973.

Song Yongyi. *Lao She yu zhongguo wenhua guannian* (Lao She and the concepts of Chinese culture). Shanghai: Xuelin chubanshe, 1985.

Song Zelai. *Penglai zhiyi* (Bizarre stories about Formosa). Taipei: Qianwei chubanshe, 1988.

Sun Changxi and Liu Xipu, "Lun *Biancheng* de sixiang qingxiang" (On the conceptual tendency of *The Border Town*), *Zhongguo xiandai wenxue yanjiu congkan* (Compendium of research on modern Chinese literature), (1985) 4:152–163.

Sun Zhongtian. *Lun Mao Dun de shenghuo yu chuangzuo* (On Mao Dun's life and works). Tianjin: Baihua wenyi chubanshe, 1980.

Sun Zongtian and Zha Guohua, eds. *Mao Dun yanjiu ziliao* (Research materials on Mao Dun), 3 vols. Beijing: Zhongguo shehui kexue chubanshe, 1983.

Todorov, Tzvetan. *The Poetics of Prose*. Richard Howard, trans. Ithaca: Cornell University Press, 1977.

Tolstoy, Leo. *What is Art?*. Aylmer Maude, trans. London: Harper and Row, 1931.

———. *War and Peace*. trans. Aylmer Maude. London: Oxford University Press, 1933.
Turgenev, Ivan. *Sketches from A Hunter's Album*. Richard Freeborn, trans. Baltimore: Penguin, 1967.
Turner, James. *The Politics of Landscape*. Cambridge, Mass: Harvard University Press, 1979.
Van Ghent, Dorothy. *The English Novel: Form and Function*. New York: Harper, 1961.
Vohra, Ranbir. *Lao She and the Chinese Revolution*. Cambridge: Harvard University Press, 1974.
Wagner, Rudolf G. *The Contemporary Chinese Historical Drama: Four Studies*. Berkeley: University of California Press, 1990.
Wang, David Der-wei. "Storytelling Context in Chinese Fiction: A Preliminary Examination of It as a Mode of Narrative Discourse." *Tamkang Review*, (1984–85) 6, 1–4:133–150.
———. "Nonconformism as Narrative Strategy: A Reappraisal of late Ch'ing Fiction." *Asian Culture Quarterly*, (1984)7, 2: 55–72.
———. "Fictional History/Historical Fiction." *Studies in Language and Literature*, (1985) 1:64–76.
———. "Mao Dun and Naturalism: A Case of 'Misreading' in Modern Chinese Literary Criticism." *Monumenta Serica*, (1986–87) 37:169–195.
———. *Cong Liu E dao Wang Zhenhe: Zhongguo xiandai xieshi xiaoshuo sanlun* (From Liu E to Wang Zhenhe: essays on modern Chinese realist fiction). Taipei: Shibao chuban gongsi, 1986.
———. *Zhongsheng xuanhua: sanshi yu bashi niandai de zhongguo xiaoshuo* (Heteroglossia: modern Chinese fiction of the thirties and eighties). Taipei: Yuanliu chuban gongsi, 1988.
Wang Huiyun and Su Qingchang. *Lao She pingzhuan* (A critical biography of Lao She). Shijiazhuang: Huashan wenyi chubanshe, 1985.
Wang Zengqi. "Shen Congwen xiansheng zai xinanlianda" (Mr. Shen Congwen at Southwestern Union University). *Lianhe wenxue* (Unitas), (1987) 27:160–164.
Wang Zhenhe. *Meigui, Meigui, Woaini* (Rose, Rose, I Love You). Taipei: Yuanjing chubanshe, 1984.
Watt, Ian, ed. The Victorian Novel. London: Oxford University Press, 1971.
Wellek, René. A History of Modern Criticism: 1750–1950: The Late Nineteenth Century. New Haven: Yale University Press, 1965.
Wen Rumin. Xinwenxue xianshi zhuyi de liubian (Changes of realism in modern literature). Beijing: Beijing daxue chubanshe, 1988.
White, Hayden. Metahistory. Baltimore: Johns Hopkins University Press, 1973.
Williams, Raymond. *The English Novel from Dickens to Lawrence*. London: Oxford University Press, 1970.
Wu Lichang, ed. *Shen Congwen*. Taipei: Haifeng chubanshe, 1989.
Wu Woyao. *Ershinian mudu zhi guaixianzhuang* (Strange things seen in the past twenty years). Taipei: Shijie shuju, 1965.

Xiao Boqing. "Lao She zai Wuhan Chongqing" (Lao She in Wuhan and Chongqing." *Xinwenxue shiliao* (Historical documents on modern literature), (1986) 2:138–146.

Xu Lin. "Lun *Luotuo Xiangzi* de jiewei ji qita" (On the ending of *Camel Xiangzi* and other revisions). *Zhongguo xiandai wenxue yanjiu congkan* (Compendium of research on modern Chinese literature), (1984) 1:255–269.

Xu Zhiying and Ni Tingting. "Zhongguo nongcun de mianying: ershi niandai xiangtu wenxue guankui" (Facets of a modern Chinese village: a general survey of native soil fiction of the twenties). *Wenxue pinglun* (Literary criticism), (1984) 5:72–82.

Yang Yi. *Zhongguo xiandai xiaoshuoshi* (A history of modern Chinese fiction). 3 vols. Beijing: Renmin wenxue chubanshe, 1986.

Ye Ziming. *Lun Mao Dun Sishinian de wenxue daolu* (On Mao Dun's forty-year literary path). Shanghai: Shanghai wenyi chubanshe, 1959.

Yin Xueman. *Kangzhan shiqi de xiandai xiaoshuo* (Modern Chinese fiction in the period of the national resistance war). Taipei: Chengwen chubanshe, 1980.

Yu, Anthony (Yu Guofan). *Yu Guofan Xiyouji lunji* (Anthony Yu's critical essays on *Journey to the West*). Li Shixue, trans. Taipei: Lianjing chuban gongsi, 1989.

Yu Guangzhong, et al., eds. *Zhonghua xiandai wenxue daxi* (A comprehensive anthology of contemporary Chinese literature in Taiwan). 15 vols. Taipei: Jiuge, 1989.

Zeng Guangcan and Wu Huaibin, eds. *Lao She yanjiu ziliao* (Research materials on Lao She). 2 vols. Beijing: Shiyue wenyi chubanshe, 1985.

Zeng Pu. *Niehaihua* (A flower in the sea of sins). Taipei: Shijie shuju, 1960.

Zhao Jiabi, ed. *Zhongguo xiandai wenxue daxi* (Compendium of modern Chinese literature). 10 vols. Shanghai: Liangyou tushu gongsi, 1935–1936.

Zhao Xiaqiu. *Zhongguo xiandai baogao wenxueshi* (A history of modern Chinese reportage literature). Beijing: Zhongguo renmin daxue chubanshe, 1987.

Zhongguo Mao Dun yanjiu xuehui, ed. *Mao Dun jiushi danchen jinian lunwenji* (Essays in memory of Mao Dun's ninetieth birthday). Beijing: Zuojia chubanshe, 1987.

Zhou Yingxiong, ed. *Chinese Text*. Hong Kong: Press of the Chinese University, 1983.

———. *Xiaoshuo, lishi, xinli, renwu* (Fiction, history, psychoanalysis, and characters). Taipei: Dongda tushu, 1989.

Zhou Zuoren. *Zhou Zuoren lunwenji* (A collection of Zhou Zuoren's critical essays). Huang Zhiqing, ed. Hong Kong: Huiwenge shuju, 1972.

Zhu Defa, A Yan, Zhai Deyao. *Mao Dun qianqi wenxue sixiang sanlun* (Essays on Mao Dun's early literary thoughts). Jinan: Shandong renmin chubanshe, 1983.

Zhuang Zhongqing, ed. *Mao Dun yanjiu lunji* (Critical essays on Mao Dun). Tianjin: Tianjin renmin chubanshe, 1974.

Index

A Cheng, 299, 312. Works: "Chess King," 299; "Tree King," 299; "Child King," 299
Aesthetic of the residue, 257ff.
Alazon, 123, 125–127, 329*n*34
Allegory, 4, 33, 102
Anderson, Marston, 318*n*4, 318*n*7, 318*n*10
Anticipatory nostalgia, 277–281
Anti-epiphany, 229
Anti-Rightist Movement, 294

Ba Jin, 187. Work: *Family*, 187 ff., 189
Bakhtin, Mikhail, 204, 252, 321*n*39, 336*n*8
Balzac, Honoré de, 11, 12, 36, 73, 118
Barthes, Roland, 317*n*1
Beijing, 127, 134, 154ff., 193, 194–195
Bible, 22
Birch, Cyril, 128
Bovaryism, 37

Boxer Rebellion, 112, 297
Braudel, Paul Achille Fernand, 226
Brooks, Peter, 118, 319*n*21
Buddhist teachings, 69

Cannibalism, 9, 214
Cao Zhi, 281
CCP (Chinese Communist Party), 38, 67, 95ff., 99, 100, 103, 107
Chandler, Frank Wadleigh, 71
Chekhov, Anton, 22, 206, 281
Chen Duxiu, 2
Chen, Yu-shih, 33, 47, 102
Chiang Kai-shek, 100
Chinese Communist Party, 38, 67, 95ff., 99, 100, 103, 107
Chinese Writers' National Anti-Aggression Association, 158
Chronotope, 50, 55, 252, 321*n*39
Chu culture, 21, 219, 263, 264, 265, 299
Classical Chinese historical novel, 28–30, 297
Coleridge, Samuel Taylor, 286

Index

Confucian teachings, 69
Confucianism, 70, 76
Conrad, Joseph, 113, 286, 330n40, 330n55
Creation Society, 161
Critical lyricism, 20, 203–210

Dai Houying, 294–296. Works: *Man ah Man!*, 294–295, *The Death of a Poet*, 295–296
Dandyism, 92
Darwin, Charles, 73
Darwinism, 71–72
Decapitation, 210, 211–219
Defamiliarization, 3, 164, 251
Derrida, Jacques, 6, 317n1
Determinism, 73, 271, 209
Deus ex machina, 40, 129, 143, 190
Dickens, Charles, 17, 113, 118, 121. Works: *Nicholas Nickleby*, 113, 114, 328n17; *The Old Curiosity Shop*, 114, 329n27; *Oliver Twist*, 328n24; *Pickwick Papers*, 121
Ding Ling, 201, 293. Work: *The Sunshine over the Sanggan River*, 293
Doleželová-Velingerová, Milena, 69, 116
Don Quixote, 129, 264
Duke, Michael, 341n7

Eros, 234, 235, 237
Expatriate Chinese syndrome, 165

Fadeyev, Aleksandr, 171. Work: *The Rout*, 172
Farce, 16, 18, 115–118, 136, 144ff., 186
Fei Ming, 22, 205
Femme fatale, 88, 192
Feng Jicai, 296–297. Works: *The Boxers*, 296–297; *One Decade, One Hundred People*, 297–298
Feuerwerker, I-tsi, 293
Fielding, Henry, 113, 139. Work: *Tom Jones*, 139, 140
First Chinese Communist Revolution, 16, 25, 35
Five Martyrs, 201

Flaubert, Gustave, 72, 118
Foucault, Michel, 216
Freud, Sigmund, 130
Frye, Northrop, 125, 207, 328n27, 329n34

Gálik, Marián, 60–61, 108
Genette, Gérard, 5, 268
Goethe, Johann, 65. Work: *Sorrows of Young Werther*, 65
Goncourts, 73
Gorky, Maxim, 45. Work: *One Day in the World*, 45
Great Cultural Revolution, 10, 112, 167, 198, 294, 296, 298, 299, 300
Gu Hua, 312

Hamlet syndrome, 126–127, 134, 180, 189–190, 194
Hanan, Patrick, 3
Han Shaogong, 299–300, 312. Works: "Papapa," 299; "Woman, Woman, Woman," 299
Hauptmann, Gerhart, 70
He Liwei, 312
Historical novel, 27–28
Howe, Irving, 68
Hsia, C. T., 34, 39, 78, 83, 94, 123, 125, 139, 156, 163, 329n33
Hsia, T. A., 8
Huang Chunming, 307, 309, 311
Huang Fan, 301, 302–303. Work: *The Opponent*, 302
Huang Yongyu, 283, 284
Hu Shi, 2
Hu Yaobang, 99, 103, 104
Hu Yepin, 201

Ibsen, Henrik, 41, 83
Imaginary nostalgia, defined, 250–253; 21, 23, 274, 281, 288–289, 307–309, 315
Iterative mode, 212, 230, 268–269, 273

Jakobson, Roman, 318n5
James, Henry, 113

Jia Pingwa, 312. Work: *Preliminary Accouts of Shangzhou*, 312
Jian Xian'ai, 249
Jingu qiguan (Wonders of the Past and the Present), 281

Kafka, Franz, 134, 302. Work: *Castle*, 302, 303
Kinkley, Jeffrey, 224, 335n1, 335n2, 335n3, 335n4, 337n34, 337n46, 337n49, 338n3, 340n52
KMT (Kuo-min-tang, Nationalist Party), 38, 95ff., 100

Lao She: concept of laughter, 17, 113, 117ff., 151, 301, 305; criticism on Chinese concept of romance, 130–134; debate with Liang Shiqiu, 161–162; depiction of the real, 23; difference from Dickens, 114, 328n27; exploration of the irrational, 15, 121, 134–135ff., 181; indebtedness to Dickens, 113, 117, 328n17; indebtedness to Lu Xun, 15–16, 111, 136, 140; London experience, 124–125, 127; major characters in wartime fiction, 179–180, 182–185; Manchu background, 112, 175, 326n2; use of melodrama and farce, 16–18, 113–119; skepticism, 15, 119, 122, 167, 183, 188, 191, 198, 332n1; source of farcical discourse, 113–114; suicide, 112, 168; suicide as a theme in fiction, 168, 197–198; wartime activities, 157–159
—Works: *Anemia*, 159, 181–185; "Bath Slaves," 179, 181; *The Biography of Niu Tianci*, 15, 135, 139–144, 303; "The Black and White Li," 168; *Camel Xiangzi*, 15, 17, 18, 111, 144–156, 174, 178, 195; *The City of Cats*, 135–139, 148–149, 164, 166–167, 182, 195, 198; *Cremation*, 159, 168–174, 191, 192, 198; "The Crescent Moon," 17, 168, 198; *Democratic World*, 159, 200; "A Different Kind of Triangle," 131; *Divorce*, 15, 18, 111, 127–130, 180, 303; *Drum Singers*, 332n7; "East Meets West," 180–181, 183; *Four Generations Under One Roof*, 168, 185–199, 303; "Grand Master Eight," 184; "Grand Opening," 115–116; "Grandson," 116, 153; *Homecoming*, 126, 190; "Killing Dogs," 179, 180, 189; "A Letter from Home," 179, 180, 189; "Little Wooden Puppet," 173, 183–184; *The Magical Boxers*, 296; *Metamorphosis*, 179, 199; "New Hamlet," 126; "An Old Tragedy in a New Time," 188; "Outside the Dabei Temple," 168; *The Philosophy of Lao Zhang*, 15, 17, 111, 114–120, 141, 148, 302; "A Piece of Pig Liver," 179, 180; "Predilection," 146, 183; *The Problem of Face*, 158; "Rabbit," 175–176; "The Romantic Fiction of the Tang Dynasty," 130; "Soul-shattering Spear," 151; *Tea House*, 151, 167, 332n1; "This Is My Life," 174–175, 195; *Train*, 159, 174–181; "Train," 176–178; *The Two Mas*, 18, 123–127, 129, 151, 164–166, 180, 189, 329n31; *Under the Red Banner*, 17, 175, 326n2, 334n37; "Unproblematic Problem," 182–183; "Vision," 15; "We Are on the Same Boat," 179, 180; "A Woman from the Liu Village," 116, 152; *Zhao Ziyue*, 120–123; 163–164

Late Qing exposé fiction, 17, 33, 46, 96, 113, 116, 128, 148, 186, 191, 306
Lau, Joseph, 14, 144, 301, 319n19, 331n77, 341n17
League of Left-Wing Writers, 10, 161
Lee, Leo, 214, 306, 317n1, 339n15, 341n13
Lenin, Vladimir, 74

Li Baojia, 128. Work: *Exposé of Officialdom*, 128
Li Daoyuan, 281. Work: *Shuijing Zhu* (A Commentary on the Classic of the Water Ways), 281
Li Dingxing, 296, 297
Li Lisan, 107, 108
Li Qiao, 301, 304–305. Work: "Phallophobia," 304
Li Shangyin, 53
Li Yongping, 309, 313–315. Work: *Jiling Chronicles*, 313–315
Liang Qichao, 2, 77. Work: "On the Relation Between Fiction and Ruling the People," 69
Liang Shiqiu, 160–161
Lin Shuangbu, 301, 305. Work: *The Final Combat on Friday*, 305
Lin, Yu-sheng, 76; cultural-intellectualistic approach, 2
Ling Yu, 340n57, 340n60
Liu Binyan, 298
Liu E, 299. Work: *The Travels of Lao Can*, 299
Liu Qing, 308
Liu Zongyuan, 268, 281
Lu Xun: as pioneer of native soil fiction, 249–250, 315; cannibalism, 9, 214; concept of the real, 2–4, 5ff.; decapitation as a theme in fiction, 213–216; influence on Lao She, 1, 14–15, 24, 111, 136, 140, 184–185; influence on Mao Dun, 1, 10–11, 24, 40, 47, 74; influence on Shen Congwen, 1, 18–19, 24, 205, 249–251; obsession with the irrational, 7–8, 9.
—Works: *A Call to Arms*, 214; "Diary of a Madman," 4–10, 11, 96, 216; "Divorce," 15; "Forging Swords," 214; "From Baicao Garden to Sanwei Studio," 216; "In the Tavern," 18, 216, 249; "Inscriptions on a Tombstone," 216; "Medicine," 213; "The Misanthrope," 6; "My Old Home," 18, 249; "The New-Year Sacrifice," 14, 18, 216, 249, 315; Preface to *A Call to Arms*, 214; "Regret for the Past," 15; "Soap," 15; "The True Story of Ah Q," 15, 136, 140, 143, 154, 184, 185, 213, 215

Lukács, Georg, 30, 74, 204
Lyrical novel, 207, 335n5
Lyricism, 203–205, 207ff., 224

Mallarméan nihilism, 209
Manichaean struggle, 119
Mao Dun: on aesthetic craftsmanship, 13–14; betrayal and self-betrayal, 89–92, 95–99; conflict between fiction and politics, 67–68, 69, 101–102; confrontation between fiction and history, 14, 27–35, 295; depiction of the real, 23, 27ff.; emplotment of revolution, 33, 77, 101–102; feminist discourse, 77–79, 82–89, 106, 325n43; influence of late Qing exposé fiction, 30, 33–34, 96; interest in urban intellectuals, 35ff., 76–77; loss of CCP membership, 68, 99, 103, 320n14; use of melodramatic device, 39; naturalism, 34, 69–70, 71–73, 75; preoccupation with the present, 12–13, 26, 32–33; Tolstoy's influence, 27, 33–35, 74–77; view of history, 11–13, 32–33, 49; view of literary history, 71–72; Zola's influence, 27, 33–35, 70–75
—Works: "Autumn Harvest," 54–55; "The Autumn of Guling," 102–103; "Creation," 80, 81–82; "Disillusionment," 37–38, 91–93; *Eclipse*, 25–26, 35–40, 43–44, 91, 104, 300; "From Guling to Tokyo," 36, 90ff., 323n10; "The Great Marsh District," 46–48, 296; "Haze," 80; "Lin Chong the Leopard Head," 46–47; "The Lins' Family Store," 56–58, 62; *Maple Leaves as Red as February Flowers*, 26, 32; *Midnight*, 59–66,

86–89, 106–109, 143; "*Multifaceted Relations*," 55–58, 61–62; "Naturalism and Contemporary Chinese Fiction," 73; "New Year's Eve in Shanghai," 44; *One Day in China: May 21, 1936*, 12, 45–46, 296, 298; "Poetry and Prose," 80; "Pursuit," 39–40, 82, 94–95; *Putrefaction*, 26, 95–101, 104; *Rainbow*, 26, 35, 40–44, 82–86, 104; "Random Notes on My Hometown," 44–45; "Spring Silkworms," 50–54, 59; "Stone Tablet," 46–49, 296; "The Story of Marsh Hay," 104–106; "Suicide," 80; "Tolstoy and Contemporary Russia," 72; "Vacillation," 38–39, 93–94; *Village Trilogy*, 49, 50–55; *Wild Roses*, 80–81; "Winter Ruins," 54–55; "A Woman," 80

Mao Zedong, 14, 294, 296, 313. Work: "Talk on Literature and the Arts in Yenan," 293

Mara Poet, 7, 10, 69

Marxism, 77, 84

Marxist-Christian ideology, 66

Marxist-Communist dialectics, 75

Marxist Humanism, 295

Marxist-Leninist ideology, 77

Marx, Karl, 75, 294. Work: *Capital*, 75

Maupassant, Guy de, 22, 221, 281

May Fourth Movement, 5, 26, 35, 41, 83, 163, 210

May Thirtieth Incident, 26, 37, 43, 83, 163, 164

Melodrama, 16, 118, 119ff., 148, 186

Melville, Herman, 286

Mimesis, 3, 4, 10, 16, 19, 29, 48, 91, 92, 109, 111, 120, 135–137, 139, 162, 208, 219, 306, 318n8, 318n9

Mimicry, 14, 98, 135–136

Ming-Qing fiction, 29

Mock Bildungsroman, 140

Moral occult, 119, 319n21

Mo Yan, 309, 312–313, 314, 315. Works: *The Red Sorghum Family*, 312; "Explosion," 313; "White Dog and Swing," 313; *Garlic-Song in Paradise City*, 313

Myth, 1, 21, 317n1

Nanchang Uprising, 26, 37, 102

Narrative domain, 291

National defense literature, 161

National Resistance War Literature, 14, 158

Nationalist Party, 38, 95ff., 100

Native soil fiction, 249–253, 307–308

Naturalism, 35, 69–70, 71–73

New Fourth Army Incident, 26, 100

New Life Movement, 277–278

Nietzschean superman, 7

Northern Expedition, 26, 37

Nostalgia, 249–250

Ouyang Shan, 293. Work: *One Generation of Noble Souls*, 293

Patriotism, 159–160, 166; "domesticated," 185, 188, 192

Pei Wenzhong, 249

Phelps, William Lyon, 71

Pinocchio, 184

Plaks, Andrew, 29

Political novel, 68

Průšek, Jaroslav, 32, 33, 113, 204, 205

Pu Songling, 281. Work: *Liaozhai zhiyi* (Strange Stories from the Leisure Studio), 281

Pygmalion myth, 81

Qian Xingcun, 40

Qian Zhongshu, 301, 306

Qu Yuan, 20, 219, 248, 255. Work: "Songs of the South," 79, 205, 219, 248, 281

Realism (Real), 1–9, 10, 15, 23, 26–28, 30–32, 35–37, 39–40, 62–64, 65, 67, 70–71, 89–92, 96–99, 109–110, 111, 120–121, 133–135, 136, 147–149, 161–162, 186–188,

Realism (Real) (*Continued*)
202, 204–208, 218–219, 228–230, 236, 239–240, 248, 258–260, 261–262, 264–265, 272–274, 280, 287–289, 291–293, 315–316, 318*n*5
Reciprocal invocation, 292
Red Guards, 198
Representation, 3–4, 15, 16, 23, 55, 63–64, 109, 111, 118ff., 122, 134, 142–143, 148–149, 160, 214–216, 248, 252, 291, 306

Sang Ye, 298
Scandinavian myth, 64
Schlemihl, Peter, 147
Schwartz, Benjamin, 71–72
Scott, Walter, 12, 30
Search for roots fiction, 312–315
Second Sino-Japanese War, 26, 96, 279
Semanov, V. I., 3
Shakespeare, William, 126
Shanghai Resistance of 1931, 26, 232
Shanhaijing (The Classic of the Mountains and Seas), 281
Shen Congwen: anticipatory nostalgia, 277–281; concept of love and passion, 234–245; concept of poetic language, 203, 204ff., 209; critical lyricism, 20, 23, 203–210; debt to Chinese literary tradition, 22, 209, 281; decapitation as a theme in fiction, 210–214, 217–218; depiction of war and lives under war, 231–234; imaginary nostalgia, 21, 23, 250–253, 274, 281, 288–289, 307–309; indebtedness to Lu Xun, 18, 213, 249–251; influence of Turgenev, 22, 206, 213, 221, 281; interaction between the lyrical and the ironical, 207; naturalization, 239; radical lyricism, 219.
—Works: "After Entering the Ranks," 231; *Autobiography of Congwen*, 210, 211, 232, 237, 282–283; "Baizi," 235, 238–240; "The Bandit King," 237; *The Border Town*, 19, 21, 203, 227, 265–275, 279, 280; "Captain," 231, 234; "Dark Night," 232; "Doctor," 285; "Fenghuang," 236, 264–265; *Fengzi*, 203, 235, 236; *Fragments of a Manuscript Surviving the Holocaust*, 242, 243ff.; "Guisheng," 235; "Huiming," 231; "Husband," 235, 240–241; "The Inn," 237; "January 18, 1934," 225–227; "The Lamp," 286–289, 311; "Little Scene in Guizhou," 210, 211; *The Long River*, 21, 227, 274–281; "Long Zhu," 235, 236, 262; "The Lovers," 238; "Material for a Legend," 283–284; "Meijin, Baozi, and the White Kid," 235, 237; "Morning, a Soldier on a Mound of Earth," 231, 232–233; "Mountain Ghost," 219–220, 263; "My Education," 210, 217, 231–232; "Night," 219, 221, 263; "The Old and New," 210, 211; "Qiaoxiu and Dongsheng," 235, 244–245; "Quiet," 203, 227–229; *Random Sketches on a Trip to Hunan*, 21, 203, 227, 254–258, 312; "Sansan," 235; "Sentry," 220–221; "Seven Savages and the Last Spring Festival," 235; "The Shaman's Love," 235, 236, 262; "Sheng," 229–230; "Spring," 203; "A Story of A Hei," 236; "The Tale of a Storyteller," 238; "Those Who Cross over the Mountains," 231, 233–234; "Three Men and One Woman," 22, 221–224, 284–286, 311; "Twilight," 210, 211, 212–213; "Under the Moonlight," 262; "Water Cloud," 266, 267; *West Hunan*, 21–22, 210, 258–265, 274, 285; "Xiaoxiao," 242–245; "Xiaozhai," 235.
Shijing (The Book of Poetry), 248
Shimamura, Hōgetsu, 71

Shu Yi, 168
Sima Qian, 22, 46. Work: *Shiji*, 28, 281
Sima Zhongyuan, 307, 308
Society of Literary Studies, 161
Song fiction, 29
Song vernacular stories, 281
Song Zelai, 309–312, 314, 315. Works: *Daniunan Village*, 309; *Bizarre Stories about Formosa*, 310–311
Soviet Comintern, 107
Storytelling, 22; in Lao She's fiction, 113, 117; in Shen Congwen's fiction, 22–23
Swift, Jonathan, 136. Work: *Gulliver's Travels*, 136

Taine, Hippolyte, 73
Tao Qian, 20, 21, 248, 282. Work: "Peach Blossom Spring," 248, 254–257, 259, 267
Thanatos, 234, 235, 237
Tian Han, 296, 297. Work: "Xie Yaohuan," 296
Tolstoy, Leo, 11, 12, 27, 30, 33, 34–35, 40, 70, 71, 72, 73, 74, 75, 76, 77. Work: *War and Peace*, 185
Turgenev, Ivan, 22, 206, 213, 221, 281. Work: *Sketches from a Hunter's Album*, 206, 213, 221, 281

Utopia, 20, 202, 258, 266

Verisimilitude, 3, 15, 16, 29, 63, 68, 96, 164, 179, 208, 222, 250, 261, 282, 292, 293, 298, 308, 315, 318*n*5, 318*n*8
Voltaire, François, 147. Work: *Candide*, 147

Wang Luyan, 211, 249
Wang Tuo, 310
Wang Wenxing, 301, 303–304. Work: *The Man with His Back to the Sea*, 303, 304
Wang Zengqi, 309, 312
Wang Zhenhe, 301–302, 303, 304, 305, 307, 309, 311. Work: *Rose, Rose, I Love You*, 302
War of Resistance literature, 14
Water Margin, 46, 48, 297
Wellek, René, 72
Wells, H. G., 136. Work: *The First Man in the Moon*, 136
Wu Han, 296. Work: *Hairui Resigns Office*, 296
Wu Woyao, 4, 33, 96–97. Work: *Strange Things Seen in the Past Twenty Years*, 33, 96, 116

Xiao Jun, 171. Work: *Village in August*, 171
Xu Qinwen, 249, 250
Xu Zhimo, 201, 335*n*2

Yan Fu, 77
Yang Qingchu, 310
Yanyi (saga) novels, 29
Yao Xueyin, 293. Work: *Li Zicheng*, 293, 296
Ye Shaojun, 205
Yu Dafu, 131, 201, 335*n*2. Work: "Sinking," 131
Yu Hua, 299, 300. Works: "Nineteen Eighty-Six," 300; "The Past Is Like Smoke," 300; "Past and Punishment," 300

Zeng Pu, 29–30. Work: *A Flower in the Sea of Sins*, 29, 88
Zhang Tianyi, 17, 301
Zhang Xiguo, 299, 306
Zhang Xinxin, 298. Work: *People in Beijing*, 298
Zhao Shuli, 308, 313
Zheng Zhenduo, 83
Zhou Zuoren, 22, 205, 323*n*15
Zhu Xining, 307
Zhuangzi, 281
Zola, Emile, 11, 12, 25, 27, 33, 34–35, 36–37, 39, 40, 60, 70, 71, 72, 73, 74, 75, 76, 77, 88, 105, 118
Zuozhuan, 28

Other Works in the Columbia Asian Studies Series

Modern Asian Literature Series

Modern Japanese Drama: An Anthology, ed. and tr. Ted Takaya. Also in paperback ed.	1979
Mask and Sword: Two Plays for the Contemporary Japanese Theater, by Yamazaki Masakazu, tr. J. Thomas Rimer	1980
Yokomitsu Riichi, Modernist, by Dennis Keene	1980
Nepali Visions, Nepali Dreams: The Poetry of Laxmiprasad Devkota, tr. David Rubin	1980
Literature of the Hundred Flowers, vol. 1: *Criticism and Polemics*, ed. Hualing Nieh	1981
Literature of the Hundred Flowers, vol. 2: *Poetry and Fiction*, ed. Hualing Nieh	1981
Modern Chinese Stories and Novellas, 1919–1949, ed. Joseph S. M. Lau, C. T. Hsia, and Leo Ou-fan Lee. Also in paperback ed.	1984
A View by the Sea, by Yasuoka Shōtarō, tr. Kären Wigen Lewis	1984
Other Worlds: Arishima Takeo and the Bounds of Modern Japanese Fiction, by Paul Anderer	1984
Selected Poems of Sŏ Chŏngju, tr. with intro. by David R. McCann	1989
The Sting of Life: Four Contemporary Japanese Novelists, by Van C. Gessel	1989
Ishikawa Jun: The Bodhisativa, trans. William Jefferson Tyler	1989
Oda Sakunosuke: Stories of Osaka Life, trans. Burton Watson	1990

Translations from the Oriental Classics

Major Plays of Chikamatsu, tr. Donald Keene. Also in paperback ed.	1961
Four Major Plays of Chikamatsu, tr. Donald Keene. Paperback text edition	1961
Records of the Grand Historian of China, translated from the Shih chi of Ssu-ma Ch'ien, tr. Burton Watson, 2 vols.	1961
Instructions for Practical Living and Other Neo-Confucisn Writings by Wang Yang-ming, tr. Wing-tsit Chan	1963
Chuang Tzu: Basic Writings, tr. Burton Watson, paperback ed. only	1964
The Mahābhārata, tr. Chakravarthi V. Narasimhan. Also in paperback ed.	1965
The Manyōshū, Nippon Gakujutsu Shinkōkai edition	1965
Su Tung-p'o: Selections from a Sung Dynasty Poet, tr. Burton Watson. Also in paperback ed.	1965
Bhartrihari: Poems, tr. Barbara Stoler Miller. Also in paperback ed.	1967
Basic Writings of Mo Tzu, Hsün Tzu, and Han Fei Tzu, tr. Burton Watson. Also in separate paperback eds.	1967
The Awakening of Faith, Attributed to Aśvaghosha, tr. Yoshito S. Hakeda. Also in paperback ed.	1967
Reflections on Things at Hand: The Neo-Confucian Anthology, comp. Chu Hsi and Lü Tsu-Ch'ien, tr. Wing-tsit Chan	1967
The Platform Sutra of the Sixth Patriarch, tr. Philip B. Yampolsky. Also in paperback ed.	1967
Essays in Idleness: The Tsurezuregusa of Kenkō, tr. Donald Keene. Also in paperback ed.	1967
The Pillow Book of Sei Shōnagon, tr. Ivan Morris, 2 vols. Also in paperback ed.	1967
Two Plays of Ancient India: The Little Clay Cart and the Minister's Seal, tr. J. A. B. van Buitenen	1968
The Complete Works of Chuang Tzu, tr. Burton Watson	1968
The Romance of the Western Chamber (Hsi Hsiang chi), tr. S. I. Hsiung. Also in paperback ed.	1968
The Manyōshū, Nippon Gakujutsu Shinkōkai edition. Paperback text edition	1969
Records of the Historian: Chapters from the Shih chi of Ssu-ma Ch'ien. Paperback text edition, tr. Burton Watson	1969
Cold Mountain: 100 Poems by the T'ang Poet Han-shan, tr. Burton Watson. Also in paperback ed.	1970
Twenty Plays of the Nō Theatre, ed. Donald Keene. Also in paperback ed.	1970
Chūshingura: The Treasury of Loyal Retainers, tr. Donald Keene. Also in paperback ed.	1971
The Zen Master Hakuin: Selected Writings, tr. Philip B. Yampolsky	1971

Chinese Rhyme-Prose: Poems in the Fu Form from the Han and Six Dynasties Periods, tr. Burton Watson. Also in paperback ed.	1971
Kūkai: Major Works, tr. Yoshito S. Hakeda. Also in paperback ed.	1972
The Old Man Who Does as He Pleases: Selections from the Poetry and Prose of Lu Yu, tr. Burton Watson	1973
The Lion's Roar of Queen Śrīmālā, tr. Alex and Hideko Wayman	1974
Courtier and Commoner in Ancient China: Selections from the History of the Former Han by Pan Ku, tr. Burton Watson. Also in paperback ed.	1974
Japanese Literature in Chinese, vol. 1: Poetry and Prose in Chinese by Japanese Writers of the Early Period, tr. Burton Watson	1975
Japanese Literature in Chinese, vol. 2: Poetry and Prose in Chinese by Japanese Writers of the Later Period, tr. Burton Watson	1976
Scripture of the Lotus Blossom of the Fine Dharma, tr. Leon Hurvitz. Also in paperback ed.	1976
Love Song of the Dark Lord: Jayaveda's Gītagovinda, tr. Barbara Stoler Miller. Also in paperback ed. Cloth ed. includes critical text of the Sanskrit.	1977
Ryōkan: Zen Monk-Poet of Japan, tr. Burton Watson	1977
Calming the Mind and Discerning the Real: From the Lam rim chen mo of Tsoṅ-kha-pa, tr. Alex Wayman	1978
The Hermit and the Love-Thief: Sanskrit Poems of Bhartrihari and Bilhaṇa, tr. Barbara Stoler Miller	1978
The Lute: Kao Ming's P'i-p'a chi, tr. Jean Mulligan. Also in paperback ed.	1980
A Chronicle of Gods and Sovereigns: Jinnō Shōtōki of Kitakabe Chikafusa, tr. H. Paul Varley	1980
Among the Flowers: The Hua-chien chi, tr. Lois Fusek	1982
Grass Hill: Poems and Prose by the Japanese Monk Gensei, tr. Burton Watson	1983
Doctors, Diviners, and Magicians of Ancient China: Biographies of Fang-shih, tr. Kenneth J. DeWoskin. Also in paperback ed.	1983
Theater of Memory: The Plays of Kālidāsa, ed. Barbara Stoler Miller. Also in paperback ed.	1984
The Columbia Book of Chinese Poetry: From Early Times to the Thirteenth Century, ed. and tr. Burton Watson. Also in paperback ed.	1984
Poems of Love and War: From the Eight Anthologies and the Ten Songs of Classical Tamil, tr. A. K. Ramanujan. Also in paperback ed.	1985
The Columbia Book of Later Chinese Poetry, ed. and tr. Jonathan Chaves. Also in paperback ed.	1986
Selected Writings of Nichiren, ed. Philip Yampolsky	1990

Companions to Asian Studies

Approaches to the Oriental Classics, ed. Wm. Theodore de Bary	1959
Early Chinese Literature, by Burton Watson. Also in paperback ed.	1962
Approaches to Asian Civilization, ed. Wm. Theodore de Bary and Ainslie T. Embree	1964
The Classic Chinese Novel: A Critical Introduction, by C. T. Hsia. Also in paperback ed.	1968
Chinese Lyricism: Shih Poetry from the Second to the Twelfth Century, tr. Burton Watson. Also in paperback ed.	1971
A Syllabus of Indian Civilization, by Leonard A. Gordon and Barbara Stoler Miller	1971
Twentieth-Century Chinese Stories, ed. C. T. Hsia and Joseph S. M. Lau. Also in paperback ed.	1971
A Syllabus of Chinese Civilization, by J. Mason Gentzler, 2d ed.	1972
A Syllabus of Japanese Civilization, by H. Paul Varley, 2d ed.	1972
An Introduction to Chinese Civilization, ed. John Meskill, with the assistance of J. Mason Gentzler	1973
An Introduction to Japanese Civilization, ed. Arthur E. Tiedemann	1974
Ukifune: Love in the Tale of Genji, ed. Andrew Pekarik	1982
The Pleasures of Japanese Literature, by Donald Keene	1988
A Guide to Oriental Classics, ed. Wm. Theodore de Bary and Ainslie T. Embree; third edition ed. Amy Vladek Heinrich	1989
Approaches to the Asian Classics, ed. Wm. Theodore de Bary and Irene Bloom	1989

Neo-Confucian Studies

Instructions for Practical Living and Other Neo-Confucian Writings by Wang Yang-ming, tr. Wing-tsit Chan	1963
Reflections on Things at Hand: The Neo-Confucian Anthology, comp. Chu Hsi and Lü Tsu-ch'ien, tr. Wing-tsit Chan	1967
Self and Society in Ming Thought, by Wm. Theodore de Bary and the Conference on Ming Thought. Also in paperback ed.	1970
The Unfolding of Neo-Confucianism, by Wm. Theodore de Bary and the Conference on Seventeenth-Century Chinese Thought. Also in paperback ed.	1975
Principle and Practicality: Essays in Neo-Confucianism and Practical Learning, ed. Wm. Theodore de Bary and Irene Bloom. Also in paperback ed.	1979
The Syncretic Religion of Lin Chao-en, by Judith A. Berling	1980
The Renewal of Buddhism in China: Chu-hung and the Late Ming Synthesis, by Chun-fang Yu	1981
Neo-Confucian Orthodoxy and the Learning of the Mind-and-Heart, by Wm. Theodore de Bary	1981

Yüan Thought: Chinese Thought and Religion Under the Mongols, ed. Hok-lam Chan and Wm. Theodore de Bary	1982
The Liberal Tradition in China, by Wm. Theodore de Bary	1983
The Development and Decline of Chinese Cosmology, by John B. Henderson	1984
The Rise of Neo-Confucianism in Korea, by Wm. Theodore de Bary and JaHyun Kim Haboush	1985
Chiao Hung and the Restructuring of Neo-Confucianism in the Late Ming, by Edward T. Ch'ien	1985
Neo-Confucian Terms Explained: Pei-hsi tzu-i, by Ch'en Ch'un, ed. and trans. Wing-tsit Chan	1986
Knowledge Painfully Acquired: K'un-chih chi, by Lo Ch'in-shun, ed. and trans. Irene Bloom	1987
To Become a Sage: The Ten Diagrams on Sage Learning, by Yi T'oegye, ed. and trans. Michael C. Kalton	1988
The Message of the Mind in Neo-Confucianism, by Wm. Theodore de Bary	1989
Learning for One's Self, Wm. Theodore de Bary	1991

Studies in Oriental Culture

1.	*The Ōnin War: History of Its Origins and Background, with a Selective Translation of the Chronicle of Ōnin*, by H. Paul Varley	1967
2.	*Chinese Government in Ming Times: Seven Studies*, ed. Charles O. Hucker	1969
3.	*The Actors' Analects (Yakusha Rongo)*, ed. and tr. by Charles J. Dunn and Bungō Torigoe	1969
4.	*Self and Society in Ming Thought*, by Wm. Theodore de Bary and the Conference on Ming Thought. Also in paperback ed.	1970
5.	*A History of Islamic Philosophy*, by Majid Fakhry, 2d ed.	1983
6.	*Phantasies of a Love Thief: The Caurapañcāśikā Attributed to Bilhaṇa*, by Barbara Stoler Miller	1971
7.	*Iqbal: Poet-Philosopher of Pakistan*, ed. Hafeez Malik	1971
8.	*The Golden Tradition: An Anthology of Urdu Poetry*, by Ahmed Ali. Also in paperback ed.	1973
9.	*Conquerors and Confucians: Aspects of Political Change in the Late Yuan China*, by John W. Dardess	1973
10.	*The Unfolding of Neo-Confucianism*, by Wm. Theodore de Bary and the Conference on Seventeenth-Century Chinese Thought. Also in paperback ed.	1975
11.	*To Acquire Wisdom: The Way of Wang Yang-ming*, by Julia Ching	1976
12.	*Gods, Priests, and Warriors: The Bhṛgus of the Mahābhārata*, by Robert P. Goldman	1977

13. *Mei Yao-ch'en and the Development of Early Sung Poetry*, by
    Jonathan Chaves   1976
14. *The Legend of Semimaru, Blind Musician of Japan*, by Susan
    Matisoff   1977
15. *Sir Sayyid Ahmad Khan and Muslim Modernization in India and
    Pakistan*, by Hafeez Malik   1980
16. *The Khilafat Movement: Religious Symbolism and Political
    Mobilization in India*, by Gail Minault   1980
17. *The World of K'ung Shang-jen: A Man of Letters in Early
    Ch'ing China*, by Richard Strassberg   1983
18. *The Lotus Boat: The Origins of Chinese Tz'u Poetry in T'ang
    Popular Culture*, by Marsha L. Wagner   1984
19. *Expressions of Self in Chinese Culture*, ed. Robert E. Hegel
    and Richard C. Hessney   1985
20. *Songs for the Bride: Women's Voices and Wedding Rites of Rural
    India*, by W. G. Archer, ed. Barbara Stoler Miller and
    Mildred Archer   1986
21. *A Heritage of Kings: One Man's Monarchy in the Confucian
    World*, by JaHyun Kim Haboush   1988

Introduction to Oriental Civilizations
Wm. Theodore de Bary, Editor

Sources of Japanese Tradition 1958; paperback ed., 2 vols., 1964
Sources of Indian Tradition 1958; paperback ed., 2 vols., 1964;
    second edition, 1988
Sources of Chinese Tradition 1960; paperback ed., 2 vols., 1964